INTERNATIONAL LIBRARY OF PHILOSOPHY

Noble in Reason, Infinite in Faculty

Themes and variations in Kant's moral and religious philosophy

A.W. Moore

Noble in Reason, Infinite in Faculty

'In *Noble in Reason, Infinite in Faculty*, A.W. Moore mines Kant for ethical insight with a sensibility informed by a wide range of recent and contemporary philosophers, from Ludwig Wittgenstein through Bernard Williams and Gilles Deleuze... a particularly helpful account of Kant's philosophy of religion...'
Paul Guyer, *Times Literary Supplement*

'... it is refreshing to encounter a book dealing with Kant's practical philosophy that does not wear its readers down with quandaries about universalizability, autonomy, and the moral law... It is time to try something different, and Moore has certainly done that.' **Robert B. Louden,** *Mind*

'... an original contribution to the ethical discussion of our time...'
Manfred Kuehn

'... deeply engages some of the most important pieces of Kant's moral and religious thinking...' **Philip Rossi**

'... clearly written... numerous provocative insights... readers will benefit from the way in which familiar themes have been deployed and reconfigured for the sake of a fairly audacious result. Moore derives something like a substitute for postmodernity's lost sense of a grounding metanarrative from the human capacity for sense making... [His] project might... be viewed as the effort to infuse our very tendency towards sense making with renewed dignity.'
Gordon E. Michalson, *Kantian Review*

'... a continuing, deep and detailed collaborative discussion with the Kant who makes best sense to [Moore] of matters of the utmost importance to them both and... to the rest of us as well... an exceptionally thought-provoking and serious book by one of our most technically proficient, but at the same time most imaginative – in short, one of our very best – contemporary philosophers... [Though this closely-argued, rich and engaging book] is, certainly and in many ways, a book for philosophers, it is equally one that may be read with much serious pleasure by anyone with a taste for reflection about the proper status of moral and religious thinking.' **Alan Montefiore,** *Balliol College Record*

A.W. Moore is Tutorial Fellow in Philosophy at St Hugh's College, Oxford. He is the author of the *The Infinite* (2nd edition, Routledge, 2001) and *Points of View*.

International Library of Philosophy
Edited by José Luis Bermúdez, Tim Crane and Peter Sullivan
Advisory Board: Jonathan Barnes, Fred Dretske, Frances Kamm, Brian Leiter, Huw Price and Sydney Shoemaker

Other titles in the ILP:

The Facts of Causation
D.H. Mellor

The Conceptual Roots of Mathematics
J.R. Lucas

Stream of Consciousness
Barry Dainton

Knowledge and Reference in Empirical Science
Jody Azzouni

Reason Without Freedom
David Owens

The Price of Doubt
N.M.L. Nathan

Matters of Mind
Scott Sturgeon

Logic, Form and Grammar
Peter Long

The Metaphysicians of Meaning
Gideon Makin

Logical Investigations, Vols I & II
Edmund Husserl

Truth Without Objectivity
Max Kölbel

Departing from Frege
Mark Sainsbury

The Importance of Being Understood
Adam Morton

Art and Morality
Edited by José Luis Bermúdez and Sebastian Gardner

Noble in Reason, Infinite in Faculty
A.W. Moore

Noble in Reason, Infinite in Faculty

Themes and variations in Kant's moral and religious philosophy

A.W. Moore

LONDON AND NEW YORK

First published 2003
by Routledge
2 Park Square, Milton Park, Abingdon, Oxon OX14 4RN

Simultaneously published in the USA and Canada
by Routledge
270 Madison Ave, New York NY 10016

First published in paperback 2005 by Routledge

Routledge is an imprint of the Taylor & Francis Group

© 2003 A.W. Moore

Typeset in Times by Wearset Ltd, Boldon, Tyne and Wear
Printed and bound in Great Britain by Antony Rowe Ltd.,
Chippenham, Wiltshire

All rights reserved. No part of this book may be reprinted or
reproduced or utilized in any form or by any electronic,
mechanical, or other means, now known or hereafter invented,
including photocopying and recording, or in any information
storage or retrieval system, without permission in writing from
the publishers.

British Library Cataloguing in Publication Data
A catalogue record for this book is available from the British
Library

Library of Congress Cataloging in Publication Data
Moore, A.W., 1956–
  Noble in reason, infinite in faculty : themes and variations in
Kant's moral religious philosophy / A.W. Moore.
    p. cm. – (International library of philosophy)
  Includes bibliographical references and index.
    1. Kant, Immanuel, 1724–1804–Ethics. 2. Ethics, Modern–
  18th Century. 3. Free will and determinism–History–
  18th Century. 4. Kant, Immanuel, 1724–1804–Religion.
  5. Religion–Philosophy–History–18th century. I. Title.
  II. Series.
  B2799.E8 M56 2003
  170'.92–dc21
                                                      2002036626

ISBN 0-415-20821-1 (hbk)
ISBN 0-415-20822-X (pbk)

For Phil

The expense of spirit in a waste of shame
Is lust in action; and till action, lust
Is perjur'd, murderous, bloody, full of blame,
Savage, extreme, rude, cruel, not to trust;
Enjoy'd no sooner but despised straight;
Past reason hunted; and no sooner had,
Past reason hated, as a swallow'd bait,
On purpose laid to make the taker mad:
Mad in pursuit, and in possession so;
Had, having, and in quest to have, extreme;
A bliss in proof, – and prov'd, a very woe;
Before, a joy propos'd; behind, a dream.
   All this the world well knows; yet none knows well
   To shun the heaven that leads men to this hell.
(William Shakespeare, Sonnet 129)

All men by nature desire to know.
(Aristotle, *Metaphysica*, Book A, Chapter 1, 98a)

Let a noise or scent, once heard or once smelt, be heard or smelt again in the present and at the same time in the past, real without being actual, ideal without being abstract, and immediately the permanent and habitually concealed essence of things is liberated and our true self which seemed – had perhaps for long years seemed – to be dead but was not altogether dead, is awakened and reanimated as it receives the celestial nourishment that is brought to it. A minute freed from the order of time has re-created in us, to feel it, the man freed from the order of time. And one can understand that this man should have confidence in his joy,... one can understand that the word 'death' should have no meaning for him; situated outside time, why should he fear the future?
(Marcel Proust, *Remembrance of Things Past*, 'Time Regained', p. 906)

Contents

Preface ix
Acknowledgements xi
Analytical table of contents xiii

Introduction 1

First theme: morality 20

First set of variations 39

Second theme: freedom 90

Second set of variations 113

Third theme: religion 147

Third set of variations 170

Notes 197
Bibliography 222
Index 239

Preface

Kant, in his moral and religious philosophy, provides the themes for this book. I attempt to do two things: to play out these themes; and to play out variations on them. At the end of the Introduction I elaborate a little on what I mean by this and on how it structures the book.

There is an analytical table of contents which charts the execution of this project through each section. Readers may find it helpful to read this before the rest of the book. Much of it, however, will make little sense on its own. It is intended primarily as an *aide-mémoire*, to be consulted retrospectively by readers whenever they want to take stock.

Many people have helped me with the writing of this book, despite being, in many cases, resolutely opposed to its main ideas. For comments on an earlier draft, and for guidance of various other kinds, I am extremely grateful to the referees appointed by Routledge, and to Pamela Anderson, Andrea Capovilla, Gordon Davis, Iskra Fileva, Katerina Ierodiakonou, Daniel Jones, Derek Parfit, Thomas Startup, Philip Turetzky, and Bernard Williams.

A.W. Moore

Acknowledgements

Most of the work on this book was done during four terms of sabbatical leave in the academic years 1999–2000 and 2000–2001. I am grateful to the Principal and Fellows of St Hugh's College, Oxford and to the General Board of Oxford University for granting me this leave of absence; to the Arts and Humanities Research Board for granting me an award under its Research Leave Scheme, which provided funding for one of these terms; and to the Mind Association for awarding me a Research Fellowship, which provided funding for another.

In the course of the book I quote extensively from Immanuel Kant, *Practical Philosophy*, translated and edited by Mary J. Gregor (Cambridge University Press, 1996) and from Immanuel Kant, *Religion and Rational Theology*, translated and edited by Allen W. Wood and George di Giovanni (Cambridge University Press, 1996). For permission to quote from the former, I am grateful to Betty Kiehl, Mary Gregor's literary executor; for permission to quote from the latter, I am grateful to Allen Wood and George di Giovanni; and for permission to quote from both, I am grateful to Cambridge University Press.

Analytical table of contents

Introduction

§1 How is it possible for us to make ethical sense of things?

§2 This question in turn raises questions about the objectivity of our ethical thinking. The fact that our ethical thinking engages us in the way it does can make the prospects for its objectivity look dim. But perhaps this is because we have in mind the objectivity of thinking that is about an independent reality. Do the prospects look brighter if we have in mind the objectivity of thinking that is constrained to go in a certain direction?

§3 It is not clear that they do. For how can thinking that engages us in the distinctive way in which our ethical thinking does be constrained to go in a certain direction? – Well, one way to answer this question would be by appeal to 'conative objectivism', the thesis that our ethical thinking depends on conative states that we all share. This would not be easy to demonstrate. But that does not mean that it is not true.

§4 Another, apparently very different way to answer the question would be by appeal to 'rationalism', the thesis that our ethical thinking consists in the exercise of pure reason.

§5 There are three principal objections to rationalism. First, it allows for ethical expertise. Second, it makes a mystery of socially grounded ethical disagreement. Third, pure reason cannot be 'practical': that is, pure reason cannot engage us in the appropriate way.

§6 Despite these objections, rationalism has considerable appeal. What follows is a study of rationalism.

§7 This study will have to be informed by the above, including the three objections to rationalism. It will be based on Kant's version of rationalism, and it will adopt a 'themes and variations' format.

First theme: morality

§1 Kant has a vision of the authority of reason that is in some respects deeply attractive, and in others deeply repugnant.

§2 He distinguishes between 'hypothetical imperatives', which apply to agents by virtue of ends they happen to have, and 'categorical imperatives', which apply to agents purely by virtue of their rationality. He further insists that the basic demands of morality are categorical imperatives. If they were not, they would have to be contingent on something, and Kant thinks that this would be intolerable. He is therefore a rationalist.

§3 He has more or less satisfactory responses to the first and second objections to rationalism. What about the third? One way to respond to this objection would be to argue that we could not put reason to practical use at all unless certain ways of acting commended themselves to us, simply as rational beings.

§4 If such an argument were to succeed, it would probably give us a characteristically Kantian loop, whereby it is a fundamental demand of pure practical reason to put pure reason to practical use. This connects with two strains in Kant's thinking: first, that the only thing that is good without qualification is putting pure reason to practical use; and second, that rational beings are to be valued for their own sake. The second of these leads to one formulation of the fundamental categorical imperative: 'So act that you use humanity, whether in your own person or in the person of any other, always at the same time as an end, never merely as a means.'

§5 A second formulation arises from the idea that rational beings regulate what they do by adopting 'maxims'. A maxim is a resolution of such a kind that to adopt it is to treat it as if it had the force of a categorical imperative, or as if it were a 'law'. If we were purely rational, we would only ever adopt maxims that really could be laws, granted what we are capable of willing. Hence the second formulation: 'Act only in accordance with that maxim through which you can at the same time will that it become a universal law.'

§6 Now among the reservations we might have about this is the following. There is no readily forthcoming substantive account of which resolutions count as maxims.

§7 The next chapter will be concerned to provide one, and thereby to provide a partial defence of Kant. Later we shall have to return to the third objection to rationalism. For, as Kant himself sees clearly, it is still nothing but an assumption that pure reason can be put to practical use.

First set of variations

§1 A starting point is the proposition that some concepts are action-guiding. That is, there are some concepts such that anyone who possesses one of these concepts thereby has certain reasons for doing things.

§2 'Some': there is no suggestion that all concepts are of this kind, though neither is that possibility excluded.

§3 'Certain': the reasons that a person has, by virtue of possessing one of these concepts, are reasons that everyone who possesses that concept has.

§4 'Doing': this is to be understood broadly enough to include 'omissions' as well as 'acts'.

§5 'Has': to have a reason, one does not have to acknowledge it, though one does have to be able to acknowledge it.

§6 'Reasons': the reasons in question are normative, they are general, and they may be defeasible.

§7 'Thereby': any dependence here is as much a dependence of possessing concepts on having reasons as of having reasons on possessing concepts, though in many cases the converse dependence holds too.

§8 'Possesses': this is to be understood in an unusually demanding way, including only the 'engaged' grasp of a concept. To possess a concept is to live by it.

§9 Let us say that an action-guiding concept 'requires' the practice of doing anything its possession gives people a reason to do. Let us say that a resolution 'involves' any concept that one must possess in order to adopt it. And let us say that a resolution 'is answerable to' any practice required by any concept it involves. Then a maxim is a resolution to do something that either counts as observing some practice to which the resolution is answerable or counts as violating some practice to which the resolution is answerable. If we further say that a 'law' is a resolution that qualifies as a maxim in the first of these two ways, then it is irrational to adopt a maxim that is not either already a law or capable of becoming a law through suitable developments in the concepts it involves, where this capability can be captured in the idea of what those who possess the relevant concepts can will. Here we have a reconstruction of Kant's rationalism.

§10 But does it yield full-blown categorical imperatives? Does it not at most yield imperatives which apply to agents who possess the relevant concepts? And does it not therefore leave us with real questions about which concepts to possess?

§11 These concerns are reflected in the debate about whether it is possible to derive an 'ought' from an 'is'. Some proposed derivations can be resisted by anyone who does not possess the relevant concepts, but not by anyone who does.

§12 Yes; this reconstruction of Kant's rationalism does leave us with real questions about which concepts to possess, questions about how to assess our 'forms of life'.

§13 This will involve reflecting on what our forms of life have been.

§14 It will involve reflecting on what our forms of life are.

§15 And it will involve reflecting on what our forms of life may yet be; on what radically new concepts we may yet possess. But to possess a radically new concept, we must be able, collectively and individually, to get from here to there. And the question whether we can get from here to there is akin to the question whether our concepts can develop in such a way that some maxim can become a law. So assessing the concepts we possess is of a piece with assessing the maxims we adopt. Both are part of trying to make sense, that is of trying to be rational. So this reconstruction of Kant's rationalism is very close to Kant's own rationalism after all – though it does call into question the idea of 'pure' reason.

§16 In both this reconstruction and the original, rationality demands that we adopt no maxims that we cannot will to be laws, though in the reconstruction this 'cannot' covers a wider range of possibilities. Some of these possibilities have an empirical element, calling the idea of 'pure' reason further into question.

§17 In the reconstruction, rationality also demands that we seek concepts that enable us to make sense. We must realize that the world itself does not make sense: we have to make sense of it.

§18 The demand to be active in making sense of the world has its own echoes in Kant. In fact this variation brings us right back to the beginning of the first theme: the authority of reason.

Second theme: freedom

§1 It is still only an assumption, however, that pure reason can be put to practical use. Even if we can now see how pure reason is able to determine certain courses of action, there remains the question, 'So what?'

§2 Kant tries to answer this question by showing that the demands of pure practical reason are the demands of freedom. To act freely is to be subject to these demands. Of course, this leaves room for a further 'So what?' But does it not in any case have the absurd consequence – call this the Radical Conception – that nobody ever freely does the wrong thing, that is the irrational thing? No; being subject to demands is different from acting in accord with them. Kant does not accede to the Radical Conception – though he does come close to doing so.

§3 Now Kant accepts a physical determinism that is incompatible with freedom. So how can he also accept that we are free? Well, he thinks that our actions can be regarded from two points of view, and that the determinism in question holds only from one of these. Indeed, he develops this picture in such a way as to rebuff any possible threat to the belief that we are free. The price he pays is to concede that the belief can never be established either. For, on his developed picture, it is a belief about how we unknowably are in ourselves – in contrast to the determinism, which is a belief about how we appear.

§4 Kant further insists that we can never fully understand the relationship between these.

§5 Among the difficulties that Kant faces, the most serious is that the freedom-precluding determinism which he champions not only leaves him with a problem of reconciliation; it challenges our understanding of what needs to be reconciled.

Second set of variations

§1 Let us return to the Radical Conception. Is the Radical Conception really 'absurd'? What if we combine it with the idea – call this combination the Radical Picture – that we can incur blame for things that we have not done freely? Provided that blame is a 'superficial' concept, the Radical Picture is just a convenient way of capturing the idea that there is a nisus in all of us towards rationality.

§2 But does it leave enough room, within freedom, for creativity and unpredictability? Yes; for being rational, that is making sense, can include creating radically new concepts.

§3 Even if creating radically new concepts is properly thought of as discovering new possibilities, rather than creating new possibilities, it still enjoys a radical unpredictability. It is like seeing certain colours for the first time.

§4 Irrationality, on this picture, involves succumbing to non-rational forces.

§5 Let us now consider an idea that is crucial to this enquiry – call it the Basic Idea – that there is a nisus in all of us, more fundamental than any other, towards rationality.

§6 This means that nothing is of greater value to us than rationality.

§7 If the Basic Idea is true, it finally enables us to address the 'So what?' questions hanging over from above. It also makes rationalism a species of conative objectivism.

§8 But is it true? It is akin to Kant's notion that supreme and unqualified value attaches to the exercise of pure practical reason and therewith to those with a capacity to exercise pure practical reason, namely people. It may also share with that notion a basicness which prevents it, even if it is true, from being established.

§9 This connects with Kant's belief that we have a fundamental 'respect' for the moral law, and that our knowing how to put pure reason to practical use is a 'fact of pure reason'.

§10 The suspicion that the Basic Idea cannot be established is reinforced by the failure of various promising ways to establish it.

§11 But provided that it is true, then there are good practical reasons to accept that it is true; and, in the absence of any way of establishing it, to hope that it is true.

Third theme: religion

§1 Kant, despite not being entirely comfortable with religion, thinks it has an important role – albeit a role subordinate to that of morality.

§2 In particular, he thinks we do well to regard the demands of morality as divine commands.

§3 Now the role which he thinks religion has he thinks it has only because of our radical evil. But why does he think we are radically evil? For various reasons, though not, as we might have expected, for the reason that any irrationality in our behaviour indicates a timeless irrationality in how we are in ourselves. That would preclude the possibility of reform, and Kant is loath to abandon hope in this possibility.

§4 In general, Kant thinks that, because of our imperfection, we need non-rational props to sustain us in any commitment to morality; and that these props include the hope that we can reform, and, as a corollary, the hope that we enjoy an immortality that will enable us to work out our reformation. We must hope and believe that we are immortal, then, just as we must hope and believe that we are free (see above) and that God exists (see below). These three propositions Kant calls 'postulates of pure practical reason'.

§5 Why must we hope and believe that God exists? Because only God can guarantee that happiness is aligned to virtue, which is itself something we must hope and believe if we are to maintain any commitment to morality.

§6 Note: our immortality need not be understood in literally temporal terms.

§7 What status do these three postulates have? Although they are propositions that we must believe, in the relevant practical sense of 'must', none of them can be proved – or, for that matter, disproved, since each of them concerns how things unknowably are in themselves.

Appendix. Note that this account glosses over various developments in Kant's thinking.

Third set of variations

§1 Now we may hope that the Basic Idea is true. If it is, it is a deep contingency that rests on further deep contingencies such as the constancy of nature.

§2 There is, however, an unresolved issue about how the Basic Idea is to be understood – whether individualistically or corporately. One very direct way to avoid this issue is to assume that the distinction is never actually operative. This assumption is part of a larger assumption: that the Basic Idea is not just true, but 'secure'.

§3 Is this larger assumption an assumption to the effect that the world makes sense? No: it is an assumption to the effect that the world fosters and protects our own sense-making.

§4 Imperfect as we are, we must hope and believe this if we are to sustain any commitment to rationality.

§5 In particular, we must hope and believe that we are never forced, at some ultimate level, into irrationality.

§6 We must likewise hope and believe that nothing will ever be of greater value to us than rationality.

§7 As with Kant's three postulates, the 'must' here is a practical 'must' grounded in our imperfection. More generally, both the Basic Idea itself and the proposition that the Basic Idea is secure share many of the lineaments of Kant's postulates.

§8 There are other ways in which this picture connects with religion. Thus the hope and the belief that the Basic Idea is secure might be sustained by belief in God, where belief in God is to be understood as a kind of commitment that is not only distinguishable from belief that God exists but, arguably, impervious to incoherence in the concept of God.

§9 However that may be, there is something in this picture corresponding to each of Kant's three postulates. Corresponding to the first, there is the Basic Idea itself; corresponding to the second, there is that aspect of the security of the Basic Idea whereby we can always make sense of things; and corresponding to the third, there is that aspect of the security of the Basic Idea whereby the world is a home for our sense-making. It remains for us to make the sense.

Introduction

> When an ethical law of the form, 'Thou shalt...', is laid down, one's first thought is, 'And what if I do not do it?'
> (Ludwig Wittgenstein, *Tractatus Logico-Philosophicus*, 6.422)

§1 How can we make sense of things?

There are countless ways in which this question might be intended. In a suitable dramatic context, someone might be asking, 'How can you and I find anything worth living for – now that *this* has happened?' Even when the question is posed in a work of philosophy, with theoretical aspirations, there are many things that might be meant. It could be a question about preconditions of the human aptitude for discovering laws of nature. It could be a question about the meaning of life.[1]

Among the dimensions of ambiguity that help to give the question its versatility, there is one that is likely to ring certain philosophical bells. The question could be understood as a 'ground-level' question: *what* sense can we make of things? Or it could be understood as an 'upper-level' or 'meta-level' question: how is it possible for us to make sense of things (at all)?

This is likely to ring certain philosophical bells because there is a broader distinction that philosophers often draw between thinking about certain issues and thinking about thinking about those issues. Thus we can think about whether God exists, about whether positive discrimination is ever justified, about whether the square of one integer is ever twice the square of another, or about whether there are any words in English that contain the consonant pair 'mt'. But we can also think about what sort of question each of these is. Is there a simple algorithm for settling it? Does it leave any room for irresoluble clashes of opinion? To what extent can views about the matter be said to be straightforwardly true or false?

This sort of ground-level/upper-level distinction is not always easy to sustain, either in theory or in practice. Certainly that is true as far as the two ways of taking the question 'How can we make sense of things?' are concerned. Making sense of things can include making sense of making sense of things. It can include establishing canons of authority and criteria of sanity for instance. Indeed, one of the reasons why I have begun with this question, and shall be using it in various ways to guide the whole enquiry, is precisely the fact that it can straddle the ground-level/upper-level divide. In so far as what follows counts as a work of ethics, I should be glad to think that it resists easy classification as either 'normative ethics' (ground-level ethics) or 'meta-ethics' (upper-level ethics). But still, I do recognize some sort of ground-level/upper-level distinction, and I do recognize the importance of something at the upper-level to orient and to motivate what follows. It is this that I shall be trying to provide in this Introduction.

How, then, is it possible for us to make sense of things? More particularly, what is involved in our being able to make ethical sense of things? What is the nature of our thinking about ethical issues?

§2 One of the first questions that anyone reflecting on these matters is likely to raise is this: 'Can our thinking about ethical issues hope to be *objective*?' But the word 'objective' is used in a bewildering variety of ways. If we are going to wield it at all, then we need to devote at least as much attention to clarifying it as to determining where it applies.

On any construal, objectivity has something to do with agreement. To say that our ethical thinking either is or can be objective is to say something positive about our chances of being able to reach ethical agreement, or of our being able to identify, explain, and eventually resolve ethical disagreement. Objectivity thus provides a kind of reassurance when it comes to broaching the corresponding ground-level issues. These issues are often, by their nature, of the utmost importance. It is reassuring to think that we can get the measure of disagreement in this way, because the apparent alternative is thoroughly alarming: namely, that disputes about these very important issues have the character, ultimately and dialectically, of a dispute about the relative merits of vanilla and chocolate ice-cream.

Nevertheless, it is very common, when people first reflect on ethical thought and confront these questions, for them to deny any such objectivity. It is common for them to think that disputes about ethical issues do indeed have the character of a dispute about the relative merits of vanilla and chocolate ice-cream; and that this sets them apart from disputes about scientific issues such as what the age of the universe is, or again from disputes about simple matters of fact such as who scored the winning goal in the 1969 FA Cup Final. In these latter cases, it will be said, one answer to the question can be 'proved', whereas, in the case of ethical disputes, 'proof' is not to the point.

This is an extremely familiar contrast. And it is an extremely dubious one, at least when it is stated so baldly. Much depends on what the criteria of successful proof are. Certainly, where the latter disputes are concerned, there is no question of forcing the agreement of someone who is not appropriately receptive (that is to say, sane, intelligent, attentive, and suchlike). But if this does not automatically count against an answer's being provable in these cases, then it cannot do so in ethical cases either. Imagine that you are an employer and that you find yourself in dispute with a fellow employer about how much compassionate leave is appropriate for one of your employees who is suffering from a bereavement: your colleague's judgement is more severe than yours. And imagine, if you can, that he (your colleague) is unwittingly betraying a kind of *Schadenfreude* at the very idea of another person's having to cope with such grief – or, less fancifully perhaps, at the very idea of *that* person's having to cope with such grief. Then certainly you are dealing with someone who is not appropriately receptive. In fact you are dealing with someone who is sick. That he can disagree with you on *this* basis has no bearing on the 'provability' of your own view. But then, what is there to say that something similar does not hold of other, apparently more reasonable bases on which he might disagree with you? Or again, consider this: which would you find easier, to demonstrate the horror of the Holocaust to a young child, or to demonstrate its historicity? We still lack a clearly enough defined conception of objectivity to be able to draw any conclusions, from these reflections, about the objectivity of ethical thinking. But they do indicate that the matter is not as straightforward as it is apt at first to appear, and that there is at any rate no *simple* reason for thinking that taking an ethical stance is dialectically akin to stating a preference as to ice-cream flavour.

Even so, people continue to find the ice-cream analogy compelling. One very basic reason for this is that our ethical views *engage* us, just as our preferences as to ice-cream flavour engage us. Thus, it might be said, if I think that the universe is fifteen thousand million years old, this is unlikely to affect my behaviour, whereas if I think that Third World debt should be cancelled, then this will naturally incline me to do certain things, say to campaign, or to vote for a suitable party, just as, if I prefer chocolate to vanilla ice-cream, this will naturally incline me to select the chocolate rather than the vanilla ice-cream.

But this is a crude oversimplification. In all three cases – that of my belief about the age of the universe, that of my conviction about Third World debt, and that of my preference for chocolate ice-cream – the most and the least that can be said, at this level of generality, is that I shall naturally be inclined to respond in certain ways to certain situations when all else is equal. Thus I shall select the chocolate rather than the vanilla ice-cream when I have the choice, and when there is nothing to hold me back (for instance, there is not some baying child with menacing parents who is about to be deprived of the last scoop of chocolate). But similarly, I shall say, 'Fifteen thousand million years', when I am asked for the age of the universe, and when there is nothing to hold me back (for instance, my answer does not give inappropriate assistance to someone in a quiz). By contrast, I shall not join in a campaign for the cancellation of Third World debt if I think that there are more pressing demands on my time, or if I am simply too lazy.

It is not just that our ethical views and our preferences engage us then. The point seems to be rather that there is something fundamental in common to the *ways* in which they engage us (however diverse these ways may otherwise be), something that makes a complete mystery of the idea that our ethical views are views about what is out there independently of us. Mackie captured this thought when he formulated what he famously called his 'argument from queerness' against the thesis that, as he put it, 'values are ... part of the fabric of the world'.[2] The argument, in a nutshell, is this: if values were part of the fabric of the world, then 'they would be entities or qualities or relations of a very strange sort, utterly different from anything else in the universe'.[3] Mackie was denying that the fabric of the world could contain anything such that, simply by knowing of it, you were impelled to act in certain ways. This was his way of denying the objectivity of ethical thinking.

Smith too has emphasized how the objectivity of ethical thinking seems to be precluded by its 'practicality'.[4] The way Smith puts it is in terms of the idea that how we think the world is is one thing, while how we want the world to be is quite another. If ethical thinking were objective, then this would suggest that our ethical views are a matter of how we think the world is; the practicality of ethical thinking suggests that they are a matter of how we want the world to be. Unlike Mackie, however, Smith does not proceed from there to a rejection of objectivism. No matter how natural or common it may be for us to reject objectivism when we first engage in meta-ethics, Smith thinks it is an unacceptable affront to our sense of what we are doing when we engage in *normative* (ground-level) ethics. We do after all argue with one another. We proceed as though there is a difference between getting it right and getting it wrong, and we fret about getting it right. So what Smith does is to reconsider the apparent incompatibility of objectivity with practicality. He argues – it is beyond the scope of this book to consider his argument[5] – that they are compatible after all. In effect, he tries to dispel any sense of queerness in ethical objectivism.

Others have tried to do the same. A striking example is Korsgaard, who writes:

> According to Mackie, it is fantastic to think that the world contains ... intrinsically normative entities. For ... they would have to meet certain impossible criteria. They would have to be entities of a very strange sort, utterly unlike anything else in the universe... [When you met one,] it would have to be – and I'm nearly quoting now – able

both to tell you what to do and make you do it. And nothing is like that.

But Mackie is wrong... [It] is the most familiar fact of human life that the world contains entities that can tell us what to do and make us do it. They are people ...⁶

This has important resonances for what is to come.

But neither Smith nor Korsgaard is trying to salvage the idea that our ethical views are views about what is out there independently of us. Here it is important to recall that objectivity can mean different things. To say that our ethical thinking is about something that is out there independently of it, or independently of us, is only one way of saying that it is objective. Here is another, quite different way: our ethical thinking is constrained to go in a certain direction. Call these two kinds of objectivity, respectively, *world-directed* objectivity and *conclusion-directed* objectivity. To see why they are different, consider our mathematical thinking. It is relatively uncontroversial that our mathematical thinking enjoys conclusion-directed objectivity. It is altogether harder to see whether it enjoys world-directed objectivity.⁷ Conclusion-directed objectivity seems to be somewhat weaker than world-directed objectivity, and less vulnerable to the charge of queerness. Admittedly, neither the metaphor of being 'out there independently of us' nor the metaphor of being 'constrained to go in a certain direction' is completely transparent. If what counts in the former case is whether values, numbers, or whatever it may be are real in anything like the way in which physical objects are real, then this raises the question of what counts as being real in 'anything like' that way. If what matters in the latter case is whether we can in the long run reasonably expect consensus, then this raises the question of who 'we' are, and of what counts as a 'reasonable expectation'. (Think again about the impossibility of securing the agreement of those who are not appropriately receptive.) Still, in so far as people's initial recoil from ethical objectivism is a recoil from queerness, the idea that ethical thinking enjoys *conclusion-directed* objectivity looks as if it might be able to draw them back to such objectivism, and back to its reassurances. Can it?

§3 There is still room for doubt. Let us assume that the conclusions towards which our ethical thinking is supposed to be directed are conclusions about reasons we have for adopting certain courses of action or living certain sorts of lives. Then one consequence of this form of objectivism seems to be this. Someone can have a reason for doing something, and can indeed be forced to acknowledge that he has a reason for doing something, even though doing that thing contributes nothing to the satisfaction of any of his 'conative states' – even though it is not in any of his interests, promotes none of his values, furthers none of his projects, realizes none of his aims, and makes none of his dreams come true. Many people find this idea baffling.

It is important here to distinguish between two ways of construing the notion of a reason. The notion can be construed explanatorily, and it can be construed normatively. Construed explanatorily, the notion of a reason is a matter of why someone does something: 'Your only reason for taking daily exercise is that you were nagged by your friends into doing so.' Construed normatively, the notion of a reason is a matter of why someone *should* do something: 'The benefits to your health give you a compelling reason to take daily exercise.' The idea that *explanatory* reasons can outstrip conative states in the way indicated is palpable nonsense. The issue is rather whether *normative* reasons can outstrip conative states in the way indicated. To say that they can may not be palpable nonsense. Even so, for many people it is still baffling. Why should anyone do anything that satisfies none of his conative states? If both he and his conative states are unlovely for one reason or another, then no doubt the rest of us will try to effect a change in him, through sanctions, blame, coercion, and the like, and no doubt this will include telling him that he should do things that he does not want to do and has no inclination to do. But however intelligible what we tell him may be as a piece of rhetoric, indeed however effective it may be, perhaps simply by virtue of registering our disapproval, there remains an unclarity concerning what purchase it has as a claim *about him* and about conclusions that he is forced to draw concerning himself. Conclusion-directed objectivity threatens to be as queer as world-directed objectivity. Is it?

As a first step towards answering this question, note that there is one extremely important way in which any queerness would in fact be dissipated. I have in mind the possibility that our ethical thinking should turn out to depend on conative states that we all share. If there were such states, and if these and these alone grounded the ethical reasons that we were supposed to have for adopting certain courses of action or living certain sorts of lives, then conclusion-directed objectivity would no longer involve normative reasons that outstripped our conative states in the supposedly objectionable way indicated. If, furthermore, the conative states in question were states that we not only shared but could not help sharing, then this would give the reasons a corresponding necessity; and this in turn would give suitable substance to the idea that our ethical thinking was 'constrained' to go in a certain direction. Since the conative states would also very likely lie deep, as would the connection between them and the reasons they grounded, it would also give substance to that powerful feeling which accompanies so much of our ethical thinking, namely that we are trying to *discover* something, something to which we are, moreover, beholden. What are the prospects for founding objectivity in *this* way? That is, what are the prospects, first, for there even being such conative states, and second, for our being able to demonstrate that there are such conative states?

Let us call such conative states – that is, conative states that we all share (perhaps as a matter of necessity) and that ground all our ethical reasons for doing things – *ethically productive* conative states. And let us call the thesis that there are ethically productive conative states *conative objectivism*. Our bipartite question, in these terms, is this. What are the prospects for the truth of conative objectivism, and what are the prospects for our being able to demonstrate its truth?

Certainly, to begin with the second of these, it would be a formidable undertaking. Great care would be required not only to identify these ethically productive conative states, but also, if the conative objectivism involved the claim that they were ours as a matter of necessity, to identify the type of necessity. Would it be conceptual? Biological? Sociological? Would it perhaps be 'dialectical', that is to say, would the conative states be ones (like due respect for reason, say) that we had to have in order so much as to engage in this type of enquiry? There would also be the question, which I mentioned in a related connection in §2, of who 'we' were. Human beings? Normal human beings? ('Normal' here should give pause.) Any animals capable of intelligent and purposive behaviour? Any beings capable of reasoning?

Throughout this, there would be an ever-present danger of question begging. Clearly, on any plausible account of what the conative states were, examples would inevitably abound of those who seemed to lack them. To show that these examples were unthreatening would be to show either that appearances were deceptive – that those concerned did have the conative states, but somewhere deep beneath the surface, and that what lay *on* the surface was the result of various processes of distortion (sublimation, acculturation, or the like) – or that the examples did not count, say, because those concerned were not included among 'us'. To try to show either of these things would be to run the clear risk of betraying both prejudice and narrow-mindedness – championing the ethical outlook, or an ethical outlook, that was grounded in one's own conative states. Especially acute, no doubt, would be the problem of circumscribing who 'we' were in a principled way, without riding roughshod over the legitimate interests of others. Here Aristotle is worth mentioning. He famously sought to defend a kind of conative objectivism; to found ethics in a shared natural '*telos*'. But this *telos* was not, on Aristotle's account, shared by everyone, or at least not fully and properly: it was not, fully and properly, shared by defectives, 'natural slaves', or women, and it was disabled even in the case of non-defective freemen who had not been properly brought up.[8] It is easy, from our vantage point in a very different cultural setting, to lambast Aristotle for being so blinkered. This would itself be blinkered. Nevertheless, it needs no further comment from me to highlight the parochialism of *that* attempt to defend conative objectivism, nor, for that matter, to highlight the unacceptability (to us) of its results. If we are to make an even half-reasonable stab at demonstrating the truth of conative objectivism, we shall need to set our universalist sights a good deal higher. But how high? And on what principles?

There remains in any case the first half of the question: what are the prospects that conative objectivism is true in the first place? Consider this. If you and I both want the government to be ousted at the next general election, do we have the same want? Do we share a conative state? Clearly we do. Now, if you want to slake your thirst and I want to slake my thirst, or if you want to win this game of chess that we are playing and I want to win this game of chess that we are playing, do we have the same want? Do we share a conative state? This is less clear. In a sense we do; in a sense we do not. These two cases point up a contrast that did not need to be drawn in the first case. In all three cases there is your individual want explaining your purposive behaviour (campaigning for the opposition party, reaching for a glass of water, concentrating hard on the game) and there is my individual want explaining my purposive behaviour (campaigning for the opposition party, reaching for a glass of water, concentrating hard on the game). In all three cases we have the same want in the sense that our individual wants are of the same *type*: they play the same explanatory role with respect to our purposive behaviour. But only in the first case do we have the same want in the sense that our individual wants have the same *content*: the same thing satisfies them. This is not true in either the second case or the third case. Indeed, in the third case – the case in which you want to win this game of chess that we are playing and I want to win this game of chess that we are playing – our individual wants have *conflicting* content. (They may do even in the second case, if there is only one glass of water.)

This distinction has a bearing on the prospects for conative objectivism, though unfortunately a negative bearing.[9] Ethically productive conative states must satisfy two criteria: they must be conative states that we all share; and they must ground all our ethical reasons for doing things. The problem is that the sense in which we are most likely to share any conative states is not the sense in which any conative states we share are most likely to ground our ethical reasons for doing things. At least, *prima facie* it is not. Again we must proceed cautiously. Still there is the question of who 'we' are; still there is the question of what sort of necessity (if any) is at stake; and now there is the question of what our criteria of likelihood are. But suppose we are talking about what can be expected of normal human beings, as a matter of biological necessity, say. Then while there are indeed good reasons to expect us to share various conative states (subject, of course, to continuing reservations about 'normal', and in particular the worry that it trivializes our expectation), this means that there are good reasons to expect us to have various conative states of the same type, playing the same explanatory role with respect to our purposive behaviour – the obvious examples, if not the only examples, being conative states connected with survival and reproduction. There are not the same good reasons to expect us to have various conative states with the same content, that is to say conative states satisfied by the same thing. *Socio*biology takes us in this latter direction, but less sure-footedly and not all the way. On the other hand, unless our shared conative states are conative states with the same content, then given some fairly minimal assumptions about the relationship between ethics and our living in harmony with one another, it is altogether harder to see why they should be expected to ground any ethical reasons we have for doing things. That is, it is altogether harder to see why they should be expected to ground any ethical reasons we have for doing things *in the relevant way*. We are of course familiar with the idea that A's conative states can ground B's ethical reasons for doing things, such as giving suitable rein to the satisfaction of A's conative states, even though doing these things satisfies none of B's conative states. But *that* way of grounding ethical reasons is beside the point here. However familiar we may be with this idea, it is just the sort of idea, baffling to many, that this whole discussion of conative objectivism was designed to circumvent.

What we are witnessing here, in small part, are general grounds for pessimism about the very project of founding ethical objectivity in human nature. These are marvellously expressed by Williams as follows:

> A correct understanding of human evolution is very relevant to projects of this kind, but ... the effect of that understanding is largely discouraging to them. This is for two [reasons]. The first is ... simply that the most plausible stories now available about that evolution, including its very recent date and also certain considerations about the physical characteristics of the species, suggest that human beings are to some degree a mess, and that the rapid and immense development of symbolic and cultural capacities has left humans as beings for which no form of life is likely to prove entirely satisfactory, either individually or socially...
>
> The second ... reason lies not in the particular ways in which human beings may have evolved, but simply in the fact that they have evolved, and by natural selection. The idea of a naturalistic ethics was born of a deeply teleological outlook, and its best expression, in many ways, is still to be found in Aristotle's philosophy, a philosophy according to which there is inherent in each natural kind of thing an appropriate way for things of that kind to behave. On that view it must be the deepest desire – need? – purpose? – satisfaction? – of human beings to live in a way that is in this objective sense appropriate

to them ... The first and hardest lesson of Darwinism, that there is no such teleology at all, and that there is no orchestral score provided from anywhere according to which human beings have a special part to play, still has to find its way fully into ethical thought.¹⁰

There are countless ways of responding to such pessimism, of course, including the two obvious extremes of rejecting ethical objectivity altogether and of attempting to found it in some other way. One response, which will be of great significance later, is well captured in a quotation from Ansell Pearson, writing about the philosophy of Deleuze. This quotation makes a striking juxtaposition with the quotation from Williams just given. Ansell Pearson writes:

> It is important to appreciate ... that nature is not constructed for our convenience, it is full of cruelty and lack of sympathy for our peculiar being and evolves without regard for our particular habitat in it. There are few deaths in nature that are not brutal, violent, and fortuitous. The task, however, is to comprehend this and to bestow upon such deaths a new meaning, which is the 'meaning' of a praxis that can only arise out of creating, and experimenting with, new possibilities of existence ... [There] is never any finality in nature or evolution, but only a musical expression of nature involving explication, implication, and complication ... [We] are to become those that we are: musicians of nature and artists of our own cultivation.¹¹

Williams says that we are given no orchestral score according to which we have a special part to play. The Deleuzian response is, 'No, indeed; we must write our own orchestral score and play our own special part according to it.'

Another way of responding to the pessimism is to try to counter it. Nothing that has been said so far shows conclusively that we cannot demonstrate the truth of conative objectivism, still less that it cannot be true, even when it is interpreted as a thesis about conative states that human beings must have as a matter of biological necessity. Nor, *a fortiori*, does anything that has been said so far show conclusively that we cannot demonstrate its truth under at least *some* reasonable interpretation. In particular, my passing reference to sociobiology above indicates one way in which it might still be thought to be demonstrable – and hence in which the ulterior project of founding ethical objectivity might still be thought to be realizable. (I emphasize the ulterior project here, because there is a popular view whereby the only project of this kind to which sociobiology, or anything like it, could be relevant would be the project of explaining away the *appearance* of ethical objectivity. That view probably rests on an inappropriately ambitious conception of objectivity. In fact, it probably rests on a conception of objectivity as world-directed. A typical expression of the view would be this: 'The most that sociobiology can show is that our ethical convictions are internalized rules by means of which society manages to hold itself together.' Whether or not that is the most that sociobiology can show, it is surely a further question whether any *more* would be required for our ethical convictions to be objective.) A quite different way in which conative objectivism might still be thought to be demonstrable, at least to those suitably open to appeals to the supernatural, would be in terms of some transcendent design. This could be supplemented by a rejection of the evolutionary stories that I have so far more or less been taking for granted, but it need not be. Suppose, however, that none of these ways of demonstrating conative objectivism met with any degree of success, and yet that there were still some hope that it was true. Then, I submit – and this too will be of great significance later – there would not only still be the hope. There would still be room for the hope.

§4 I now want to consider an apparently very different way of trying to found the objectivity of ethics, in its conclusion-directed form. (The importance of the qualification 'apparently' will be clear later.[12]) I shall call it *rationalism*. Rationalism has been of unsurpassed significance in the history of ethics (both at ground-level and at upper-level). The rest of this Introduction will be devoted to presenting it. And most of the rest of the book will be devoted to exploring it.

When I first introduced conclusion-directed objectivity, in contradistinction to world-directed objectivity, I did so in relation to mathematics. I suggested that it would be much bolder to attribute the latter kind of objectivity to our mathematical thinking than it would be to attribute the former kind. That our mathematical thinking enjoys conclusion-directed objectivity is, roughly, the default view: something very powerful and independently motivated would be required to overturn it. That our mathematical thinking does not, on the other hand, enjoy world-directed objectivity is, roughly, the upshot of a Mackiean recoil from queerness: if there were mathematical entities out there, they would be entities of a queer sort. However, if our mathematical thinking does enjoy the former kind of objectivity without the latter, then the fact that we can do mathematics at all is a very striking fact. Or rather, since it is a very striking fact that we can do mathematics on any account, it becomes striking in a distinctive way. This comes out in relation to the suggestion made by Williams, in the light of what we know about human evolution, 'that human beings are to some degree a mess, and that the rapid and immense development of symbolic and cultural capacities has left humans as beings for which no form of life is likely to prove entirely satisfactory'.[13] For our mathematical thinking is itself a paradigmatic expression of such symbolic and cultural capacities. If it enjoys conclusion-directed objectivity without world-directed objectivity – if it is constrained in how it proceeds, but not by a subject matter that is out there independently of it – then its constraints must be internal. So there must be certain deep confluences in how we exercise the capacities to which Williams alludes, confluences whose existence his suggestion prevents us from regarding as a matter of course. They are *not* a matter of course. It is not a matter of course that humans agree about patterns of symbol manipulation, about how these control the application of different syntactic rules and the implementation of different syntactic procedures, and about how these in turn register the exercise of formal concepts, all to the extent of being able to sustain mathematics as a serious collective enterprise.[14] As it is, there are plenty of people who fail to see what is going on in mathematics beyond a certain rudimentary level. Had their failure been both more serious and more widespread, then, in the absence of world-directed objectivity, there would have been nothing there to see.

World-directed objectivity, if only it were not queer, would have obvious explanatory potential here. If there were a mathematical reality out there independently of our mathematical thinking, populated by numbers, matrices, geometrical figures, and the rest, and if we were in some sort of knowledgeable contact with it, then there would be little wonder, or less wonder, or at any rate not the same wonder, that we agreed about how to proceed in mathematics, to the extent of being able to sustain mathematics as a serious collective enterprise. For we would simply be agreeing about what this mathematical reality was like. This would be akin to the fact that we agree about what physical reality is like, to the extent of being able to sustain physics as a serious collective enterprise. And in the mathematical case, as in the physical case, there might be good reason to think that being in some sort of knowledgeable contact with this reality had been of evolutionary benefit to us, say because physical reality was in some sense modelled on it and we were thereby better able to negotiate our way round physical objects. But without world-directed objectivity, all there is to sustain mathematics as a serious collective enterprise is our own concerted endeavour – our own capacity, through shared practices and a shared understanding of them, to generate mathematical concepts and *to make shared mathematical sense of things*. How can we make sense, in turn, of that?

This is a genuine question. I do not mean to suggest that we *cannot* make sense of it. If that were true, then we might just as well trade this queerness for the queerness of world-directed objectivity and avail ourselves of *its* explanatory potential. My question is a genuine question, and various kinds of answers suggest themselves. One possibility would be to see our capacity to make shared mathematical sense of things as an integral part of our capacity to make shared physical sense of (physical) things. Another would be to see the former as a by-product of the latter. Each of these would need to be supplemented by an account of the applicability of mathematics. Each of them would also need to be supplemented by an account of what we are actually doing when we engage in mathematics: modelling the structure of our own thought, playing games with symbols, or whatever. My point is not to cast doubt on whether any such answer can be given. My point is only that one needs to be given. It is indeed striking, in the absence of a mathematical reality out there, that such higgledy-piggledy products of nature as us, with, as Hollis puts it, 'our ... two eyes, thirty feet of digestive tract and opposable thumbs',[15] can nevertheless, when we set to it, attain to such sublimities of mathematical thinking as that $e^{i\pi} + 1 = 0$.[16]

But suppose that mathematics does enjoy conclusion-directed objectivity without world-directed objectivity, and that this striking fact can ultimately be explained. Now mathematics is an *a priori* discipline. Whatever role experience may play in generating it, or in facilitating its practice, or in assessing its applicability, there is an important sense in which mathematics proceeds without reference to experience, through the sheer *a priori* exercise of concepts. This exercise places those who engage in it firmly within what Sellars called 'the logical space of reasons'.[17] Having mathematical concepts involves acknowledging that certain judgements, say the judgement that there are two apples and two bananas in the bowl, are reasons for certain others, say the judgement that there are at least four pieces of fruit in the bowl. Exercising mathematical concepts – without recourse to experience – involves making such reasons explicit,[18] and engaging in mathematics involves exercising mathematical concepts – without recourse to experience. I say this without prejudice on the question to which I alluded a little earlier, of what we are actually doing when we engage in mathematics (whether we are modelling the structure of our own thought, playing games with symbols, or whatever). That question remains open, because the question of what the character of our mathematical concepts is remains open. The point is: whatever their character, mathematics proceeds through the sheer *a priori* exercise of them – through the unaided use of reason. And this must be part of the story about why it enjoys conclusion-directed objectivity without world-directed objectivity.

Part of the *story*, I say; not part of the explanation. The fact that mathematics proceeds through the unaided use of reason belongs as much to the *explicandum* as it does to the *explicans*. The striking fact that we are able to do mathematics is but one manifestation of the striking fact that we are able to reason at all. But we are; and this in turn means that, however much of a mess we are, we are able, to some degree, to attain to that orderliness and coherence that constitutes living by concepts – that constitutes making sense of things.

Rationalism is the thesis that this ability to reason embraces not only our mathematical thinking but our ethical thinking too. It is the thesis that we can attain to just such an orderliness and coherence by making *ethical* sense of things, and that we can determine what to do and how to live by the use of pure reason. This means that if our mathematical thinking does enjoy conclusion-directed objectivity without world-directed objectivity, then so too does our ethical thinking.

The analogy with mathematics does not solve all the problems that this raises of course. This is not least because of how many of these problems remain to be solved in the case of mathematics itself. The point of this excursion on mathematics has not been that we can see clearly enough how our mathematical thinking enjoys conclusion-directed objectivity without world-directed objectivity to be able to see how rationalism might secure the same combination for our ethical thinking. The point has not even been that we can see clearly enough *that* our mathematical thinking enjoys conclusion-directed objectivity without world-directed objectivity to be able to see that rationalism might secure the same combination for our ethical thinking. What we can see (and indeed what we can see *less* clearly than we would wish) is just our mathematical thinking. The point of the excursion has been simply that, *if* our mathematical thinking enjoys conclusion-directed objectivity without world-directed objectivity, which – despite the contingencies of nature that make this a matter for special explanation – it certainly seems to, then rationalism might indeed secure the same combination for our ethical thinking. This is enough for rationalism to be worth exploring. It is not enough for rationalism to be spared the formidable problems about the nature of rationality that afflict the philosophy of mathematics.

§5 But are there in any case some simple and decisive objections to rationalism? There are three principal objections which are worth mentioning straight away.

The first is this. Rationalism has the absurd consequence that there can be ethical expertise, rather like mathematical expertise, the sort of thing that might be fostered through teaching and research in relevant university departments. People's untutored views about ethical issues are then of use only up to a certain basic level. Beyond that, the careful ratiocination of those clever enough and suitably trained is all that can settle ethical questions. Where appropriate, the rest of us must just accept the authority that such people have for the answers they give.

Some rationalists would concede that rationalism has this consequence but deny that it is absurd. It seems so, they might say, only because of the value and importance that we attach to individuals thinking about ethical questions for themselves. But there are ways of accounting for this without denying that experts are more reliable arbiters of what is right and wrong. (We do after all attach *some* value and importance to non-experts, children say, thinking about mathematical questions for themselves. This helps them to develop their understanding both of the relevant concepts and of mathematical practice. It does not follow that their views are to be taken as seriously as those of experts.)

But whether or not this would be an absurd consequence for rationalism to have, there is in any case a question about whether it has it.[19] That ethical thinking is fundamentally a matter of reasoning leaves open the possibility that it is a matter of simple native reasoning, using concepts whose creation, dissemination, appropriation, and application in the first place are what constitute the significant ethical work, work which has next to nothing in common with proving mathematical theorems and which does not in any other way suggest an analogy with mathematical expertise. (Yet again I am alluding to something that will be of great significance later.)

The second objection is one that Mackie levels (along with his objection on the grounds of queerness) against *any* version of objectivism. It is based on what he describes as 'the well-known variation in moral codes from one society to another and from one period to another, and also the differences in moral beliefs between different groups and classes within a complex community'.[20] As Mackie observes, mere disagreement does not preclude objectivity. There are disagreements about scientific matters, and, we might add, about mathematical matters. (Some mathematicians object to the use that other mathematicians make of the concept of infinity. Some accept and others deny that there can be unprovable mathematical truths, a disagreement that translates into disagreement about the validity, within mathematics, of certain basic methods of proof.[21]) What matters is not whether there are in fact disagreements. What matters is how the disagreements are to be understood. The difference between ethical disagreements and these other disagreements, according to this Mackiean objection, is that the latter can be understood in a way that is suitably related to our chances of being able to eliminate them, and to what would be involved in our eliminating them. Specifically, they can be understood in terms of some conception of *error*: of what error is, and of how it can arise. Thus scientific disagreement, according to Mackie, 'results from speculative inferences or explanatory hypotheses based on inadequate evidence'.[22] 'It is hardly plausible,' he continues, 'to interpret moral disagreement in the same way. Disagreement about moral codes seems to reflect people's adherence to and participation in different ways of life.'

One response to this second objection is to try to defend the objectivity of our ethical thinking by combining it with a kind of relativism. Such a combination, which has the effect of making our ethical disagreement look merely apparent, is by no means untenable. Here again it helps to think about the mathematical case. There is Euclidean geometry, according to which there cannot be more than one straight line between any two points. And there are non-Euclidean geometries, according to which there *can* be more than one straight line between two points. *Prima facie* a mathematician who adopts Euclidean geometry is disagreeing with a mathematician who adopts one of these non-Euclidean alternatives. In fact, however, it is possible to view the two mathematicians as operating with different systems of concepts, albeit concepts that are sufficiently closely related, in sufficiently important ways, for it to be natural to use the same vocabulary to express them. This enables us to see the disagreement between the two mathematicians as merely apparent. (I am assuming that they are not in dispute about how to apply these concepts in the description of real physical space.) This issues in a kind of relativism that is no threat to the objectivity of our mathematical thinking. Each of the two mathematicians can accept that there is never more than one *Euclidean* straight line between two *Euclidean* points. The idea, then, is that something similar holds of apparent disagreements in ethics: what Mackie calls 'people's adherence to and participation in different ways of life' is just an analogue of mathematicians' adoption of different systems of geometrical concepts.

Still, there are many problems with this response. The most serious is that in certain cases – in the cases that are of greatest theoretical interest and of greatest practical concern – 'people's adherence to and participation in different ways of life' are the source of real practical conflicts, conflicts in which there are disagreements about *what to do* and in which those concerned may literally be killing one another as a result. Plainly, no analogue of explicitly relativizing principles of geometry to some system of geometrical concepts is going to bring peace in such cases. That is a tragic fact of life. At the theoretical level, it means that such disagreements have still not been understood in a way that can be clearly reconciled with the objectivity of ethical thinking. The second objection is one that we shall have to come back to.

The third objection is one that likewise relates to the impact of our ethical thinking on *what to do*. I talked in §2 about the tension between the objectivity of our ethical thinking and its practicality. That was when the objectivity in question was world-directed objectivity. The tension is part of what makes world-directed objectivity queer. Later, in §3, I discussed conative objectivism, whereby the objectivity of our ethical thinking is conclusion-directed objectivity and the tension disappears. But it does not disappear *just because* the objectivity is conclusion-directed. It disappears because of the appeal that conative objectivism makes to ethically productive conative states. According to the third objection, when the conclusion-directed objectivity of our ethical thinking is to be secured not by appeal to ethically productive conative states but by appeal to the use of pure reason, as it is in rationalism, then the tension re-appears. For the use of pure reason can have no jurisdiction over what to do. Its jurisdiction is rather over what to *think*. Thus, for instance, it can determine what follows from what and what is inconsistent with what. In doing this, it may indeed combine with our conative states to issue in various decisions, choices, courses of action, and the like – or even to issue in further conative states. (If I want to achieve some goal, and I come to think, as a result of reasoning, that it is impossible to do so without achieving some subsidiary goal, then it is likely that I shall end up wanting to achieve that subsidiary goal too.) But the use of pure reason cannot itself, ultimately, dictate what we are to do. In so far as we can reason about what to do, this is always a matter of determining the means to an end, never of determining the end itself. As Hume memorably and vividly put it, 'Reason is, and ought only to be the slave of the passions, and can never pretend to any other office than to serve and obey them.'[23]

I shall make no attempt to answer this third objection here. Like the second, it is one that we shall have to come back to. The basic challenge for any species of rationalism is to answer the question: how can pure reason be practical?

§6 These three objections notwithstanding, rationalism has its appeal, quite apart from the appeal of securing conclusion-directed objectivity for our ethical thinking without world-directed objectivity. The demands of ethics do seem to share with the demands of reason a certain laser-beam quality which Murdoch so wonderfully sums up as follows: 'very clear, narrow, strong, coming from an unseen source, illuminating a point in [the] world'.[24] The compulsion to accept, say, that Mary is mortal, granted that Mary is a human being and granted that all human beings are mortal, has a feel of unyielding focused intensity about it which is not unlike the feel of the compulsion to accept that one should abide by a promise. Again, rationalism seems to do justice to that sense of discovery which accompanies much of our ethical thinking, and to which I said in §3 that conative objectivism does (a different kind of) justice: the sense of trying to discover something to which we are beholden.

I by no means want to cast such feelings in the role of data that must be respected at all costs. Meta-ethics has to reckon with the possibility that ordinary (ground-level) ethical thinking is accompanied by all sorts of feelings, conceptions, and convictions that must ultimately be exposed as illusory. But if exposing these things as illusory is in turn going to have an unsettling effect on ethical thinking itself, perhaps even to the point that we can no longer engage in it in good faith, at least not in the same way and to the same extent, then there are some basic questions that need to be addressed about what is answerable to what.

The same questions arise in the philosophy of mathematics. It is a popular view, most famously expressed by Wittgenstein, that the philosophy of mathematics must be non-revisionary; that, to reverse Marx's dictum, it is not the business of philosophers to *change* mathematics, only to interpret it.[25] Lewis also expresses the view, with characteristic wit. He writes:

> I'm moved to laughter at the thought of how *presumptuous* it would be to reject mathematics for philosophical reasons. How would *you* like the job of telling the mathematicians that they must change their ways, ... now that *philosophy* has discovered [the errors of those ways]? Can you tell them, with a straight face, to follow philosophical argument wherever it may lead? If they challenge your credentials, will you boast of philosophy's other great discoveries: that motion is impossible, ... that it is unthinkable that anything exists outside the mind, that time is unreal, ... that it is a wide-open scientific question whether anyone has ever believed anything, and so on, and on, *ad nauseam*?[26]

To be sure, the rhetoric here masks numerous complications and subtleties. There may after all be philosophical errors to which mathematicians are especially prone and which they infiltrate into their own discipline. The fact remains that, whenever philosophical reflection has an unsettling effect on our mathematical thinking – for instance, when it fastens on the finitude of our resources to deal with the positive integers 1, 2, 3, ... and leads to doubts about whether there really are infinitely many of them[27] – then there is, *prima facie*, at least as much reason to be suspicious of the philosophical reflection as there is to be suspicious of our mathematical thinking. And the same sort of thing is true when philosophical reflection has an unsettling effect on our ethical thinking. To that extent, if only perhaps to that extent, it is a virtue of rationalism to respect the feelings which I have said naturally accompany much of our ethical thinking.

Rationalism's credentials extend as far back as Plato, and beyond. Plato was one of the great champions of the view that pure reason can be practical (even if this is not a particularly Platonic way of putting it);[28] and his associated veneration of mathematics was given celebrated expression in the inscription which he placed over the doorway of the academy he founded: 'Let no-one enter here who is ignorant of geometry.' Ever since then, rationalism, in one form or another, has been a mighty force in ethics, variously applied, exposed, expounded, resisted, or reinforced by successive generations of ethicists as they have seen fit. My aim in what follows is to probe rationalism more fully, in certain connections and in certain applications, taking as my starting point its most famous incarnation.

§7 Before I proceed, there are two remaining tasks for this Introduction. I have already made a number of promissory claims. These will structure the enquiry in various important ways. I think it will be instructive to have them out in the open. The first task is simply to list them. They are:

i that I shall be using as a guide for the enquiry the question, 'How can we make sense of things?' (§1);
ii that Korsgaard's riposte to Mackie, in which she cites people as 'entities that can tell us what to do and make us do it', has important resonances for what is to come (§2);
iii (in the wake of Williams' pessimism about founding objectivity in human nature) that the Deleuzian response to Williams which can be found in Ansell Pearson – the response that we must as it were write our own orchestral score and play our own special part according to it – will be of significance later (§3);
iv that the idea that there is room for hope, where the truth of conative objectivism is concerned, will be of significance later (§3);
v that it will be clear later why I describe rationalism as 'apparently' very different from conative objectivism (§4);
vi (in response to the first objection to rationalism) that the idea that ethical thinking is a matter of simple native reasoning, and that the significant ethical work is done in providing and implementing the concepts that are its raw material, is an allusion to something that will be of significance later (§5);
vii that we shall have to come back to the second objection to rationalism, namely that there are disagreements in ethics that cannot be understood in terms of any conception of error (§5);
viii that we shall have to come back to the third objection to rationalism, namely that pure reason cannot be practical (§5).

It ought to be possible, by the end of the book, to return to each of these and to see how I take myself to have vindicated or satisfied it.[29]

The second task is to say a little about the format of the book. In one fairly straightforward sense this is a book about Kant. It is Kant's version of rationalism that I shall be taking as my starting point. As the book progresses I shall be looking at aspects of his moral and religious philosophy. But 'aspects' is the operative word. This book is not intended as a comprehensive study. (In three short annotated bibliographies at the end of the three chapters principally on Kant I shall cite a small sample of the many excellent books that already provide that.) Nor does it involve any serious exegesis. My aim is rather, in a spirit of selective appropriation, to rehearse some of Kant's ideas, then to explore possibilities that they open up and to work around possibilities that they close off. The format of the book is therefore that of themes and variations. (The variations will themselves often draw on themes from other great philosophers.) There will be three chapters presenting the main themes, alternating with three chapters presenting the variations on them.[30]

First theme: morality

> How recognizable, how familiar to us, is the man so beautifully portrayed [by Kant] in the [*Groundwork*], who confronted even with Christ turns away to consider the judgment of his own conscience and to hear the voice of his own reason... [This] man is with us still, free, independent, lonely, powerful, rational, responsible, brave.
> (Iris Murdoch, 'The Sovereignty of Good over Other Concepts', p. 80)

§1 In Kant we find epitomized all that is deeply attractive and all that is deeply unattractive about rationalism. At the beginning of his essay 'An Answer to the Question: What Is Enlightenment?' he writes:

> *Enlightenment is the human being's emergence from his self-incurred minority. Minority* is inability to make use of one's own understanding without direction from another. This minority is *self-incurred* when its cause lies not in lack of understanding but in lack of resolution and courage to use it without direction from another. *Sapere aude!* Have courage to make use of your own understanding! is the motto of enlightenment.[1]

Here Kant is celebrating what he sees as our (humanity's) recent awakening to the realization that the only authority, where ultimate matters of truth and value are concerned, is our own authority, the authority of our own unaided reason. The exigent demand to work things out for ourselves is at the same time the liberating reassurance that we *can* work things out for ourselves. We have both the duty and the privilege to direct our own lives and to make our own sense of things, which we can do through the exercise of that faculty which quintessentially distinguishes us from other animals: the faculty of reason. There is something uplifting and ennobling about Kant's vision. In its portrayal of a single supreme source of value, tapped by reason, inherent in reason, transcending all but reason, and freely available to each of us, it has an almost solacious quality. And yet, at the same time, Kant's vision has appeared to many as a repugnant mockery of all that is important in our lives. It has seemed hide-bound, cold, calculating, abstract, monolithic, devoid of compassion, an empty formalism. Most of Kant's admirers insist that this is itself a repugnant mockery of Kant. The fact remains that what Kant has bequeathed to us has been of almost equal significance in its capacity to repel as in its capacity to engage, a fact which is part of its enduring fascination.

§2 We begin with a distinction that Kant draws between 'hypothetical imperatives' and 'categorical imperatives'. Rational beings differ from other beings capable of purposive behaviour in that they can reflect on their behaviour and act *for reasons*. Whenever there is a reason to act in a certain way, we can say that there is an *imperative* to act in that way. The imperative is *hypothetical* when the reason is to procure some further end that the agent may have: acting in that way is a means to that end. The imperative is *categorical* when the reason is independent of any such end: acting in that way is 'good in itself' and commends itself to any rational being, simply *qua* rational.[2]

To adapt an example from Wittgenstein, imagine someone who is being urged to take tennis lessons. He may demur on the grounds that he is not particularly concerned to improve his game. If he is being urged to stop telling outrageous lies, on the other hand, then he does not seem to have any analogous way of demurring.[3] In the former case there is a hypothetical imperative. Since the man lacks the relevant end, the imperative does not apply to him. In the latter case there seems to be a categorical imperative. The imperative seems to apply to him willy-nilly.

The terminology is not altogether happy. For one thing, the sheer fact that an imperative can be hypothetical means that the word 'imperative', with its connotations of (inescapable) obligation, is misleading. Moreover, to express an imperative, it is not necessary to use a sentence with the grammatical form of an imperative. Someone can say to the man just considered, 'You must stop telling these lies.' Again, to express a hypothetical imperative, it is not necessary to make explicit mention of the relevant end, still less to make explicit mention of it in the antecedent of a conditional. Someone can say (truly) to a man who does want to improve his tennis, 'You ought to take lessons.' There is no need to say, 'You ought to take lessons if [*or:* given that] you want to improve your game.' Conversely, it is possible to cast a categorical imperative as an injunction to do what is necessary to realize some aim – if the aim is one which is itself unavoidable for any rational being. Someone could say to the man considered previously, 'If you want to reform, you must stop telling these lies.' Let the terminology be as it may: the distinction itself certainly has some intuitive appeal.

Now it is Kant's view that morality (or ethics – unlike other writers I intend no distinction between these two terms[4]) is characterized by the categorical imperative. In other words, if there is a moral reason to act in a certain way, then the corresponding imperative is a categorical one. And vice versa: if there is a categorical imperative to act in a certain way, then the corresponding reason is a moral one. Such is Kant's rationalism.[5]

Why does Kant take the rational and the moral to be aligned in this way? In part, because he takes morality to be non-contingent. He thinks it would be absurd to claim that there is a basic (non-circumstantial) moral precept to act in a certain way though there might not have been. But this in turn means that (unless morality is a chimera, or unless it is in some way beyond our grasp – possibilities to which Kant is alive and to which we shall return, especially in Theme Two), any such precept needs to be discoverable by pure reason. The alternative is that experience is needed to discover it. But what experience is needed to discover could have been otherwise. It is contingent.[6]

Very well then; but why does Kant take morality to be non-contingent? One way to see why is by pressing the question, 'What could it be contingent on?' This is not just a rhetorical question, however. It has had plenty of historically and philosophically significant answers. The most noteworthy, perhaps, is: 'The will of God.' But Kant recoils from this answer, on the grounds that nothing short of God's goodness could give Him any authority to determine what we ought to do. What God wills is answerable to (antecedently given) moral standards, not vice versa. To put the point with a crudity that ought to help focus the attention: if God decreed tomorrow that we should castrate all non-Aryan males, this would not create a moral obligation to do so; it would create a moral obligation to rebel.

There has been much written about these issues.[7] A natural reaction to such crudity, on the part of those who think that morality *is* contingent on the will of God, is to say that this is not the sort of thing that God *could* decree. But this of course invites the question, 'In what sense of "could"?' If God's goodness is simply being taken for granted as something fixed, or again if there is something in the very conception of God that allows us to infer His goodness *a priori*, then this reaction is in effect a concession to Kant. The issues are subtle. And the added subtleties in Kant's own handling of them are exacerbated by the fact that he does, ultimately, acknowledge a sense in which morality depends on God's will – but only the sense in which it depends on your will or my will or the will of any other rational being. There remains a clear sense in which Kant subordinates divine authority to the authority of reason. And, despite the subtleties, this subordination has an appeal that is in many ways very basic. As Kant puts it:

> Even the Holy One of the Gospel must first be compared with our ideal of moral perfection before he is cognized as such; even he says of himself: why do you call me ... good? none is good (the archetype of

the good) but God only ... But whence have we the concept of God as the highest good? Solely from the *idea* of moral perfection that reason frames *a priori*.⁸

Another significant way of answering the question, 'What could morality be contingent on?' is: 'Shared conative states,' – that is, by appeal to what I called in the Introduction conative objectivism. Indeed, as I emphasized when I first introduced conative objectivism, in §3 of the Introduction, this answer can be embellished to: 'Necessarily shared conative states.' When it *is* thus embellished, even if the necessity in question is not the necessity that Kant takes to be characteristic of morality – even if it is biological necessity, say, and hence discoverable only through experience – we might wonder whether, were he to consider such an answer, it would be enough to appease him. But no. Kant writes:

> Suppose that finite rational beings were thoroughly agreed with respect to what they had to take as objects of their feelings of pleasure and pain and even with respect to the means they must use to obtain the first and avoid the other; ... the determining ground would still be only subjectively valid and merely empirical and would not have that necessity which is thought in every [moral] law, namely objective necessity from *a priori* grounds ... [This] seems at first glance to be mere cavilling at words; but it defines the terms of the most important distinction that can ever be considered in practical investigations.⁹

In fact Kant goes further and turns appeals to human nature on their head. Granted that human beings do have a faculty of reason, and assuming that 'in the natural constitution of a [living being] ... there will be found ... no instrument for some end other than what is also most appropriate to that end and best adapted to it',¹⁰ we cannot but be struck (Kant says) by how poorly suited our faculty of reason is to helping us satisfy our conative states; and indeed by its capacity to create in us new conative states and, with them, new frustrations and heartaches. Kant sees only one possible conclusion. He writes:

> Since reason is nevertheless given to us as a practical faculty, that is, as one that is to influence the *will* [sc. if only in the generation of hypothetical imperatives,] ... the true vocation of reason must be to produce a will that is good ... [And] in attaining this purpose [it] is capable only of its own kind of satisfaction, namely from fulfilling an end which in turn only reason determines.¹¹

§3 For Kant, then, there is nothing that morality could be contingent on. Hence his commitment to rationalism.

How then would he respond to the three principal objections to rationalism which I set out in §5 of the Introduction?

The first – that rationalism allows for ethical expertise – he would simply deny. He regards it as more or less a datum that people have a natural facility (no doubt absent in defectives and no doubt suppressed by all sorts of social and psychological forces in many non-defectives) to exercise pure reason in determining what is morally required of them. True, he thinks that, for any moral requirement, a quasi-mathematical demonstration can be given that it *is* a moral requirement, and such a demonstration will presumably be more accessible to some people than to others. But that is not the point. For what such a demonstration will do, in Kant's view, is to justify what in a sense needs no justification: it will explain *why* we should think something which, after suitably conscientious reflection, and quite independently of this demonstration, we can already see that we should think. Thus Kant writes:

> It would be easy to show how common human reason ... knows very well how to distinguish in every case that comes up what is good and what is evil, what is in conformity with duty or contrary to duty, if, without in the least teaching it anything new, we only, as did Socrates, make it attentive to its own principle; and that there is, accordingly, no need of science and philosophy to know what one has to do in order to be honest and good, and even wise and virtuous. We might even have assumed in advance that cognizance of what is incumbent upon everyone to do, and so also to know, would be the affair of every human being, even the most common.[12]

Again:

> What *duty* is, is plain of itself to everyone ... [The] moral law commands compliance from everyone, and indeed the most exact compliance. Apprising what is to be done in accordance with it must, therefore, not be so difficult that the most common and unpractised understanding should not know how to go about it.[13]

And in that famous and moving passage in the conclusion of his *Critique of Practical Reason* Kant leaves us in no doubt that he takes the moral law within us to be as open to (awestruck) view as the starry heavens above us.[14]

For all that, Kant freely admits the effort that is sometimes required to determine what we ought morally to do. (The quasi-mathematical demonstration may even be of help in such a case.[15]) He also admits the importance of education in fostering the natural facility that we have to determine what we ought morally to do. (He has a good deal to say about this.¹⁶) He is at liberty to admit these things because they concern what is involved in individuals exercising, or coming to exercise, or being helped to exercise, their own authority on matters of morality. There is no question of that deference to the authority of another which *is* suggested by the notion of ethical expertise and which, as we have seen, Kant would be the first to repudiate. In any case, it would be so much the worse for the first objection if it were an objection to his admitting *these* things. The fact remains that, once Kant has made the alignment between the rational and the moral, it seems to be something of an article of faith on his part that there is not *some* sort of analogue, in morality, of mathematical expertise.

Kant's answer to the first objection serves also to illustrate a very general difficulty for rationalism, namely that the first two objections significantly buttress each other. Answering either is liable to aggravate the problem of answering the other. The second objection is that rationalism makes a mystery of socially grounded moral disagreement. The better a case Kant makes for our having a natural facility to determine what is morally required of us, the more of a mystery this becomes.[17]

It is a mystery that is related to, though importantly different from, another mystery which lies at the heart of Kant's moral and religious philosophy and to which we shall return in Themes Two and Three, the mystery of immorality. If rationality and morality are aligned in the way that Kant says they are, how are rational beings able to act immorally? Kant has much to say about this. Ultimately, he concedes, immorality is inexplicable. Even so, he does give, in outline, explanations of some of its specific manifestations. And some of these explanations – explanations of why people indulge in various particular violations of the dictates of morality – might readily be converted into explanations of why they make various particular errors about what those dictates are.[18] However that may be, there is a real issue for Kant about why so many people in so many places and at so many times have had ethical outlooks that have been at such radical variance with one another (including many that have been at radical variance with his own: that uncompromisingly deontological, utterly pietistic code of conduct emblematic of his own place and time[19]). Kant is not as green as he is usually portrayed as being. Nevertheless, it is hard to escape the feeling that his biggest problem, as far as this second objection and the attendant need to explain socially grounded moral disagreement are concerned, is a somewhat closeted unawareness of how much needs to be explained.

The third objection is the most basic. It is the objection (in effect) that categorical imperatives are not possible; that no way of acting can commend itself to rational beings simply because they are rational.

Hypothetical imperatives, and the use of reason to generate them, are relatively unproblematical. Suppose I already have a reason to do x, which I acknowledge. And suppose I come to see that I cannot do x without doing y. Then, to the extent that I am rational, I shall come to acknowledge that I have a reason to do y too (a reason that may well of course be overridden). As Kant puts it, 'whoever wills the end also wills (insofar as reason has decisive influence on his actions) the indispensably necessary means to it that are within his power'.[20] Relatedly, if there *were* any categorical imperatives, then the use of reason to apply them would be relatively unproblematical. If there were a categorical imperative for me to do z, which I acknowledged, and if I came to see that I could not do z without doing w, then, to the extent that I was rational, I should come to acknowledge that I had a reason to do w too. But how can pure reason dictate what I am to do in the first place? How are categorical imperatives possible?

Reconsider the man telling outrageous lies. I said in §2 that there seems to be a categorical imperative for him to stop. But is there? Really? It is important here not to beg questions about the alignment of the rational with the moral. A categorical imperative, remember, is one that it would be *irrational* to flout.[21] Suppose this man has not the least inclination to reform. There are all sorts of charges that can be brought against him; but do they really include the charge of irrationality?

It is not just a question of whether reason can be put to practical use beyond the simple generation of hypothetical imperatives. Of course it can. Sometimes, through the exercise of reason, we see that two or more of our conative states have conflicting content. We then decide, perhaps again with the help of reason, how much store to set by each of them. And we act accordingly. (We differ in this respect from non-rational beings who act simply on the pristine strength of their conative states.) This certainly illustrates a practical use of reason beyond the simple generation of hypothetical imperatives; but not to generate categorical imperatives; not to determine ends of its own. It is the latter that still needs to be accounted for. Somehow Kant needs to show how, in addition to the comparatively unproblematical uses of reason, there is this contested use; how, as well as a practical use of reason, there is a practical use of *pure* reason.

This is just what, according to the third objection, cannot be done. Still, we must not acquiesce in this objection until we have considered putative ways of doing this thing which it says cannot be done. One such would be the following: to argue, first, that a necessary condition of putting reason to practical use is valuing certain things, and, second, that a necessary condition of valuing such things is acting in certain ways (say, ways that promote or preserve or cherish these things). An argument of this kind, if successful, would give substance to the idea that acting in such ways commended itself to any rational being. It would follow that if we were purely rational – if reason had complete control over what we did – then those, all else being equal, would be the ways in which we would act. Categorical imperatives would have been vindicated.

Call such a vindication of categorical imperatives a 'transcendental' vindication of them. (This is a very Kantian label for a very Kantian style of argument.[22] I am not saying that Kant himself uses the label in this way, nor indeed that he ever gives such an argument, at least not explicitly. But in the next section we shall see important connections between this style of argument and Kant's own conception; and these will give the former a useful heuristic role. Later, in Theme Two, we shall turn to something similar that can be found in Kant.) What are the prospects for a transcendental vindication of categorical imperatives?

§4 Consider first the following subsidiary question: what is the most obvious candidate for something that would necessarily be valued by any being putting reason to practical use? A plausible answer is: putting reason to practical use. Indeed, if there *were* a transcendental vindication of categorical imperatives, then there would be such a thing as putting *pure* reason to practical use, in which case a second obvious candidate that we could (non-question-beggingly) insert into the vindication would be: putting pure reason to practical use. What would this give us? Roughly, that there is a fundamental categorical imperative to implement (or promote, or preserve, or cherish) the practical use of pure reason. This is an extremely tight loop. It may seem too tight to have any content. But it is just the sort of extremely tight and seemingly contentless loop that characterizes Kant's moral philosophy. And it connects with two of the most dominant strains in that philosophy.

The first of these strains is the idea that the only unqualified good is a good will. That is, the only thing that must be valued, as a matter of pure reason, and whose value cannot be enhanced, diminished, or compromised by anything else, is, precisely, putting pure reason to practical use (where, for Kant, putting pure reason to practical use means neither more nor less than determining, by pure reason, what to do, and thereby forming the intention to do it: it does *not* require the carrying out of the intention, which may be thwarted by various unforeseen circumstances or by various sorts of incompetence).[23]

This idea has a number of important consequences for Kant. One is that the moral worth of an action depends solely on the agent's motive. And the only laudable motive, morally, is to act from duty (that is, granted Kant's rationalism, to do what pure reason requires). If someone lacks this motive, yet for extraneous reasons does the very thing that he would have done if he had had the motive, still no merit accrues. Such a person has acted *in conformity with* duty, but not *from* duty.[24]

A second consequence is that what is morally right, in other words what is the mark of a good will, cannot be subordinated to any other good. For suppose it could. Suppose, in other words, that there were some fundamental good, such as happiness or the glory of God, that did not itself have to be understood in terms of what is morally right, but rather that doing what is morally right were to be understood as pursuing this good. Since this good could not be determined *a priori* – *ex hypothesi*, the *only* good that can be determined *a priori* is a good will – then neither could what is morally right. In other words, what is morally right would have to be determined empirically. And this is contrary to the very basis of Kant's rationalism.[25]

A third consequence is encapsulated in a formula that is often attributed to Kant though he never puts in so many words: '*ought* implies *can*'.[26] For if what one ought morally to do is what pure reason requires one to do, then it makes no sense to say that one ought morally to do something that one is incapable of doing. (This in turn has obvious and important consequences concerning the differences between guilt and shame. For Kantians there is a moral significance that attaches to the former but not to the latter, which is connected with the fact that the latter can be targeted at what is not in one's control. Thus if Uncle George misbehaves I may feel ashamed. If I have an attack of hiccups I may feel ashamed. Indeed if I am caught carrying out some petty theft I may feel ashamed. But any *guilt* I feel will be targeted at the theft itself.[27] We shall come back to this and related contrasts in Theme Two. It is worth noting that some non-Kantians see such contrasts as symptomatic of all that is least helpful in Kant's moral philosophy.[28])

The second dominant strain in Kant's moral philosophy with which the tight loop connects is the idea that people, or rational beings in general if these are different,[29] are to be valued for their own sake. This is because, for Kant, valuing the practical use of pure reason is inseparable from valuing (as such) those with a capacity for the practical use of pure reason. Those with a capacity for the practical use of pure reason may not actually implement this capacity. That is, they may not have good wills. They are not good without qualification. But they are the ground of that which is good without qualification, and they are to be valued as such. This means that they must never be exploited. That is, they must never be treated as mere means. To treat a person as a mere means is to prescind from that person's own practical rationality, which is precisely what is proscribed.

It is in these terms that Kant is able to extract from the apparently meagre resources assembled so far something that is recognizably a moral injunction. He writes: '*So act that you use humanity, whether in your own person or in the person of any other, always at the same time as an end, never merely as a means.*'[30] This is the first of two formulations that we shall be considering of what, after all this, Kant takes the fundamental categorical imperative to come to.[31] He gives several formulations, but the two we shall be considering are the two best known. We shall turn to the second shortly.

But first, notice something that happens the moment *any* such formulation is given; the moment *anything* concrete is said about what Kant's conception actually demands of us. The differences between categorical imperatives and hypothetical imperatives begin to seem much less marked. Let us return once more to the man telling outrageous lies. Suppose we can convince him that his lying involves manipulating other people in a way that runs directly counter to Kant's injunction. And suppose we can convince him that he really is thereby being irrational. (These are large suppositions. It is a large enough supposition, come to that, that he can be bothered to listen to any attempts on our part to convince him of anything. But suppose he can.) What if he replies, 'Very well, I'm being irrational,' and sets off to tell further outrageous lies?[32] An imperative that it would be irrational to flout begins to look no different, in terms of the kind of force that it exerts, from an imperative that it would be unfashionable to flout. Just as a given individual may not care about being fashionable, or may care minimally about it but care much more about other things, so too there may be an individual whose other objectives eclipse any concern that he or she has to be rational.

Of course, there is nothing here to foreclose the possibility that, as a matter of brute fact, or even as a matter of some kind of necessity, we (whoever 'we' are) do attach a fundamental and overriding significance to being rational. But if *that* is what makes categorical imperatives special, then rationalism is not after all so very different from conative objectivism, the thesis that morality is grounded in shared conative states: indeed, the former is a species of the latter. (I emphasized in §4 of the Introduction that any apparent gap between rationalism and conative objectivism may be only apparent. Here is why.) This is an *extremely* important idea to which we shall return in Variations Two.

As I said, the differences between categorical imperatives and hypothetical imperatives (and thus between rationalism and conative objectivism) begin to seem much less marked the moment any flesh is put on the osteal idea that the fundamental categorical imperative is to implement (promote, preserve, cherish) the practical use of pure reason – the idea that emerged from the envisaged transcendental vindication of categorical imperatives. A small price, it might be said, for succeeding in putting *some* flesh on those bones! The greatest problem for Kant's rationalism, as presented so far, is not that it looks as if it can be refuted but that it looks as if it *cannot* be refuted: it looks as if there is nothing there to refute. Let us turn, then, to the second of Kant's attempts to put flesh on the bones. It is the most famous of all.

§5 Kant holds that putting reason to practical use, if only in the unproblematical way that has nothing yet to do with categorical imperatives, involves actively determining what to do on the strength of one's conative states. Actively determining what to do on the strength of one's conative states contrasts with passively succumbing to their strength. (Of course, the suggestion that our conative states are like alien forces by which we are beset is caricatural at best.[33] The suggestion is there in what I have just said partly because I am giving a mere sketch of Kant. It is there partly because of Kant.[34]) Actively determining what to do on the strength of one's conative states in turn involves making resolutions (however tacitly, however unself-consciously) and then acting on them. Such resolutions include what Kant calls *maxims*. Maxims are resolutions that serve as principled rules of conduct. A simple example of a maxim is to keep any promise one has made. Another is never to waste any natural resources.[35]

Now maxims provide reasons for what we do. But what sort of reasons? I distinguished in §3 of the Introduction between what I called explanatory reasons (reasons that we actually have for doing what we do) and normative reasons (reasons that we should have for doing what we do). If someone does something because of some maxim that she has adopted, then the maxim has clearly provided an explanatory reason for what she does. But by adopting it, and thereby letting it serve as a principled rule to guide her behaviour, she is also thereby treating it as though it had provided a normative reason for what she does (again, however tacitly, however unself-consciously). That is, she is treating it as though it were a resolution that she *should* abide by. Indeed, she is treating it as though it were a resolution that *anyone* should abide by. For part of what makes something a principled rule, as opposed to the encapsulation of just another conative state pitching in alongside all the others, is its claim to be apt to regulate the behaviour of anyone, irrespective of that person's (non-rational) conative states. To adopt a maxim, and then to act accordingly, is to act as though the maxim has provided a normative reason for what one does which carries the force of a categorical imperative, not just that of a hypothetical imperative.[36]

But 'as though' is the operative phrase. For one thing, it would be question-begging at this stage to suppose that any such reason *could* carry the force of a categorical imperative. But also, more significantly, there are many cases in which it could not. To take an instructively absurd example, consider the maxim to speak less than anyone else in any conversation in which one participates. This could not be a maxim that everyone should abide by, because it is not a maxim that everyone *could* abide by: if they did, the very practice of having conversations would disintegrate and the maxim along with it. Sometimes, less extremely, one could not *will* that everyone should abide by a certain maxim. Thus consider the maxim to put one's own interests, however small, above those of anyone else, however great. This is not self-stultifying in the way in which the maxim to speak less than anyone else in any conversation in which one participates is. But one could not will it to be a maxim by which everyone should abide since, if they did, one would be forsaken on those many occasions on which one relied on others to subordinate their interests to one's own.

Rules that do yield reasons with the force of a categorical imperative (if such there be) Kant calls *practical laws*, or sometimes just *laws*.[37] In adopting a maxim, one is thus treating it as a law. But now we can return to the core idea that the fundamental categorical imperative is to implement the practical use of pure reason. The practical use of pure reason involves submitting to the force of a categorical imperative to whatever extent it is possible to do so – no more, no less. Therefore it involves treating as laws only those maxims that really could be laws, compatibly with what agents are capable of willing. In other words, it involves, for any maxim that one might adopt, actually adopting it only when it could also be a law, and indeed only when one could also will that it be a law. It is in these terms that Kant arrives at the second, and most famous, of his formulations of the fundamental categorical imperative: '*Act only in accordance with that maxim through which you can at the same time will that it become a universal law.*'[38]

Kant considers various examples of actions that, in his view, are wrong, and argues that this formulation of the fundamental categorical imperative can be used to explain what is wrong with them. Thus suppose that I adopt a maxim that sanctions my making a promise with the intention not to keep it if I am in difficult circumstances, and suppose that I act on this maxim. Kant takes this to be wrong, and he takes his formula to show that it is wrong. He writes:

> To inform myself ... whether a lying promise is in conformity with duty, I ask myself: would I be content that my maxim (to get myself out of difficulties by a false promise) should hold as a universal law (for myself as well as for others)?... Then I soon become aware that I could indeed will the lie, but by no means a universal law to lie; for in accordance with such a law there would properly be no promises at all, since it would be futile to avow my will with regard to my future actions to others who would not believe this avowal or, if they rashly did so, would pay me back in like coin; and thus my maxim, as soon as it were made a universal law, would have to destroy itself.[39]

Kant also considers someone who, because it would be a hardship to develop his talents, duly neglects them, acting on a maxim that sanctions his doing this. Again Kant takes this to be wrong, and again he takes his formula to show that it is wrong – this time, by showing that the maxim cannot be *willed* to be a law. He writes:

> [This man] asks himself whether his maxim of neglecting his natural gifts, besides being consistent with his propensity to amusement, is also consistent with what one calls duty. He now sees that a nature could indeed always subsist with such a universal law...; only he

cannot possibly *will* that this become a universal law... For, as a rational being he necessarily wills that all the capacities in him be developed, since they serve him and are given to him for all sorts of possible purposes.[40]

We can see, then, that, for Kant, whereas practical reason enables us to control our actions in accordance with maxims, *pure* practical reason operates, as it were, up a level and enables us to control our maxims in accordance with the purely rational demands of consistency and fitness to regulate. It enables us to filter out and reject maxims that we cannot use to make (full, coherent, shared) sense of things, maxims that, in short, do not themselves make sense. It imposes order and unity on the chaos and multiplicity of our conative states. In Kant's words, it 'subject[s] *a priori* the manifold of desires to the unity of consciousness of a practical reason commanding in the moral law'.[41]

Note how Kant's conception straddles the distinction between normative ethics and meta-ethics. He is offering us an ethic of principle, whereby we must always do what is right *because* it is right *because* it is what we would do if we were purely rational. He is also offering us a relative of the so-called golden rule, to do as we would be done by. (But note: I do not say a close relative. Kant himself warns against too readily assimilating them. He derogates the golden rule, somewhat sophistically it must be said, with the complaint that 'many a man would gladly agree that others should not benefit him if only he might be excused from showing them beneficence', adding that 'a criminal would argue on this ground against the judge punishing him'.[42] It is interesting to note also the very un-Kantian context in which the phrase 'Do as you would be done by' first occurs. It is in a letter from Philip Stanhope, the fourth Earl of Chesterfield, to his son. He writes, 'Do as you would be done by is the surest method that I know of pleasing.'[43] Whatever else it is intended to do, Kant's formula is assuredly not intended to specify a method of pleasing. But, for all that, there is, between Kant's formula and the golden rule, a definite kinship.) For these and other reasons, Kant's conception resonates at a very deep level for many of his readers. This is partly because of how well attuned it is to the ethical understanding of its own time and place, and partly because of the enormous impact it has had on the ethical understanding of other times and places.

§6 There are nevertheless many obvious qualms that we might have about it. I shall cite just four. First, how well does Kant's invocation of what we are capable of willing to be a law, where this is explicitly intended to include less than what is capable of *being* a law, square with his rationalistic insistence that any basic moral precept needs to be discoverable by pure reason? Is it not an empirical question what we are capable of willing?

Kant is alive to this worry. He thinks it is not an empirical question, because the capacity concerned is that of non-contradiction: that is to say, the question is what we are capable of willing without our will 'contradicting itself'.[44] But this notion is not well explained. It is obscure in what way our will is supposed to 'contradict itself' when we show no interest in developing our talents for example.[45]

Second, what if someone acts on more than one maxim, one of which she can will to be a law, one of which she cannot? (Imagine someone who takes a single opportunity both to assist a colleague and inappropriately to promote her own career prospects.) Has she, in Kant's terms, done something both right and wrong?

Some commentators would reply on Kant's behalf that nobody can in fact act on more than one maxim, for to act on a maxim is to make it the decisive influence on what one does: if two maxims sanction what someone does, the one on which the person acts (if either) is the one that would have prevailed if there had been a conflict between them.[46] Others would say on Kant's behalf that, although someone *can* act on more than one maxim, for an action to be wrong is simply for at least one of the maxims on which it is performed to be such that the agent cannot will it to be a law. (We are familiar enough with the many ways in which wrong-doing can wear a cloak of righteousness.) Both these responses raise myriad further questions about Kant's conception. For instance, does Kant's conception guarantee, or even require, that there be some unique rational way to resolve any conflict between maxims? Can there be, on Kant's conception, a situation in which someone is forced to do something wrong, because whatever he does will involve acting on some maxim that he cannot will to be a law? (Consider Herod when, having promised to give Salome whatever she asks for, he is confronted by a request for the head of John the Baptist.[47]) If Kant's conception does allow for such a situation, does it nevertheless provide some safeguard against anyone's finding himself in such a situation except as a result of his own prior wrong-doing? Or except as a result of *someone's* prior wrong-doing? Kant addresses such issues,[48] but he does so inchoately. We shall return to some of them later.

Third, why exactly is it irrational to act as though something is a law even when it could not be one?

This question has an *ad hominem* force against Kant because of his own insistence elsewhere that we are required by reason to act as though certain concepts apply in ways in which they never could.[49] A central example is the concept of the infinite whole. Kant says that we should treat this concept as having empirical application to the physical universe, even though we can derive various contradictions from the supposition that it does. Treating it in this way will both direct us and sustain us in the endless quest for a deeper and more extensive knowledge of nature. It will ensure that, however much we have explored, we shall be propelled to explore further, in pursuit of complete systematic unity in our understanding. (The concept of moral perfection can play a similar inspirational-cum-regulative role in ethics.[50]) To be sure, treating the concept of the infinite whole in this way is a world apart from making a false promise. But the former does seem to share with the latter that selective use of the 'as if' mode – acting *as if* something is what it could never be, when there is an advantage to be gained from doing so – which is supposed to make the latter irrational.

The fourth qualm is the most serious, and it will provide the principal motif for the next chapter. Before I present it, we need to consider the most basic possible objection to Kant's view: namely, *that there is nothing wrong with adopting a maxim that one could not will to be a law*. People regulate their lives in all sorts of ways that are tailored to their own particular conative states – their own values, preferences, goals, ambitions, and the like – as moulded by their own particular circumstances. And it is entirely reasonable for them to do so. Thus imagine a war widow who resolves to spend a few moments, at a specific time each day, in quiet reflection at the war memorial. She has adopted a maxim which she patently could not will to be a law, indeed which patently could not *be* a law, and which is none the worse for that. Her reason for visiting the war memorial at that time each day clearly has, and can in no way be criticized for having, the force of a hypothetical imperative. Or again, imagine someone who resolves to pay off his credit card each month.[51] He too has adopted a maxim which could not be a law: the institution of credit cards depends on there being people who do not do what he has resolved to do. Yet there is nothing wrong with his resolution, nor with his acting on it.

What are we to make of this objection? The examples certainly give pause. Yet it is hard to escape the feeling that they somehow miss the point.

Kant's formula forces us to ask the familiar question, 'What if everyone did that?' Sometimes it is perfectly acceptable to deflect this question by responding, 'Not everyone *will* do that.' The two examples above illustrate this. But sometimes, for instance when someone has given false information on a tax return, or indeed when someone has told a lie of any kind, the question can be asked in a way that makes this response inappropriate. Kant's formula surely invites us to ask the question in this second way. And the examples above seem irrelevant to that. But how can we substantiate this sense of irrelevance?

Presumably we need some way of showing that the woman's resolution to visit the war memorial each day, and the man's resolution to pay off his credit card every month, do not (after all) count as maxims. But why not? So far all we have been told about maxims is that they are 'resolutions that serve as principled rules of conduct'. But how are we to distinguish between those resolutions that serve as principled rules of conduct and those that do not? This is the focus of the fourth qualm. The fourth qualm is that we cannot find, in the full light of the objection just considered, either with Kant's help or using our own independent resources, a suitable account of what a maxim is.[52]

What about Kant's own explicit definitions? These, as they stand, are of little help. A maxim, he tells us, is 'the subjective principle of acting ... in accordance with which the subject *acts*', as opposed to a (practical) law, which is 'the objective principle valid for every rational being, in accordance with which he *ought to act*'.[53] What can we glean from this? That a maxim *purports* to be a law? That it purports to have a claim on others in a way in which the resolution to pay a daily visit to the war memorial does not? If so, in what sense? It cannot be a question of how agents themselves view their resolutions. The malicious prankster who resolves never to give correct directions to strangers, and whose resolution Kant would surely want his account to proscribe, precisely does not see his resolution as having a claim on others. He views it as a way of exploiting the greater co-operation of others. Is he being irrational, then, not only in acting on his resolution, but even in viewing it in this way? If so, why? Perhaps it is a question of generality. Perhaps the resolution never to give correct directions to strangers has a generality which means that, willy-nilly, it purports to be a law, unlike the resolution to visit the war memorial each day (whose underlying maxim, if there is one, might be to pay due obeisance to the dead). But then surely the resolution to pay off one's credit card each month is at least as general as the resolution never to give correct directions to strangers. Furthermore, if what distinguishes maxims from other resolutions is that they purport to have a claim on other people – that they are not just private recipes for organizing one's own affairs – then why need a rational agent adopt any maxims at all? (Kant says that 'a rational being must always regard himself as lawgiving in a kingdom of ends'.[54] Why?[55])

The fact is that we do not have at this stage – and we seem far short of having – a satisfactory account of what a maxim is.

§7 In the next chapter I shall try to provide one. In particular, I shall try to provide an account which will be sensitive to what might be called the 'sociology' of maxims (an account, in other words, which will be sensitive to where maxims come from, to how they are inculcated, and to why it is absurd to imagine any given individual either dispensing with them or, conversely, conjuring them up for himself in complete independence of other people) and which will at the same time enable us to rebut the above objection to Kant's view. This will constitute a partial defence of Kant.[56]

I say 'partial' for two reasons. First, there are other objections (some of which we have already seen, some of which will emerge later). Particularly noteworthy is a variation on the above objection, subtler and altogether more interesting than the original, whereby a person may quite properly adopt a maxim precisely *because* it could not be a law. How so? Well, someone may be concerned, not to satisfy his or her own private conative states, but to subvert the institution or practice that (provisionally) makes the maxim possible. A relatively simple example would be somebody's adopting the maxim never to accept a tip. This objection will prove significant later.

(Incidentally, my description of this example as *relatively* simple is advised. The example actually harbours all sorts of complexities, and it is worth pausing to reflect on some of them. I am taking for granted that the maxim never to accept a tip could not be a law. But why not? A natural answer is that, if everyone adopted this maxim, there would be no such thing as tipping. But is this true? Could the practice not survive as a kind of affectation, with no presumption of take-up, simply to betoken appreciation or gratitude? It might be objected that this would not count as tipping, properly so called. Very well; suppose it would not. Even then, perhaps the most that can be said is that, if everyone *knew* that everyone had adopted the maxim never to accept a tip, there would be no such thing as tipping. And even *then*, perhaps there would still be such a thing as tipping in principle, merely not in practice. Which of these – if any – would suffice to show that the maxim could not be a law? I here simply raise these questions. There is little in Kant, I think, to help us answer them. In the next chapter I hope to develop an approach to these issues that entitles us more or less to bypass such questions.)

The second reason that I apply the word 'partial' to my defence of Kant is in acknowledgement of the fact that I shall be following the themes and variations format. I shall be trying to adapt Kant's ideas, quite possibly taking them in directions in which he himself would resist taking them. I shall be putting exegesis largely to one side. I hope that, by the end of the next chapter, what may have seemed initially like a tiresomely uncharitable cavil about Kant's conception will have turned out to connect with ethical issues of the first importance.

Finally – and this adumbrates the two chapters after the next – I must emphasize that everything that we have been discussing in this chapter, ever since we first looked at the core idea that there is a fundamental categorical imperative to implement the practical use of pure reason, and then considered Kant's two best-known attempts to put flesh on that idea (and much of what we shall be discussing in the next chapter too – subject to reservations that will emerge about the very idea of 'pure' reason), depends, effectively, on the supposition that pure reason can be put to practical use. The third objection to rationalism, namely that this supposition is false, remains to be addressed.

Kant himself is very clear about this. Having argued in his *Groundwork of the Metaphysics of Morals* for the following conditional – that *if* pure reason can be put to practical use, then the fundamental categorical imperative can be formulated in the various ways he says it can – he insists that a 'critique' of pure practical reason is still required to establish the antecedent of the conditional. 'That morality is no phantom,' he writes, '[which] follows if the categorical imperative ... [is] absolutely necessary as an *a priori* principle[,] ... requires a possible *synthetic use of pure practical reason*, which use, however, we cannot venture upon without prefacing it by a *critique* of the rational faculty itself.'[57] At the end of §3 I sketched one way in which the critique might be given, namely by means of a transcendental vindication of categorical imperatives. (This rested on the idea that a necessary condition of putting reason to practical use is valuing putting reason to practical use.) We shall look at Kant's own (related) way of providing such a critique in Theme Two, when we turn to his theory of freedom.

Further reading

Further work in moral philosophy by Kant himself, beyond that already cited, includes 'A Supposed Right', *Perpetual Peace*, and 'Theory and Practice'.

Fine introductory books on Kant's moral philosophy are Acton (1970), Aune (1979), Sullivan (1994), Teale (1951), Walker (1998), and [T.C.] Williams (1968). Two useful introductory articles are Korsgaard (1997) and Schneewind (1992). More advanced books, with varying foci reflected in their titles, include Allison (1990), Auxter (1982), Baron (1995), Louden (2000), Munzel (1999), Nell (=O'Neill) (1975), Seidler (1986), Stratton-Lake (2000), Sullivan (1989), and Wood (1999).

The best English-language commentaries on Kant's three greatest works in moral philosophy are: on *Groundwork*, Paton (1947); on 2nd *Critique*, Beck (1960); and on *Metaphysics of Morals*, Gregor (1963). Three further notable commentaries on *Groundwork* are Duncan (1957), Ross (1954), and Wolff (1973).

There are many collections of essays on different aspects of Kant's moral philosophy. Especially noteworthy are: Guyer (1993), which relates Kant's moral philosophy to his aesthetic theory; Guyer (2000a), with a focus on Kant's veneration of freedom and its relation to his liberalism; Herman (1993a), with an unusual and very helpful emphasis on the role of context in Kantian moral reasoning; Hill (1992), which highlights the importance of respect for persons in Kantian morality; Hill (2000), which uses a Kantian framework for moral deliberation to address social and political issues; Korsgaard (1996b), which deals with various implications of the categorical imperative; and O'Neill (1989a), which combines interpretation of Kant's moral philosophy with application of it. Also, providing very instructive comparisons between Kant, Aristotle, and the Stoics, there is Engstrom and Whiting (1996). (For an account of the Stoics that brings out further comparisons with Kant, though not explicitly, see Frede (1999).)

Further work relating Kant's moral philosophy to that of Aristotle includes Hursthouse (1999), Chapter 4, Korsgaard (1996f), Louden (1986), McDowell (1998a), [A.W.] Moore (1990), and Sherman (1997).

Two fascinating articles relating Kant's moral philosophy to that of Hume are Wiggins (1995) and Wiggins (1998).

Books in moral-cum-political philosophy that in one way or another have a broadly Kantian inspiration include [R.M.] Hare (1952), [R.M.] Hare (1963), Hollis (1987), Nagel (1970), and Rawls (1999).

First set of variations

> Either ethics makes no sense at all, or this is what it means and has nothing else to say: not to be unworthy of what happens to us... 'Become the man of your misfortunes; learn to embody their perfection and brilliance.' Nothing more can be said, and no more has ever been said: to become worthy of what happens to us, and thus to will and release the event, to become the offspring of one's own events, and thereby to be reborn, to have one more birth, and to break with one's carnal birth – to become the offspring of one's events and not of one's actions, for the action is itself produced by the offspring of the event.
> (Gilles Deleuze, *The Logic of Sense*, 21st Series, p. 149)

§1 What is a maxim? That is the question that will motivate this chapter.

I begin with a fundamental proposition which I am going to take for granted. *Some concepts are action-guiding.*[1]

In due course I shall explain what I mean by this. But first, a word or two about the status of this proposition. It is not so fundamental that it cannot or need not be justified. On the contrary, much could legitimately be written in defence of it. Indeed, that is part of the reason why I am going to take it for granted. The alternative would be to write a quite different book. But the proposition will, I hope, seem plausible. And in any case, if what follows is even broadly correct, then it will itself help to substantiate the proposition.

Very well, what does the proposition mean? As a first approximation, it means that there are some concepts such that anyone who possesses one of these concepts thereby has certain reasons for doing things.[2]

For instance, anyone who possesses the concept of *blasphemy* thereby has a reason not to blaspheme; anyone who possesses the concept of a *swear word* thereby has a reason not to utter swear words in certain circumstances; anyone who possesses the concept of a *promise* thereby has a reason to keep any promise he or she has made; anyone who possesses the concept of *privacy* thereby has a reason to respect other people's privacy;

anyone who possesses the concept of *compassion* thereby has a reason to be compassionate; anyone who possesses the concept of *truthfulness* thereby has a reason to be truthful; anyone who possesses the concept of *cowardice* thereby has a reason to avoid doing what is cowardly. These examples should give some idea of what I am talking about. But they also, in all kinds of ways, show how much clarification is still required. (Am I claiming that *only* those who possess these concepts have the corresponding reasons; that, as it were, *ignorantia juris excusat*? Am I claiming that those who have no inhibitions about swearing, say, do not really understand what swearing is? Or that, if they do, they have somehow managed to block reasons they have, willy-nilly, to refrain from swearing in certain circumstances? In what follows I shall try to address just such questions.)

To return to my paraphrase: something needs to be said about each of 'some', 'possesses', 'thereby', 'has', 'certain', 'reasons', and 'doing'. I shall say something about each of these, in order, roughly, of decreasing straightforwardness. I begin with 'some'.

§2 *'Some'*: The proposition is that *some* concepts are of a certain kind. I do not intend to rule out the possibility that all are. There are ways of construing the proposition, looser than anything suggested by the examples above, whereby they clearly are. For example, anyone who possesses the concept of *nitrogen* thereby has a reason to demur at an application of the concept to what he or she knows to be oxygen. But even with such trivial construals somehow ruled out, I am not ready to dismiss the idea that all concepts are of this kind. Be that as it may, all I am assuming, and all I need assume, is that some are; and the clearest examples will be of the broadly 'ethical' sort indicated above, the sort most relevant to our concerns.

§3 *'Certain'*: The proposition is not merely that, for each of the relevant concepts, anyone who possesses it thereby has reasons for doing things, where these may be different reasons in the cases of different people. It is rather – and this is what 'certain' is meant to indicate – that, for each of the relevant concepts, there are reasons for doing things such that anyone who possesses the concept thereby has *them*. In other words, all those who possess one of these concepts thereby *share* reasons for doing things.

For the time being I do not need to go much beyond this purely structural point. Later I shall need to consider the various preconditions and implications of different people's sharing a reason. But I ought already to make a couple of observations about what it is for people to share a reason. First, it certainly does not suffice that the reason be in the public domain. *Any* reason is in the public domain. A reason is something that must in principle be recognizable by anyone, not just by the person whose reason it is, as explaining or justifying something that the person does or could do. If, in particular, it justifies something that the person could do, in other words if it is what I called in §3 of the Introduction a normative reason, then the person must in principle be able to offer it to other people *as* a justification for doing that thing, and they in turn must in principle be able to acknowledge it as such.[3] Indeed, for the person actually to act on the reason is, in part, for him or her to be prepared to offer it to other people in this way. But none of this entails that other people must share the reason.[4] Given Mary's aspiration to play the piano, she has a normative reason to take regular piano lessons. But Jonathan, who can see perfectly well that Mary has such a reason, does not himself have any reason to take regular piano lessons, since he does not likewise aspire to play the piano.

One might go further. One might say that, if it is a matter of complete indifference to Jonathan whether or not Mary ever plays the piano, then neither does he have any reason to do whatever is necessary to promote *her* taking regular piano lessons. This highlights an ambiguity in the phrase 'share a reason', similar to the ambiguity that I discussed in §3 of the Introduction in the phrase 'share a conative state', and it brings me to the second of my two observations. It is possible for two people to share a reason in the sense that they have individual reasons of the same type. For instance, Mary has a reason to take regular piano lessons and Christopher, who is equally keen to play the piano, has a reason to take regular piano lessons. It is also possible for two people to share a reason in the sense that they have individual reasons with the same content. Thus Mary has a reason to take regular piano lessons and Catherine, who has Mary's interests very much at heart, has a reason to ensure that Mary takes regular piano lessons.[5] The first sense, I think, is slightly more natural than the second. At any rate it is the one I intended two paragraphs back – and the one I shall appropriate from now on. The proposition is that there are some concepts such that all those who possess one of these concepts thereby share reasons in the sense that they have individual reasons *of the same type*.

§4 *'Doing'*: This word is to be understood very broadly. As both the example of blaspheming and the example of swearing indicate, it is to be understood as including 'omissions' as well as 'acts'.[6] Anyone who possesses the concept of blasphemy thereby has a reason *not* to blaspheme. Anyone who possesses the concept of a swear word thereby has a reason *not* to swear in certain circumstances.

It is when the word is understood more broadly still that the proposition is in danger of being trivially true of every concept. As my comments in §2 may already have suggested, I am not unduly concerned about ruling out such a trivial interpretation of the proposition, and I shall not spend time trying to do so. It is true that other, less trivial interpretations are more clearly related to the Kantian ideas that I am hoping to develop. But it is also true that the main use to which I want to put the proposition I can put it to anyway.

However, before leaving this issue, I do want to consider one very broad way of understanding the word 'doing' which, while it may not make the proposition trivially true of every concept, does significantly enlarge the range of concepts of which the proposition is true. I have in mind an interpretation whereby 'doing' something can include drawing a conclusion from given premises, or more specifically (and with less threat of triviality – after all, from the premise that the gas in the container is oxygen we can draw the conclusion that it is not nitrogen) drawing a conclusion from given premises that do not strictly entail that conclusion. On this understanding, anyone who possesses the concept of *greenness*, say, thereby has certain reasons for doing things. In particular, and famously, anyone who possesses the concept of greenness thereby has a reason to conclude that the first emerald to be examined after today will be green, given that all the emeralds that have been examined up until now have been green.

I say 'famously' because this example is well known from Goodman's discussion of such inferences.[7] Goodman's discussion seems to me to have a significant if unexpected bearing on our own discussion, which is why I have introduced the example. I shall not say much about it now – we shall come back to it later – but I can already sketch what I have in mind.

Goodman devises the word 'grue', which can be defined as applying to anything examined before tomorrow if and only if it is green and to anything else if and only if it is blue.[8] He then observes that we have no reason to conclude that the first emerald to be examined after today will be grue (which is to say, blue) despite the fact that all the emeralds that have been examined up until now have been grue (which is to say, green). The question that exercises Goodman is this: what is it about the concept of grueness that makes it differ in this respect from the concept of greenness?

The intuitive answer is that the former is somehow gerrymandered. But this is not as straightforward as it seems. If 'bleen' is defined analogously to 'grue', then we can say that something is green if and only if it is either examined before tomorrow and grue or not examined before tomorrow and bleen.

I am attracted to a broadly Goodmanian answer: what distinguishes the concept of greenness from the concept of grueness is precisely the fact that we possess the concept of greenness but do not possess the concept of grueness. And as for what I mean by 'possess' here, see below (§8) for my gloss on this word.

§5 *'Has'*: Someone who possesses one of the relevant concepts thereby *has* certain reasons for doing things. I do not say that he acknowledges these reasons. All sorts of factors, such as insensitivity, selfishness, and simple stupidity, as well as distractions of various kinds, may prevent him from doing so. What I do say is that he must in principle be *capable* of acknowledging these reasons, by a process that does not itself involve his coming to have them.

The point of this qualification – 'by a process that does not itself involve his coming to have them' – is so that I can discount, for instance, the case in which someone possesses the concept of a swear word, cannot at first see why he should not swear in one of the relevant situations, but sees well enough once he has been threatened with some very severe punishment if he does so. For this is not a reason he already had. However, I do *not* discount the possibility that his being threatened in this way, in the past, was a significant contributory factor in his coming to possess the concept of a swear word in the first place. The matter is therefore both complex and hazy. For there will not have been any definite cut-off point at which he suddenly counted as possessing the concept.

Why do I insist that a person who possesses one of the relevant concepts should be capable, in principle, of acknowledging each of the reasons that he thereby has? Roughly, because there would otherwise be something hollow and unexplanatory about the claim that he has them. In fact I would further insist that each of the reasons must be grounded in the person's conative states. This is because I side with Williams in a debate which he initiated, and towards which I gestured in §3 of the Introduction, the debate about whether, whenever anyone has a reason for doing anything, the reason must be grounded in the person's conative states.[9] Following Williams, I say it must. I shall have a little more to say about this in my next gloss, on 'reasons'. But the debate in question is a large debate, and I do not need to enter into it now.

§6 *'Reasons'*: Three features of my use of the word 'reasons' in this context need to be emphasized. First, to revert once more to the distinction that I drew in §3 of the Introduction between explanatory reasons and normative reasons, I mean *normative* reasons. Second, I mean *general* reasons. And third, I do *not* mean *indefeasible* reasons: in other words, I do not exclude reasons that are defeasible.

Each of these labels is more or less self-explanatory. Nevertheless, a word or two of elucidation is called for.

The normativity, to recapitulate, means that such reasons are a matter of what people *should* do. That is, the proposition is that anyone who possesses one of the relevant concepts thereby should do certain things.

The generality is really just a reflection of the point I made in §3 in my gloss on 'certain'. The things a person should do by virtue of possessing one of the relevant concepts are things that anyone who possesses that concept should do. The reasons in question are reasons of a sort fit to be shared.

This is not to deny that a person who possesses one of the relevant concepts also thereby has reasons of a sort *not* fit to be shared. On the contrary, the general reasons he or she has will themselves, in suitable situations, yield such non-general reasons. (By virtue of possessing the concept of privacy, I not only have a general reason to respect other people's privacy. I have a non-general reason to return unread your diary which I have just found.) But these non-general reasons are obviously not included among those that everyone who possesses the concept thereby has. This in turn is why I can afford to be rather nonchalant about what exactly the notion of generality comes to. Roughly, a general reason is a reason that can be specified without appeal to particular people, places, times, or situations. If I wanted to put the notion to significant philosophical work, I should need to offer something much less rough. But I do not want to put the notion to significant philosophical work. The work is done by the sheer fact that the reasons in question are shared by all those possessing some given concept. This is enough to guarantee them the required generality.

Typically, in specifying one of these reasons, one will exercise the corresponding concept. I myself have done so for each of the examples I have given so far. Thus anyone who possesses the concept of privacy thereby has a reason to respect other people's *privacy*; anyone who possesses the concept of truthfulness thereby has a reason to be *truthful*. By contrast, in specifying one of the non-general reasons that one of these general reasons yields, one is liable not to exercise the corresponding concept. Thus, by virtue of possessing the concept of privacy, I have a reason to return your diary without reading it; by virtue of possessing the concept of truthfulness, Alison has a reason to admit to her brother what she has discovered about his wife's infidelities. The general reasons that someone has by virtue of possessing one of these concepts are reasons that are shaped by the concept itself, irrespective of its application in particular circumstances. The non-general reasons that these in turn yield are reasons that are determined by the concept's application in particular circumstances, and may well be most naturally specified in terms that bypass the concept itself, in favour of the peculiarities of the circumstances. But this is all still very rough. And it still counts for less, as far as grasping the general/non-general distinction is concerned, than the sheer fact that the former reasons are the ones that everyone possessing the concept thereby has.

The defeasibility, or rather the non-exclusion of defeasibility, is a corrective to the normativity. In saying that anyone who possesses one of the relevant concepts thereby has certain (normative) reasons for doing things, I do not exclude the possibility that he or she also has, on occasion, some overriding reason not to do one of these things. For instance, even though anyone who possesses the concept of privacy thereby has a reason to respect other people's privacy, there may, in certain circumstances, be some other overriding reason not to do so, say the need to gain information about someone that will save his or her life. Again, even though anyone who possesses the concept of a swear word thereby has a reason not to swear in certain circumstances, there may, in such circumstances, be some other overriding reason to do so, say the need to register anger or disapproval. For anyone who possesses the concept of privacy, the fact that an act would show respect for someone else's privacy counts *in favour of* doing it, but not conclusively. For anyone who possesses the concept of a swear word, the fact that an act would be an act of swearing in one of the relevant contexts counts *against* doing it, but not conclusively. Thus defeasibility.

The point that I am insisting on here is that I do not exclude defeasible reasons. But it is worth making explicit that I do not exclude indefeasible reasons either. I do not *exclude* them, though in fact I have an open mind about whether any of the reasons in question are indefeasible. If they are, it will be because they involve virtues whose exercise already, so to speak, allows for all contingencies. Thus perhaps anyone who possesses the concept of compassion thereby has an indefeasible reason to be compassionate. Perhaps it is of the very essence of compassion that there is never any reason not to be compassionate, but at most a reason to rein the way in which one shows one's compassion (say, the need to cope with competing claims on it, or the need 'to be cruel to be kind').[10]

Before I leave the word 'reasons' I should say a little more about the question, which I mentioned in the previous section, of whether a person's (normative) reasons need to be grounded in his or her conative states. In §3 of the Introduction I signalled the disquiet that many people feel about the idea that they need not; that it can be truly said of someone that she should do something even though doing that thing satisfies none of her conative states (is not in any of her interests, promotes none of her values, furthers none of her projects, realizes none of her aims, makes none of her hopes come true). In my previous gloss, on 'has', I signalled my own disquiet about this idea. Here I should like simply to add that I see nothing in the proposition that some concepts are action-guiding, as I have been explaining it, to make me resile. If all those who possess a certain concept thereby share certain (normative) reasons, this can be because all those who possess the concept thereby share certain conative states. In fact, to echo another point that I made in the previous gloss, instilling those conative states in a person, perhaps brutally instilling them, may be an integral part of bringing her – of bringing her up, indeed – to possess the concept. None of this is meant to suggest that those who possess one of the concepts must straightforwardly want to do the things that they thereby have reasons to do, any more than they must acknowledge those reasons. But if they do not, this must be because of some dissonance in their conative states, or some gap in their knowledge, or some unclarity in their understanding, or something of the sort. I do not want to reduce the notion of a reason to that of a conative state: I doubt very much that the notion of a reason can be reduced to any other notion.[11] But I do want to acknowledge its dependence on the notion of a conative state. And there is nothing in my fundamental proposition, so far as I can see, to prevent me from doing so.[12]

§7. *'Thereby'*: There are two worries that we might have about the inclusion of this word. The first is that it suggests a kind of magic. It suggests that concepts, abstract objects, somehow give us reasons to live our lives in certain ways. How? With what authority? The second worry is that it suggests that *only* concepts give us these reasons (a variation on the idea, as I put it in §1, that *ignorantia juris excusat*). Yet surely even those who lack the concept of compassion, say, have, or can have, a reason to be compassionate.

As far as the first worry is concerned, the suggestion of magic can readily be annulled. What I said towards the end of my previous gloss is relevant here. It is not that concepts give us reasons for doing things. It is rather that, included in the processes that do give us reasons for doing things (ultimately, by instilling conative states in us, if what I said above is correct) are processes of socialization and acculturation that at the same time lead to our possessing concepts. Thus children are taught what a promise is in part by being made to abhor, or at any rate to have negative feelings towards, promise breaking. The word 'thereby' does register a kind of dependence, but it is as much a dependence of possessing concepts on having reasons as it is of having reasons on possessing concepts.[13] (To think that there is an asymmetric dependence of having reasons on possessing concepts is to make the same sort of mistake as, I think, certain positivists used to make when they thought that some assertions, say an assertion of 'Aunts are female', were true in virtue of what the words meant. We should rather say that, in asserting, 'Aunts are female', we are articulating a rule for our use of the words 'aunt' and 'female' which itself contributes to their meaning.[14]) We do well for these purposes to regard the reasons in question as a kind of normative bedrock. This is reflected in the fact that often those reasons will not themselves admit of any more basic justification, still less a more basic justification in terms of how they relate to the corresponding concepts. As Williams memorably says, '"You can't kill that, it's a child" is more convincing as a reason than any reason which might be advanced for its being a reason.'[15] (Anyone who possesses the concept of a child thereby has a reason not to kill one.)

But now the second worry looks all the more serious. Does not the word 'thereby' suggest that to have one of the relevant reasons one must possess the corresponding concept, which seems not only dubious in itself but also at variance with what has just been said? For is it not a clear implication of what has just been said that the reasons are there to be had anyway?

The first point to be made in response to this is that 'thereby' can be understood without carrying any such suggestion. Anyone with a British parent thereby qualifies for British citizenship. We are not tempted to conclude that this is the *only* way of qualifying for British citizenship. The second and converse point that needs to be made is that it is *not* a clear implication of what has just been said that the reasons in question are 'there to be had anyway'. In describing these reasons as a kind of normative bedrock I did not mean to imply that they are like ground on which the corresponding concepts are to be constructed. Those concepts may themselves be part of the normative bedrock. There is in many cases a reciprocal dependence. Possessing the concept, in such a case, is of a piece with having the reasons. More fully, possessing the concept involves participating in a way of life whose complex interlocking structures of mutually supporting evaluations in turn involve having the reasons, these reasons themselves being unavailable and perhaps even unintelligible in isolation from the overall structure. So to return to the worrying suggestion: although that suggestion can be excised from anything I have said so far, I am not at all reluctant to admit that in many cases, if not in all cases, it is correct. To take one of the clearest examples: only someone who possesses the concept of a promise has a reason to keep any promise she has made, since only someone who possesses the concept of a promise can make a promise in the first place. Someone cannot make a promise if she has no idea what it would be to do so. And it would be vacuous to retort here, 'She can still have a reason to keep any promise she makes, since this means only that, *if* she were to make a promise, something that would admittedly require her first coming to possess the concept of a promise, she should then keep it.' Recall what I said in §5 in my gloss on 'has'. To make such a claim about her would be hollow and unexplanatory. She could not acknowledge the reason, save by a process that would involve her coming to have it.

In many of the examples that I have given so far, perhaps in all of them, something similar holds. Even in the case of the concept of compassion, and indeed that of the concept of a child which I mentioned parenthetically above, it is worth asking how far the reasons in question, with all their peculiar contours, and with all the associations and connotations that they (inevitably) have, are really available even to those who have no idea what it would be to respect such reasons. This is not to say that someone who lacks the concept of a child is therefore at perfect liberty to kill a child. It would be better to say that only of someone who possesses the concept of a child does it so much as make sense to suppose that he or she has a reason not to kill a child. Someone who lacks the concept is, in this respect, like a brute – like a non-rational animal, that is. But as before, these are questions on which I do not need to arbitrate.

§8 *'Possesses'*: Here, perhaps, I should acknowledge that I am putting a familiar word to unfamiliar use. Not that there is some standard everyday notion of what it is to possess a concept which I am flouting. Anyone with any notion at all of what it is to possess a concept is already operating at a level of reflection above the everyday, it seems to me. Nor do I see any reason to suppose that there is only one viable account of what it is to possess a concept, still less a single account that is appropriate for all concepts.[16] The fact remains that I intend 'possess' in an unusually demanding way, and I perhaps do best to admit that I am using it as a term of art.

To convey what I intend I need to draw a distinction. Many concepts, if not all concepts, can be grasped in two ways, an engaged way and a disengaged way. To grasp a concept in the disengaged way is to be able to recognize when the concept would (correctly) be applied, to be able to understand others when they apply it, and so forth. To grasp a concept in the engaged way is not only to be able to do these things, but also to feel sufficiently at home with the concept to be prepared to apply it oneself, where being prepared to apply it oneself means being prepared to apply it not just in overt acts of communication but also in how one thinks about the world and in how one conducts one's affairs. What this requires, roughly, is sharing whatever beliefs, concerns, and values define the outlook that gives application of the concept its point.

Take the concept of *the Sabbath*. Those who are not Jewish have no difficulty in grasping this concept in the disengaged way. A person who is not Jewish can understand perfectly well what somebody means when she says that her birthday this year falls on the Sabbath. But only a Jewish person recognizing an obligation to keep the Sabbath can grasp the concept in the engaged way. We might say, a little grandiloquently, that such a person *lives by* the concept.

Again, take the concept of *a typical Capricorn*. Someone who has no truck with astrology can still grasp the concept in the disengaged way, and may indeed be very good at distinguishing between those who would count as typical Capricorns and those who would not. But only someone who has a belief in astrology can grasp the concept in the engaged way. Only such a person will be prepared to count the fact that someone has the characteristics of a typical Capricorn as a reason for thinking that he or she has a birthday between 23 December and 19 January.

To be sure, this distinction is one of degree, not of kind. Borderline cases can readily be constructed: think of the grasp that non-orthodox Jews have on the concept of the Sabbath. Furthermore, each of the two ways of grasping a concept itself clearly admits of degrees. Thus a non-

Jewish person may understand what somebody means when she says that her birthday this year falls on the Sabbath, but not quite what she means when she says that she always keeps the Sabbath: his grasp of the concept, even *qua* disengaged, is imperfect. And it is important to note that someone who grasps a concept in the disengaged way may yet apply the concept ironically, or as part of playing some kind of role, or as a pretence, or even in the process of attributing certain beliefs or values to someone else, who grasps the concept in the engaged way: we might call these *vicarious* applications of the concept, as opposed to *in propria persona* applications of it. But none of these complications prevents the distinction from being a relatively robust one.[17]

By *possession* of a concept I mean grasp of it in the engaged way. To possess a concept is to enter into the spirit of that concept, to have whatever outlook gives the concept its point, to *live by* the concept as I put it above.

This is why I said in §4 that we possess the concept of greenness but do not possess the concept of grueness. It is not that we have any trouble in grasping the concept of grueness in the disengaged way, nor in vicariously applying it for that matter. For instance, we have no trouble in recognizing emeralds we have come across as grue. But in order to possess the concept we should need to see some point in so recognizing them (beyond whatever theoretical point there is to be made in discussions such as this, that is), which we do not. That we possess the concept of greenness but do not possess the concept of grueness is reflected in the brute fact that we exercise the former in all sorts of ways in which we do not exercise the latter – for instance, and most notably, in arriving at expectations.

Similarly, possession of the concept of a swear word requires more than merely knowing which words count as swear words. It requires more even than knowing, in some aloof, anthropological way, that the use of these words in certain contexts will shock certain people. To possess the concept of a swear word one must have *some* tendency to share that shock, even if one habitually and enthusiastically flouts it, or even if one habitually and nonchalantly flouts it. A casual swearer, however casual, typically overcomes *some* resistance to swearing, and may even be stimulated, in some minimal way, by the friction of doing so. Someone who genuinely did not possess the concept of a swear word might find it opaque that there was a taboo against uttering a given word in circumstances in which there was no taboo against uttering one of its synonyms.

Let us stay a while with this idea that a swearer may be stimulated by having to overcome some resistance to swearing – the first indication of many, in this and subsequent chapters, that there is a difference between possessing a concept and always abiding by it. There is a graphic illustration of something similar, though much more extreme, in the work of Diamond. Referring to various cases in which human beings deliberately fail to treat their fellow human beings as such, for instance cases in which they kill their enemies in the way in which they would kill non-human animals, she writes:

> Of course, even in these cases, a great deal of the response to 'human being' may remain intact, as for example what may be done with the dead body. Or again, if the enemyhood is so deep as to remove even these restraints, and men dance on the corpses of their enemies, as for example in the 1970s in the Lebanon, the point of this can only be understood in terms of the violation of what is taken to be how you treat the corpse of a human being. It is because you know it *is* that, that you are treating it with some point as that is *not* to be treated. And no one who does it could have the slightest difficulty – whatever contempt he might feel – in understanding why someone had gone off and been sick instead.[18]

Such cases illustrate just how poignantly possessing a concept can differ from actually abiding by it, even though – in fact, precisely because – the former provides impetus towards the latter.

Between a fully committed engaged grasp of a concept and an utterly aloof disengaged grasp of it there is indeed a large and multifarious range of cases. Thus there is the relaxed liar, who, although he possesses the concept of a lie (he is not a pathological liar, he refrains from lying when all else is equal, he is resentful when he discovers that others have been lying to him), has nevertheless managed to achieve enough distance from the concept to be able to lie without compunction. Conversely, there is the virulent lapsed Catholic whose erstwhile possession of the concept of sin (say) has become, in effect, its possession of her. Although she deliberately and persistently acts in ways that are intended to indicate her distance from that concept, and from other related concepts, all she succeeds in doing is making clear how close to them she still is. She does not possess them any longer. But nor does she have the kind of detached grasp of them that, say, a lifelong atheist with a knowledgeable interest in the Catholic Church might have. (An incidental caveat that I ought to enter in connection with this second example is that the words 'engaged' and 'disengaged', just like the word 'possess', are serving a somewhat specialized function for me. There is a natural way of understanding them whereby this person's grasp of the concept of sin is not at all disengaged. That, indeed, is her problem.)

One thing that such examples help to show – and this is something to which we shall return – is that, although it is individuals whose grasp of a concept is either engaged or disengaged, this contrast cannot ultimately be understood except in terms of how those individuals, and the concept, stand in relation to certain social groups. The relaxed liar counts as having an engaged grasp of the concept of a lie, despite the distance he manages to keep from it, because of his participation in a social world that is defined, in part, by that very concept. By contrast, one of the reasons why the lapsed Catholic counts as having a disengaged grasp of the concept of sin, despite the profound influence that it still exerts on her, is, quite simply, that she has renounced her faith: she has left the Church. No doubt she is now swimming against the tide, not just standing on the bank. But she certainly is not swimming *with* the tide.

I hope it is now reasonably clear what possession of a concept, on my understanding, requires: less than total allegiance to the concept (witness the relaxed liar, and witness those who dance on corpses); but more than mere grasp of it; and more even than grasp of it under the life-imbuing influence of whatever outlook gives application of the concept its point (witness the lapsed Catholic).

With possession so understood, it is highly plausible that possession of certain concepts comes with reasons for doing things. Concepts, to quote Wittgenstein, 'help us to comprehend things. They correspond to a particular way of dealing with situations.'[19] Those who possess a given concept thereby participate in what he elsewhere famously calls a 'form of life'.[20] In possessing the concept – in being ready to think and speak in those terms – they must make some of the same connections between things, they must be struck by some of the same similarities and differences, they must find some of the same things natural foci of attention, they must structure the world, to some extent, into the same foreground and background. In Cavell's words, they must share 'routes of interest..., modes of response, senses ... of significance and of fulfilment, of what is outrageous, of what is similar to what else'.[21] That they do so will be partly a matter of biology, partly a matter of inculcation, and it will be reflected in their taking certain things for granted, interpreting situations in certain ways, and, very often, valuing certain things. Those who grasp the concept in the disengaged way must share some of this too. But they will lack something in the outlook of those who possess the concept, something that makes full participation in the relevant form of life an option. What they will lack, and what those who possess the concept will have, is a way of making collective and individual *sense of things*. And it is highly plausible that, in some cases at least, this will involve their having reasons for doing certain things, the purport of my fundamental proposition.

§9 Having now clarified that proposition, I am in a position to proffer an account of what a maxim is. (But I repeat that I am not proffering it as exegesis, or at least not as pure exegesis.)

Given an action-guiding concept – that is, given a concept such that anyone who possesses the concept thereby has certain reasons for doing things – let us say that the concept *requires* the practice of doing any one of these things. Thus, for instance, the concept of a promise requires the practice of keeping any promise one has made. And given a resolution such that it is impossible for anyone to adopt that resolution (however tacitly, however unself-consciously) without possessing a certain concept, let us say that the resolution *involves* the concept. Thus, for instance, the resolution to keep any promise one has made involves the concept of a promise. Finally, running these two ideas together, given a resolution which involves a certain concept which in turn requires a certain practice, let us say that the resolution *is answerable to* the practice. Thus the resolution to keep any promise one has made is answerable to the practice of keeping any promise one has made. Then my proposal is this: *a maxim is a resolution to do something that either counts as observing some practice to which the resolution is answerable or, conversely, counts as violating some practice to which the resolution is answerable.*

The resolution to keep any promise one has made is clearly a case in point. That resolution is answerable to the practice of keeping any promise one has made. And it is a resolution to do precisely that. Hence it is a resolution to do something that counts as observing some practice to which the resolution is answerable. Hence, on my proposal, it is a maxim.

The resolution to break any promise one has made if this will be to one's financial advantage is a further case in point. That resolution likewise involves the concept of a promise. So it is likewise answerable to the practice of keeping any promise one has made. And it is a resolution to do something that counts as violating that practice. Hence, on my proposal, it too is a maxim.

On the other hand, the resolution never to make a promise to someone whose own promises cannot be trusted is not a case in point. This resolution involves the concept of a promise, along with other concepts such as that of trust and indeed that of a person. But none of the concepts it involves requires a practice that would be either observed or violated by acting on the resolution. Hence, on my proposal, it is not a maxim.

Nor, similarly, are the resolutions considered in §6 of the previous chapter, whose apparently unexceptionable non-universalizability was what prompted this whole discussion in the first place: the woman's resolution to visit the war memorial at a certain time each day; and the man's resolution to pay off his credit card each month.

So far, so good. Now consider the resolution to break any promise one has made if this will save someone's life. (The case of Herod and Salome is obviously relevant once again: see §6 of the previous chapter.) This is more interesting. Clearly this resolution is answerable to the practice of keeping any promise one has made. And it is a resolution to do something that counts as violating that practice. On my proposal, then, it is a maxim, and straightforwardly so. But this is only part of the story. To leave the matter there would be to suggest that there is something wrong with the resolution. It would indicate that anyone who adopts the resolution and acts on it thereby does something that he or she has a normative reason not to do. However, here we must remember one of the three features of my understanding of reasons to which I drew attention in §6 above: *the reasons associated with action-guiding concepts may be defeasible.* While it is true that anyone who possesses the concept of a promise should keep any promise he or she has made, the 'should' here carries with it an implicit 'all else being equal' rider. It may also be true that such a person has a normative reason, indeed an overriding normative reason, on occasion, to break some promise he or she has made. Not only that; a fuller exception-specifying reason may *itself* be associated with the concept of a promise. Thus we must allow for the possibility that the concept of a promise requires *both* the practice of keeping any promise one has made *and* the practice of breaking any promise one has made if this will save someone's life (and indeed, there being no limit to the number of layers of complexity that can be added, the practice of keeping any promise one has made if, even though breaking the promise will save someone's life, it will do so only at the cost of someone else's life). Whether the concept does require these practices or not is a matter of substantive debate. But suppose, for the sake of argument, that it does. Suppose, say, that one does not count as properly possessing the concept of a promise if one invests promises with such significance that one's reason for keeping any promise one has made takes precedence even over reasons of life and death. Then the resolution to break any promise one has made if this will save someone's life fits both ways of being a maxim on my proposal. It is a resolution to do something that counts as violating some practice to which the resolution is answerable, namely the practice of keeping any promise one has made. But it is also a resolution to do something that counts as observing some practice to which the resolution is answerable, namely the practice of breaking any promise one has made if this will save someone's life. Moreover, it is both of these things with respect to one and the same concept. There is nothing awry in this. Nor does it indicate any incoherence in the concept. It simply registers the defeasibility of one of the relevant reasons. (I take for granted, incidentally, that resolutions can likewise be defeasible. Someone who adopts a resolution can quite consistently think it right, on occasion, to act against that resolution. This means that someone can quite consistently, and quite reasonably, adopt both the resolution to keep any promise he or she has made and the resolution to break any promise he or she has made if this will save someone's life.)

Although I am eschewing simple exegesis here, it is interesting to note, in passing, that Kant himself is alive to the complexities of defeasibility, or at any rate more alive to them than is often recognized. Though he famously castigates taking one's own life 'as a mere means to some discretionary end',[22] he also raises, as genuine, hard, casuistical questions, whether certain cases of suicide are permitted. He asks:

Is it permitted to anticipate by killing oneself the unjust death sentence of one's ruler – even if the ruler permits this (as Nero did with Seneca)? Can a great king who died recently be charged with a criminal intention for carrying a fast-acting poison with him, presumably so that if he were captured when he led his troops to battle he could not be forced to agree to conditions of ransom harmful to his state? ... A man who had been bitten by a mad dog already felt hydrophobia coming on. He explained, in a letter he left, that, since as far as he knew the disease was incurable, he was taking his life lest he harm others as well in his madness ... Did he do wrong?[23]

True, the qualification 'as a mere means to some discretionary end' can always be so interpreted as to anticipate whatever answers to these questions we are disposed to give – as, more obviously still, can the qualification 'when ... [the] longer duration [of one's life] threatens more troubles than it promises agreeableness', which is how Kant puts it elsewhere.[24] The fact remains that Kant recognizes a prohibition against suicide to which it is a real question whether certain specified acts constitute exceptions.[25]

We saw above that a concept may require two practices, one of which incorporates exceptions to the other; and, as a corollary, that a resolution may be answerable to two practices, one of which incorporates exceptions to the other. But there is a yet more interesting possibility. And it is this possibility which is most relevant to the use to which I want to put Kant's ideas.

Let us say that a concept *encompasses* a practice when it does not actually require the practice though it could, without loss of identity, develop in such a way that it did. Quite how much a concept can develop without loss of identity is a vague matter. It is akin to the question of how much a game can develop without loss of identity. (When, some time in the fifteenth century, the pawn was first allowed to move forward two squares in chess, did this create a new game, what we now call chess? Or did that very game undergo a change? It would at any rate be odd, and unsatisfactory, *simply* to say that chess was invented in the fifteenth century.) *Some* development in a concept is certainly possible without loss of identity. Vague concepts themselves provide an interesting model of what I have in mind here. On one very plausible view, a vague concept, such as the concept of a child, allows for some discretion in its application. Thus anyone who possesses the concept of a child, and who is asked to give a verdict, must apply the concept to a 4 year old, and must not apply it to a 44 year old (subject to various qualifications ruling out metaphorical applications and suchlike); but it may be that he can apply it or not apply it, with equal right, to a 14 year old. And whichever he does, it may further be true that the concept could develop, without loss of identity, in such a way that what he did was mandatory. That is, the concept could be honed, or refined, in such a way that it came definitely to include, or definitely to exclude, 14 year olds. It is just such a combination of indeterminacy and determinability that I have in mind with my idea of a concept's encompassing a practice. Granted this idea, the interesting possibility to which I refer is this: that a concept which requires one practice may encompass a second practice which incorporates exceptions to the first – a corollary of this being that a resolution which is answerable to the first practice may, through a development in the relevant concept, come to be answerable to the second.

For example, the concept of a promise, which requires the practice of keeping any promise one has made, may also encompass the practice of breaking any promise one has made if this will avert a serious risk to one's own life – the practice of subordinating promises to safety, as I shall say for short. If this is so, it means that the concept of a promise, as it stands, does not actually require the practice of subordinating promises to safety. That is to say, someone can possess the concept of a promise without thereby having a reason to subordinate promises to safety. On the other hand, it also means that the concept could so develop that this was no longer true. It could so develop, or be so refined, that anyone who possessed it did thereby have a reason to subordinate promises to safety. And if this did happen, then the resolution to subordinate promises to safety would come to be answerable to that very practice.

How then is this relevant to what I want to do with Kant's ideas?

Suppose that some person A adopts some maxim m, which in turn involves some concept c. Then A must possess c. So if A is rational, he will not do anything that cannot be reconciled with possession of c. (There are analogues at the theoretical level. If someone possesses a concept, and is rational, then he or she will not think anything that cannot be reconciled with possession of that concept. Thus if someone possesses all the relevant concepts, and is rational, and knows that the Principal is an aunt, then he or she will not think that the Principal is also a man. Again, if someone possesses all the relevant concepts, and is rational, and knows that all hitherto examined emeralds have been green, then, all else being equal, he or she will not think that the first emerald to be examined after today will be blue. There are even theoretical analogues of defeasibility, as the phrase 'all else being equal' indicates. Thus such a person *may* think that the first emerald to be examined after today will be blue if news comes through of the discovery of some previously unknown region where there are all sorts of familiar gemstones with unfamiliar colours.[26]) That A will not do anything that cannot be reconciled with possession of c does not mean that A will not do anything that counts as violating a practice that c requires: such is the lesson of defeasibility. But it does mean that A will not do anything that counts as violating a practice that c requires unless that violation either constitutes observation of some other practice that c requires or, at the very least, constitutes observation of some other practice that *c* encompasses. (In the latter case, *A* will be like someone counting a 14 year old as a child. He will be acting in accord with possession of *c* by electing to treat it as if it had already been refined in one of the many ways in which it could be refined. If this sort of thing happened sufficiently often, it might even contribute to an eventual refinement of *c* whereby it did require the practice in question.) Let us now return to the idea of a maxim. A maxim, to repeat the definition that I am proposing, is a resolution to do something that either counts as observing some practice to which the resolution is answerable or counts as violating some practice to which the resolution is answerable. I further propose that a *law*, in the broadly Kantian sense,[27] is a resolution that qualifies as a maxim in the first of these two ways. That is, a law is a resolution to do something that counts as observing some practice to which the resolution is answerable. Given this definition, it follows from what has been said so far that *A*'s maxim *m*, if it is not already a law, must at the very least be capable of becoming a law, through suitable developments in the concepts it involves. The alternative is that *m* is a resolution to do something that counts as violating some practice to which it is answerable even though there is no relevant extenuation; and worse, even though *m* does not so much as allow for the possibility, through suitable developments in the concepts it involves, of there being relevant extenuation. *A* is then a little like someone possessing the concept of greenness yet counting the fact that all hitherto examined emeralds have been grue as a reason for thinking that the first emerald to be examined after today will be grue; or again, a little like someone accepting the privileges of membership of some institution yet flouting the corresponding duties. The upshot of the discussion, then, is that a rational person will act on a maxim only when that maxim is either a law or capable of becoming a law, through suitable developments in the concepts it involves.

Now, 'capable of becoming a law': quite what sort of capability this is is a deep and important question to which we shall return. But we can already hazard that it is itself partly a conceptual matter, partly a matter of the forms of life open to those who possess the relevant concepts, and partly a matter of the sociohistorical parameters within which the concepts are situated. We can also hazard that this may, without too much violence, be encapsulated in the idea of what those who possess the relevant concepts *can will*. So a rational person will act on a maxim only when he or she can will that it become a law. And here at last I arrive at my reconstruction of Kant.[28]

Practical reasoning, on this reconstruction, includes a pure element: keeping faith with concepts. Theoretical reasoning likewise involves keeping faith with concepts. What makes it possible for keeping faith with concepts to have a practical dimension as well as its more familiar theoretical dimension is, ultimately, the fact that some concepts are action-guiding. This is of course the fundamental proposition that I am using as a premise for this discussion. And we now see why.

§10 There seems to be some real prospect, then, for a vindication of Kantian rationalism – if not a total vindication, then still enough of a vindication to buttress rationalism in general. The ethical 'must' looks to have been assimilated to the logical 'must', each expressing demands placed on us by the concepts we possess. As Kant himself says, 'we can become aware of pure practical laws just as we are aware of pure theoretical principles, by attending to the necessity with which reason ascribes them to us'.[29] This in turn may inspire in us further rationalistic ambitions. Various possibilities suggest themselves. Just as we may want to say that only thinking which can be reconciled with concepts one possesses is genuine thinking, so too we may want to say that only acting which can be reconciled with concepts one possesses is genuine acting. Again, just as we may want to say that respecting the logical 'must' turns mere flights of fancy and associations of ideas into genuine thoughts, so too we may want to say that respecting the ethical 'must' turns mere caprices and unregulated responses to the force of conative states into genuine actions.

But before we get carried away, we must note one obvious and crucial gap in the vindication we have so far. Kantian rationalism, like any other species of rationalism, requires the possibility of a categorical imperative: the possibility that a certain course of action should commend itself to any rational being. But the closest we seem to have got to this is the possibility that a certain course of action should commend itself to any rational being *who possesses all the relevant concepts*. Thus it may be that if I am rational, and if I possess the concept of a promise, then I shall acknowledge the value of promise keeping. But this leaves open the possibility that someone who is rational, but who does not possess the concept of a promise, does not acknowledge the value of promise keeping – and not just because he or she is incapable of even thinking in those terms; for it leaves open, more specifically, the possibility that someone who is rational, and who does not possess the concept of a promise, *but who does grasp the concept of a promise in the disengaged way*, does not acknowledge the value of promise keeping. Such a person may think that the concept itself, and with it the whole institution of promising, is an anathema of some sort, a concept that we are better off not possessing. (Jesus thought this.[30]) The closest we seem to have got to a categorical imperative, then, still looks decidedly hypothetical.

This is in fact an exceedingly important check on any rationalistic excesses that may be tempting us, and it will in effect structure the whole of the rest of this chapter. It echoes an old criticism of Kant's rationalism that goes back at least to Hegel. Hegel decried the abstract nature of Kant's ethical work. He wrote, 'Kant's ... formulation [of the categorical imperative, in terms of] the possibility of visualizing an action as a *universal* maxim, ... in itself contains no principle beyond abstract identity and ... "absence of contradiction".'[31] Then, fastening on the concepts of property and of human life, he continued:

> The absence of property contains in itself just as little contradiction as the non-existence of this or that nation, family, etc., or the death of the whole human race. But if it is already established on other grounds and presupposed that property and human life are to exist and be respected, then indeed it is a contradiction to commit theft or murder; a contradiction must be a contradiction of something, i.e. of some content presupposed from the start as a fixed principle.[32]

In sum: yes, it is a requirement of rationality that we adhere consistently to the concepts we possess, but that still leaves open the concrete question of which concepts we are to possess.

But the issues are more complex than this suggests. Notice first that there are theoretical analogues of this sort of hypotheticality. For instance, whereas it is tempting to say that anyone who is rational must acknowledge that twice two is four, we should rather say that anyone who is rational and who possesses the relevant arithmetical concepts must acknowledge that twice two is four. We cannot rule out the possibility of a rational being who does not possess these concepts, and who therefore does not acknowledge this truth, perhaps operating with some rival arithmetic instead. To operate with a rival arithmetic instead would not be to deny such truths. It would not even be to deny their necessity. It would be to decline to think in those terms, in favour of something which, though no doubt bearing some intimate relation to our own arithmetic, nevertheless differed from it.

In the case of geometry, this sort of abstract possibility is a historical reality. For centuries it would have been agreed that anyone who was rational must acknowledge that between any two points there is one and only one straight line (to return to the example that I used in §5 of the Introduction). The truth, however, is rather that anyone who is rational and who possesses the relevant geometrical concepts, those of Euclidean geometry, must acknowledge that between any two points there is one and only one straight line. There are non-Euclidean geometries that allow us to say that between two points there can be more than one straight line (though it is something close to a pun that makes this look like a matter of genuine disagreement). Moreover, in the wake of relativity theory, it is now one of these rivals that is reckoned to provide the best tools for describing real physical space.[33] (Kant himself, it should be noted, stands in a fascinating and curiously ambivalent relation to this particular example. For while he was the first, both temperamentally and historically, to emphasize the relativity of our acknowledging Euclidean geometry to our possessing the relevant geometrical concepts, he nevertheless took that acknowledgement to be, already, an acknowledgement of truths about real physical space: he would have been utterly disconcerted by subsequent advances in physical theory.[34])

Again, to take this time an example of a way of thinking from which we are already naturally disposed to keep our distance, it is clearly not rational *simpliciter* to think that, if all hitherto examined emeralds have been grue, then we should expect the first emerald to be examined after today to be grue, but it is rational to think this if one possesses the concept of grueness.

For that matter, it is not rational *simpliciter* to think that, if all wogs have flat noses, then no-one with a protruding nose is a wog – there are many rational people who find it offensive to think in such terms and who are not prepared even to reckon with such propositions – but it is rational to think this if one possesses the concept of a wog. Here someone might object, 'So long as one is thinking *purely* rationally, one has no choice but to accept that this conditional is true.' But the fact is that the notion of *pure* rationality is looking increasingly suspect.[35]

(As an aside: does the preparedness to think in certain terms to which this kind of relativization is required include not only the possession of certain concepts but the willingness to juxtapose concepts in certain ways? A famous logic textbook of the mid-1960s attracted opprobrium from feminists for including a host of sample sentences – 'All women are featherbrained', 'Only women are featherbrained', 'No man is featherbrained' – whose subliminal effect, however unintended, now seems all too clear.[36] Those who wanted to resist the opprobrium insisted that the logical form of the sentences, which was all that mattered in this context, was quite independent of any such effect and must be acknowledged by anyone who viewed the sentences purely rationally. Was this just as wrong as insisting that anyone who is purely rational must acknowledge the truth of the conditional that, if all wogs have flat noses, then no-one with a protruding nose is a wog? No; not *just* as wrong. There are a number of pertinent differences between the two cases. One is that the offence in the use of these sentences, such as it was, was actually compounded by the fact that the sentences served their logical function unexceptionably. Another difference – the most pertinent – is that even those who objected to the use of these sentences would have had to agree that it is sometimes acceptable to think in such terms, for instance, and most notably, when denying that all women are featherbrained. Even so, it is worth considering whether such differences are differences of degree rather than of kind. Would the differences have been so marked if one of the sample sentences had been 'Only dead Jews are good Jews'?)

In conclusion, then, theoretical rationality is subject to the same sort of relativism as, on my reconstruction of Kant's rationalism, practical rationality is. This makes the vindication of rationalism look more impressive. It seems unreasonable to expect practical rationality to meet demands of absoluteness that theoretical rationality cannot meet (though we should note that Kant himself, in various ways, some of which were reflected in his views about geometry, did have that expectation[37]). Furthermore, in both the theoretical case and the practical case, there is still the unrelativized demand to keep faith with one's concepts, whatever they may be. So there might after all be a fundamental categorical imperative to act only according to a maxim that one can will to be a law.[38]

The fact remains that, because of the distinction between grasping a concept in the engaged way, in other words possessing it, and grasping a concept in the disengaged way, a person can quite reasonably flout some of the demands of practical rationality to which other people are subject, and even try actively to combat those demands. For instance, it may be that anyone who possesses the concept of a wog thereby has a reason to treat black people with disdain; even so, there is nothing irrational about *not* acknowledging that one has a reason to treat black people with disdain, nor indeed about doing what one can to unseat the concept.

The matter is made yet more complex by the fact that someone can both possess a concept and, perfectly reasonably, want to be rid of it. Someone can have decided that there is something petty or degrading or pernicious about thinking in terms in which she herself still naturally thinks. She has not yet reached the detachment to which she aspires. And the best way to try to reach that detachment, and to try to get others to reach it too, may well be by being *subversive* – adopting maxims which involve the concept but which, by design and without relevant extenuation, flout practices that the concept requires, maxims which therefore cannot be laws. A very simple model of this would be someone's resolving to shock people as often as possible by violating some taboo, with the aim of subverting the taboo and ultimately of depriving its violations of any capacity to shock. Another simple model to which I alluded in §7 of the previous chapter would be somebody's resolving never to accept a tip. Arguably one cannot do this without possessing the concept of a tip, and without thereby having some reason, however minimal, to accept any tip one is offered. Someone who genuinely did not possess the concept of a tip would arguably not need to adopt the resolution. Such a person would already treat any offer of a tip with suitable detachment, as part of some more or less quaint institution to which he or she had not the least inclination to subscribe. Resolving never to accept tips may be a step on the way to achieving that sort of detachment.[39] But the resolution to shock people as often as possible by violating a taboo and the resolution never to accept a tip involve the same (relativized) irrationality as the resolution never to keep any promise one has made. It is as if some local irrationality is being put to the service of some higher reason, rather as an isolated dissonance in music can be put to the service of some more complete harmony, or again, rather as an inoculation in medicine can be put to the service of someone's greater health.[40]

Be that as it may, the upshot of these ruminations appears to be that, however much of a vindication of Kantian rationalism we have, all the interesting and substantive questions, both in normative ethics and in meta-ethics, have merely been transferred to the non-rational arena of how we are to assess the concepts we possess in the first place.

§11 There is a debate in philosophy which nowadays seems a little dated but which is worth a digression to consider because it illustrates well the issues that have now come to the fore. This debate was fiercely contested in the 1960s, and it was couched in terms of whether it is possible to derive an 'ought' from an 'is'.[41] Hume is often cited in connection with the debate, as one of the first and clearest exponents of the view that it is not possible to do this, and, while acknowledging that the exegesis is delicate, I can think of no better way of introducing the debate than by following suit. Here is what Hume says:

> In every system of morality, which I have hitherto met with, I have always remark'd, that the author proceeds for some time in the ordinary way of reasoning, and establishes the being of a God, or makes observations concerning human affairs; when of a sudden I am surpriz'd to find, that instead of the usual copulations of propositions, *is*, and *is not*, I meet with no proposition that is not connected with an *ought*, or an *ought not*. This change is imperceptible; but is, however, of the last consequence. For as this *ought*, or *ought not*, expresses some new relation or affirmation, 'tis necessary that it shou'd be observ'd and explain'd; and at the same time that a reason should be given, for what seems altogether inconceivable, how this new relation can be a deduction from others, which are entirely different from it.[42]

Searle famously challenged this view, something of an orthodoxy by the time he was writing, by presenting what he took to be a simple derivation of an 'ought' from an 'is'. This derivation was captured in the following sequence of statements:

1 Jones uttered the words 'I hereby promise to pay you, Smith, five dollars'.
2 Jones promised to pay Smith five dollars.
3 Jones placed himself under (undertook) an obligation to pay Smith five dollars.
4 Jones is under an obligation to pay Smith five dollars.
5 Jones ought to pay Smith five dollars.[43]

Searle was quick to concede that not each of these statements strictly entailed its successor. But he argued that it was possible to add statements which did yield a sequence of entailments and which were themselves free of any 'ought', explicit or implicit. Thus, for instance, in the case of the step from (1) to (2), he argued that the following pair of statements fitted the bill:

1a   Under certain conditions C [Searle indicated how these should be specified] anyone who utters the words... 'I hereby promise to pay you, Smith, five dollars' promises to pay Smith five dollars.
1b   Conditions C obtain.[44]

In an article written in response to Searle's argument, Hare presented a counter-argument which he summarized as follows:

It may seem as if the 'brute fact' that a person has uttered a certain phonetic sequence entails the 'institutional fact' that he has promised, and that this in turn entails that he ought to do a certain thing. But this conclusion can be drawn only by one who accepts, in addition, the non-tautologous principle that one ought to keep one's promises. For unless one accepts this principle, one is not a subscribing member of the institution which it constitutes, and therefore cannot be compelled logically to accept the institutional facts which it generates in such a sense that they entail the conclusion, though of course one must admit their truth, regarded purely as pieces of anthropology.[45]

Though he did not put it in these terms, Hare was effectively arguing that only those who possess the concept of a promise, and who have therefore already implicitly acknowledged certain 'ought'-statements, should accede to Searle's proposed derivation. This seems to me entirely right. To borrow an example of Mackie's, consider a parallel proposed derivation proceeding from the statement 'John uttered the words "Bags I have the chocolate cake"', via the statement 'John bagged the chocolate cake', to the conclusion 'John has a right to (John ought to be given) the chocolate cake'.[46] This, surely, will be quite properly resisted by anyone who does not possess the concept of bagging.

That only those who possess the concept of a promise should accede to Searle's proposed derivation explains, I think, the undoubted impression of sleight in Searle's argument. At any rate I think the proposed derivation can be resisted. To that extent I side with Hare in this debate.

However, I would straightaway insist on the converse, that the *only* way of resisting the proposed derivation is by not possessing the concept of a promise; in other words, that all those who do possess the concept should accede to the proposed derivation. And this, I think, explains the equally undoubted appeal of Searle's argument. After all, we all do possess the concept, on some non-trivial understanding of who 'we' are. Furthermore, Searle explicitly anticipated the possibility of a counter-argument such as Hare's. He acknowledged that someone could challenge the whole institution of promising. He even envisioned the kind of disengaged counterpart of his proposed derivation that such a person might give, in which the conclusion was merely 'According to them he ought to pay Smith five dollars.'[47] He was not *simply* trading on the fact that we possess the concept of a promise, then. He was self-consciously and openly trading on that fact. At any rate it seems to me that, while his proposed derivation can be resisted, it cannot be resisted (so to speak) by us. To *that* extent I side with Searle in this debate.

Moreover, Searle went on to make the exceedingly important point, to which we shall return, that while there is indeed scope for challenging the whole institution of promising (just as there is scope for challenging the whole institution of bagging), there is no scope for simultaneously challenging *all* such institutions.[48] Human beings must have some institutions of this kind. They must possess *some* action-guiding concepts.[49] That human beings must possess some action-guiding concepts, to function as human beings at all, is a consequence of something to which our discussion has continually returned and to which it will continue to return, namely the need that human beings have, as finite rational beings, *to make collective and individual sense of things*. This phrase 'collective and individual', which I have used before, should be thought of as picking out two sides of a single coin. For a group of human beings to make collective sense of things, for instance through the institution of promising, is for each of them to be enabled to make individual sense of things, for instance by having the opportunity both to make promises and to rely on other people to keep promises they have made. Conversely, for one human being to make individual sense of things, for instance by treating some course of action as taboo, is for a group to which that person belongs to be enabled to make collective sense of things, for instance by having the opportunity not only to interpret this person but to come to share what makes him or her interpretable. We are, as Aristotle observed, not only rational animals but political animals, where what the latter means, roughly, is that we are animals who can flourish only in communities.[50] There is, furthermore, good reason to believe, though Aristotle himself may have had difficulties coming to terms with this, that these two defining characteristics of human beings cannot ultimately be separated from each other.[51] An excellent illustration of all of this, including the possibility that individuals can find themselves making sense of things in ways from which they would rather keep their distance, is provided by the fact that communities comprise individuals with all manner of *roles* to play (parents, pupils, judges, voters, referees, trustees, ministers, *et cetera*). For these roles are very often unchosen; they help to define the outlooks of those who occupy them; these outlooks in turn comprise various action-guiding concepts; and, for any given community, other communities can readily be imagined in which the roles available to be played are very different.[52]

As for the debate between Searle and Hare, its principal lesson, I suggest, is the very relativism on which I have been insisting. The debate provides a graphic illustration of how even the question whether or not one should accept the validity of an inference is relative to what concepts one possesses.

But I see a further lesson. I think the debate shows that we must resist a certain account of action-guiding concepts. According to this account, action-guiding concepts combine, separably, a factual component and an evaluative component, where it is the latter that makes them action-guiding. This account is enormously enticing.[53] It is very tempting, for instance, to think that the concept of cowardice has a factual component, whereby it denotes those who have a certain attitude to danger, and an evaluative component, whereby whoever non-vicariously applies the concept registers his or her disapproval of that attitude; or that the concept of a swear word has a factual component, whereby it denotes words whose utterance is tabooed in a certain way, and an evaluative component, whereby whoever non-vicariously applies the concept registers his or her endorsement of the taboo. If this were correct, it would be natural to think further that the difference between grasping the concept in the engaged way (possessing it) and grasping it in the disengaged way consisted, precisely, in the difference between being in a position to exercise both components and being in a position merely to exercise the first. But a number of philosophers have argued forcibly that this is an unworkable account of action-guiding concepts. In particular, they have focused on the supposed factual components and challenged the idea that these can be divorced from whatever approval or disapproval is supposedly being attached to them.[54] As Williams puts it, while it is true that someone can grasp an action-guiding concept in the disengaged way, he must do this by imaginatively grasping its evaluative point: 'he cannot stand quite outside the evaluative interests of [those who possess the concept], and pick up the concept simply as a device for dividing up in a rather strange way certain neutral features of the world'.[55] I certainly applaud these arguments. But I want to focus here on the other supposed components of action-guiding concepts, the evaluative ones. For this is where I think the debate we have been considering has greatest impact.

Consider: what sort of evaluation could turn the disengaged judgement that, 'according to them', Jones ought to pay Smith five dollars into the engaged judgement that, simply, Jones ought to pay Smith five dollars? One obvious proposal, suggested by the quotation from Hare above, is: the judgement that one ought to keep one's promises. But it is surely impossible to hear this as anything other than an application of the concept of a promise by one who already possesses it. (*Why* ought one to keep one's promises? This would simply make no sense as an unsupported addendum to an otherwise disengaged view of promising.) If questions are not to be begged, the evaluation needs to be a judgement that can be couched in terms available to one who grasps the concept only in the disengaged way. It needs, basically, to express approval of the institution of promising. However, if it *merely* does that, it will be too weak. People can see all sorts of good in institutions to which they nevertheless do not subscribe. If, on the other hand, it casts the institution of promising as somehow indispensable, on the grounds, say, that it is superior to any promise-free alternative, then it will be too strong. People can subscribe to institutions to which they nevertheless recognize equally fine alternatives. The problem is that there is no reason to suppose that the balance between these can be struck. And if it cannot, in this case or in others, then action-guiding concepts do not, after all, consist of two separable components, one factual and one evaluative.[56]

§12 Let us take stock. We have seen some scope for a vindication of Kantian rationalism. The ethical 'must' and the logical 'must' can be assimilated. The reason why I must not act on a maxim to break promises when this will be to my financial advantage is of a piece with the reason why I must not accept that the Principal is both an aunt and a man. The alternative, in each case, would be to flout concepts I possess. But in both cases there remain questions about whether I do well to possess those concepts. In the ethical case such questions are themselves the stuff of ethics, so much so that real doubt must be cast on how much of a vindication this vindication of Kantian rationalism is. For unless those questions can themselves be settled by the exercise of pure reason – and to establish that they can would either launch us on an awkward regress or involve considerations of an entirely new kind – then ethical thinking does not, after all, consist only in the exercise of pure reason. Indeed, the notion of *pure* reason is beginning to look suspect, not just in connection with ethics. Reason requires the use of concepts. But which concepts is surely always at the mercy of non-rational factors.[57]

Furthermore, notwithstanding my ruminations about human beings having no choice but to possess action-guiding concepts, and notwithstanding my recurrent use of certain examples (the concept of a promise and the concept of a swear word, for instance), we should not forget that the assumption on which this discussion has been based is merely that *some* concepts are action-guiding. I do believe that there is a much deeper and much more ambitious thesis to be argued. And I would justify my use of the examples on the grounds that, if any concepts are action-guiding, these are. But still, if all that is being granted is that some concepts are action-guiding, then the use of such concepts to generate maxims, and the use of reason to repudiate maxims that cannot be willed to be laws, may be very limited.

We must in any case query how much of ethics is taken up by deciding which resolutions to act on. Is ethics primarily a matter of deciding how to *act* at all? Perhaps it has much more to do with deciding what sort of person to be,[58] or what sort of institutions to have,[59] or how to affirm life[60] – any of which can be seen as a variation on the ancient concern with *how to live*.[61] And this in fact brings us back to the need to assess the concepts we possess. For the concern with how to live also embraces questions about when, how, and whether to abandon, challenge, confront, endorse, protect, nurture, reinforce, or adapt the concepts we possess.

How are such questions to be tackled? They have a significant ethical dimension, but they have other significant dimensions too. They cannot ultimately be divorced from questions about what sorts of concepts we do currently possess, how we came to possess them, and what sorts of concepts we are capable of possessing. And these questions are in turn a compound of the political, the sociological, the anthropological, the historical, the technological, the psychological, and indeed the biological.[62] They also involve exercises of the imagination, especially and most obviously when it comes to considering alternatives to the concepts we currently possess. These alternatives may be borrowed or adapted from our own past. They may be borrowed or adapted from the past or present of others. (Both of these raise further non-trivial questions, as I have already indicated more than once, about who 'we' are and who therefore count as 'others'.) They may be of some entirely new kind, fashioned not just by drawing new boundaries in conceptual space (which is how, for instance, the concept of grueness was fashioned), but by actually enlarging conceptual space – that is, not just by classifying extant possibilities in new ways, but by creating new possibilities.[63] (The emergence of the concept of a promise did not just mean that people began to think about promises. It meant that they began to be able to make them.) In general, assessing the concepts we possess will involve making sense of how we make sense. It will involve self-consciously reflecting on our forms of life, and on their different phases: on what they have been; on what they are; and on what they may yet be. Let us consider each of these in turn.[64]

§13 *Reflecting on what our forms of life have been*: This will mean thinking about how we got to be where we are. In thinking about this we are liable to be struck by the sheer contingency of where we are; by the complex social and historical accidents that have conspired to put us there. We are liable to realize, salutarily, that there is nothing sacrosanct about the concepts we possess, nor therefore about all sorts of things that we unthinkingly take for granted.

We may also see that some of the concepts we possess have their origins in a larger scheme, the rest of which we have abandoned or lost, with the result that those concepts neither make sense any longer nor enable *us* to make sense any longer, or at least not in the way in which they once did. Nietzsche was scathing about attempts (specifically, English attempts) to preserve Christian morality without Christianity. He wrote:

> When one gives up Christian belief one thereby deprives oneself of the *right* to Christian morality. For the latter is absolutely *not* self-evident... Christianity is a system, a consistently thought out and *complete* view of things. If one breaks out of it a fundamental idea, the belief in God, one thereby breaks the whole thing to pieces: one has nothing of any consequence left in one's hands... [The] origin of English morality has been forgotten... [The] highly conditional nature of its right to exist is no longer felt.[65]

Interestingly, something similar has been endorsed more recently by philosophers who are themselves Christians. Anscombe writes:

> The concepts of ... moral obligation and moral duty ... ought to be jettisoned if this is psychologically possible; because they are survivals, or derivatives from survivals, from an earlier conception of ethics which no longer generally survives, and are only harmful without it...
>
> To have a *law* conception of ethics is to hold that what is needed for conformity to the virtues ... is required by divine law. Naturally it is not possible to have such a conception unless you believe in God as a law-giver; like Jews, Stoics, and Christians...
>
> It is as if the notion 'criminal' were to remain when criminal law and criminal courts had been abolished and forgotten.[66]

A related argument, not specifically concerned with Christianity (though likewise, as it happens, coming from the pen of a Christian), can be found in the opening pages of MacIntyre's *After Virtue*.[67] MacIntyre there presents us with a very striking image. He invites us to imagine a public reaction against the natural sciences as a result of which 'laboratories are burnt down, physicists are lynched, books and instruments are destroyed ... [and] science teaching [is abolished] in schools and universities'.[68] He then asks us to imagine that, later:

> enlightened people seek to revive science, although they have largely forgotten what it was... [All] they possess are fragments ... [which] are reembodied in a set of practices which go under the revived names of physics, chemistry and biology... [But] everything that they do and say conforms to certain canons of consistency and coherence and

those contexts which would be needed to make sense of what they are doing have been lost, perhaps irretrievably.[69]

After giving further details and ruminating further on them, he continues:

> What is the point of constructing this imaginary world...? The hypothesis which I wish to advance is that in the actual world which we inhabit the language of morality is in the same state of grave disorder as the language of natural science in the imaginary world which I have described. What we possess ... are the fragments of a conceptual scheme, parts which now lack those contexts from which their significance derived. We possess indeed simulacra of morality, we continue to use many of the same expressions. But we have – very largely, if not entirely – lost our comprehension, both theoretical and practical, of morality.[70]

Nietzsche, Anscombe, and MacIntyre all indicate one important way in which reflecting on what our forms of life have been can itself force us into a self-conscious reappraisal of what they now are. This is a suitable cue for the next section.

§14 *Reflecting on what our forms of life are*: Anything that brings home the contingency of our forms of life will start us thinking about alternatives, and about whether some of these alternatives are preferable. How far is what we currently have satisfactory? Ought we to be trying, perhaps through the kind of subversion that I described in §10, to dismantle some of it? And, more fundamentally and more importantly as far as this discussion is concerned, how are such questions themselves to be addressed?

They are not peculiar to ethics. Scientists frequently confront such questions. In §10 I mentioned the fact that non-Euclidean concepts are now reckoned to be the most appropriate geometrical concepts for describing physical space, though for centuries Euclidean concepts were assumed to have title to that claim. And we have several times touched on the issue – not a live issue, to be sure, though of great theoretical interest – whether we would be better off possessing the concept of grueness than that of greenness. Two things about these non-ethical examples are worth noting. First, when questions about the possible advantages of new concepts arise in a scientific context they are themselves scientific questions. This helpfully models the fact that when such questions arise in an ethical context they are ethical questions. Second, if Goodman's own assessment of the issue about grueness is correct, then, despite the mood of insurrection that any discussion of this sort is liable to inspire, we must appreciate the merit that there can be in a brute conservatism. The sheer fact that a concept is one that we already possess very often tells in its favour over various mooted rivals.

Here it is worth remembering Austin's comment that, 'if a distinction works well for practical purposes in ordinary life (no mean feat, for even ordinary life is full of hard cases), then there is sure to be something in it'.[71] True, Austin does add that 'this is likely enough to be not the best way of arranging things if our interests are more extensive or intellectual than the ordinary'. But later, he helpfully summarizes his ambivalent message by saying, 'Certainly ... ordinary language is not the last word: in principle it can everywhere be supplemented and improved upon and superseded. Only remember, it *is* the *first* word.'[72] I shall return to the merits of conservatism in the next section.

Meanwhile, there are three broad ways in which we may think that revision of our current concepts is called for. First, we may think that there is unnecessary clutter in a certain area; that we need to simplify what we have.[73] Second, and conversely, we may think that certain needs are not being met; that we need to enrich what we have.[74] In the first of these two cases our thought is that we need to eliminate some of our current concepts, though not in favour of new ones. In the second case our thought is that we need to devise new concepts, though not at the expense of any current ones. The third case is where we think that we need to *replace* some of our current concepts *by* new ones.

On what grounds might we think this? On all sorts of grounds. The concepts that we are interested in replacing may do work of a kind that certainly needs to be done. For instance, they may govern how men and women, or parents and children, interact with one another. Yet they may also strike us as naïve or crude, as confused or confusing. They may seem to rest on faulty presuppositions. They may – this was the principal lesson of the previous section – appear to have floated dangerously free of their original historical mooring: Nietzsche, Anscombe, and MacIntyre all *bemoaned* what they saw. They may seem to be demeaning, deadening, or discriminatory. (These last terms of appraisal are of the sort most likely to figure in an ethical context, and they are themselves of course ethical. This is a further indication of how assessing ethical concepts is an ethical enterprise, a matter of thinking ethically about how to think ethically. There is no Archimidean point.[75])

It will help if we consider some examples. Many people nowadays feel uncomfortable with traditional concepts of masculinity and femininity. Korsgaard expresses well the dissatisfaction they feel:

> If someone says that aggressiveness is not feminine the response to him will not be that aggressiveness *is* feminine or that aggressiveness is great. The response is 'let's not talk that way'. The complaint that has been launched against [the values embodied in the evaluative concepts 'masculine' and 'feminine'] is not that they were false or misleading but that they were straitjackets, stunting everybody's growth. It is that

people who hold themselves and others to these ideals do not flourish. They must therefore be abandoned or revised.[76]

Another example is a certain pseudo-scientific concept of welfare which, explicitly in the thinking of some utilitarians, and implicitly in the deliberations, both public and private, of many other people, is taken to register the *telos* of everything we do, something that we ought constantly to strive to maximize. On reflection, it seems plain that no one concept can do all the work that this concept is supposed to do. In particular, it seems plain that nothing which is maximizable (and hence quantifiable) is pre-eminently worth maximizing. Consider in this connection Anscombe's memorable complaint about extreme hedonistic utilitarians: 'They were saying that something which they thought of as like a particular tickle or itch was quite obviously the point of doing anything whatsoever.'[77]

A closely related criticism of the concept is this. It purports to be *the* action-guiding concept *par excellence*. But unless people have more specific guidance, in the form of projects other than to maximize welfare, and indeed in the form of action-guiding concepts other than the concept of welfare – unless they have reasons for doing things that sometimes outweigh any reasons they have to 'maximize' *anything* – then we can have no grip on the concept of their welfare at all. In other words, unless the concept is not all it purports to be, then it cannot be anything it purports to be. It ends up giving us, far from the supreme directive that it is supposed to give us, no directive at all.

Not that assessing the concepts we currently possess will always mean finding fault with them of course. Sometimes, on the contrary, it will reinforce our confidence in them.[78] And sometimes such confidence will be best expressed through re-exercise of the very concepts in question. A case in point is a concept that seems to me to be paradigmatically action-guiding, that of a need. We would certainly not be better off without this concept. Indeed – and this is the point – we need it. Furthermore, we need it for the simple but vital reason that people have needs, needs which themselves – again there is no better way of putting this – need our attention.[79]

The concept of a promise is another that most people will want to retain, though this time anyone trying to express confidence in the concept does better to tell a story about how possession of the concept helps us in the conduct of our affairs. Hume tells such a story:

> In order ... to distinguish [interested commerce from disinterested commerce], there is a *certain form of words* invented for the former, by which we bind ourselves to the performance of any action. This form of words constitutes what we call a *promise*, which is the sanction of the interested commerce of mankind. When a man says *he promises*

any thing, he in effect expresses a *resolution* of performing it; and along with that, by making use of this *form of words*, subjects himself to the penalty of never being trusted again in case of failure... [Promises] are the conventions of men, which create a new motive, when experience has taught us, that human affairs wou'd be conducted much more for mutual advantage, were there certain *symbols* or *signs* instituted, by which we might give each other security of our conduct in any particular incident.[80]

In general there will be as many effective ways of expressing our approval of what we see as there will of expressing our disapproval.

§15 *Reflecting on what our forms of life may yet be*: This is the hardest and most important part of the process. (That is, it is the hardest and most important part of the process to the extent that the three parts can be separated from one another. Reflecting on what our forms of life may yet be is impossible without reflecting on what they are, since what matters is where we can go *from here*. Reflecting on what our forms of life are is impossible, in any really effective way, without reflecting on what they have been, for reasons that the discussion of Nietzsche, Anscombe, and MacIntyre in §13 illustrated: reflecting on what they have been can be the key to making sense of what they are. Reflecting on what our forms of life have been is impossible without reflecting imaginatively on what they might have been, a kind of deferred reflection on what they may yet be. And there are plenty of other connections besides.)

Attention shifts not just from the past and present to the future, but to possible futures. Our interest is in what forms of life we *can* have. We shall need to survey a range of possibilities then. But there are at least two crucial respects in which we shall need to do something more basic than that. First, it is not obvious what species of possibility is relevant here. Some of what is biologically possible, for instance, will not be technologically possible. Some of what is technologically possible will not be economically possible. Some of what is economically possible will not be politically possible. Some of what is politically possible, in some abstract atemporal sense, will not be politically possible any longer (for us, here, now). Part of our effort, then, must be devoted to determining which species of possibility to reckon with in the first place. There is no point in considering what is biologically impossible of course. But we might seriously consider what is politically impossible. Much depends on how political impossibility is itself being understood. If it is defined, in part, by what would involve the incurring of certain political costs, such as the suppression of certain freedoms, or the abolition of certain privileges, then we might seriously think of incurring those costs; of doing what is impossible merely in the sense that it is currently beyond this or that political pale.

We might, as people say, seriously think the unthinkable. (Of course, there are questions about whether any given form of life *is* impossible in any given sense, questions about which we can be mistaken and whose answers, in some cases, are liable to change with changing circumstances.[81])

The second respect in which we shall need to do something more basic than survey a range of possibilities is just as significant. It is natural to assume that one ultimate constraint on all our deliberations in these matters will be what is *conceptually* possible. And it is certainly true that, if something is not conceptually possible, such as there being promises that are simultaneously both broken and unbroken, then we need not and indeed must not reckon with it. But let us not forget that, in considering what forms of life we can have, we are considering what *concepts* we can possess, and, more to the point, what new concepts we can possess. And this may involve us in coming to grasp, if only in the disengaged way, concepts that no-one has ever grasped before. But coming to grasp concepts that no-one has ever grasped before will involve us in coming to acknowledge new conceptual possibilities. By this I do not mean that it will involve us in coming to acknowledge the conceptual possibility of what we currently acknowledge to be conceptually impossible, for instance that there be promises that are at once broken and unbroken: that makes no sense. I mean that it will involve us in coming to acknowledge the conceptual possibility of what we cannot currently acknowledge to be either conceptually possible or conceptually impossible, or indeed anything else, because we do not currently have the wherewithal even to think in those terms – the kind of thing that I had in mind when I talked in §12 about our not just drawing new boundaries in conceptual space but enlarging conceptual space.

There is more, then, to reflecting on what our forms of life may yet be than surveying some antecedently given, fixed range of possibilities. There is an innovative element too, an element that needs to be capable of yielding something that is, in the deepest sense of the word, new.

Here someone might ask, 'If what is ultimately at issue is what new concepts there can be, the second of these two points, then why think we need to reckon with anything more restrictive than conceptual possibility, the concern behind the first of these two points?'

But in so far as there is any one thing that is 'ultimately at issue', then it is not what new concepts there can be. It is what new concepts we can possess, where our possession of concepts, whatever the truth about concepts themselves, will always be a concrete socio-historical reality. Reflecting on what things of *that* sort are possible, as a propaedeutic to considering whether or not to try to realize some of those possibilities, cannot but take into account the more restrictive species of possibility which, in one way or another, govern all such practical deliberations.

Here it is worth thinking once again about what it is to possess a concept, something about which I have already said much but about which there is still far more to say. There are two important contrasts that must govern any adequate account of what it is to possess a concept. First, there is the contrast between, on the one hand, the fact that it is individuals who ultimately possess concepts and, on the other hand, the fact, to which I have alluded more than once, that their doing so is not only inseparable from their being comprehensible to other individuals but is only possible, at a very deep anthropological level and arguably at much deeper levels too, in the context of some community.[82] Second, there is the contrast between, on the one hand, the fact that concepts have nothing to answer to and, on the other hand, the fact, to which I keep returning, that they need to provide individuals with a way of making sense – on both interpretations of that fittingly ambiguous phrase: they need to provide individuals with a way of being comprehensible; and they need to provide individuals with a way of comprehending. These two contrasts are themselves two variations on a single theme. They both pit personal freedom of some sort against social constraint of some sort, at the same time drawing attention to their mutual dependence.

Let us focus on each of these in turn, beginning with personal freedom. Concepts have nothing to answer to. This is not to say that they are beyond criticism. On the contrary: the whole point of this part of the discussion is that they are not beyond criticism. But they are beyond a certain kind of criticism. While a concept can be crude, unjust, outmoded, difficult to handle, and countless other objectionable or disadvantageous things, it cannot be false. It cannot misrepresent anything. It provides those who possess it with a way of making sense, but there is no question – with one important qualification that I shall mention shortly – as to whether it provides them with a way of making 'correct' sense. Even if we should regard possession of a concept as a kind of knowledge, which I myself think we should, this does not tell against the point that I am making here. For it is knowledge how to do various things. It is knowledge, for instance, how to process information, how to interpret other people, how to reason about certain matters. It is not knowledge *that* anything is the case.[83] (This connects with something that Neiman says is fundamental to the whole of Kant's philosophy, both theoretical and practical, namely 'the denial that the rational is, or is centrally concerned with, the cognitive'.[84] For by 'the cognitive' she means knowledge of the latter kind.[85]) In light of this, I want to say that personal freedom finds expression, indeed that it finds supreme expression, in the possession of concepts. Possession of concepts is what makes possible the autonomous, unconstrained (except by the constraints of rationality) creation-cum-discovery – in a word, the *making* – of sense.[86]

But there is an obvious worry about this. Do not some concepts rest on false presuppositions and/or engender false expectations – the concept of phlogiston, for example, or that of a typical Capricorn, or indeed that of grueness?

They do. Possession of some of these concepts certainly entails having false beliefs. (This was the qualification to which I referred above. We may want to say, of such concepts, that they provide those who possess them with a way of making 'incorrect' sense.) But note that, even in these cases, the concepts themselves cannot be said to be false. For the mere disengaged *grasp* of them does not entail having false beliefs. Furthermore, in some of the cases mentioned in the previous paragraph, not even possession of the concepts entails having false beliefs. It merely entails having reasons to think things that are false. But these reasons are defeasible. It seems to me conceivable, however hard it is to imagine, that someone who possessed the concept of grueness might nevertheless have enough substantial countervailing reasons never to be led astray. But the price that the person would have to pay for this would be that of having to wield a considerable amount of supplementary heavy-duty complex conceptual machinery (rather like the price that someone would have to pay in order to give an accurate description of physical space using the concepts of Euclidean geometry). It would be much easier for that person if he or she simply possessed the concept of greenness instead. And what this goes to show is that what is wrong with the concept of grueness is not that it is false but that there would be horrendous difficulties for anyone who possessed it in putting it to satisfactory use.[87]

Concepts are immune to a certain sort of criticism then. But the fact that they are not immune to all sorts of criticism means that there can be reasons for or against possessing them. And this brings us to the second element in possession of concepts, the element of social constraint – as well as bringing us to the most fundamental point of contact between the two elements. Any individual has good reason to possess concepts that will help him or her both to make sense to other individuals and to make sense *of* other individuals. In practice, of course, this means that any individual has good reason to possess the concepts possessed by most of the other people roundabout, the concepts enshrined in the traditions, the culture, and the language of his or her community (or communities). Indeed, initially at least, the individual will have no choice but to possess these concepts, and it will be a sign of some maturity if he or she ceases to possess any of them or comes to possess concepts that most of those roundabout do not possess.

'The traditions, the culture, and the language of his or her community,' I said. It is perhaps the third of these, the language of the community, that most clearly illustrates the sort of social cohesion that is at issue here. For instance, consider yet again the fact that we possess the concept of greenness but do not possess the concept of grueness; that we exercise the former in all sorts of ways in which we do not exercise the latter. Nowhere is this more blatant than in the fact that the word 'green', but not the word 'grue', is part of our everyday language. For anyone in our community to grasp the concept of grueness, even in the disengaged way, and *a fortiori* in the engaged way, he or she must first be exposed to some explicit definition of the concept in terms of 'green' and 'blue'.

Furthermore, a community's language embodies, in effect, rules by which its members live. Kant, as we saw in the previous chapter, thought that rational beings should, simply *qua* rational, regard themselves as members of a community of self-legislators. This idea has seemed obscure to many. But granted even a minimal connection between the rational and the linguistic, does it not begin to look almost truistic? What clearer example of a community of self-legislators could there be than a linguistic community? And the rules of the community's language help to shape the concepts that its members possess. To take a comparatively trivial example that we have already used a number of times, there is a rule in our community not to call anybody an aunt whom one is not prepared to call female. There are myriad ways in which such rules come about. Often primitive patterns of action and reaction evolve into practices that in turn get reinforced and 'hardened' into such rules.[88] But whatever their genealogy, they are part of the sociolinguistic structure which both determines how any individual member of the community is to exercise his or her freedom, in order to participate in all that renders members of the community mutually intelligible, and makes possible certain exercises of that freedom, through just such participation.

Sharing possession of concepts is part of sharing a form of life. An individual, through possession of concepts, is enabled to make sense of things, and more particularly to tell various stories, and more particularly still to tell his or her own story, the telling of which is inseparable from acting it out – from living a life. But so too, a community, through shared possession of concepts, is enabled to make collective sense of things, and more particularly to propagate various stories, and more particularly still to propagate its own story. As I emphasized in §11, in connection with Searle, our making individual sense of things and our making collective sense of things should be thought of as two sides of a single coin. It is much the same thing to say that the two interpretations of the unadorned phrase 'making sense' which I distinguished a little while ago – being comprehensible and comprehending – register two sides of a single coin.[89] Furthermore, our making sense of things, and in particular our passing on our own stories, includes our making sense of how we make sense of things. It includes our indulging in precisely the sort of self-conscious reflection on our own concepts and our own forms of life that is the focus of this part of the discussion, in such a way that individuals are free both to suggest reforms of various sorts and – this is just as significant – to champion the *status quo*. We need to be aware that our concepts themselves have stories to be told, and that we are the authors of those stories.

This further indicates why the element of social constraint is so important. We do not and cannot possess our concepts *in vacuo*. We do not and cannot pick them up at will. Each individual comes to possess concepts by being immersed in a community, and each individual makes his or her contribution to telling the stories of these concepts, occasionally by helping to bring the stories to an end, occasionally by helping to initiate them, but most often by simply carrying them on, and most interestingly, from our point of view, by adopting suitable maxims.[90]

We can now return to the main topic of this section: reflection on what our forms of life may yet be. One implication of the latter part of this discussion is that, in reflecting on what our forms of life may yet be, we shall find ourselves forced into a certain short-term conservatism. Immediate changes are possible. Major changes are possible. But changes that are both immediate and major are not possible, not without catastrophic effect. There are some forms of life which, though they are certainly attainable, and attractive, are attainable only *via* suitable transitional forms of life, through long processes of attrition and accretion. In the famous image of Neurath, as expressed by Quine, we are in 'a boat which, if we are to rebuild it, we must rebuild plank by plank while staying afloat in it'.[91]

Moreover, this short-term conservatism is, it seems to me, contained within another, broader conservatism that we likewise cannot realistically escape. As I have already said, there seems to me to be no question of our ceasing to possess action-guiding concepts altogether. Only action-guiding concepts, I suggest, afford us the kind of participatory involvement in a shared form of life that properly equips us to make sense of things. If I am right about this, then neither is there any question of our escaping the practical demands of rationality by trying to make *detached* sense of things, using only concepts that are not action-guiding. Nor, relatedly, is there any question of our escaping the practical demands of rationality by adopting only resolutions that are not maxims. (Perhaps there is more than one truth in Williams' witty gloss on 'the moral law', conceived in a broadly Kantian way: it is, Williams writes, 'more exigent than the law of an actual liberal republic, because it allows no emigration'.[92])

However that may be, one thing that these reflections on conservatism certainly serve to remind us is that, when we envisage new possibilities, with a view to trying to realize some of them, we must consider not only how they compare with what we already have, but what would be involved in our realizing them. Thus the fundamental objection to my reconstruction of Kant's rationalism – that rationality, though it requires us to keep faith with the concepts we possess, leaves us free to stop possessing them – however damning it may be at a theoretical level, cuts very little practical ice. Stopping possessing any given concept is not the sort of thing we can just do; not simply, not effortlessly, not gratuitously.

Similarly as far as Kant's own rationalism is concerned. I do think that Kant had what I described in the previous chapter as 'a somewhat closeted unawareness' of rival moral outlooks. And there is no denying that his own rationalism was compromised by the parochialism of the examples by which he sought to defend it.[93] But none of this detracts from the casuistical significance that the examples may have had for those who, by virtue of sharing Kant's situation, also shared possession of the relevant concepts.

In reflecting on what our forms of life may yet be, then, we shall be exercising our imaginations within a fairly rigid framework determined partly by what our forms of life already are and partly by the constraints set by whatever species of possibility we deem most relevant to this exercise. We shall be addressing questions of the form, 'Would this work?', 'Could we live with that?', 'At what cost?', 'With what gain?', 'How could we get from here to there?' It will be largely a matter of envisaging, or trying to envisage, routes from concepts we currently possess to concepts we may yet possess, thinking about how the former may evolve into the latter.

But now: what is *that* reminiscent of if not the process whereby, on the reconstruction of Kant that I have offered, we consider whether some maxim that we have adopted is capable of being a law? That process too requires us to address such questions. Specifically, it requires us to address questions of the form, 'Could this concept so develop that this maxim counted as observing some practice to which the maxim was answerable?' Could the concept of a promise, for instance, so develop that it required the practice of breaking any promise one had made if this was to one's material advantage? Could it so develop that it required the practice of breaking any promise one had made if this averted a serious risk to one's own life? In the first case, certainly not. There could not be a form of promising of that kind. The fact that somebody had 'promised' to do something, on that construal of a promise, would not give other people sufficiently firm expectations for them to be able to make the kind of sense of the situation that would be required to sustain such a practice. We might say: such a concept of a promise would not give people enough in the way of directives to be able, by keeping faith with it, to act in 'the logical space of reasons'.[94] Whatever seemed right, to half-quote Wittgenstein, would be right, which means that we could not properly talk about 'right' at all.[95] By contrast, there could perhaps be a form of promising of the second kind. And perhaps our form of life could yet come to incorporate just such a concept of a promise.

What originated fundamentally as a criticism of my reconstruction of Kant's rationalism, then – that not only the maxims we adopt but also the concepts we possess stand in need of assessment – has turned out, in practice, to be itself a variation on the same theme. Assessing our concepts is of a piece with assessing our maxims. They are both part of trying to make sense. They are both part of trying to be rational. *To make sense* **is** *to be rational*.[96]

Reconsider a dilemma I posed for my reconstruction of Kant's rationalism in §12. Given that assessing our concepts, in an ethical context, is itself an ethical exercise, rationalism demands that it, no less than assessing our maxims, be something that can be done by the use of pure reason; but the task of establishing that it can be done by the use of pure reason will either launch us on an awkward regress or involve considerations of some entirely new kind. I think we get a good sense of how the discussion has panned out if we reflect on why this dilemma now looks less of a threat to my reconstruction of Kant's rationalism than it did before, at least subject to reservations I have voiced about the very idea of pure reason. To amplify: assessing a given concept, in an ethical context, may take a very different form from assessing a given maxim – though equally, it may not. It may not, because it may itself, first and foremost, involve determining the rationality of adopting some maxim. An obvious candidate is the maxim to abhor any concept that is sexist, in tandem with the judgement that the concept in question is indeed sexist. We may decide that it is perfectly rational to adopt this maxim, so long as we possess the concept of sexism. But then there will be questions about whether we do well to possess *that* concept. This clearly marks the beginning of a regress. What is not so clear is that it need be an 'awkward' regress, nor even a particularly long one. We may have ways of expressing confidence in our concept of sexism that are *not* primarily a matter of determining whether it is rational to adopt some maxim.

But what then about the case where assessing a given concept, in an ethical context, does take a very different form from assessing a given maxim, as it may in the case of assessing our concept of sexism? Well – and this is the key point – it still comes within the purview of making sense. It still comes within the purview of directing our activities in accord with where they can be placed in conceptual space; of tailoring how we think and how we act in accord with what forms of life we can have, and more generally in accord with how it would be possible for everyone willingly to think and act; of being, in a word, rational.

I am not saying that the upshot of the discussion is that Kantian rationalism has been fully vindicated after all, still less that Kant's own rationalism has been. This is not least because of the reservations I mentioned above about the idea of pure reason: further reservations will emerge in the next two chapters. But I do think the upshot of the discussion is that, in order to find what is wrong with Kantian rationalism, we have to dig very *very* deep.

§16 'What a piece of work is a man!' declaims Hamlet, 'How noble in reason! how infinite in faculty!'[97]

'How noble in reason': that, surely, registers the profound attraction of Kantian rationalism.[98] There is something at once comforting, challenging, and, above all, ennobling about the idea that our rationality, that which quintessentially distinguishes us from other animals and allows us to direct our own lives rather than just respond to the various imperatives of our biology, creates imperatives of its own, and gives us the means to answer all the most fundamental questions about how to live. It elevates us. In Kant's own words:

> [it] infinitely raises our worth ... by our personhood, in which the moral law reveals to us a life independent of animality and even of the whole sensible world, at least as far as this may be inferred from the purposive determination of our existence by this law, a determination not restricted to the conditions and boundaries of this life but reaching into the infinite.[99]

Our rationality points us towards the infinite, then. But it is also grounded in the infinite. It is grounded in our unlimited capacity, not just to apply concepts, but to create new concepts; to develop extant concepts; to contemplate different forms of life; to respond to whatever befalls us, both by making sense of it and, correlatively, by making sense in the face of it. 'How infinite in faculty!' Our rationality *is* our unlimited capacity to do these things. To be rational *is* to make sense.

I have been arguing latterly that these connections can find expression both in our assessment of the maxims we adopt and in our assessment of the concepts we possess. The first of these marks a point of contact with Kant's own rationalism. The second is a defence against the most obvious objection to my reconstruction of that rationalism. In this and the following section I want to say a little more, in turn, about each of these.

To begin, then, with our assessment of the maxims we adopt. Both in my reconstruction of Kant's rationalism and in Kant's own account, rationality demands that we adopt no maxim that we are not capable of willing to be a law. But what sort of capability is this? In my reconstruction, it is, as I put it in §9, partly conceptual, partly a matter of the forms of life open to those who possess the relevant concepts, and partly a matter of the sociohistorical parameters within which the concepts are situated. The subsequent discussion has, I hope, helped to elucidate this.

In Kant's own account the capability can be of two sorts; and he accordingly recognizes two sorts of duty. He writes:

> Some actions are so constituted that their maxim cannot even be *thought* without contradiction as a universal law..., far less could one *will* that it *should* become such. In the case of others that inner impossibility is indeed not to be found, but it is still impossible to *will* that

their maxim be raised to the universality of a law ... because such a will would contradict itself... [The] first is opposed to strict or narrower ... duty, the second only to wide ... duty.[100]

It would appear, then, that whereas for me there is one messy sort of capability involved, for Kant there are two clearly distinguished and much cleaner sorts of capability involved. In fact, however, in light of the discussion in this chapter, I submit that Kant has merely identified two points on a messy spectrum. (I do not say that Kant himself would be happy to see it in these terms. Also, I should perhaps qualify my suggestion: Kant has identified two points on a messy spectrum in so far as he has identified anything. For, as I complained in the previous chapter, he does not sufficiently clarify his notion of what we are capable of willing without our will 'contradicting itself'.)

More fully, my suggestion is this. What we are capable of willing, in any sense that is relevant in the present context, must at the very least be conceivable, or conceptually possible. Thus everyone can agree that, if there would be some conceptual impossibility in a given maxim's being a law, then we are not capable of willing it to be a law. But there are other species of possibility, as I urged in the previous section. And just as these give different senses to the question of what our forms of life may yet be, so too they give different senses to the question of what we are capable of willing. Indeed one consequence of what I am arguing in this chapter is that these amount to much the same thing, a crucial intermediary being the fact that the different species of possibility give different senses to the question of how our concepts are capable of developing. Moreover, here, much as before, part of our effort, when it comes to determining whether or not we are capable of willing a given maxim to be a law, must be devoted to determining which of the species of possibility to reckon with. Kant has merely singled out one (in so far as he has singled out anything), a species of possibility that lies a little way along the spectrum from the end point of conceptual possibility with which he contrasts it. But there are other points in-between. And there are other points further along.

For my own part I prefer to operate with a single unrefined conception of capability corresponding to the entire spectrum, a conception which I see as admitting of different refinements in different contexts for different purposes. I am also happy to include, among these refinements, some that are a good deal further along the spectrum than whatever Kant intends, and indeed sufficiently far along it to have a substantial empirical element. For reasons that I hope already to have made clear, this need not compromise any rationality involved. To refuse to adopt a maxim that one is not capable of willing to be a law, even by the lights of one of the more empirical of these refinements, can still count as rational. It can still be a matter of respecting the various demands that one is placed under, given one's circumstances, by the overarching demand to make sense.

And note: the fact that some of these refinements have a substantial empirical element not only need not compromise any rationality involved; it need not compromise the necessity of whatever necessities we, in the various corresponding senses of 'can', can grasp. Thus the fact that certain empirical conditions must be satisfied for us to grasp that promises are binding, or indeed to grasp that aunts are female, in no way threatens the conceptual necessity of these propositions. Had these conditions not been satisfied, the propositions would not thereby have been false. Promises would not have failed to be binding. Aunts would not have failed to be female. At most the issues would not have arisen for us. Aunts would not have *failed* to be female, because aunts *must* be female. And this 'must' is as hard as it either can or need be.[101] It is a common mistake to think otherwise.[102]

To recapitulate: the empirical element in rationality, on my reconstruction of Kant's rationalism, arises because the demand of reason to keep faith with concepts one possesses must take into account how those concepts may develop, and this is partly an empirical matter. But I wonder whether Kant's own rationalism is not afflicted by a similar empirical element. I have already expressed doubts about his notion of what we are capable of willing without our will 'contradicting itself'. But what about what we are capable of willing in the other sense that Kant recognizes? What would count as an example of a maxim that we could not will to be a law in that sense, or, as Kant puts it, a maxim that we could not will to be a law because we could not even *think* it to be a law without contradiction? He seems to count the maxim to make false promises whenever this is expedient as an example.[103] At any rate, if it is not – and it is as compelling a candidate as any he considers – then yet more doubts attach to the notion of what we are capable of willing without our will contradicting itself. This is because the reason that Kant gives for thinking that we could not will this maxim to be a law is that

> in accordance with such a law there would properly be no promises at all, since it would be futile to avow one's will with regard to one's future actions to others who would not believe this avowal or, if they rashly did so, would pay one back in like coin.[104]

'It would be futile,' he says. Has this *nothing* to do with the empirically determined constitution of human beings: with how they learn from experience, with how they arrive at their expectations, with what risks they are prepared to take?[105]

What, then? Am I saying that neither my reconstruction of Kant's rationalism nor yet Kant's own version is really worthy of the title 'rationalism'?

Well, given that rationalism is the thesis that *pure* reason can be used to determine how we ought to act, then, yes, I am inclined to say that. Certainly each of them leaves rationalism, in its most extreme form, unvindicated. But the real lesson, as I have already intimated, is this: there is something deeply suspect about the very idea of 'pure' reason.

§17 We turn next to our assessment of the concepts we possess, and, correlatively, to our vision of what new concepts we may yet possess. What we want, above all, are concepts that enable us to make sense, on each of the interpretations of this phrase that I distinguished in §15: we want concepts that enable us to be comprehensible; and we want concepts that enable us to comprehend, to make sense *of things*. This desire is not peculiar to ethics. Our reason for spurning the concept of grueness is that it does not enable us to make sense of things, or at least not except in an absurdly convoluted way.

In saying that we want concepts that enable us to make sense, I mean that we want concepts that enable *us* (here, now) to make sense. As I have already indicated, this raises difficult questions about who 'we' are. (Twenty-first-century human beings? 'Normal' twenty-first-century human beings? English speakers? Members of this particular culture, or state, or society?) These questions will have to be settled in different ways for different purposes. And part of the process of assessing our concepts must be to attend to them; to take due account of the fact that our enquiry needs to have a particular historical focus.

One thing that we may find, as the discussion of Nietzsche, Anscombe, and MacIntyre in §13 showed, is that concepts that once enabled us to make sense do not any longer do so, or perhaps rather that concepts that once enabled forebears of ours to make sense do not enable *us* to do so. Changing circumstances demand new concepts. For example, it is a notable feature of a good deal of impressive recent writing in Christian ethics that it does not try to force contemporary problems into old categories, but tries rather to adapt old categories to suit contemporary problems. Elford, in one such book, takes as one of his background assumptions 'that even the best of our moral endeavours will remain provisional ones: will remain, that is, continually subject to review and revision in the light of new knowledge and needs'.[106] And Holloway, in another such book, acutely aware of the fact that Christians are increasingly having to articulate their moral views in contexts in which Christianity is not common coinage, takes as one of his background assumptions that the moral views of Christians are worthless unless they make sense to non-Christians.[107] (This gives an interesting twist to Nietzsche's insistence that the moral views of *non*-Christians are worthless unless they make sense to non-Christians. It also, I think, gives the lie to Nietzsche's uncharacteristically imperceptive claim – which is what it surely is – that Christianity is 'a consistently thought out and *complete* view of things',[108] which almost suggests that Christianity is some self-contained metaphysical system or quasi-scientific theory, possibly even a system or theory with deductive consequences for all circumstances, past, present, and future.[109]) Holloway uses a jazz metaphor. He says that we must 'listen and adapt to one another, to keep the melody flowing'; and that this will involve 'respecting themes we ourselves do not choose to follow' and finding 'common themes in which many of us can participate'.[110] He wants to show how we can carry on making good ethical music even after it has become apparent that no-one is following a score – a striking echo of Williams' claim, to which I referred in §3 of the Introduction, that nature does not give us any score to follow; and of the Deleuzian reaction to that claim, which I found in Ansell Pearson, that we must (therefore) write our own score. It is worth quoting Ansell Pearson again: 'we are to become those that we are: musicians of nature and artists of our own cultivation.'[111] In other words, we are to make sense of things.

To do this we need to find a way forward from here, cherishing the concepts that already enable us to make sense of things, adapting the concepts that could better enable us to make sense of things, looking to create new concepts that may yet enable us to make greater sense of things. And note: among the 'things' of which we need to be able to make sense are our own basic reactions to situations, whether these be hard-wired, inculcated, or some mixture of the two.[112] The concept of a *person*, for instance, is largely moulded around basic reactions of compassion, envy, pity, fear, and suchlike that we have to one another.[113] Thus consider a very premature baby who, though capable of surviving for two or three days on a life-support machine, has no prospect of living beyond the end of the week. The fact that all concerned, not just the parents for whom the baby is naturally an object of love, spontaneously respond to her with an emotion for which the best word is probably 'respect', and thereby accord her a special dignity – it is non-trivial, for instance, that they have a name by which they refer to her – is a significant part of what makes that baby a person. In more ambiguous cases, notably in the case of a very young fetus, it may be that the concept of a person awaits further concerted and considered refinement. Note also: if the concept of a person is an action-guiding concept, as it seems to me paradigmatically to be, then there may be as great a dependence of the concept on the associated reasons as vice versa. (This connects with what I said in §7 about the concept of a child.) Thus imagine a man who undergoes some violent and radical personality change. The fact that his wife has a reason to remain faithful to him – I am not just talking about sexual fidelity – seems to me to contribute as much to his being the same person as vice versa. Indeed I would go further: the fact that she is not entitled to remarry contributes as much to his being the same person as vice versa. I think we do well to remember Locke's famous observation that 'person' is a forensic term.[114]

Even in formal contexts there seem to me to be illustrations of the need to develop concepts in such a way as to make sense of our basic reactions to situations. In 1931 Gödel proved a ground-breaking theorem in mathematical logic, which had the consequence that all the formal systems of arithmetic that were then standardly recognized needed to be supplemented.[115] (By a formal system of arithmetic I mean a set of axioms and rules governing such basic arithmetical concepts as addition and multiplication.) Moreover, he was able to describe some of the available supplements in such a way that they appeared utterly compelling. So these supplements were, quite properly, accepted. And, I would contend, our arithmetical concepts underwent a corresponding development.

A particularly interesting feature of this example is the fact that the development in question came about as a result of our keeping faith with our arithmetical concepts as they had been. For what Gödel's description of the relevant supplements did was this: it showed that accepting them was equivalent to sanctioning the formal systems of arithmetic that had been standardly recognized up until then (specifically, that it was equivalent to acknowledging their consistency). There may seem to be a contradiction in terms here. It may seem that, if accepting these supplements constituted a development in our arithmetical concepts, as I am claiming, then it cannot also have constituted fidelity to what the concepts had been, as I am further claiming: if our earlier use of the concepts did not determine that these supplements should be accepted, then it is futile, and it was futile at the time, to look at our earlier use of the concepts to see whether the supplements should indeed be accepted. (Peacocke essentially argues this.[116]) But this seems to me to be on a par with the claim that, if our reaction to an arrangement of lines on a piece of paper helps to determine that there is a picture of a face there, rather than being determined by it – which it surely does – then it is futile to look at the lines themselves to see whether there is indeed a picture of a face there – which it manifestly is not.[117]

The Gödel example is instructive partly because of light that it casts on what it is for a concept to undergo development, which is so crucial to my reconstruction of Kant's rationalism. But it is instructive also as an illustration of a much broader and very important idea: that included among the 'things' of which we need to make sense are our own past practices, and, more generally, all that has shaped our lives hitherto. We owe to Nietzsche the most powerful expression of this idea. Nietzsche describes 'It was' as 'the will's teeth-gnashing and most lonely affliction'.[118] True redemption of 'It was' requires not penitence or contrition, but triumphant affirmation. It requires a transformation of the 'It was' into a 'Thus I willed it.' We must live in such a way that we can make sense of our own pasts, and can thus accept them, as an integral part of the overall narrative structure of our lives. Our biographies, or autobiographies, must become works continuously in the writing, drawing on whatever concepts we need to sustain their plots.[119]

In general, we must look for concepts that enable us actively to interpret things rather than passively to undergo them. Only then can we be, in Deleuze's phrase, 'worthy of what happens to us'.[120] Only then can we overcome what Nietzsche calls *ressentiment*: a morbid failure to come to terms with the possibility that what happens to us does not make sense.[121] *It* does *not* make sense; *we* have to make sense *of it*. To quote Deleuze again:

> There resounds today the news that sense is never a principle or an origin, but that it is produced. It is not something to discover, to restore, and to re-employ; it is something to produce by a new machinery... An empty square for neither man nor God; singularities which are neither general nor individual, neither personal nor universal... Today's task is to make the empty square circulate and to make pre-individual and nonpersonal singularities speak – in short, to produce sense.[122]

This goes some way towards explaining a very striking feature of Deleuze's philosophy, namely how thoroughly miscellaneous are his various idols and mentors. Deleuze recognizes what Turetzky has appositely called 'a distaff tradition' in philosophy, a tradition which includes the Stoics, Spinoza, Leibniz, Nietzsche, and Bergson.[123] To pick just one pair from these, Spinoza and Nietzsche, it may seem obscure what fundamental themes or concerns or precepts two such diverse thinkers might be thought to share. But they share a preoccupation with the question: how can we welcome the arrival of the future with a sense of triumph? How can we accept the past in a way that constitutes, not a passive resignation, but an active affirmation of the future? We have glimpsed how Nietzsche approaches such questions. His approach has something deep in common with Spinoza's. For Spinoza, we become truly active when, under the guidance of reason, we *understand* what happens to us. Here are his definitions of action and passion:

> I say that we act or are active when something takes place within us or outside of us whose adequate cause we are, that is, when from our nature anything follows in us or outside us which can be clearly and distinctly understood through that alone. On the other hand, I say we suffer or are passive when something takes place in us or follows from our nature of which we are only the partial cause.[124]

In other words, we are active to the extent that we *appropriate* what takes place. Or in other words again, we are active to the extent that we *make sense of* what takes place.[125]

Of course, our making sense of what takes place is not completely unconstrained. Above all it is constrained by what takes place. I trust that nothing I have said will be seen as abnegating this obvious fact, nor as belittling its importance. Here is Williams, speaking from a somewhat different vantage-point but in a way that I think is highly pertinent:

> We do not want our freedom to be limitless... Some things, clearly, are accessible to an agent at a given time and others are not. Moreover, what is accessible, and how easily, depends on features both inside and outside the agent. He chooses, makes up plans, and so on, in a world that has a certain practicable shape, in terms of where he is, what he is, and what he may become. The agent not only knows this is so (that is to say, he is sane), but he also knows, on reflection, that it is necessary if he is indeed going to be a rational agent. Moreover, he cannot coherently think that in an ideal world he would not need to be a rational agent... We may sometimes think that we are dismally constrained to be rational agents, and that in a happier world it would not be necessary. But that is a fantasy (indeed it is *the* fantasy).[126]

That our freedom is limited in this way should check any suggestion that making sense of what happens means living in some kind of pollyannaish dream-world. It is in any case important to appreciate that one way of making sense of what happens is by making sense of it as an abomination. In so far as we must 'accept' what happens, this does not mean that we must unthinkingly take for granted its beneficence, *à la* Pangloss.[127] Nor does it mean that we must be resigned to it. Resignation is another form of *ressentiment*.[128] No; what it means is that we must locate what happens in a narrative. And this narrative may well develop in such a way that we strive to ensure, through the learning of suitable lessons, that nothing of the like ever happens again.

It is perhaps helpful to think in this connection about the processes whereby a young child learns a language. At first it is confronted by mere noise. Then, in tandem with developing concepts, it comes to make sense of that noise. It acknowledges that people are saying things. But some of the things that it acknowledges that people are saying it may be minded to contradict.

If we can ensure, by making sense of some grievous thing that has happened, that nothing of the like ever happens again, then we shall in a way have overcome it, and not it us. To quote Camus, 'one might think that a period which, within fifty years, uproots, enslaves, or kills seventy million human beings, should only, and forthwith, be condemned. But also its guilt must be understood.'[129]

I am reminded, in these latter reflections, of the moving and humbling words of one concentration camp survivor: 'The question is not why the righteous suffer; the question is how to suffer righteously.'[130] But of course, there is no harder question. And when the focus of the question is not one's own suffering, nor yet the suffering of one's loved ones, as it was for the person who said this remarkable thing, but the suffering of strangers, as it is for most of us reflecting on what he said, then its hardness is compounded by the fact that even to think in these terms seems intrusive and arrogant. There is more than one kind of challenge in the demand to make sense of things.

§18 Let us consider finally how these ideas relate back to Kant. How much of the original theme can be discerned in these variations? Or, for that matter, of them in it? Is there perhaps a Spinozistic–Nietzschean ethic of joy in the following quotation from Kant?

> Now, if we ask, 'What is the *aesthetic* constitution, the *temperament* so to speak *of virtue*: is it courageous and hence *joyous*, or weighed down by fear and dejected?' an answer is hardly necessary. The latter slavish frame of mind can never be found without a hidden *hatred* of the law, whereas a heart joyous in the *compliance* with its duty ... is the sign of genuineness in virtuous disposition, even where *piety* is concerned, which does not consist in the self-torment of a remorseful sinner..., but in the firm resolve to improve in the future.[131]

To be sure, we should beware of glib assimilations. To hear much more than an interesting echo of Spinoza or Nietzsche in this quotation would be forced. Even so, there is much in Kant to relate the idea of assessing and devising concepts, so as to make sense of things, to his conception of rationality. In his *Critique of the Power of Judgment* Kant revealingly lists what he takes to be three fundamental principles of thought: first, that one should think 'for oneself'; second, that one should think 'in the position of everyone else'; and third, that one should think 'in accord with oneself'.[132] Thinking for oneself is exercising the personal freedom that I claimed in §15 is a crucial element in possessing concepts, a necessary condition of having autonomous thoughts and thus of having any thoughts at all: the first principle connects with the fact that to make sense of things is to *make* sense of things. Thinking in the position of everyone else is respecting the social constraint that I claimed in §15 is a crucial element in possessing concepts, a necessary condition of having publicly shareable thoughts and thus, again, of having any thoughts at all: the second principle connects with the fact that to make sense of things is to make *sense* of things. Thinking in accord with oneself is keeping faith with the concepts one possesses, a necessary condition of having rational thoughts and thus, once again, of having any thoughts at all: the third principle connects with the fact that to make sense of things is to *make sense* of things. (As Kant says, the third principle 'can only be achieved through the combination of the first two and after frequent observance of them has made them automatic'.[133])

There are three corresponding principles of action. Kant himself does not put it in these terms, but I do not think that this does undue violence to his overall conception. First, one should adopt one's own maxims. Second, one should consider whether one can will one's maxims to be laws. Third, one should act on one's maxims only when one can indeed so will them. In sum, one should act rationally: one should act in a way that makes sense. So far as the first of these is concerned, one may need to create new concepts. And so far as the second is concerned, at least on my reconstruction of Kant, one will certainly need to envisage developments in one's concepts. Both of these exemplify something that is central to Kant's *Critique of the Power of Judgment*, namely what he calls the 'reflecting' power of judgement. The power of judgement in general he defines as 'the faculty for thinking of the particular as contained under the universal,' and the *reflecting* power of judgement as the power of judgement when 'only the particular is given, for which the universal is to be found.'[134] This of course requires creativity. And in a discussion of what he calls 'genius', he talks about what is, in effect, an extreme version of such creativity, which in turn he relates back, again in effect, to the first and second principles. Here is what he says:

> Genius 1) is a *talent* for producing that for which no determinate rule can be given, not a predisposition of skill for that which can be learned in accordance with some rule, consequently ... *originality* must be its primary characteristic. 2) ... [S]ince there can also be original nonsense, its products must at the same time be models, i.e., *exemplary*; hence, while not themselves the result of imitation, they must yet serve others in that way, i.e., as a standard or a rule of judging.[135]

However – and this is a fundamental point to which we shall return in Variations Three – there is no *a priori* guarantee that we and the world will be 'made for each other' to whatever extent is necessary for us to be able to find the universal for the particular; for us to be able to make sense of things. Whenever we do succeed in making sense of things, this will be by virtue of a happy confluence of radical contingencies. That seems to me to be one of the basic lessons, if not the basic lesson, of Kant's *Critique of the Power of Judgment*.[136] This may seem a surprising claim about what is largely a work in aesthetics. But the connection with aesthetics is not hard to see: the pleasure that we cannot help but feel when we do succeed in making sense of things is, in Kant's scheme, a feeling of beauty.[137]

But to return to the first principle of thought: there is an obvious connection between this and what Kant calls 'enlightenment', a connection which he himself explicitly draws. By 'enlightenment', as we saw at the beginning of the previous chapter, Kant means the dawning of courage in individuals to think for themselves. Later in the essay in which he gives that definition, he also gives various examples of the form that such courage can take. These examples are wonderfully resonant of motifs that I have been trying to develop in this chapter. They concern individuals who, by virtue of holding certain offices or playing certain roles, have reason to follow certain directives, but who also recognize themselves as free (subsequently) to step back from their offices or roles and query the directives. This is very reminiscent of the way in which we are free to step back from, and to query, the various institutions and action-guiding concepts that give us reasons for doing things. Here are two of Kant's examples:

> A citizen cannot refuse to pay the taxes imposed upon him ... But the same citizen does not act against the duty of a citizen when ... he publicly expresses his thoughts about the inappropriateness or even injustice of such decrees. So too, a clergyman is bound to deliver his discourse to the pupils in his catechism class and to his congregation in accordance with the creed of the church he serves, for he was employed by it on that condition. But ... he has complete freedom and is even called upon to communicate to the public all his carefully examined and well-intentioned thoughts about what is erroneous in that creed.[138]

Furthermore, Kant is adamant that no institution can bind itself against such challenges from within:

> This is quite impossible. Such a contract, concluded to keep all further enlightenment away from the human race forever, is absolutely null and void, even if it were ratified by the supreme power, by imperial diets and by the most solemn peace treaties. One age cannot bind itself and conspire to put the following one into such a condition that it would be impossible for it to enlarge its cognitions ... and to purify them of errors, and generally to make further progress in enlightenment.[139]

Those who, by virtue of possessing certain concepts, make a certain sense of things, are always free to assess those very concepts and, by envisioning developments in them or modifications to them or replacements for them, to see their way to making better sense of things. That is the challenge of enlightenment. The end of this first set of variations has brought us full circle to the beginning of their theme.

Second theme: freedom

> To be free ... is to be able to bind oneself by the norms that are concepts. The *only* thing that Kantian agents can *do*, in the strict sense of *do* that involves the exercise of freedom, is apply concepts – whether theoretically in judgment, or practically in action. Activity that consists in the application of concepts is *rational* activity. So we are free exactly in so far as we are rational.
> (Robert Brandom, 'Some Pragmatist Themes in Hegel's Idealism', note 2)

§1 At the end of Theme One I emphasized that Kant's formulations of the fundamental categorical imperative depended, as he himself saw clearly, on the supposition that pure reason can be put to practical use. One of the main objections to rationalism is that this supposition is false. In Variations One I went some way towards addressing this objection. Only some way, however. There remain the worries about the very idea of 'pure' reason.

Do there remain other worries? Indeed. Perhaps the most basic, and the most relevant to Kant's own view of what still needed to be done, is the following. If pure reason is to be of practical use, then it must be capable of achieving two things. It must be capable of determining certain courses of action. And it must be capable of exerting some motivational power with respect to whatever courses of action it determines. To see the distinction between these, suppose that the issue had been, not whether pure reason can be of practical use, but whether consulting Uncle George can be of practical use. And suppose that, in the first respect, it can. Perhaps Uncle George is rarely short of advice about what to do. Even so, this manifestly leaves open the possibility that consulting Uncle George fails in the second respect, there being nothing, in general, to commend following his advice. (By contrast, seeking the will of an inscrutable and powerful tyrant might succeed in the second respect but fail in the first.) The worry is simply that I have concentrated exclusively on the first respect. I have provided a positive answer of sorts to the question, 'Can pure reason determine certain courses of action?' but no answer at all to the question, 'So what?' We tend to overlook this second question because we take it to be obvious that 'rational', or 'determined by reason', are terms of commendation. But recall the case of the man envisaged in Theme One, §4, who, having been persuaded that he was being irrational in telling outrageous lies, turned out to be impervious to this fact and set off to tell further outrageous lies.[1]

To be sure, the matter is not quite as straightforward as this example suggests. Consider a theoretical analogue. Imagine someone who, in the course of weighing two opposing views about an issue, becomes persuaded that it would be irrational to adopt one of them. Can we really make sense of his simply being impervious to this fact and adopting it none the less?

We cannot. That is, we cannot make sense of his *simply* being impervious to this fact. If he adopts the view which he knows it would be irrational to adopt, this requires explanation. In acknowledging that it would be irrational to adopt this view, he is acknowledging that there is a reason not to adopt it. And in acknowledging that there is a reason not to adopt it, he is already part way to not doing so. (It is of the essence of normative reasons that their being recognized as such tends to make explanatory reasons of them.)

Still, he can be part way to not doing something yet still recoil and do it. Explicable self-conscious irrationality, even in the theoretical case, is not, I think, precluded. Quite how much can be explained is a large and complex matter that I cannot hope to settle here. An extreme case is that of Tertullian, who famously embraced the doctrine of the incarnation on the grounds that it was 'certain because impossible'.[2] A less extreme case would be that of somebody believing something because of a *hunch*, a hunch which he knew ran contrary to all the available evidence.[3]

To explain such cases of self-conscious irrationality one needs to locate them in broader patterns of rationality in the thinking of the individuals concerned. This is for reasons that Davidson has emphasized. As he puts it:

> crediting people with a large degree of [rationality] ... is unavoidable if we are to be in a position to accuse them meaningfully of ... irrationality. Global confusion ... is unthinkable, not because imagination boggles, but because too much confusion leaves nothing to be confused about.[4]

Similarly, if someone self-consciously and explicably does something irrational, this does not mean that he is not (really) a rational being. On the contrary. It is only because he is a rational being that he can do something irrational in the first place. In other words, it is only because he is capable of respecting the demands of rationality that he is capable of flouting them. If he could not respect them, then whatever he did would be, not irrational, but non-rational. That is, it would be outside 'the logical space of reasons' altogether.[5] (Only someone who knows how to play chess can make what is genuinely a bad chess move. Someone who does not know how to play chess can at most go through the physical motions of making a bad chess move. But this does not itself, strictly speaking, constitute making any move at all.)

All of this entails that there are limits to how much irrationality can intelligibly be ascribed to someone. *A fortiori* it entails that there are limits to how much self-conscious irrationality can intelligibly be ascribed to someone. But it does not entail that none can. And this suggests that, even to the extent that we have shown pure reason to be capable of determining certain courses of action, we still need to confront the question, 'So what?'

Someone might say, 'But have you not in effect addressed this question, perhaps even suppressed it, in your very effort to substantiate the possibility of self-conscious irrationality? For surely the tenor of these remarks is that what that possibility *is* is the possibility of deliberate abnormal resistance to the demands of reason. This reinforces the common-sense view that "rational" is a term of commendation; that one does not count as acknowledging the rationality of something unless one has some inclination, albeit an inclination that one can overcome, to pursue it.'

Well, yes, such is the tenor of the remarks at the theoretical level. In fact we can go further: one does not count as *thinking* unless one has an inclination of this sort, an inclination to yield to the demands that rationality places on thought. This is, in part, what thinking is. Thinking essentially involves the exercise of concepts. And the exercise of concepts is not possible without due respect for the demands of rationality, since these determine what counts as keeping faith with concepts and thus what counts as exercising them at all. (To put the point in the terms of the previous chapter: one does not count as thinking except in so far as one *makes sense*. Exceptional episodes of irrationality in one's thinking must be precisely that: exceptional. They must be episodes in which some isolated failure on one's part to make sense fits into a larger pattern of sense that one makes.) However, it would be begging all sorts of questions to suppose, without further ado, that something analogous holds at the practical level. The most we can say so far is that, granted the existence of action-guiding concepts, there is an analogue, at the practical level, of thinking irrationally, something that deserves to be called acting irrationally, namely acting in a way that is contrary to possession of some concept one possesses. But it is too soon to say that one does not count as acting at all unless one has some inclination to eschew this sort of thing. It is too soon to say even why one has any reason to eschew it. If someone acts in a way that is contrary to possession of some concept he or she possesses, or indeed in a way that *accords* with possession of some concept he or she possesses, then there will be reasons enough in play, for instance whatever reasons he or she has by virtue of possessing the concept and, in the former case, whatever reasons he or she allows to override these. What is not yet clear is why there is, over and above such reasons, a reason to act in accord with possession of the concept just because it counts as acting in accord with possession of the concept. (If the concept of an action-guiding concept were itself action-guiding – if anyone who possessed the concept thereby had a reason to act in accord with any action-guiding concept she possessed – then there would be such a reason. But we would be begging the same questions if we assumed that the concept of an action-guiding concept were indeed action-guiding in this way.) We still need some account, then, of why agency is as beholden to the demands of rationality as thought is, perhaps an account whereby, as in the case of thinking, one does not count as *acting* unless one has some inclination to yield to such demands.

§2 This is just the kind of thing that Kant provides.

So far we seem to have nothing but an empty tautology: 'To act in accord with the demands of pure practical reason would be to act in accord with the demands of pure practical reason.' But Kant finds something underpinning this tautology, a condition of its very intelligibility, namely our *freedom*. Indeed, he takes freedom and pure practical reason to be prerequisites of each other. And it is in these terms that he tries to convey the force that the demands of pure practical reason exert. They are nothing less than the demands of our being free agents, of our acting freely at all.[6]

At different points in his writing he expresses this connection between freedom and pure practical reason, or rather the impact that it has on us, in different ways, tending sometimes to the view that we can regard ourselves as free because we can regard ourselves as subject to the demands of pure practical reason (which are also, of course, on Kant's conception, the demands of morality)[7] and sometimes to the view that we can regard ourselves as subject to these demands because we can regard ourselves as free.[8] At one point he puts it as follows:

> Lest anyone suppose that he finds an inconsistency when I ... call freedom the condition of the moral law and ... the moral law ... the condition under which we can first become aware of freedom, I want only to remark that whereas freedom is indeed the *ratio essendi* of the moral law, the moral law is the *ratio cognoscendi* of freedom. For, had not the moral law *already* been distinctly thought in our reason, we should never consider ourselves justified in assuming such a thing as freedom... But if there were no freedom, the moral law would *not be encountered* at all in ourselves.[9]

Nevertheless, even if there are changes of emphasis and viewpoint here, indeed even if there are, *pace* Kant, changes of view, the basic connection between freedom and pure practical reason remains a fundamental constant.[10]

That freedom requires pure practical reason Kant argues as follows. Freedom is the capacity to act independently of alien causes. Now this is a negative definition of freedom. As such it is perfectly acceptable. But we need to offer something more positive if we are to show how an exercise of freedom is more than as it were an inexplicable twitch, something random and unprincipled. We need to say what makes it properly an *act*, that is an act *of will*. If it is not subject to the lawlike determination of alien causes, then it must be subject to the lawlike determination of causes of some other kind. It must be subject to the lawlike determination of *its own* causes. The will must be 'a law unto itself'. This yields the positive definition we require: freedom is the capacity to act in accord with the will's own laws. (This is reflected in the fact that an act of will, unlike an event of any other kind, is not merely governed by laws. It is governed by the agent's conception and recognition of laws, or, in Kant's own word, by the agent's 'representation' of laws.[11] The agent acts *for* a reason.) But the will's own laws, practical laws, are none other than the demands of pure practical reason (see Theme One, §5). So freedom requires pure practical reason.[12]

That pure practical reason requires freedom Kant argues as follows. If pure reason is to be put to practical use, it must be able to determine what an agent does independently of alien causes. The agent must therefore be able to act independently of alien causes. That is, the agent must be free.[13]

For Kant, then, acting is indeed on a par with thinking in that one does not count as fully and properly doing it – one does not count as *freely* doing it – except in so far as one is subject to the corresponding demands of rationality and is capable of yielding to those demands. But does this give us what we need? Not yet. The capacity to yield to the demands of pure practical reason falls short of an inclination to do so.

At times in Kant's writing there is a suggestion of something more radical, a conception whereby only agency in accord with the demands of pure practical reason counts as genuinely free agency.[14] Call this the Radical Conception. Let us leave aside for the time being the question whether Kant does in fact accept the Radical Conception. Does *it* give us what we need?

There are two basic reasons for thinking that it does not. First, even granted the Radical Conception, there is an issue about why anybody should mind forfeiting his or her own freedom. If it can be shown that acting irrationally, or immorally, somehow involves surrendering to alien forces (where 'alien' forces are to be understood as including the forces of one's own conative states[15]), does this not still leave room for the question, 'So what?'?

This is an issue that will occupy us in the next chapter. But it is worth signalling already one broadly Kantian response to it. Kant thinks that a rational being cannot act except 'under the idea of freedom':[16] in acting, a rational being takes himself to be freely determining what to do. This means that a rational being cannot act in a way that he takes to constitute subjection to alien forces. If he is to act at all, never mind for the time being whether with genuine freedom, then he must act against what he takes to constitute such subjection. But this is just another way of saying that he has a tendency to eschew such subjection. (This is connected to Kant's further claim that any being which cannot act 'otherwise than under the idea of freedom is just because of that really free in a practical respect, that is, all laws that are inseparably bound up with freedom hold for him just as if his will had been validly pronounced free also of itself'.[17])

The second and converse reason for thinking that the Radical Conception still does not give us what we need is that it involves, not too little, but too much. For to say that only agency in accord with the demands of pure practical reason counts as genuinely free agency looks like another way of saying that only rational acts properly count as acts. And that in turn looks far too large a claim. It seems to eclipse altogether the category of the irrational. What is not rational, on this conception, seems to be non-rational, in other words outside the logical space of reasons altogether. (It is as if we are being invited to deny the possibility of a bad chess move. Anything less than a perfect chess move is the product of distraction, or fatigue, or carelessness, or some such. If a player transfers his bishop from one square to another in such a way as to give his opponent mate in six, then he might just as well have had his arm knocked by a bystander. In other words, anything less than a perfect chess move is not properly a *move* at all.)

Worse, perhaps, granted Kant's equation of (pure practical) rationality with morality, the Radical Conception seems to eclipse altogether the category of the morally blameworthy. It looks as if anything less than moral perfection is, like height or shoe size, not the sort of thing for which anyone can be held responsible. The fact that I am too greedy to take active part in a just distribution of the goods at our disposal seems to be no more my fault, on this conception, than the fact that I am too short to reach up for the medicine that you so urgently need. But this is surely rationalism gone crazy.

Well, this too is an issue that will occupy us in the next chapter. But in any case there remains the exegetical question that we temporarily put to one side: does Kant accept the Radical Conception? It is certainly not a conception that he ever explicitly endorses, however much there is in his work pointing in the direction of it. The most he endorses is that a free will is a will subject to its own rational laws. This does not entail that for the will to be *exercised* freely is for it to be exercised in accordance with those laws. Moreover, there are places where Kant insists on the opposite – in line with common sense. Thus in *Critique of Practical Reason*, having described an irrational or immoral act as one that is 'pathologically affected', he straightway adds in parenthesis: 'though not thereby determined, hence still free.'[18]

There is a distinction that Kant sometimes draws, using two words that can both be rendered in English as 'will', between '*Wille*' and '*Willkür*'. Although this distinction is somewhat more prominent in some of his commentators than it is in Kant himself,[19] there is no doubt that it plays a significant role in underpinning his conception of these matters. Kant defines the distinction as follows:

> Insofar as [the faculty of desire in accordance with concepts] is joined with one's consciousness of the ability to bring about its object it is called *Willkür*; if it is not joined with this consciousness its act is called a *wish*. The faculty of desire whose inner determining ground, hence even what pleases it, lies within the subject's reason is called *Wille*. *Wille* is therefore the faculty of desire considered not so much in relation to action (as *Willkür* is) but rather in relation to the ground determining *Willkür* to action. *Wille* itself, strictly speaking, has no determining ground; insofar as it can determine *Willkür*, it is instead practical reason itself.[20]

What this comes to – and here I quote from Allison's helpful gloss – is that '*Wille*' and '*Willkür*' 'characterize respectively the legislative and executive functions of a unified faculty of volition.'[21] An agent's *Wille* is the source of the laws she sets herself (irrespective of any particular ends she happens to have): these are what determine what she ought to do. Her *Willkür*, which is her power to choose how far she will adhere to these laws, is the source of the maxims she adopts: these are what determine what she actually does.[22]

The way in which the agent's *Wille* registers her freedom is by setting its own laws, and by setting only its own laws. These, as noted above, are none other than the demands of pure practical reason. The agent's *Wille* and her pure practical reason are one and the same on Kant's conception. And this goes a long way towards explaining why there is indeed a constant hint in Kant of the Radical Conception.

By contrast, the way in which the agent's *Willkür* registers her freedom is simply by allowing her to choose whether or not to act in accord with the laws which her *Wille* sets. And this goes a long way towards explaining how Kant nevertheless manages to keep the Radical Conception at bay.

However, even as far as the agent's *Willkür* is concerned, the Radical Conception remains clearly visible in the background. For the connection that Kant draws between the agent's *Willkür* and her freedom is severely compromised by Kant's further insistence that it is only because the agent is subject to various non-rational forces (needs, appetites, ambitions, and other such conative states) that she ever chooses *not* to act in accord with the laws which her *Wille* sets.[23] As Kant says, referring to the 'ought' that characterizes statements of moral obligation (the 'ought' in 'I ought to keep any promise I have made'):

> this 'ought' is strictly speaking a 'will' that holds for every rational being under the condition that reason in him is practical without hindrance; but for beings like us – who are also affected by sensibility, by incentives of a different kind, and in whose case that which reason by itself would do is not always done – that necessity of action is called only an 'ought'.[24]

In other words, the 'I ought' of rational animals such as us is the 'I will' of beings (if such there be) who are purely rational. It is only because we are *not* purely rational that we have any such concept as 'the morally obligatory'. If we were purely rational, if we could see with utter reason-illumined clarity all that we did and why we did it (and thus always did as we ought), then, and only then, would it be true to say that our actions were in no way constrained or conditioned or befuddled; that they answered to nothing and to no-one but ourselves; that they had their motivating source in that within us which was completely autonomous and self-sufficient, namely our *Wille*. But this, surely, is but one step away from saying that only if we acted in a way that was purely rational would our actions be truly free. Shades of the Radical Conception!

In sum, then, there are grounds for describing the Radical Conception as Kantian, even if not for imputing it to Kant; but there are also grounds for thinking that, although the Radical Conception is just the kind of thing to meet the basic need that the partial defence of rationalism so far has left us with, it contains both too little and too much properly to do so.[25]

§3 Let us now turn to the *metaphysics* of Kant's conception of freedom.

Kant, inspired by the success of Newtonian mechanics, holds that every event in the physical world is completely determined by antecedent physical causes. Not only that. He has arguments of great power and depth for the conclusion that there could not so much as *be* a physical world, a world of the only kind that we can make sense of, unless it were governed in this way by inexorable causal laws.[26]

However, he also holds that such determinism is incompatible with libertarianism, the doctrine that we are free.[27] This incompatibilism is reflected in the first of his two definitions of freedom to which I referred in the previous section, the negative definition of freedom as the capacity to

98 Second theme: freedom

act independently of alien causes. The same incompatibilism finds expression in the following passage from his *Critique of Practical Reason*:

> If I say of a human being who commits a theft that this deed is, in accordance with the natural law of causality, a necessary result of determining grounds in preceding time, then it was impossible that it could have been left undone; how, then, ... can that man be called quite free at the same point of time and in regard to the same action in which and in regard to which he is nevertheless subject to an unavoidable natural necessity?[28]

There is a tradition in philosophy, of which Hume is perhaps the most notable representative, according to which there is no incompatibility here at all.[29] The capacity to act independently of alien causes is not the capacity to act independently of *all* causes. (This, as we have seen, is something that Kant himself emphasizes.) Does free agency not therefore tolerate – does it not indeed require – the determination of what the agent does by his or her wants, choices, decisions, and the like, in other words by causes that are suitably 'internal' to the agent? This idea is well expressed by Quine as follows:

> For hundreds of years it has been thought by some philosophers, and not by others, that determinism in the natural world is incompatible with freedom of the will ... I count myself among the others. One is free, in the ordinary sense of the term, when one does as one likes or sees fit; and this is not altered by the fact, if fact it be, that what one likes or sees fit has had its causes.[30]

But Kant, whose positive definition of freedom, as the capacity to act in accord with the will's own laws, might be thought to make him a natural ally of this tradition – Hume, after all, proffers a definition of freedom, as 'a power of acting or not acting, according to the determination of the will,' which sounds very like this positive definition of Kant's[31] – nevertheless wants none of it. With Hume and his followers no doubt in mind, Kant continues the quotation above as follows:

> It is a wretched subterfuge to seek to evade this [sc. incompatibilism] by saying that the *kind* of determining grounds of [a human being's] causality in accordance with natural law agrees with a *comparative* concept of freedom (according to which that is sometimes called a free effect, the determining natural ground of which lies *within* the acting being ...). Some still let themselves be put off by this subterfuge and so think they have solved, with a little quibbling about words, that difficult problem on the solution of which millennia have worked in vain

and which can therefore hardly be found so completely on the surface. That is to say, in the question about that freedom which must be put at the basis of all moral laws..., it does not matter whether the causality determined in accordance with a natural law is necessary through determining grounds lying *within* the subject or *outside* him,... if, as is admitted by these men themselves, these determining representations have the ground of their existence in time and indeed in the *antecedent state*, and this in turn in a preceding state, and so forth ...; they are always *determining* grounds of the causality of a being ... under the necessitating conditions of past time, which are thus, when the subject is to act, *no longer within his control* ...; and they therefore leave no ... *freedom* ... (in the ... proper sense) ... If the freedom of our will were none other than [our being driven by suitably 'internal' causes], then it would at bottom be nothing better than the freedom of a turn-spit, which, when once it is wound up, also accomplishes its movement of itself.[32]

Quine is completely unmoved by this sort of alarmism. He continues *his* quotation as follows:

The notion that determinism precludes freedom is easily accounted for. If one's choices are determined by prior events, and ultimately by forces outside oneself, then how can one choose otherwise? Very well, one cannot. But freedom to choose to do otherwise than one likes or sees fit would be a sordid boon.[33]

The debate is a live one then. But if Kant is right, then he is in a serious quandary. For, as we have seen, the determinism and the libertarianism that he insists are incompatible with each other are also, each of them, doctrines to which he is non-negotiably committed. He needs to effect *some* sort of reconciliation.

The way in which he does this is by assimilating the incompatibility in question, or rather, the incompatibility of determination and freedom upon which it rests, to the incompatibility of rest and motion. There is a sense, a perfectly straightforward sense, in which rest and motion are incompatible with each other. We can all agree that a physical object which is at rest cannot at the same time be in motion. Nevertheless, a physical object, a luggage rack, say, can be both at rest relative to a train and, at the same time, in motion relative to an embankment. The same sort of relativism, Kant thinks, applies in this case. He believes that an event can be both completely determined by antecedent physical causes, when considered from one point of view, and free, when considered from another. And the determinism and the libertarianism to which he is committed then hold from different points of view. His quarrel with the

Humean tradition is thus that it espouses a simple absolute compatibilism, whereby determinism and libertarianism can hold even from the same point of view. He offers a more oblique relativistic compatibilism.³⁴

There is certainly something appealing about this conception.³⁵ Consider a case of theoretical reasoning. Consider yourself reaching a verdict on the validity of the following inference.

> I have no brothers or sisters.
> The father of the man in the picture is my father's son.
> Therefore the man in the picture is my son.

It seems contrary to your whole sense of what you are doing to regard your verdict as nothing but the product of physical processes in your brain. As Kant says, you 'would then attribute the determination of your judgment not to your reason but to an impulse'.³⁶ On the other hand, there seems no obvious impediment to admitting that your verdict *is* the product of physical processes in your brain, perhaps even processes that allowed for no other possible outcome. Assuming that you arrived at the correct verdict, it is not as if you need bemoan the fact that, at some level, you could have done no other. The point seems to be that, just as certain marks on a sheet of paper can be regarded now as strokes and squiggles and now as writing conveying a message, so too your reaching the end of your deliberations can be regarded now as your brain's coming to be reconfigured in a certain way as a result of a complex concatenation of physical causes and now as your arriving at a particular judgement as a result of ratiocination. When you balk at the idea that your verdict is *nothing but* the product of physical processes in your brain, it is because you have your own (alternative) view of the matter whereby, in exercising certain concepts, you have an (alternative) sense of *why* you arrived at that verdict, which sense was itself instrumental in leading you to do so.

To see more fully what this conception comes to let us think again about the possession of concepts. As I urged in the previous chapter, to possess a concept is to make sense of things in a certain way. To think or act in accord with the concept is to negotiate the logical space of reasons under the guidance of that sense. The subject thinks or acts as she does because, through exercise of the concept, she acknowledges that there is a reason to think or act as she does. In Kant's terms, she thinks or acts not just 'in accordance with laws' but 'in accordance with the representation of laws'.³⁷ Sometimes, when she is reflective about what she is doing, she thinks or acts in accordance specifically with the representation of laws of reason, laws which as it were define the geometry of the logical space of reasons and are thus partly constitutive of any concept she possesses. She does what makes sense because she recognizes it as what makes sense. Higher-order concepts are at work here: concepts such as those of consistency, autonomy, and sense itself. To put it again in Kant's terms, 'reason is by means of [such higher-order concepts] itself an efficient cause.'[38] And this very concept of causality by reason is in turn one of the higher-order concepts at work.[39] But such causality is none other than the causality which, in contrast to that which binds together separate items (the heating of some water and its boiling, say), binds the subject's will to itself and, as Kant persuasively insists, constitutes exercise of freedom.[40] Hence anyone who possesses any concept at all, and who also possesses this concept of freedom, cannot but see thought or action that is in full accord with the former as an instance of the latter. No-one can engage in rational activity of any kind 'otherwise than under the idea of freedom'. And no-one can recognize anyone else as engaging in rational activity of any kind 'otherwise than under the idea of freedom'.[41]

There is an ideal implicit in this discussion which it is worth a brief digression to make explicit, an ideal which I have elsewhere called, using a deliberately Kantian label, *unconditionedness*.[42] Exercise of a concept, whether in thought or in action, is unconditioned in this sense when its (third-personal) explanation and its (first-personal) vindication come together; or in other words, when its best explanation cites, as the subject's own reason for exercising the concept in that way, rational self-conscious reflection on that very explanation. This means that the subject's own insight into why he is exercising the concept in the way he is is part of the story about why he is exercising the concept in the way he is. He is acting in accordance with laws *by* acting in accordance with their representation; making sense of things *by* making sense of that very way of making sense of things. This is a paradigm of rationality. It is also, on the Kantian conception that we are currently exploring, a paradigm of freedom, that freedom under whose concept (or idea) all rational activity must be regarded.

But, to return to the main idea, possession of this concept of freedom involves, like possession of any other concept, making sense of things in a certain way. In particular it involves making sense of things in terms of the logical space of reasons. And this is just one of indefinitely many ways of making sense of things. Another is making sense of things in purely physical terms. Neither is intrinsically superior to the other. The former has only the distinction of being linked inseparably to any other way of making sense of things, at a certain level of reflection. But this does not preclude making suitably non-reflective sense of things in a way that leaves freedom completely out of the picture. Making sense of things in purely physical terms, and specifically in terms of complete physical determinism (if that is what all the available empirical evidence combined with the best conception of the physical that we can form gives us reason to do), is a case in point. Freedom is not and cannot be part of the resultant picture. But it can still be part of other pictures.

Such, at any rate, is Kant's conception – suitably recast and supplemented to make it chime with some of the variations of the previous chapter. To the (very large) extent that I am attracted to it, I have my own reasons for thinking that it is better not couched in terms of the notion of a point of view. (I think there are compelling arguments for regarding one of these ways of making sense of things, namely the physical one, as being, not from some distinctive point of view, but from no point of view at all.[43]) I also have reasons, which I shall try to make clear at the end of this chapter and at the beginning of the next, for thinking that we need to interpret the idea that freedom 'cannot be part of the deterministic picture' somewhat differently from Kant. However that may be, we can see broadly how Kant thinks he can have his libertarian cake and eat it.

Still, if I may be excused some stretching of this metaphor, to say that he can have his libertarian cake and eat it, though it may entail that the cake is eatable, does not entail that the cake is edible – *fit* to be eaten. Kant is as clear about this as anyone. Far from regarding his reconciling project as a vindication of the concept of freedom, he thinks there is a deep sense in which the concept cannot be vindicated. He writes:

> Freedom ... is a mere idea, the objective reality of which can in no way be presented in accordance with laws of nature and so too cannot be presented in any possible experience; and because no example of anything analogous can ever be put under it, it can never be comprehended or even only seen.[44]

That the cake is not just eatable but edible – that not only does the reconciling project leave room for our freedom but we are actually free – is something which, as we have seen, Kant thinks we cannot help thinking. This is partly for the basic reason that we cannot act except on that conviction. But it is partly also because of the demands of morality that we feel impinging on us, demands whose most fundamental presupposition is that we are free.[45] Kant even goes as far as to say that 'freedom is real, for this idea reveals itself through the moral law,... which we ... know',[46] and again, that a man 'judges ... that he *can* do something because he is aware that he *ought* to do it and cognizes freedom within him, which, without the moral law, would have remained unknown to him'.[47] However, the knowledge or cognition that Kant is talking about here is that which he elsewhere calls 'practical'.[48] It is not the discursive knowledge which would settle any theoretical doubts. The fact remains that, in so far as we are reflective and self-conscious about our arrogation of freedom to ourselves, then we must accept it as an article of faith.[49]

The most Kant can do, therefore – and his reconciling project is the principal component in his campaign to do it – is to show that at least this article of faith cannot be confuted.[50] What the reconciling project does, if successful, is to show that it (the article of faith, our conviction that we are free) is under no threat from the fact of physical determinism. In the final section of his *Groundwork of the Metaphysics of Morals* he argues that it is under no threat from any other source either.

The way in which he does this is by locating the reconciling project in a broader metaphysical framework. He proceeds as follows. He first insists that there is a quite general reason for drawing a distinction between appearance and reality. He then urges that there is, in addition and more specifically, a reason for assimilating to this distinction the distinction on which we have been focusing between the two ways of viewing our own actions (in purely physical terms, and in terms of the logical space of reasons). Here is the crucial passage:

> No subtle reflection is required to make the following remark...: that all representations which come to us involuntarily (as do those of the senses) enable us to cognize objects only as they affect us and we remain ignorant of what they may be in themselves so that, as regards representations of this kind,... we can achieve only cognition *of appearances*, never of *things in themselves*. As soon as this distinction has once been made..., then it follows of itself that we must admit and assume behind appearances something else that is not appearance, namely things in themselves... This must yield a distinction, although a crude one, between a *world of sense* and the *world of understanding*... Even as to himself, the human being cannot claim to cognize what he is in himself through the cognizance he has by inner sensation... [Thus,] as regards mere perception and receptivity to sensations he must count himself as belonging to the *world of sense*, but with regard to what there may be of pure activity in him (what reaches consciousness immediately and not through affection of the senses) he must count himself as belonging to the *intellectual world* [i.e. the world of understanding]...
>
> Now, a human being really finds in himself a capacity by which he distinguishes himself from all other things, ... and that is *reason*. This ... shows in what we call ['concepts of reason'] a spontaneity so pure that it thereby goes far beyond anything that sensibility can ever afford it...
>
> Because of this a rational being must regard himself *as intelligence* ... as belonging not to the world of sense but to the world of understanding; hence he has two points of view from which he can regard himself and cognize laws for ... all his actions; *first*, insofar as he belongs to the world of sense, under laws of nature...; *second*, as belonging to the intelligible world [i.e. the world of understanding],

under laws which, being independent of nature, are not empirical but grounded in reason.[51]

On Kant's view, then, our conviction that we are free is a conviction about how things are in themselves, not about how they (empirically) appear.[52] Kant is adamant, however, that we can never discover anything about how things are in themselves. This means, in particular, that we can never discover anything that is incompatible with our conviction.

Does this give us the security we require? Almost. It certainly precludes one way of refuting our conviction, namely by discovering something that is incompatible with it. But there does remain another way, namely by showing that it is internally inconsistent, as it were incompatible with itself. Can Kant avert *this* threat?

He believes he can. For these purposes, however, he has to rely on details of his own particular conception of the appearance/reality distinction. This conception is altogether more radical than anything we have mooted or seen Kant mooting so far. He holds that things in themselves are not even spatial or temporal; in other words, that even space and time are part of the 'lens' through which we view things. Also part of this lens, on Kant's conception, are various fundamental concepts such as those of unity, plurality, substance, and, crucially, causality. We do not read these concepts off from experience. They are part of our innate cognitive equipment, that which makes our experience, and with it our capacity for empirical knowledge, possible at all. (In one of the most famous, most important, most recondite, and most demanding passages in the whole of Western philosophy, Kant explores what this doctrine comes to and why we are thereby justified in exercising these concepts in the way we do. This passage, commonly referred to as 'the Transcendental Deduction', occurs in his masterwork *Critique of Pure Reason*.[53] Discouragingly, in the later *Critique of Practical Reason* he prefaces a related undertaking, itself part of the defensive project which we are currently considering, by comparing it with that of the Transcendental Deduction, and commenting that, this time, 'one cannot hope to have everything as easy'![54])

Now I said above that the concepts in question 'crucially' include that of causality; crucially, because, for Kant, free exercise of the will is, precisely, a certain kind of causality. It is causality in which the cause is not itself determined by some antecedent cause.[55] Hence it is causality in which the cause must be understood as a feature of how things are in themselves, not of how they spatio-temporally appear.[56] (Kant sometimes calls the cause in such a case a *'causa noumenon'* to reflect this fact.) This, of course, reinforces what we have already seen Kant insist on, that our conviction that we are free is a conviction about how things are in themselves. For Kant, any application of the concept of freedom is, ultimately, an application of the concept of causality to things in themselves.

Does this enable him to avoid the threat of internal inconsistency? On the contrary, it seems to exacerbate that threat. For if the concept of causality is part of the lens through which we view things, then how *can* it be applied to things in themselves?

Kant has a ready reply. (I do not say that it is an entirely unproblematic reply, though I shall sketch it here without dwelling on the problems: these have to do with how invariant a concept can be across radically different applications of it.) To say that a concept is part of the lens through which we view things is to say that it is one of the innate tools that equip us to arrive at knowledge of how things appear. This does not preclude our putting the concept to extended use, in thinking about, if not in arriving at knowledge of, how things really are.[57] The very fact that the concept is not read off from experience allows for this possibility. What is more, the very fact that the concept equips us to arrive at knowledge of how things appear in the way it does testifies to its internal consistency – and thus, indirectly, to the internal consistency of the concept of freedom which is defined in terms of it. This safeguards us from the one remaining threat to our conviction that we are free.

Kant summarizes his argument as follows:

> [The] concept of a being that has free will is the concept of a *causa noumenon*; and one is already assured that this concept does not contradict itself since the concept of a cause, as having arisen wholly from the pure understanding, also has its objective reality with respect to objects in general assured by the [Transcendental Deduction] inasmuch as, being in its origin independent of all sensible conditions..., the concept could certainly be applied to things as beings of the pure understanding.[58]

§4 Kant believes, then, that 'noumenal' exercises of freedom somehow ground the 'phenomenal' antics of human beings, the various goings-on in space and time for which we can be praised or blamed. But how are we to understand this?

Kant has a simple answer to this question. We are not to understand it in any precise way at all. As he famously says of the related doctrine that the moral imperative enjoys 'practical unconditioned necessity', 'we do not ... comprehend [this], but we nevertheless comprehend its *incomprehensibility*; and this is all that can fairly be required of a philosophy that strives in its principles to the very boundary of human reason'.[59] To concede more would be to jeopardize his fundamental tenet that we can have no discursive insight into how things are in themselves.

Still, discursive insight is one thing. An inchoate understanding of what is going on (just focused enough to entitle us to say that we comprehend its incomprehensibility) is quite another. How far can we advance beyond the bare apprehension that things appear the way they do because things are the way they are?[60] If this whole conception is to withstand any scrutiny at all, then we had better be able to get at least as far as making sense of people's *individual responsibility* for some of the things they do.

Very well; but is it not enough to say the following? It is in part because of how people are in themselves, and in particular because of how they exercise their freedom, that the physical world and all its laws are the way they are, and in particular that people's bodies undergo some of the microscopic and macroscopic rearrangements of their parts that they do.

There are various reasons for doubting that it is enough to say this. The mere dependence of appearance on reality does not secure the dependence of *specific* features of appearance on *specific* features of reality which is so crucial to this conception. It is supposed to be because of how I and I alone exercise my freedom that I promise to meet you at the station at six o'clock, say. We still need some idea of how such specific dependence is possible.

Perhaps the greatest obstacle to our attaining any such idea is the atemporality of things in themselves. Suppose I not only promise to meet you at the station at six o'clock, but also, subsequently, arrange to be somewhere else at six o'clock. Then there are not, on this conception, two corresponding sequential exercises of my freedom at the level of things in themselves. There is no *sequence* at that level at all.[61] One wonders whether it even makes sense to talk of there being 'two' exercises of my freedom. Is there perhaps some single primordial exercise of my freedom, blazoned across the entire complex saga of my life?

There are times, indeed, when Kant suggests that this is precisely what he thinks. Thus in *Critique of Practical Reason* he writes that God,

> to whom the temporal condition is nothing, sees in what is to us an endless series the whole of conformity [or lack of conformity] with the moral law, and the holiness that his command inflexibly requires ... [or its lack] is to be found whole in a single intellectual intuition of the existence of rational beings.[62]

Be that as it may, there is still the question of how the exercise of my freedom can help to dictate what the physical world is like, in such a way that I am responsible for making and breaking my promise, but not for the fact that I came down with flu shortly after breaking it – except, possibly, in as much as I chose to go into that crowded room with all those coughing people – and certainly not for the fact that water expands when it freezes.

A partial answer to this question (though only partial) is that the exercise of my freedom determines my *character*, where this in turn can be thought of, from the point of view of how things are physically, as a set of dispositions in my body ensuring that it (my body) will respond in certain ways to certain changes in its internal and external conditions. Thus just as a lump of sugar will dissolve when it is put in water, so too I, in my cowardice, will flee when I am put in a position of manifest danger.

There is a link here with what Kant calls my '*Gesinnung*' – usually translated as my 'disposition' – which he defines as 'the ultimate subjective ground of the adoption of [my] maxims'.[63] Following this link, we can say a little more fully what this partial answer might come to. In determining my character I determine which maxims I will adopt; and in determining which maxims I will adopt I determine how changes in my conative states and in my other circumstances shall combine to cause me to act. If I were completely rational I would ensure that I only ever adopted maxims that made sense, which is to say, maxims that enabled *me* to make sense. My conative states, or some of them at least, are themselves beyond my control. They are part of that to which my character makes me respond. If I irrationally satisfy one of these conative states, my fault lies not in what I want to do but in the fact that I allow what I want to do to stop me from making sense. In Kant's own words:

> I do not hold myself accountable for [these conative states] or ascribe them to my proper self, that is, to my will, though I do ascribe to it the indulgence I would show them if I allowed them to influence my maxims to the detriment of the rational laws of my will.[64]

My irrationality is a kind of weakness against the force of my conative states then. If I were completely rational I would be master of these states, resisting, directing, and re-directing their force as and where appropriate.[65]

There is much here to give pause, obviously. Many people will regard this picture as a travesty of our ethical lives. Many, come to that, will regard it as a travesty of Kant.[66] But to the extent that it can serve as a quasi-Kantian answer to the question of how the exercise of my freedom is able to render me responsible for various things I do, it also perhaps makes Kant's reconciling project somewhat easier to grasp. For the fact that an object has a certain physical constitution, whereby events and processes in and around it have whatever effects they have, clearly allows for the possibility that those events and processes, and indeed their effects, are completely physically determined. Consider in this connection the following quotation from *Critique of Practical Reason*:

> A rational being can ... rightly say of every unlawful action he performed that he could have omitted it even though as appearance it is sufficiently determined in the past and, so far, is inevitably necessary; for this action, with all the past that determines it, belongs to a single phenomenon of his character, which he gives to himself and in

accordance with which he imputes to himself, as a cause independent of all sensibility, the causality of these appearances.[67]

Still, those who are unsympathetic to the reconciling project will remain exercised by the thought that, granted determinism, the fact that there is this object (my body) with this physical constitution in this portion of space and time was itself ordained by the physical state of the universe millions of years ago. Also, of course, there remains the difficulty of understanding how an atemporal exercise of my freedom, or indeed more than one atemporal exercise of my freedom, can translate into *changes* of character on my part – just as there remains the yet more basic difficulty of understanding how exercise(s) of my freedom can be specifically directed at my body. The first of these difficulties is one that occupies Kant himself, and we shall return to it in Theme Three. The second serves to remind us just how extraordinary Kant's conception is.

It is hard to know quite how charitable we should be here. On the one hand, Kant himself insists that his conception is not fully intelligible. And it is not as if we have shown it to be positively incoherent. It is not even as if we have forestalled all possible attempts to show it to be coherent. Walker mentions one such, though without attributing it to Kant.

> [This] would be to suppose that my noumenal self plays no part in deciding what the phenomenal world is like, or what the people in it are like, but chooses which of the available characters is to be *mine*, as in Plato's myth of Er at the end of the *Republic*.[68]

On the other hand, if Kant is right that, ultimately, it is only in these terms – only in terms of this extraordinary conception – that we can retain faith in our own freedom, and if, moreover, this is the sole reason or even the principal reason for our taking the conception seriously, then he must not be allowed to hide behind his own concessions of incomprehensibility from the huge obligation that he is under to explain why, in that case, we should take the conception any *more* seriously than we should the possibility that we are not, after all, really free.

§5 I want finally to consider three difficulties that Kant faces, taking my cue from this last point.

As we have seen, Kant has a response of sorts to the challenge just issued. He holds that there is a practical level at which we cannot but think of ourselves as free; and indeed that we are therefore 'really free in a practical respect'. Even so, at another level, a level of suitable reflection, we are still entitled to ask, if not bound to ask, whether what we cannot help thinking at that practical level is really true.[69]

This point has an *ad hominem* force against Kant which is evidenced by the following quotation. (Note: by 'categories' in this quotation Kant means the *a priori* concepts which I described in §3 as 'part of the lens through which we view things';[70] and by '(transcendental) ideas' he means what result when such *a priori* concepts are applied beyond possible experience, for instance to things in themselves.[71])

> Human reason has a natural propensity to overstep all [the boundaries of possible experience], and ... transcendental ideas are just as natural to it as the categories are to understanding, although with this difference, that just as the categories lead to truth, ... the ideas effect a mere, but irresistible, illusion, deception by which one can hardly resist even through the most acute criticism.[72]

Given that the concept of freedom is just such a (transcendental) idea, Kant has here signalled the very possibility that is of concern, the possibility that our belief in our own freedom is an irresistible illusion.

Moreover, the context in which this quotation appears adds to the *ad hominem* force of the point. Kant is considering various antinomies in which we are embroiled, including that of determinism and libertarianism. And he proffers the following general diagnosis. We recognize that the conditioned ultimately presupposes the unconditioned.[73] And we have an engrained craving for insight into the latter, a kind of intellectual thirst for ultimate explanation. So we assume that the unconditioned exists somewhere within the bounds of possible experience (within the bounds of what we can know). But it does not. Within these bounds everything is conditioned. So our assumption leads us into confusion. To escape the confusion we must recognize that all our ideas of unconditionedness are precisely that: *ideas*, concepts that can have application only beyond the bounds of possible experience.[74] We must also repudiate any concept in which one of these ideas is conflated with something empirical. Any such hybrid is by its very nature incoherent. A prime example is the concept of the (entire) physical universe, an amalgam of the idea of the unconditioned whole with the concept of physical reality. There cannot be such a thing.[75]

Nothing would have been more natural within this framework than for Kant to say the same about our concept of freedom. That is, nothing would have been more natural than for him to declare our concept of freedom, or more specifically our concept of a free exercise of the will, as an amalgam of the idea of uncaused causality with the concept of a physical occurrence, and then to deny that there can be such a thing.

But no. Kant champions our concept of freedom as a pure idea with no empirical element, and then relegates free exercise of the will, or rather, perhaps, promotes free exercise of the will, to the realm of the transcendent. For if freedom is an illusion, then so is morality;[76] and Kant cannot

110 Second theme: freedom

bring himself to accept *that*. He does say at one point, having outlined the 'natural dialectic in the speculative use of pure reason' and the 'natural illusion' to which it gives rise, that 'reason in its practical use is no better off.'[77] But elsewhere he insists that, in its practical use, through our awareness of the moral law, reason gives us a kind of commerce with the transcendent which affords 'objective and undoubted reality' to our concept of freedom.[78]

It is clear, then, *why* Kant thinks that the metaphysical price of his extraordinary conception of freedom is a price worth paying. The difficulty for him is this. He himself has tailor-made resources for challenging all that he is thereby trying to preserve; for explaining how there can come to be such illusions as freedom and morality, and indeed for explaining how there can come to be such *powerful* illusions, 'deception by which we can hardly resist even through the most acute criticism.'[79]

The second difficulty is a corollary of the transcendence that Kant assigns to our freedom. It relates back to the Radical Conception which I introduced in §2, the conception whereby only fully rational agency is genuinely free. I said that Kant rejects this conception, despite pressures within his own system to accept it. The difficulty is that the transcendence of freedom adds to these pressures. This is because it makes our freedom, and therewith our rationality, our very quintessence. What we most fundamentally are, for Kant, are free rational agents, beings capable of abiding by self-imposed laws of reason. It is various accidents of ours, deriving from our existence in the physical world, which interfere with our rationality: conative states competing with the demands of reason. This already has the unsettling consequence that how things appear is capable of exercising an influence on how they really are. But even if we waive that worry – after all, we are happy to admit that how things appear to an hallucination victim, say, can (really) agitate him[80] – there remains the mystery of how an act of irrationality, a compromise of a person's quintessence, can itself be an exercise of freedom, an expression of that person's quintessence.[81]

As before, Kant disarmingly sidesteps this difficulty by conceding, not only that there is a mystery, but that the mystery is beyond our understanding. He writes:

> The rational origin ... of this disharmony in our power of choice [*Willkür*] with respect to the way it incorporates lower incentives in its maxims and makes them supreme, i.e. this propensity to evil, remains inexplicable to us, for, since it must itself be imputed to us, this supreme ground of all maxims must in turn require the adoption of an evil maxim. Evil can have originated only from moral evil (not just from the limitations of our nature); yet the original predisposition (which none other than the human being himself could have cor-

Second theme: freedom 111

rupted, if this corruption is to be imputed to him) is a predisposition to the good; there is no conceivable ground for us, therefore, from which moral evil could first have come in us.[82]

Indeed, there is not.

The third difficulty concerns the ambit of (justified) praise and blame. That is, it concerns the question *which* of the goings-on in space and time result from exercises of our freedom (supposing that the problems considered in the previous section do not undermine Kant's entitlement to talk in these terms at all). Once again Kant looks to be pre-emptive. He writes:

> The real morality of actions (their merit and guilt), even that of our own conduct, ... remains entirely hidden from us. Our imputations can be referred only to the empirical character. How much of it is to be ascribed to mere nature ... no one can discover, and hence no one can judge it with complete justice.[83]

This, of course, is just what he must say. Yet the difficulty goes deeper than this. For if Kant's conception is to have any chance of being taken seriously, then it must also have some chance of connecting with the imputations that we are antecedently inclined to make. It cannot be my fault that I blinked when an object suddenly came flying towards my face, nor that I came down with flu last week. It cannot be my fault that water expands when it freezes. But now: what *are* the imputations that we are antecedently inclined to make? If there is anything in this area that we are antecedently inclined to do, then it is to revise our assessments in the light of further knowledge. Thus suppose we discover that a shoplifter has been acting under hypnosis, or under duress, or under extreme stress for that matter. Then we shall think twice about blaming her for her thefts. We shall likewise think twice about blaming her for her thefts if we discover that she is a kleptomaniac. However – and this is the crucial point – what we are antecedently inclined to do, if we become persuaded of determinism *and* become persuaded of the incompatibilism on which Kant insists, is to repudiate praise and blame altogether. It is of no avail for Kant to argue that his reconciling project shows that we do not need to do this. The reconciling project comes one consideration too late. It is what we are *antecedently* inclined to do that dictates what is available to be reconciled.

Kant heroically tries to resist this line of argument. He writes:

> One may take ... a malicious lie ...; and one may ... investigate its moving causes, through which it arose, judging on that basis how the lie and its consequences could be imputed to the person... [One] goes into the sources of the person's empirical character, seeking them in bad upbringing, bad company, and also finding them in the wickedness

of a natural temper insensitive to shame, partly in carelessness and thoughtlessness; in so doing one nonetheless blames the agent... This blame is grounded on the law of reason, which regards reason as a cause that, regardless of all the empirical conditions just named, could have and ought to have determined the conduct of the person to be other than it is.[84]

But what Kant says one does in such a case is precisely what one does not do if one has only his incompatibilism as one's guide. The third difficulty, it seems to me, is insurmountable.

Further reading

General commentaries on Kant's theory of freedom include, in addition to Allison (1990), to which I have already made several references: Carnois (1987), which is an attempt to impose systematic order on Kant's many diverse uses of the term 'freedom'; Hudson (1994), which defends Kant's reconciling project in broadly contemporary terms; Jones (1940), which provides an introduction to Kant's theory of freedom in connection with his morality; and Velkley (1989), which looks at the role of freedom in the foundations of Kant's entire philosophical system, adopting a largely historical perspective. Michalson (1990) is worth a mention here, though it is somewhat more relevant to Kant's religious philosophy to which we shall be turning in Theme Three: it grapples with the problem of how, in Kant's terms, we ever come to abuse our freedom in the way we do.

Many general commentaries on Kant have helpful chapters or sections dealing with his theory of freedom. See, for example, Allison (1983), Chapter 15; Bennett (1974), Chapter 10; and Walker (1978), Chapter X. See also Sidgwick (1962), Book I, Chapter V, §1, and Appendix.

Among relevant collections of articles, notice should be given of: Allison (1996a), Part II, which develops some of the material in Allison (1990); Guyer (2000a), which relates Kant's veneration of freedom to his liberalism; and Harper and Meerbote (1984), a collection of essays on aspects of Kant's accounts of causality and freedom.

Two individual articles of note are: Körner (1967), which contains an exposition of Kant's theory of freedom and a proposal about how to avoid its noumenal element; and Wood (1984), which defends the coherence of Kant's theory of freedom.

Finally, see again note 35 for material on freedom with a more or less Kantian inspiration.

Second set of variations

> Man is only a reed, the weakest in nature, but he is a thinking reed. There is no need for the whole universe to take up arms to crush him: a vapour, a drop of water is enough to kill him. But even if the universe were to crush him, man would still be nobler than his slayer, because he knows that he is dying and the advantage the universe has over him. The universe knows none of this.
>
> Thus all our dignity consists in thought. It is on thought that we must depend for our recovery, not on space and time... Let us then strive to think well; that is the basic principle of morality.
>
> (Blaise Pascal, *Pensées*, §200)

§1 The third of the difficulties facing Kant that I considered at the end of the previous chapter suggests that, whatever prospect we have of reconciling determinism and libertarianism, we have no prospect of reconciling determinism, libertarianism, and incompatibilism.[1] This is not to say that his 'two points of view' conception – or his 'two ways of making sense' conception, if that is a better way of construing it – must be rejected. Perhaps there *is* a way of making sense of things whereby everything is completely physically determined (or at least determined to whatever extent is necessary for there to be an issue here). And perhaps there *is* a way of making sense of things whereby we are free. The point is only that the first of these ways of making sense of things cannot then be combined with the claim that the determinism in question precludes our freedom.

This may be because it cannot be combined with *any* claim about our freedom. The first way of making sense of things may leave freedom entirely out of the picture, neither precluding it nor accommodating it. Thinking in those terms may mean not thinking in terms of freedom at all. (If this *is* the case, then the correct view of the relationship between freedom and determination is no more straightforwardly compatibilist than it is straightforwardly incompatibilist. It is certainly not compatibilist in the Humean/Quinean sense considered in Theme Two, §3, whereby freedom is an empirically identifiable species of determination.)

It is worth a brief digression to consider this possibility. Call the thesis that there is indeed such a gap between these two ways of making sense of things the Incommensurability Thesis. The Incommensurability Thesis gives an importantly new twist to the idea that freedom cannot be part of the deterministic picture.[2] What Kant means when he says that freedom cannot be part of the deterministic picture is simply that physical determinism precludes freedom. But what anyone who accepts the Incommensurability Thesis means is that *exercise of the concept of* physical determinism precludes *exercise of the concept of* freedom; or rather, more strictly, that exercise of the former precludes exercise of the latter with respect to the same subject matter, at the same time. (By way of analogy, consider the contrast between the two following: 'The next move in this game cannot be a pawn move because if White moves any of his pawns, then he will place himself in check'; 'The next move in this game cannot be a pawn move because it is a game of draughts.')

I myself think that the Incommensurability Thesis, suitably construed, is correct (though I am not concerned to argue for that now). It certainly provides a way of saying many of the things that Kant says without facing the third of the difficulties that he faces. But one question that this immediately raises – and this is part of the reason why the thesis is worth this brief digression to consider – is whether we ought, in that case, to invoke a principle of charity and say that it is what Kant really has in mind. (Kant himself once advised, 'Many historians of philosophy ... let the philosophers speak mere nonsense... They cannot see beyond what the philosophers actually said to what they really meant to say.'[3]) For that matter, is there good reason for saying that the Incommensurability Thesis is what Kant has in mind even apart from any principle of charity? Consider the following quotation from *Critique of Pure Reason*:

> In nature the understanding can cognize only *what exists*, or has been, or will be. It is impossible that something in it *ought to be* other than what ... it in fact is; indeed, the *ought*, if one has merely the course of nature before one's eyes, has no significance whatever. We cannot ask at all what ought to happen in nature, any more than we can ask what properties a circle ought to have.[4]

Well, there is certainly plenty in Kant that is conducive to this alternative interpretation. But there is too much, in my view, that is antithetical to it. In particular there is the material towards the end of Book One of *Critique of Practical Reason*, from which I quoted in the previous chapter. There Kant writes:

> If one takes the determinations of the existence of things in time for determinations of things in themselves..., then the necessity in the

causal relation can in no way be united with freedom; instead they are opposed to each other as contradictory.[5]

And a little later he refers to 'the natural necessity which cannot coexist with the freedom of the subject'.[6] Although Kant's own theme allows for, and indeed makes possible, this important variation, the theme and the variation are nevertheless distinct.

Be the exegesis as it may, the Incommensurability Thesis has much to commend it. But it also has certain inherent *limits*: limits, that is, to how far it can be extended. It is by raising a question about these limits that I want to bring the discussion back to my main concern.

According to the Incommensurability Thesis, thinking about things in terms of physical determination means not thinking in terms of freedom at all. The same cannot be said of thinking about things in terms of, say, coercion, compulsion, constraint, and suchlike. Thinking in these terms can have definite implications for freedom. Any of these conditions can be 'freedom-precluding', by which I mean simply that to show that someone has done something under any of these conditions can be a way of showing that he or she has not done the thing freely. (Not that this is any threat to our freedom more generally – not unless a reason can be given for thinking that everything we do we do under some such condition.[7]) The question that I wish to raise is this. Is whatever interferes with our rationality 'freedom-precluding' in this sense? That is, does whatever gets in the way of our paying due heed to the dictates of reason, or of our acting in accord with those dictates (say, fatigue, distraction, fear, or even the force of our own conative states) mean that we are not in complete control of what we do, and ultimately that what we do we do not do freely?

To answer yes to this question is to endorse what I called in the previous chapter 'the Radical Conception', the conception whereby it is only when we act rationally that we act in a way that is genuinely free. I expressed some of the outrage that we are liable to feel when we first encounter this conception, and I tried to explain why Kant, despite pressures within his own system to accept it, nevertheless does not do so. But perhaps it deserves more of a hearing.

The outrage is due to the apparent vanishing of the category of the irrational. This seems bad enough. Worse, when the Radical Conception is combined with some form of rationalism, the category of the morally blameworthy appears to vanish too. But do these categories really vanish in the way they appear to? Only if irrationality and moral blameworthiness themselves require freedom. It may seem too obvious to be worth disputing that they do. But there is a picture whereby they do not.

This picture, which I shall call the Radical Picture, is as follows. (I call it 'the Radical Picture' simply to register that it incorporates the Radical Conception. In due course I hope that neither the picture nor for that matter the conception will look all that radical.) A person has no control over what she does except in so far as she has rational control over what she does. She does not act freely except in so far as she acts rationally. (This is the Radical Conception.) Even so, in circumstances where there is a suitably salient possibility that she does act rationally, she can, by realizing some other possibility, still be said to have acted *ir*rationally and (thereby) to deserve (moral) blame. True, she is not then acting freely. She is not in control of what she does. But *that* is why she deserves blame. She is to blame *for* not being free, *for* her loss of control. Freedom, on this picture, is a kind of strength. It is exercised in overcoming the power of non-rational forces. It is not exercised in some prior choice about whether to act rationally or not. It is exercised *in* acting rationally.[8]

This picture, appearing as it does so utterly exigent, so utterly puritanical, has a corresponding capacity, which we have already seen in a number of related contexts, to repel and to inspire in equally profound measure. For some it will have hideous connotations of something that is all too familiar in various institutionalized forms, an ethos that is at once brutal, stifling, and disturbingly androcentric.[9] For some it will evoke an ideal of uncompromising commitment to the True, the Good, and the Right. For others it will seem simply comical.

I do not myself believe that it has enough concrete content to warrant any of these reactions. I see it as not much more than an imposition of structure on to a set of familiar concepts (the concept of being rational, the concept of being to blame for what one does, and the like). Whatever significance it has must derive, in ways that I hope will be clear by the end of the chapter, from the concrete content that these concepts themselves have. Be that as it may, we can still ask whether there is anything wrong with imposing this structure on to them.

One reason for thinking that there is harks back to the third of the difficulties facing Kant. A similar difficulty afflicts the Radical Picture. What is the ambit of (justified) blame? If blame can attach to someone for something that she has not done freely, indeed if it can attach to her *only* for something that she has not done freely, then what determines when and where it attaches? Is she to blame for something that she does under threat of her life? Or when she is both physically and emotionally exhausted? Or because she feels broody? Or because she does not feel broody? Is an alcoholic to blame for taking another drink? How far into the domain of what is not rational does the irrational extend?

According to the Radical Picture, as sketched above, in order for someone to deserve blame for some (irrational) thing that she has done, her doing the rational thing needs to be (needed to be? needs to have been?) a 'suitably salient possibility'. But what does this mean, if the sort of possibility in question is not physical possibility (which it had better not be if the Radical Picture is not to beg questions about physical determinism)? Mere conceivability seems not to be enough, on pain of our having to admit that someone can be to blame for developing a brain tumour. For surely it is *conceivable* that she should have had powers to prevent this, and, had she been in control of what she was doing, that she would thereby have done so. Or is 'suitably salient' somehow supposed to block this kind of absurdity? If so, how?

One response to this difficulty would be to stand by the imputations that we are ordinarily inclined to make, granted, as I tried to make clear at the end of the previous chapter, that these are revisable in the light of further knowledge. This response, I insisted then, was unavailable to Kant because of his further commitment to both determinism and incompatibilism. However, in the absence of any such commitment, standard practice may be as much of a basis as is required.

But is it secure enough? Is it not too shifting and contextual and messy and indeterminate to carry metaphysical weight?

No doubt it is. But 'metaphysical' weight is not what it needs to carry, if indeed it needs to carry any weight at all. The concept of blameworthiness is *superficial*. That is, it is superficial in the thoroughly non-pejorative sense that judgements of blameworthiness neither answer to hidden facts about the inner workings of reality nor express some overarching philosophical world-view. Whatever significance the concept has lies 'on the surface'.[10] This is not to deny that the significance it has is huge. The concept of blameworthiness both shapes and controls some of the most fundamental beliefs, attitudes, and feelings governing our interpersonal relations,[11] as well as being arguably our single most powerful social tool for change at the personal level. Learning that some practice is blameworthy, paradigmatically by being blamed for it, can not only change a person's ways. It can change his conative states and, in the long term, help him on his way to the possession of new action-guiding concepts (see Variations One, §§6 and 7). The point is not to belittle such processes. Quite the contrary. The point is to insist that we need neither scientific investigation nor philosophical system-building, but sympathetic attention to the processes themselves, in order to see what their significance is. There is no reason whatsoever why standard practice, in all its complexity and subtlety, with its highly sophisticated mechanisms of internal revision, should not have the resources to fix the contours of the concept of blameworthiness with as much precision as could reasonably be expected of them.[12]

Very well; but why then is the difficulty facing Kant not just as serious for the Radical Picture? Is it not part of standard practice to withhold blame when someone is seen not to be in control of what she is doing?

Well *is* it? There is clear provision within standard practice for the idea that somebody can be to blame *for* not being in control of what she is doing (a drunk driver, say). However, while that raises all sorts of interesting moral (and legal) questions of its own, it is not the main point. The main point, which will sound mildly shocking when I state it, is this. Neither standard practice nor the Radical Picture makes all that much capital out of the concept of freedom. What I mean is that the important conceptual work, in both cases, is done by other categories. In the case of the Radical Picture it is done above all by the category of the rational and the category of culpable departures from the rational. These two categories also do significant work in our standard practices of assessing one another's *thinking* of course. And as far as that (assessing one another's thinking) is concerned, questions of freedom are certainly peripheral. When we criticize a mistake of logic, in a way in which we would never dream of criticizing a slip of the tongue, this is because we take the former, unlike the latter, to be what was *meant*, the point being that one ought not to mean any such thing: it does not make sense. Whether the mistake was due to carelessness, fatigue, nervousness, wishful thinking, the effects of some drug, or any of countless other possible factors is immaterial as far as that goes (though it is clearly not immaterial as far as our attitude to the person who made the mistake goes, nor as far as any efforts at correction go). To ask whether the mistake was made 'freely' – whether the making of it was an 'exercise of freedom' – would sound, to most ears, very strange.[13] Of course, the concept of freedom in play might be an artefact, something purpose-built. If so, then some account would need to be given of what work it was supposed to be doing. And if that work was of a broadly organizational kind, as it were concerned with drawing new boundaries on a conceptual terrain that was already operational, then the situation would be very much like that which, I suggest, obtains with the Radical Picture. This is why I said earlier that I saw the Radical Picture as not much more than an imposition of structure on to a set of familiar concepts.

Not *much* more than that. But of course, it *is* more than that. It places a special emphasis on the distinction between what is rational and what is not rational, an emphasis which it does not place on the distinction between what is either rational or irrational (what is within the logical space of reasons) and what is non-rational. Moreover it does this in a way that is not, and is not intended to be, entirely independent of the connotations that talk of freedom ordinarily has. The point is, given that freedom is ordinarily regarded as a clear desideratum of agency, the Radical Picture helps to capture the idea that there is a nisus in all of us towards rationality; the idea that being rational does count in favour of a proposed course of action. (This is not to deny that the idea still needs independent motivation. As I pointed out in the previous chapter, saying that a proposed course of action would involve forfeiture of freedom is every bit as vulnerable to the question 'So what?' as saying that it would be irrational.

But the Radical Picture may provide a useful framework within which to address that question. I shall return to these issues in §§5–11 below.) This helps to explain, I think, why there are constant pressures within Kant's system to endorse something like the Radical Picture. He too wants to use the connection between rationality and freedom to express the value of the former.[14] Even so, he resists the pressures. For he also wants to preserve the idea that the demarcation between what is irrational and what is non-rational is just as much concerned with exercise of freedom, the very freedom that makes the former (what is irrational) bad. Irrationality, for Kant, is an *abuse* of freedom, not a loss of freedom. Those who likewise find the Radical Picture unpalatable, for whatever reason, and yet see something worth salvaging in its particular gilding of rationality, may find a suitable compromise in a conception whereby irrational acts do involve exercise of freedom, but only rational acts involve that exercise in its fullest and most perfect form.[15] Or indeed they may invoke some additional categories at this point and say something like this: both irrational acts and rational acts qualify as exercises of freedom, but whereas the former qualify simply through the agent's choice to act in one way rather than another, the latter qualify in another way too, namely through the agent's compliance with his own or her own most fully autonomous judgement about how that choice is to be made. (And here, of course, the terms '*Wille*' and '*Willkür*' come to mind: see §2 of the previous chapter.) Anyone who does talk in these terms, it seems to me, will be disagreeing with the Radical Picture in letter only, not in spirit. For my own part, I think the Radical Picture has a simplicity and a power that make it worth retaining, and I shall adopt it in what follows.[16]

§2 To be free is to be rational, and to be rational is to make sense. Making sense involves adhering to whatever concepts one possesses and doing so, at least in part, *to* make sense (however tacitly, however unselfconsciously). If a person, by adhering to some concept he or she possesses, does make sense, then this will enable others who possess the same concept in turn to make sense – *of him or her*. It will enable them to see him or her as moving within the logical space of reasons, a space in which their grasp of this and other concepts enables them likewise to move. But all the sense-making involved in this solidarity of mutual rationalization is superficial, in the sense of 'superficial' that I indicated in the previous section. Our making sense of one another in this way is part of our making sense of things in general through the exercise of precisely such concepts as freedom and rationality, concepts whose content and significance lie open to view in the practices that sustain them.

It is here, if anywhere, that this variation differs most markedly from its original Kantian theme. For Kant, these concepts had in them something that was deep; so deep, in fact, as to be unfathomable.[17] Or should we say rather that they had in them something that was so lofty as to be transcendent? At any rate they had in them, and needed to have in them, something that separated them off from the surface phenomena – what Kant himself would have called, simply, the phenomena – of which he thought he could make nothing but deterministic sense.[18] Kant had his own complex and weighty reasons for thinking that such a separation was necessary. But he may also have been susceptible, at least in part, to a common illusion, namely the illusion of thinking that, when one makes sense of things, the things one makes sense of are inseparable from the sense one makes of them – so that there cannot be two quite different ways of making sense of the same things. There can. To say that someone is rational does not preclude a completely deterministic story about the physical processes in which the person's rationality manifests itself.[19]

But still, if the conception of freedom in the Radical Picture is to be even remotely orthodox, then to say that someone is rational had better preclude a completely deterministic story, or anything like a completely deterministic story, about the rational processes themselves. For surely freedom, on any orthodox conception, must allow for some creativity, which must in turn entail a kind of unpredictability: not the unpredictability of what is random, but the unpredictability of what is new. Even if physical determinism, in the absence of any reduction of rational processes to physical processes, allows for unpredictability of movement within the logical space of reasons, still there will be something seriously wrong with the Radical Picture if it turns out that such unpredictability is due merely to the fact that movement within the logical space of reasons can include movement which is irrational (so that what cannot be predicted is merely how, if at all, the movement will deviate from the path of rationality). There will be something seriously wrong if rationality itself entails predictability.

How might a defender of the Radical Picture try to deflect this worry? One way would be with the following argument, designed to show that rationality does not entail predictability. Suppose we confine attention to cases of the kind most favourable to the view that it does, namely exercises of theoretical reasoning where the task in hand is to determine a unique solution to a given problem. Not even cases of *that* kind admit, in general, of prediction. Or at least, they do not admit of prediction if prediction requires advancing in some algorithmic way from knowledge of 'input' to knowledge of 'output'. (*Does* prediction require this? One problem with the worry is that, without considerable gloss, questions of predictability are not at all well defined.) There is no algorithm for advancing from knowledge of 'input' to knowledge of 'output' because – and here we can confine attention still further, to exercises in mathematical reasoning – there is no algorithm for advancing from knowledge of any given mathematical problem to knowledge of its solution. That is itself a deep mathematical truth.[20] Determining the solution to a mathematical problem may require insight, ingenuity, inspiration. To be sure, when a particular person is trying to determine the solution to a particular mathematical problem, and when we ourselves have got there first, then there is a sense in which we can predict what the person will come up with (provided that the person undertakes the task with perfect rationality; and modulo differences of approach that he or she may take in giving the same solution to the same problem; and prescinding from other such irrelevancies as the person's losing interest in the problem and coming up with nothing at all). But this is a rather feeble sense of predictability. It amounts to little more than the idea that the problem in question has a unique solution.

But, an opponent of the Radical Picture might reply, that is bad enough. The unpredictability that freedom requires is that of an 'open' future, the unpredictability, in other words, that consists in there being more than one relevant possibility concerning what will occur, none of which can yet be said to be the one that will be realized. But if the solution to the problem in this case is s, then there is only one relevant possibility concerning what will occur, namely that the person will come up with s.

Well, yes, if the solution to the problem is s, then a perfectly rational person cannot come up with anything other than s as a solution to the problem. That is more or less tautological.[21] If an opponent of the Radical Picture considers this to be predictability of a freedom-threatening kind, so be it. There is a much more powerful defence of the Radical Picture available.

Remember, making sense of things is not confined to adhering to whatever concepts one possesses. It includes creating new concepts. And this in turn, as I emphasized in Variations One, §§12 and 15, is not confined to drawing new boundaries in conceptual space. It includes enlarging conceptual space – creating *radically* new concepts, as I shall say. But this is the *ne plus ultra* of creation. Unlike other kinds of creation it is not just a matter of combinatorics (the rearrangement of elements that already exist). It issues in what was previously, quite literally, unthinkable.[22] And it has an unpredictability about it which is therefore equally extreme. When a radically new concept is created, it is not just that, before the act of creation, there were different possibilities waiting to be realized with nothing yet to determine which would be. Before the act of creation there was nothing yet to determine even what the possibilities were. The creation was at the same time the creation of the very possibility of what was created. It was the creation of its very *own* possibility. The *ne plus ultra* of creation; and the *ne plus ultra* of unpredictability.[23]

This is enough, I think, to demonstrate that the Radical Picture allows for as much in the way of unpredictability as any libertarian could possibly hope for. But just to ice the cake, notice two things. First, these cases in which radically new concepts are devised overlap with the cases that we earlier took to be maximally congenial to the view that what is rational is predictable, the cases where a unique solution to a given problem was being sought. For sometimes, in mathematics, the techniques used to solve a problem involve radically new concepts, even though neither the posing of the problem nor the stating of the solution does.[24] Second, for reasons touched on in Variations One and familiar to any student of Wittgenstein,[25] adhering to a concept that one already possesses is sometimes not much different, or different only in degree, from inventing a radically new concept. In particular, this is true when the concept has to be adapted to suit circumstances of some previously unknown kind, circumstances that may themselves arise through the invention of a radically new concept. Concepts form a network. When one is created, others must evolve accordingly. (Think also of the case in which someone adopts a maxim which, though not already a law, is capable of becoming a law through suitable developments in the concepts it involves: see Variations One, §9.) In sum, rationality allows for as much creativity and unpredictability as freedom of any kind ever could.

§3 Someone might object that it is inappropriate to talk of possibilities being 'created'. It is of the nature of a possibility, they might say, as it is of the nature of anything abstract, to be atemporal.

I have no particular axe to grind about this. Suppose the objection is conceded. Suppose the metaphors that I have been using to characterize radical conceptual innovation are to be replaced accordingly. Thus we are to speak, not of the 'creation' of possibilities, but of their 'discovery'; not of the 'enlargement' of conceptual space, but of the 'exploration' of previously unknown regions of it. The fact remains that there is an unpredictability about these things which is of the purest and deepest kind. Beyond that fact, which is all that ultimately counts here, any dispute about these matters is largely verbal.[26] (Even so, it is worth asking how far the objector is prepared to take the objection. Is the only genuine creation the creation *ex nihilo* of something concrete, anything else being – at most – the discovery of possibilities of reconfiguration? Does a sculptor, by chipping away at a block of marble, discover a statue inside? Does painting consist in discovering one of the possible arrangements of pigment on one's canvas? Are symphonies discovered?[27])

This objection is little more than a challenge to my terminology then. But lurking behind it is a more substantial point, a point as it were about topology. There *is* a sense, which is related to but different from that adverted to in the objection, in which the metaphor of enlarging conceptual space is inappropriate; a sense in which, whether we say that new possibilities are created or discovered, the *space* of possibilities, conceptual space, is always the same and always completely open to view. What changes, or what comes to be newly recognized, is how that space is divided. By this I do not mean simply that new boundaries get drawn in the space. (That is the mark of *non*-radical conceptual innovation.) I mean rather that the space is seen to have a finer grain. Thus, to pick a technical example that illustrates the point very precisely, when Cantor argued in the nineteenth century that some infinite sets are bigger than others, and introduced the concept of an infinite cardinal – a number designed to measure how big an infinite set is – this enabled mathematicians to make finer discriminations of size than they had previously been able to.[28] They came to see that, among the various possibilities of size for a set that they had previously recognized (such as having at least one member, having exactly twelve members, or being finite), one, namely being infinite, admits of sub-divisions that they had not previously recognized. Think also of the way in which grasp of the concept of a swear word enables you to make finer discriminations of meaning than you would otherwise be able to. If someone tells you that a word in a foreign language has the same sense as 'vagina', say, then you can see straight away that there is something crucial about the meaning of the word that you have still not been told. Having the same sense as 'vagina' is one possibility of meaning for a word, but it is not so to speak a 'monadic' possibility. It admits of sub-divisions according to what sort of taboo, if any, attaches to use of the word.[29]

Now up to a point this is still a matter of terminology. That is to say, the advantages of the 'fineness of grain' metaphor for characterizing radical conceptual innovation are, up to a point, the advantages of a more perspicuous way of speaking rather than those of a more accurate account of the phenomenon. But even up to that point they include at least one advantage that is considerable. The metaphor helps us to an understanding of what remains stubbornly liable to resist understanding, namely how the following two ideas consist: first, that exercises of reason enjoy an unpredictability which is of the purest and deepest kind; and second, that there is a completely deterministic story to be told about the physical processes that constitute those exercises of reason. To say that we have two ways of making sense of the same things, neither of which is reducible to the other, does not foreclose the following recurring doubt: the second of these ideas implies that if one knew all the relevant physical facts prior to some radical conceptual innovation, then one could in a sense know not just what all the relevant possibilities were concerning what was to come, but also which of them was going to be realized. How is *that* the *ne plus ultra* of unpredictability? Well, leaving aside the thousands of obscurities in the notion of 'knowing all the relevant physical facts', we can now see how one might indeed be in a position to know which of the relevant possibilities was going to be realized and yet not be in a position to know quite what the innovation was going to produce, precisely because the innovation was going to slice all the relevant possibilities in ways of which one currently had not the least inkling. Here is an analogy. Imagine a congenitally blind person who is thoroughly acquainted with all the physical facts of vision. He knows all about pigment, wavelengths, retinas, and the rest. Even so, there is plenty that he does not know, and cannot know. He does not know, and cannot know, what a cloudless midday sky looks like. If at some later time he is to be given the faculty of sight, then he will come to know such things. But he currently cannot so much as imagine them. He is in principle incapable of predicting what the world will be like for him once he has acquired the faculty of sight. It is not just that he cannot know whether a cloudless midday sky will look like *this* or like *that*. He does not even have a sense of what the possibilities are. Yet, for all that, there may be a completely deterministic story to be told about all the physical processes involved, and he himself may be fully acquainted with that story. Coming to make sense of things in some radically new way is like coming to *see* for the first time.[30]

Let us stay with this analogy for a while. A person who makes sense of things in a certain way is like someone who can sense chromatic differences between things. He knows what it *is* for something to be this 'colour' or that 'colour'. And when he both thinks and acts in accord with his way of making sense of things, then others who make sense of things in the same way can make sense in particular of him. They can see, for example, that it is because of his different attitudes to different 'colours' that he treats things in the ways he does. They can see him as, say, revelling in this 'colour' and abhorring that one; as pursuing this 'colour' and eschewing that one. A purely physical way of making sense of the same things might at one level be exhaustive. But at another level it would leave room for ignorance about what was going on here. Specifically, it would leave room for ignorance about how what was going on exhibited this person's rationality. Because his rationality expresses itself in his dealings with *'colour'*, this can be acknowledged and understood only by someone with suitable 'colour vision'. It is as if his rationality consists in his engaging with a certain *form* that the physical facts have, a form which he to some extent imposes on to them (through how he sees things) and which, in its own self-contained way, transcends what those facts actually are.

How fanciful is it to read something like this picture into the following quotation from Kant?

> The moral law ... provides a fact absolutely inexplicable from any data of the sensible world [i.e. the physical world] and from the whole compass of our theoretical use of reason, a fact that points to a pure world of the understanding and, indeed, even *determines* it *positively* and lets us cognize something of it, namely a law.
>
> This law is to furnish the sensible world, as a *sensible nature* (in what concerns rational beings), with a form of the world of the

understanding, that is, of a *supersensible* nature, though without infringing upon the mechanism of the former... The supersensible nature of [rational] beings ... is their existence in accordance with laws that are independent of any empirical condition and thus belong to the *autonomy* of pure reason.[31]

Or how fanciful is it to read something like this picture into the views of Spinoza that we glimpsed in Variations One, §17? Spinoza, I said, takes us to be active (and thereby free) when we make sense of what happens; when 'from our nature anything follows in us or outside us which can be clearly and distinctly understood through that alone'.[32] Thus, for instance, when someone sees certain things as this 'colour' and certain other things as that 'colour', this supplies both him and other people with a way of understanding, *through an understanding of him*, why he pursues these things and eschews those. In Lloyd's words, rather than 'passively [undergoing] the power of an "external" determining cause ... [, he wrests] from it, as it were, the status of determining cause'.[33]

Or how fanciful is it to read something like this picture into the views of the early Wittgenstein? Wittgenstein, in his *Tractatus Logico-Philosophicus*,[34] makes play with the idea that acknowledging the various facts which constitute 'the world' leaves us free to take different attitudes to those facts (that is, to the world). It leaves us free to see things as variously 'coloured', as admitting of a greater range of possibilities than is implicit in the acknowledgement of the facts. To take such an attitude to the world is not to acknowledge any further facts. There *are* no further facts. ('The world,' Wittgenstein famously says at the beginning of his book, 'is all that is the case.'[35]) Nor is it to determine what the facts actually are. It is rather to exercise one's will in such a way that the world 'becomes an altogether different world. It must, so to speak, wax and wane as a whole.— The world of the happy man is a different one from that of the unhappy man.'[36] (The world must 'wax and wane as a whole'. This reinforces my suggestion that the 'expansion' metaphor and the 'fineness of grain' metaphor are not really in competition. Wittgenstein's image, which evokes the opening up and the closing off of possibilities, resonates with both.)

§4 Let us reflect further on how irrationality fits into the Radical Picture. Despite the myriad forms that irrationality can take, it always involves some loss of control. It always involves someone succumbing, at some level, to some non-rational force, or some combination of non-rational forces, such as fear or lethargy or recklessness or (for that matter) stubborn insensitive adherence to rules.

Kant illustrates well the contrast between being at the behest of such forces and being in control of what one does, in the following passage from *Critique of Practical Reason*.

> Suppose someone asserts of his lustful inclination that, when the desired object and the opportunity are present, it is quite irresistible to him; ask him whether, if a gallows were erected in front of the house where he finds this opportunity and he would be hanged on it immediately after gratifying his lust, he would not then control his inclination. One need not conjecture very long what he would reply. But ask him whether, if his prince demanded, on pain of the same immediate execution, that he give false testimony against an honourable man whom the prince would like to destroy under a plausible pretext, he would consider it possible to overcome his love of life, however great it may be. He would perhaps not venture to assert whether he would do it or not, but he must admit without hesitation that it would be possible for him. He judges, therefore, that he can do something because he is aware that he ought to do it and cognizes freedom within him, which, without the moral law, would have remained unknown to him.[37]

Here Kant distinguishes between a motivation such as lust, which prevails only when it is not in competition with anything stronger, and a motivation such as the desire to do one's duty, which can annul all other forces.[38] That capacity to annul all other forces, and to enable the subject to do what he does because he can see that it is what he must do, is the very hallmark of freedom. On the Radical Picture, unless the capacity is active, then the subject is not free.

Take someone who unjustifiably breaks a promise. This is irrational. He possesses the concept of a promise but fails to adhere to it – in a situation where adhering to it is, in the phrase I used in §1, a 'suitably salient possibility'. What he does is at the behest of various non-rational forces, ultimately, perhaps, the sheer fact that he wants something badly enough. No doubt this way of putting it, along with the crudely mechanistic metaphors that I have been using, does scant justice to the intricacies of the situation. Perhaps he thinks long and hard and carefully about whether to pursue what he wants, wrestling in particular with the fact that this will mean breaking a promise, and wrestling with this fact not just because of its potential damage to his reputation but also, at whatever unprincipled level, because of the value which, as someone who possesses the concept of a promise, he attaches to promise keeping. But this serves only to illustrate how subtle and complex the processes can be whereby non-rational forces come to hold sway over what a person does.

If someone in such a case does think hard about whether to break a promise, pitting the various disadvantages of doing so against the advantages, then his possession of the concept of a promise becomes just another of the forces in play. And this serves to illustrate something else: that not only can non-rational forces take all sorts of forms, they can involve the very stuff of rationality, namely concepts. This may sound paradoxical. But concepts can have as powerful a non-rational grip on us as anything can. Concepts are tools. We use them to deal with the world, above all to make sense of things. They provide us with a way of being masters and mistresses of what happens, not its slaves. But like any other tools, they carry their own dangers of more or less limited enslavement. Used properly, they give us a certain control. Abused, they have a certain control over us.

This is why the irrationality involved in a mistake of logic – say, the mistake of thinking that, if everything has an explanation, then there must be an explanation of everything – is fundamentally of a piece with the irrationality involved in doing something one wants even when one has an overriding reason not to. In both cases there is an ultimate failure to make sense, a failure which can be attributed to the strength of non-rational forces (the bewitchment of surface grammar, the lure of whatever is wanted). In both cases there is a loss of control. (And yes, I continue to be only too aware of the hideous connotations that this way of putting it has.)

Wittgenstein had a particularly lively sense of the ways in which confusion can make us captives of our own concepts. Indeed, he thought that this was how all the traditional problems of philosophy arose.[39] He also had a particularly lively sense of the importance of the phenomenon. Here is a pertinent quotation:

> The problems arising through a misinterpretation of our forms of language have the character of *depth*. They are deep disquietudes; their roots are as deep in us as the forms of our language and their significance is as great as the importance of our language.[40]

Hacker, commenting illuminatingly on this attitude of Wittgenstein's, writes:

> Work on philosophy is often more a work on oneself, on the way one sees things and what one demands of them... It leads one to abandon certain combinations of words as senseless, and that involves a kind of resignation, not of intellect but of feeling. For it can be as difficult not to use an expression as to hold back tears... – hence Wittgenstein's daunting remark that every philosophical error is the mark of a character failing.[41]

This is moving stuff!

Wittgenstein may, however, have had a much less lively sense of another of the ways in which we can become captives of our own concepts, namely through undue conservatism. If he did, then his sensitivity in the one case and his lack of sensitivity in the other were surely not unconnected. It is easy enough to see how a lively sense of the dangers of conceptual confusion can issue in a fear of conceptual innovation: new concepts bring with them new possibilities of confusion. Thus Wittgenstein was deeply suspicious of Cantor's work to which I referred in the previous section. He complained, 'One pretends to compare [one infinite set] in magnitude with [another]... I believe, and hope, that a future generation will laugh at this hocus pocus.'[42] In fact, however, Cantor's work is sufficiently rigorous to justify the kind of impatient retort that Wittgenstein himself might have given if the use of a more homespun concept had been at issue: 'One *pretends* no such thing. One does it.' There is something bordering on the paranoiac in some of Wittgenstein's hostility to new ways of thinking. We must be constantly open to new ways of thinking; not, of course, uncritically open to them, but open enough to avoid the converse error of being uncritically closed to them. Being uncritically closed to new ways of thinking is another way of being less in control of one's concepts than in their thrall. It is another way of being irrational.

§5 Let us take stock. In this chapter I have adopted the Radical Picture, whereby we do nothing freely except in so far as we do it rationally. That we do nothing freely except in so far as we do it rationally is what I have called the Radical Conception. What the Radical Picture adds to the Radical Conception is the idea that there is nevertheless such a thing as irrationality, and that irrationality, in at least some of its myriad forms, is the target of (justified) blame.

This alignment of freedom with rationality, I have suggested, gives freedom little more than a structural role; but a structural role that helps to capture the idea that there is a nisus in all of us towards rationality (towards making sense). The time has come to investigate this idea.

In fact I want to investigate something stronger, which, in recognition of its importance to this enquiry, I shall call the Basic Idea: namely, that *there is a nisus in all of us,* **more fundamental than any other**, *towards rationality*.[43] There are three questions concerning the Basic Idea that I want to consider. First, what does it mean? Second, what is its significance if it is true? And third, *is* it true (and, if it is, how might its truth be established)?

§6 *What does the Basic Idea mean?*: It means that there is nothing of greater value, from our point of view, than rationality. This requires a good deal of further elucidation of course. Some of this I hope will be provided in the ensuing discussion. (I shall also try to say more in Variations Three.) But two observations are in order straight away. First, something will obviously need to be said about who 'we' are. This is an issue that has already arisen in various forms and in various contexts. Any assessment of the Basic Idea must keep the issue clearly in focus. Second, the Basic Idea does *not* mean that we never value what is irrational over what is rational. But it does mean that, if ever we do do this, then there must be some special explanation.

This explanation can be of one of two broad kinds. The first possibility is one to which I have alluded at various points in previous chapters, namely that the irrationality fits into larger patterns of rationality. I mentioned this possibility in Theme Two, §1, in connection with self-conscious irrationality in our thinking. And in Variations One, §10, I suggested that irrationality can be put to service in subverting concepts that are abhorrent or otherwise unsatisfactory, for instance through the resolution to shock people as often as possible by violating some absurd taboo, or even through the resolution never to accept a tip. The second possibility is that we have been deflected from valuing what, from our own point of view, is most to be valued, by something which therefore counts, again from our point of view, as a corruption. This is where the Radical Picture has greatest heuristic impact. For this possibility obviously sits well with the idea that we never freely pursue what is irrational; that we pursue what is irrational only in so far as we are under the control of something. (The first possibility may seem to sit less well with this idea. But they can be reconciled. The key to their reconciliation is that we are able freely to sacrifice our own freedom.) Of course, since our point of view is indeed ours – whoever 'we' may be – these references to our point of view can be eliminated. What is most to be valued, from our point of view, is most to be valued; and what is a corruption, from our point of view, is a corruption. If the references to our point of view *are* eliminated in this way, as it were by taking up that point of view, then what already sounds Aristotelian in these ideas will sound all the more so.[44] And it can be made to sound yet more so by the addition of the following crucial concession: that, even to the extent that we do freely and uncorruptedly value what is most to be valued, we may well have been brought to this point by forces beyond our control, above all by the forces of education and upbringing.[45]

Very well; but is the Basic Idea, so construed, not just false? To be sure, no final assessment is possible while an answer to the question of who 'we' are is still pending. But surely, on any interesting interpretation of 'we', rationality is of value to us only up to a point; that is to say, rationality is of value only up to a point. There are many other things that are of value. And surely some of these can sometimes count for more than it does, in conflicts between them and it. The increasingly Manichean language that I have been using to talk about the 'non-rational forces' that lead us away from rationality prejudices this thought. But a more textured understanding of these forces, and especially of our emotions, can make it seem utterly compelling. To take just one notable example, what about *love*? Are there not certain sorts of 'loss of control', to use the loaded term that I have been using, which are to be both celebrated and cherished?

Nobody in his right mind will deny that there is much in our lives which, though it is non-rational, is of value; nor, for that matter, that this includes untold varieties of love.[46] But to say that something is of value is one thing. To say that sometimes we are to pursue it even though there is an alternative that enables us to make better sense of things is quite another. Let us not be seduced at this point by the siren call of romanticism. To make better sense of things is to make *better* sense of things. It is not to make more impassive, less responsive, less caring sense of things. (It is not to make loveless sense of things. People often have to resist impulses of love to show greater love for one another. Think in particular of parents and their children.) The cardinal point here is that making sense of things includes making sense of the non-rational forces in our lives. And making sense of these *can* involve nurturing them and rejoicing in them. It can involve developing concepts that come to embrace them, for instance, in the case of our emotional reactions, by transforming them into the exercise of those concepts. (See again the discussion of these matters in Variations One, §17. But note: making sense of the non-rational forces in our lives can equally involve shunning or combating them. If it does, and if the non-rational forces in question are themselves conceptual forces, then that is when we are most likely to find ourselves freely sacrificing our own freedom, making sense of things by allowing ourselves temporarily not to make sense.) There is much in our lives which, though it is non-rational, is to be both celebrated and cherished. But this is not to say that there is anything in our lives which, though it is *ir*rational – though it constitutes a culpable 'loss of control' – is to be both celebrated and cherished. Nor is it any threat to the Basic Idea.[47]

§7 *What is the significance of the Basic Idea if it is true?*: If the Basic Idea is true, then it finally enables us to address the 'So what?' questions that have been nagging since the beginning of the previous chapter.

I tried to argue in Variations One that it is a requirement of rationality that we adhere consistently to the concepts we possess. But, as I emphasized then, this still leaves us vulnerable to the question of whether we do well to possess those concepts. It also leaves us vulnerable to the question of whether we do well to be rational. The bulk of Variations One was concerned with how to address the first of these questions. The second question, which is the ultimate 'So what?' question, of which all the others are variants, is the one that has been waiting to be addressed ever since. And the Basic Idea constitutes a direct answer to it. (At least it does relative to an answer to the question of who 'we' are. The Basic Idea says nothing, directly, about anyone who is not one of 'us'. Nor does it have much, if anything, to offer to anyone who *is* one of 'us', but who wishes, at some profound level, to cease to be so. But perhaps there is nothing to offer to such a person. Perhaps ceasing to be one of 'us' is tantamount to ceasing to be.[48])

A further and related significance attaching to the Basic Idea, if it is true, is this. If there is this nisus in all of us towards rationality, then it will certainly be what I called in §3 of the Introduction an 'ethically productive conative state', that is to say a conative state that we all share and that grounds our ethical reasons for doing things. And this in turn will make the rationalism which it underpins a species of what I called in that same section 'conative objectivism', the thesis that there are such states. (As I have intimated more than once concerning the apparent gap between rationalism and conative objectivism, 'apparent' is the operative word.) What makes this particularly significant is that conative objectivism, as I urged at the end of that section, is not a hopeless thesis. That is to say, quite literally, there is room for the hope that it is true. We shall come back to this in the final section of the chapter, and again in Variations Three.[49]

§8 *Is the Basic Idea true (and, if it is, how might its truth be established)? – Part I*: I do take the Basic Idea to be true. But I am also acutely aware that there may be no way to establish its truth; that those who accept it may have to accept it as a kind of axiom.

Sometimes Kant gives the impression that he treats the supreme and unqualified value of the exercise of pure practical reason, in the form of a 'good will' – which is in effect a corollary of the Basic Idea – as axiomatic. The famous opening sentence of his *Groundwork of the Metaphysics of Morals* is: 'It is impossible to think of anything at all in the world, or indeed even beyond it, that could be considered good without limitation except a *good will.*'[50] And in *Critique of the Power of Judgment* he writes:

> If it thinks over the existence of things in the world and the existence of the world itself, even the most common understanding cannot reject the judgment that all the many creatures, no matter how great the artistry of their arrangement and how manifold the purposive interconnections by which they are related to each other may be, ... would exist for nothing if there were not among them human beings (rational beings in general), i.e., the judgment that without human beings the whole of creation would be a mere desert, existing in vain and without final end. But ... it is not well-being, not enjoyment (whether corporeal or spiritual), in a word it is not happiness by means of which we estimate that absolute value. For the fact that if the human being exists he makes this itself his final aim does not yield any concept of why he should exist at all... [It] is the value that he alone can give to himself, and which consists in what he does, in how and in accordance with which principles he acts,... in the *freedom* of his faculty of desire; i.e., a good will is that alone by means of which his existence can have an absolute value and in relation to which the existence of the world can have a *final end.*[51]

True, the reference to freedom here reminds us of the basic project that we spent most of the previous chapter watching Kant trying to execute: the project as it were to burrow beneath the value of rationality in order to locate, precisely in our freedom, the source of that value. The following eloquent passage from *Critique of Practical Reason* is relevant here.

> *Duty!* Sublime and mighty name that embraces nothing charming or insinuating but requires submission, and yet does not seek to move the will by threatening anything that would arouse natural aversion or terror in the mind but only holds forth a law that of itself finds entry into the mind and yet gains reluctant reverence (though not always obedience), a law before which all inclinations are dumb, even though they secretly work against it; what origin is there worthy of you, and where is to be found the root of your noble descent which proudly rejects all kinship with the inclinations, descent from which is the indispensable condition of that worth which human beings alone can give themselves?
>
> ...It is nothing other than ... *freedom* and independence from the mechanism of the whole of nature, regarded nevertheless as also a capacity of a being subject to special laws – namely pure practical laws given by his own reason...[52]

But as I have repeatedly said, in connection with my own similar if comparatively artless alignment of rationality with freedom, this only really replaces questions about the value of rationality with questions about the value of freedom. In §2 of the previous chapter I sketched a broadly Kantian response to questions of this latter kind, based on Kant's conviction that a rational being cannot act except 'under the idea of freedom'. But is this conviction much different from the conviction that a rational being cannot act except under the idea of rationality? And if not, is the broadly Kantian response much different from a reaffirmation of the Basic Idea? It is hard to escape the feeling that our spade is being turned.[53]

To say that our spade is being turned is not to say that this nisus in us towards rationality is some kind of surd, unconnected with any of our other conative states, as if like some predilection for a certain flavour of ice-cream. It is clearly not like that. Valuing rationality, like being rational (if indeed these are two separate things), is a matter of how a subject organizes whatever else he or she values, and what he or she thinks, and how he or she acts. Indeed, as I suggested in §1 of the previous chapter, specifically in connection with thinking, someone who did not value rationality, at least to the minimal extent of being inclined to respect its demands, would not count as *thinking* at all. I would say the same about being in various conative states, for instance having goals, aims, and projects. In fact I would say the same about acting (see again §1 of the previous chapter). But even if I am right to say these things, this does not vindicate the Basic Idea. The Basic Idea is not just that we value rationality, nor even that there is a nisus in us towards rationality. The Basic Idea is that there is a nisus in us, *more fundamental than any other*, towards rationality. And this extra element does have the character of a surd.

It is worth noting incidentally that even the weaker idea that we value rationality is vindicated only in a rather special sense. It is vindicated as part of a particular way we have of making sense of ourselves, rather than as a belief about how we are anyway. The idea that any given individual values rationality is of a piece with the idea that some of what that individual does counts as thinking or as acting. It is a matter of how he gets treated and interpreted. To half-quote Wittgenstein, I am not of the *opinion* that other people think and act: rather, my attitude towards them is an attitude towards those who think and act.[54]

It is instructive at this point to invoke the concept of a person. (I shall use the word 'person' in what has become a fairly standard philosophical sense, allowing for the possibility that there are persons who are not human beings – aliens, say, or even God – but disallowing the possibility that there are human beings who are not persons.[55]) I claim, in line with what I have just been saying, that to value rationality is part of what it is to be a person. Or rather, continuing to sound the Aristotelian note, to value rationality is part of what it is to be a normally functioning, fully developed person: the *capacity* to value rationality is part of what it is to be, simply, a person. These qualifications are intended to cater for babies and those with various mental impairments. However, I am well aware that, in making them, I may be involved in all sorts of question begging. For instance, is somebody to be deemed abnormal just *because* he or she fails, in some sense, to value rationality? And in what sense of 'capacity' does a person in a persistent vegetative state have the capacity to value rationality, while a tankful of gunk consisting mostly of water, together with the other raw materials needed to constitute a human being, does not? (The fact that the latter question sounds mildly offensive is itself of some relevance here.) Some of the potential question begging is serious, and makes much of what I am about to say a good deal less straightforward than it will appear. Unfortunately, it is beyond the scope of the current discussion to do more than register this fact.[56] Some of the potential question begging, on the other hand, does not concern me at all. On the contrary, it reinforces the main point that I now want to make, namely that possession and exercise of the concept of a person, and more specifically of the concept of a normally functioning, fully developed person, are possible only from a certain point of view defined, in part, by the valuing of rationality. (This bears out what I said in Variations One, §17, about the concept of a person being action-guiding.) In fact possession and exercise of these concepts are possible only from the point of view of a *person*. To recognize someone as a person, and to know what it would be for that person to function normally and to be fully developed, and in particular to know that this would involve the person's realizing his or her capacity to value rationality, one must oneself be a person who values rationality. Conversely, to be a person who values rationality is to make sense of others in those terms. It is to recognize other people *as* other people, and to know what it would be for them to function normally and to be fully developed. Valuing rationality and recognizing the capacity in others to value rationality are reciprocal parts of what it is to be a normally functioning, fully developed person.[57]

But valuing rationality is inseparable from valuing, as such, those whom one recognizes as having the capacity to value rationality. It is inseparable from valuing people. (Kant invoked a similar inseparability to argue that one formulation of the fundamental categorical imperative was never to treat people merely as means: see Theme One, §4.) Valuing other people is thus part of what it is to be a normally functioning, fully developed person. Such mutual valuation is in turn part of what constitutes the shared point of view of persons, from which alone persons can be recognized, that which actually binds them together in their personhood. This is one of the many reasons why Korsgaard is quite right to insist (as we saw her do in §2 of the Introduction, in reply to Mackie) that 'the world contains entities that can tell us what to do and make us do it ... [, namely] people'.[58] To be a normally functioning, fully developed person is to set a value that one shares with other people on the rationality that one shares with other people, and thereby to set a value on them too, responding naturally to what one recognizes them as valuing.[59]

But given that the valuing of rationality is part of the nisus in us which, according to the Basic Idea, is more fundamental than any other, it follows from these considerations that the Basic Idea itself now assumes another aspect. It now appears equivalent to the claim that *people* have a unique, and uniquely fundamental, place in our estimation. As before (see above, §6) it is important to emphasize that this does not mean that we never value anything else above people. But it does mean that, if ever we do do this, then there must be some special explanation, having to do either with some larger pattern of sense that we are making or (far more probably, the second of these being all too easily mistaken for the first) with our depravity. Nor does it mean that people are the only things of value in creation. (Not even Kant thought that.[60] Consider, for instance, non-human animals. Indeed it should be noted in this connection that the quotation from Korsgaard above continues: '...and the other animals'.[61]) But it does mean that the value of other things is secondary, and perhaps even (as Kant did think) derivative.

That the Basic Idea has assumed this new aspect does not, however, put us any nearer to being able to establish it. It reinforces the feeling that there is no deeper to dig. What is there to say when the special value of *people* is at issue?[62]

§9 *Is the Basic Idea true (and, if it is, how might its truth be established)? – Part II*: That Kant himself feels that he has reached explanatory bedrock here or hereabouts is borne out by a number of features of his own account of these matters. In *Critique of Practical Reason* he writes: 'The objective reality of the moral law cannot be proved by any deduction, by any efforts of theoretical reason, speculative or empirically supported.'[63] He does acknowledge, in *Groundwork of the Metaphysics of Morals*, that

> in order for a sensibly affected rational being to will that for which reason alone prescribes the 'ought,' it is ... required that his reason have the capacity to *induce a feeling of pleasure* or of delight in the fulfilment of duty, and thus there is required a causality of reason to determine sensibility in accord with its principles.[64]

But this acknowledgement does not take us any further down in the strata of explanation, for two reasons. First, there is no explaining how the feeling of pleasure is induced. 'It is quite impossible,' he continues, 'to see ... how a mere thought which itself contains nothing sensible produces a feeling of pleasure or displeasure... [It] is quite impossible to explain how and why ... morality interests us.'[65] And second, more importantly, this feeling of pleasure is in any case parasitic on the fact that we have reason to do as we ought, not vice versa. 'It is not *because the law interests* us that it has validity for us,' he writes in the very next sentence; '... instead, the law interests us because it is valid for us as human beings, since it arose from our will as intelligence and so from our proper self.'[66]

There are two special ideas that Kant makes use of in this connection. Each of them represents an exegetical quagmire, and I shall not now attempt to wade through either of these quagmires. But I do want to say just enough about each idea to indicate its relevance.

First, pursuing this concern with the 'phenomenology' of morality, Kant talks about our 'respect' for the moral law. He defines this as the 'immediate determination of our will by means of the law and our consciousness of this'.[67] Our respect for the moral law is a *feeling*. It is partly humiliating and partly elevating. It is targeted on the moral law (though also, derivatively, on people). It is occasioned by the moral law. And it has the capacity, evidenced in Kant's example of the person deciding that he could sacrifice his own life to avoid giving false testimony against another person (see above, §4), to induce action in accord with the moral law, by overcoming all other motives.[68]

All *other* motives? Does this mean that our respect for the moral law is itself a motive? And if so, does it follow that acting in accord with the moral law out of respect for the moral law is not truly praiseworthy, there being, in Kant's rationalism, only one morally praiseworthy motive for acting in accord with the moral law, namely, and simply, to act in accord with the moral law?

No, this does not follow. Kant avoids any awkward proliferation of motives here by taking respect for the moral law to *be* that morally laudable motive, as it appears to finite beings such as us who have various competing motives. He defines *incentive* as 'the subjective determining ground of the will of a being whose reason does not by its nature necessarily conform with the objective law',[69] then goes on to say that:

> respect for the law is not the incentive to morality; instead it is *morality itself subjectively considered as an incentive* inasmuch as pure practical reason, by rejecting all the claims of self-love in opposition with its own, supplies authority to the law, which now alone has influence.[70]

But he denies that we can give any deeper explanation of the capacity of the moral law to constitute such an incentive. We must just accept

> consciousness of this fundamental law ... [as] a fact of reason... [We] cannot reason it out from antecedent data of reason, for example, from consciousness of freedom (since this is not antecedently given to us)... [It] instead forces itself upon us of itself as a synthetic *a priori* proposition that is not based on any intuition, either pure or empirical... [It] is ... the sole fact of pure reason.[71]

And this is the second of the two ideas that I referred to above.

'The sole fact of pure reason,' Kant says. This is an idea that he appeals to many times, especially in *Critique of Practical Reason*. He formulates it in sufficiently diverse ways to make interpreting him more than usually difficult, but I hazard that he means something like this: the fact that we know how to put pure reason to practical use; or equivalently, the fact that we know how properly to exercise our freedom.[72] This knowledge is not knowledge that anything is the case. If it were, that would jeopardize Kant's insistence that we can have no discursive insight into how things are in themselves (see §3 of the previous chapter). It is knowledge how to do something. Or more fully, it is knowledge which can be characterized as knowledge how to do something.

But any use of the construction ' "know" + interrogative + infinitive' to characterize knowledge presupposes some good, that is some value, set of values, norm, or suchlike. (Consider, for instance, 'She knows when to stir in the cream', or, 'He knows whom to suck up to', or, 'I don't know whether to believe you.'[73]) The good presupposed here is the good implicit in the Basic Idea: the supreme value of rationality. (The knowledge could just as well have been characterized as knowledge of the difference between right and wrong.) And the point of view from which this presupposition is made – the point of view of anyone prepared to characterize the knowledge in this way – is also, if the Basic Idea is correct, the point of view of those to whom the knowledge is actually ascribed, 'us'.

Kant's own appeals to the fact that we have this knowledge are similarly value-laden, and from a point of similar immersion. And he makes them in such a way as to cast the fact as some kind of datum. The upshot of the discussion in this section, then, is that Kant's spade is turned at something very like the place at which I have suggested ours is; or, to revert to the musical metaphor in terms of which I have been casting the whole enquiry, that this particular theme of Kant's stops in something very like the way in which my variation on it stops.[74]

§10 *Is the Basic Idea true (and, if it is, how might its truth be established)? – Part III*: What I am suggesting, then, is that there is no way to establish the truth of the Basic Idea – even though I hold it to be true. But I can hardly be said to have established, in turn, this negative claim. I now want to lend further credence to it (the negative claim) by looking at what I take to be the five most promising ways to establish the truth of the Basic Idea and arguing that each of them fails.[75]

> *The first way*: This is to derive the Basic Idea from the Radical Conception. The derivation is very simple. The Radical Conception, in its alignment of freedom with rationality, entails that, whenever we have completely free rein, we do what is rational. But that is tantamount to the Basic Idea.

What is to be said about this simple derivation? One immediate objection is that, if it is correct, attention simply shifts to the Radical Conception. The issue now is whether *that* can be established. (Indeed I have been quite candid about the fact that I have adopted the Radical Conception because it helps to capture the idea, of which the Basic Idea is a variant, that there is a nisus in all of us towards rationality.) But the second step in the derivation can in any case be resisted. This is the step that equates our doing what is rational, whenever we have completely free rein, with the Basic Idea. And it will be resisted by anyone whose opposition to the Basic Idea is matched by opposition to the idea that there is any kind of nisus in us towards *freedom*. (Here once again we confront the issue of what is so good about being free. Perhaps freedom is some terrible burden that we will do whatever we can, however irrationally, to avoid. Perhaps we would rather be given directives, even from some completely untried source, than incur the awesome responsibility of determining what to do for ourselves.[76])

The second way: This has its origins in Kant. It is to argue that there is indeed a nisus in all of us towards freedom and rationality, a nisus more fundamental than any other, because free rational beings are what we quintessentially *are*. (That is, freedom and rationality are that part of our essence which distinguishes us from all else. If 'we' are understood to be human beings, then Kant would arguably have been prepared to make the stronger claim that freedom and rationality are the *whole* of our essence, or at any rate that they, together with our finitude, are the whole of our essence – thereby excluding, counter-intuitively, and in notable contrast to Aristotle, our animality.[77]) To forfeit either our freedom or our rationality is to fail to be true to ourselves. In Kant's own words, 'the law interests us because it is valid for us as human beings, since it arose from our will as intelligence *and so from our proper self.*'[78] He goes on, '*What belongs to mere appearance is necessarily subordinated by reason to the constitution of the thing in itself.*'[79]

As I indicated in §5 of the previous chapter, the idea that what we quintessentially are are free rational beings creates a major difficulty for Kant concerning free acts of irrationality. This is not a difficulty given the Radical Conception, however. On the Radical Conception there are no free acts of irrationality. The problem with this second way of establishing the Basic Idea is not that. It is rather something very like the problem with the first way. Either it is question-begging to say that what we quintessentially are are free rational beings or the issue arises of what is so good about respecting our quintessence, about being 'true to ourselves'. Is there a nisus in all of us towards *that*?[80]

The third way: This is to argue, again in roughly Kantian vein, that the Basic Idea is a necessary condition of something about us that we cannot coherently deny, perhaps because denying it would be a direct testament to its truth. A case in point might be simply that we make judgements. The argument in that case would be that we cannot so much as make judgements unless there is this fundamental nisus in us towards rationality.

Many instances of this style of argument – which bears an obvious affinity with what I called a 'transcendental' vindication of categorical imperatives in Theme One, §3 – have been propounded in moral philosophy.[81] Two in particular are worth mentioning in this connection. Williams presents an argument designed to show that a necessary condition of our being rational agents is that we want to be free.[82] And Korsgaard presents an argument designed to show that a necessary condition of our being rational agents, where 'we' in this case are explicitly understood to be human beings, is that we value our own humanity, and therefore that we value ourselves.[83] Given the link that I am recognizing between our rationality and our freedom, Williams' argument is clearly close to the kind of thing that we are currently envisaging. And given the link that I am recognizing between valuing rationality and valuing people (see above, §8), so too is Korsgaard's. A third argument that is perhaps even closer is the one I derived from Kant himself, in §2 of the previous chapter, and to which I referred again in §8 of this chapter: the argument, namely, that a necessary condition of our being rational agents is that we act 'under the idea of freedom', where this in turn (according to the argument) is equivalent to the claim that we have a special concern to act freely.

But, as I went on to point out after citing the Kantian argument in §8, there is no reason to suppose that anything of this kind will serve to vindicate the Basic Idea. It may vindicate the idea that we value rationality, where this idea is part of our way of making sense of one another and is itself something that we cannot coherently deny.[84] This would be a highly significant result. But the Basic Idea, as I have repeatedly emphasized, requires more. It requires that rationality is of greater value to us than anything else.

Before I leave this third way of establishing the Basic Idea, I want to highlight one of its most interesting features. It is a way of establishing not just the truth of the Basic Idea but its necessity. The necessity here is a very distinctive Kantian form of necessity. It is the necessity of that which is an inescapable condition of our being able to engage in this sort of critical reflection in the first place. All the ways of establishing the Basic Idea that we are considering in this section are ways of establishing that it enjoys *some* form of necessity. But this form of necessity is somewhat starker than in the other cases. Now my reason for wanting to highlight this feature is its bearing on a debate in moral philosophy to which I have gestured a couple of times (in §3 of the Introduction and again in Variations One, §§5 and 6), namely the debate about whether, whenever anyone has a normative reason for doing anything, that reason must be grounded in the person's conative states. Just as the Basic Idea has the capacity to dissolve the distinction between rationalism and conative objectivism (see above, §7), so too, and relatedly, it has the capacity, if it enjoys some form of necessity, to dissolve certain applications of this debate. In particular, it has the capacity to dissolve applications of this debate to reasons that we have for doing what accords with this nisus in us. For, concerning any such reason, it is vacuous to argue about whether we would have had that reason had it not been for the nisus. On the one hand, we can say that we have the reason *because of* the nisus. And this makes it sound for all the world as if we are taking one side in the debate. On the other hand, we can say that we would have had the reason no matter what our conative states had been (the point being that, no matter what our conative states had been, there would have been this nisus in us: it is there as a matter of necessity). And this makes it sound for all the world as if we are taking the other side in the debate.[85] The fact of the matter is that the debate, in this particular application, comes to nothing.

And lest the full significance of this be missed, note two things. First, the sort of reason in question here, granted the Basic Idea, is the most fundamental sort of reason that we ever have for doing anything: it includes all our ethical reasons. And, second, the dissolution of the debate is not parasitic on the success of any of these ways of establishing the truth of the Basic Idea. The Basic Idea may enjoy some form of necessity even if (as I am trying to show) all these ways of establishing its truth fail.[86]

> *The fourth way*: This is unique among the ways of establishing the Basic Idea that I am considering in that it has a substantial empirical element. It involves an appeal to natural selection. Roughly, the idea is that we would not have survived had it not been for this fundamental nisus in us towards rationality.

It seems to me that the Basic Idea is simply too strong to be established in this way. Ironically, there is support for this verdict in something that Kant himself says towards the beginning of *Groundwork of the Metaphysics of Morals*. I say 'ironically' because Kant is there arguing that reason is poorly suited to help us survive, which suggests that the Basic Idea is in a sense too *weak* to be established in this way. Here is the crucial passage:

> In the natural constitution of an organized being, that is, one constituted purposively for life, we assume as a principle that there will be found in it no instrument for some end other than what is also most appropriate to that end and best adapted to it. Now in a being that has reason and a will, if the proper end of nature were its *preservation*, ... then nature would have hit upon a very bad arrangement in selecting the reason of the creature to carry out this purpose. For all the actions that the creature has to perform for this purpose ... would be marked out for it more accurately by instinct, and that end would have thereby been attained much more surely than it ever can by reason.[87]

In fact Kant is both underestimating what reason can do to help us survive and overestimating what reason needs to do to help us survive. But that is not the point. The point is this. Even if reason does help us survive, and more pertinently, even if the Basic Idea plays a role in explaining how we survive, this is not enough to establish the truth of the Basic Idea. The truth of the Basic Idea can be established in this way only if it is possible to rule out an explanation of how we survive in which the Basic Idea does *not* play a role. And this is why the Basic Idea seems to me to be too strong. It is also why the quotation from Kant is pertinent. The quotation reveals how something much weaker than the Basic Idea – say, that there is a nisus in us towards rationality that we subordinate to various pleasure drives in various more or less systematic ways – may play just as effective an explanatory role here. Bluntly, we do not need to set such store by rationality simply in order to pass on our genes.

But now a worry arises. If the Basic Idea is too strong to be established by such considerations as these, then is it perhaps so strong that it can be refuted by them? Perhaps we would not have survived if we *had* set such store by rationality, and in particular if we had set more store by rationality than by self-preservation. Indeed, surely if there is any plausible candidate for 'the most fundamental nisus in us', then it is the nisus towards simply keeping going.

Well, tempting though this thought is, it is noteworthy how rarely one can say of someone that he would not be ready to sacrifice his life for *anything* that manifests his rationality; that he would never, for instance, be prepared to lay down his life for his friends.[88] (Nagel writes, 'Anyone incapable of caring enough about something outside himself to sacrifice his life for it is seriously limited.'[89]) To be sure, this is not decisive. If the Basic Idea can be reconciled with the fact that we sometimes value what is irrational over what is rational (either because we can see some relevant larger pattern of rationality or because we have been suitably corrupted – see above, §6), then so too the idea that there is this fundamental nisus in us towards self-preservation can be reconciled with the fact that we sometimes value something outside ourselves over our own lives. For the fact that we sometimes do this may just show how powerful social conditioning can be. It *may* just show how powerful social conditioning can be even if the Basic Idea is true – not only because social conditioning is so integral to developing our nisus towards rationality, but also, contrastingly, because social conditioning is so integral to disguising our suppression of that nisus. It is so integral to the variety of devices we use to fake rationality. Think of the countless familiar ways in which less extreme acts of self-sacrifice can result from people's obsequiousness, their craving for approval, their desire to humiliate others: socially constructed forces channelled, with socially constructed artfulness, into the production of what appears straightforwardly commendable. The fact is that neither the Basic Idea nor any rival idea about our most fundamental nisus is ever going to be established by simple appeal to what people do or do not do, what they would or would not do. That further supports the main thesis that I wish to defend in this section, that there is no establishing the truth of the Basic Idea. (There is of course another worry: that it supports this thesis only by supporting the suspicion that the Basic Idea is without real content. I shall attempt to allay this suspicion in §11 below, and again in Variations Three.)

I have been casting this part of the discussion in Darwinian terms. But there is no reason to suppose that any other teleological outlook can be used to establish the truth of the Basic Idea either, not least because there is no reason, nowadays, to suppose that any other teleological outlook can itself be established. Among the other teleological outlooks that I have in mind are appeals to transcendent design, broadly Aristotelian stories, and indeed whatever Kant himself has in mind in the quotation above, and shortly afterwards when he enquires into the 'true function' of reason.[90] My use of the phrase 'whatever Kant himself has in mind' is not meant to suggest any evasiveness on his part. The second half of his *Critique of the Power of Judgment* is devoted to a sustained and forceful account of precisely what he has in mind.[91] It would be beyond the scope of this discussion, however, to try to expound Kant's understanding of these matters. Suffice to say that not even Kant is talking about something that he thinks can be *established*.[92] His understanding of these matters is conducive to my scepticism about whether any firm non-Darwinian framework is available within which to settle the truth or falsity of the Basic Idea.

We saw Williams expressing scepticism about non-Darwinian teleological outlooks in §3 of the Introduction. I quoted a passage from Williams in which he says that the 'best expression [of such an outlook], in many ways, is still to be found in Aristotle's philosophy', but then goes on to say that 'the first and hardest lesson of Darwinism [is] that there is no such teleology at all, and that there is no orchestral score provided from anywhere according to which human beings have a special part to play'.[93] In between Williams characterizes Aristotle's teleology as the view that 'there is inherent in each natural kind of thing an appropriate way for things of that kind to behave'. 'On that view,' he continues, 'it must be the deepest desire – need? – purpose? – satisfaction? – of human beings to live in a way that is in this objective sense appropriate to them,' immediately adding in parenthesis: 'the fact that modern words break up into these alternatives expresses the modern break-up of Aristotle's view'.[94] If Williams' scepticism in this regard is justified, as I am inclined to think it is, then among the many things that follow is that the rather singular word that I have been using to express both the Basic Idea and various related ideas – this word 'nisus' – had better not be intended to put those Aristotelian pieces back together again.[95]

Before I finish with the fourth way of establishing the Basic Idea I want to mention a variant on it that fails in pretty much the same way. 'Variant on it' is the critical phrase. What I have in mind is akin to the use of a teleological outlook, but is nevertheless different from it and withstands Williams' scepticism. It is the use, rather, of a method that Nietzsche calls *genealogy*.[96] (That this is different from the use of a teleological outlook is evidenced not least by Williams' own enthusiasm for genealogy.[97]) Genealogy is a way of explaining some aspect of our lives by telling a story about how it might have come about, and perhaps also, in part, about how it did come about. Nietzsche himself tells such a story to explicate our very system of morality.[98] Hume tells such a story to explain our sense of justice.[99] Craig tells such a story to explain our concept of knowledge.[100] And Williams tells such a story to explain the value that we place on truth and truthfulness.[101] The thought occurs that we may be able to tell such a story to explain this fundamental nisus in us towards rationality. And so we may. But as a way of establishing *that there is* such a nisus in us, any such story must fail. The point of a genealogical story is typically to give us a better understanding of some aspect of our lives whose existence we already acknowledge. If such a story is to serve as a way of establishing the existence of the aspect of our lives it concerns, then it must include an element of inevitability. That is, it must block any rival story whereby we live lives free of the aspect in question. There is no reason in general to suppose that a genealogical story will do this. And there is reason in particular to suppose that a genealogical story about our fundamental nisus towards rationality will *not* do it. This reason, as before, is the fact that the most in our lives that can be expected to enjoy such inevitability is our having a nisus towards rationality, not our having a nisus towards rationality which is more fundamental than any other.

Before I turn to the fifth and final way of establishing the Basic Idea I must remind you of something that may in any case by now be all too obvious: I *still* have not said who 'we' are. The discussion in §8 may have suggested that I take 'us' to be people. But I have never committed myself to this. And indeed there would be a serious problem with doing so. This problem was adumbrated by some of the complexities of that very discussion. It is this. If 'we' are people, and if the Basic Idea is true, then the fundamental nisus towards rationality must be present in babies and people who are severely mentally handicapped. And this reinforces the suspicion that the Basic Idea is without real content; or worse, that it is an instrument of prejudice used to dismiss those who fail to conform in one way or another as somehow either not fully developed or abnormal. (Recall Aristotle's exclusion of 'natural slaves' and women from those who, at least fully and properly, shared the natural human '*telos*': see §3 of the Introduction.) On the other hand, to restrict 'us' to only certain people would be severely to compromise the supposed impact of the Basic Idea, and would still allow it to serve as an instrument of prejudice ('*You're* not one of *us*'). The fifth way of establishing the Basic Idea, if successful, serves a double function. It establishes the Basic Idea, but it also, at last, provides an answer to the question of who 'we' are.

> *The fifth way*: This is simply to make the Basic Idea true by definition – defining 'us' as whoever have the relevant kind of nisus.

If the fourth way of establishing the Basic Idea was unique in the extent of its empirical content, then the fifth way certainly lies at the other end of the spectrum. It makes the Basic Idea utterly vacuous. That, however, is not why I wish to reject it. I see no objection to the project of making an idea like this true by suitable definition of one of its key terms; exploring its consequences; allowing it thereby to provide a framework, or part of a framework, for discussion; and leaving open the question of how and where it might eventually be applied.[102]

The problem with pursuing such a project in the present context is twofold. First, various things are antecedently expected of the Basic Idea. In particular, it is meant to play a role in buttressing rationalism. This means that pursuing such a project in this context would merely be another onus-shifting device, such as made me reject the first and second ways of establishing the Basic Idea. The onus this time would shift from the question of whether the Basic Idea was true to the question of whether suitable ethical significance attached to whoever 'we' were.

Second, if the Basic Idea were made true by definition, then it would be impossible to know how much latitude should be allowed in ascribing this fundamental nisus towards rationality to those in whom it was at best latent. Thus suppose we already know that babies are included among 'us'. Then we also know that, if the Basic Idea is true, it allows for some of 'us' to be still at a level of unrealized potential, albeit potential that can be realized through normal processes of education and upbringing. Without any such anchorage, however, there would be nothing to stop the compass of the Basic Idea from contracting to include no-one at all; or indeed from expanding to include the tankful of gunk that I mentioned in §8. I conclude that the fifth way of establishing the Basic Idea must be rejected along with all the others.

§11 Who *are* 'we' then? I shall resort to the answer which my discussion in §8 may have suggested, and which may indeed have been suggested all along. We are people.[103] Not that it is always entirely clear what counts as a person. To pick just one problematic case of particular ethical significance, there is familiar controversy about fetuses. (Also, as I said in §8, I do not rule out the possibility of non-human people.) But the answer 'We are people' is clear enough for current purposes, and it provides enough anchorage to prevent the concept of unrealized potential from floating away into absurdity in the way envisaged at the end of the previous section.

But what about the problem with this answer mentioned above, namely that, because of babies and those who are severely mentally handicapped, it (this answer) reinforces the suspicion that the Basic Idea is either without content or an instrument of prejudice?

As far as the first of these threats – the threat of lack of content – is concerned, I shall say a little now and reserve fuller discussion for Variations Three. Notice first that the Basic Idea is certainly not without content in the sense in which it would have been without content if it *had* simply been made true by definition. The most that can be said to be without content in that sense – and here I echo a point that I made in the previous section in connection with the fourth way of establishing the Basic Idea – is that there is a nisus in us towards rationality, not that there is a nisus in us towards rationality which is more fundamental than any other. Still, there had better be more to dispel the first threat than that.

I think there is. I see the Basic Idea as something like what Kant might have called a regulative ideal. The term is not one that he ever actually uses. But the *notion* is of great importance for him. I have in mind a species of what he does label 'regulative principle'. By a regulative principle he means a rule directing us to act in accord with a given supposition.[104] A *regulative ideal* is a regulative principle whose associated supposition is that some 'idea', that is some *a priori* concept freed of whatever conditions allow it to be applied empirically (see §5 of the previous chapter), nevertheless can be applied empirically.[105] We encountered this notion in Theme One, §6, where I cited as a central example the rule to act in accord with the supposition that the concept of the infinite whole has empirical application to the physical universe: if we abide by this rule, then we shall never give up in the quest for a deeper and more extensive knowledge of nature.

The Basic Idea, although it is unlike a regulative ideal in being true or false, is like a regulative ideal in the following respects. Its truth or falsity can never be settled empirically. In particular, its truth or falsity can never be settled by appeal to what we do or do not do. (This is one of the chief grounds for the suspicion that the Basic Idea is without real content of course.) But to accept it as true is to accept, among other things, that we should never give up in our efforts to account for cases in which it appears false, cases in which either there is unrealized potential (babies) or we positively elevate the irrational over the rational. And in cases of the latter kind, that is to say cases in which we positively elevate the irrational over the rational, what this means is that we should never stop looking for the larger patterns of rationality into which this irrationality fits or the forces of corruption that have brought us to this point. This makes the Basic Idea into a heuristic device, and gives it very real practical content.

The disappearance of that threat, however, merely exacerbates the other. For the very fact that the Basic Idea has content with a significant practical dimension means that there is a question whether we do well to accept it (as we do seem to do well to accept that we should strive for an ever deeper and ever more extensive knowledge of nature). We do not do well to accept the Basic Idea if we are thereby using it as an instrument of prejudice against those who fail to conform in one way or another. Even if this does not involve 'dismissing' such people, which is how the threat was expressed in the previous section, nevertheless it can hardly fail to involve dismissing some of their legitimate interests.

Well, yes, there is a question about whether we do well to accept the Basic Idea or not; about whether we can accept it and avoid the charge of inappropriately using it as an instrument of prejudice or not. But this is no different, ultimately, from the question whether it is true or not. (This is where the difference between the Basic Idea and a regulative ideal is crucial.) If it is true, then nothing is more valuable (from our point of view) than rationality. So we are right to look for explanations for why we sometimes value what is irrational over what is rational. And, in cases where the explanation is not to be found in some higher rationality, we are right to regard whatever has brought us to this point as a corruption. To be sure, 'corruption' is a value-laden term. It would not be appropriate to use such a term in this context if we were not speaking from the point of view of those for whom rationality is supremely valuable. But if the Basic Idea is true, then we *are* speaking from that point of view, and we are quite right to talk of corruption here. Similarly, but conversely, if the Basic Idea is false, then accepting it as true, with all that this commits us to, may just reduce both us and our efforts at understanding our own irrationality to a sad mockery.

So we are back where we were three or four sections ago, wondering whether the Basic Idea is true and entertaining the suspicion that there may be no way of telling. But an additional suspicion that we must now entertain is this: the only satisfactory way of discussing some of the implications of the Basic Idea is in terms that make no real sense unless it is true, from a point of view that is not ours unless it is true. If this is right, and if we accept the Basic Idea, then we cannot avoid question begging when it comes to pitting it against rival views about what we are like. (This was the sort of predicament I took myself to be in when I claimed in §8 that valuing rationality is part of being a fully developed, normally functioning person; and the sort of predicament I took Kant to be in in §9 when I discussed his appeals to 'the fact of pure reason'.) If that is our predicament, we must just acknowledge it and be unashamed about it. We must also, of course, hope that we are not thereby betraying a delusion; that the Basic Idea is indeed true.

But we must hope this anyway if we accept the Basic Idea without any way of establishing its truth. Hope, I think, is the crucial and proper attitude for us to take to the Basic Idea. I said in §3 of the Introduction, and repeated in §7 above, that there is room for the hope that conative objectivism is true. That hope has now been transposed into the hope that the Basic Idea is true. I still believe there is room for it. I no more think that the Basic Idea can be refuted than I think that it can be established – obviously not, since I take it to be true. But I shall leave the matter there for now. This is a good cue for the two remaining chapters.

Third theme: religion

> A religion which executes its obsolete sovereign must now establish the power of its new sovereign; it closes the churches and this leads to an endeavour to build a temple... An era blindly embarks on an attempt to discover a new illumination, a new happiness, and the face of the real God. But what will this new God be?...
>
> Seventeen eighty-nine does not yet affirm the divinity of man, but the divinity of the people, to the degree in which the will of the people coincides with the will ... of reason. If the general will is freely expressed, it can only be the universal expression of reason. If the people are free, they are infallible... [The people] are the oracle that must be consulted to know what the external order of the world demands... External principles govern our conduct: Truth, Justice, finally, Reason. There we have the new God.
>
> (Albert Camus, *The Rebel*, Chapter 3, pp. 91–92)

§1 Kant's attitude towards religion was one of profound ambivalence. On the one hand, he never relinquished the fundamental moral outlook that had been instilled in him by his pietistic upbringing.[1] Nor did he ever stop cherishing certain characteristic images, narratives, and concepts of mainstream Christianity. He was especially concerned to protect what he saw as its three most important and most efficacious ideas: *freedom*, *immortality*, and *God*.[2] For reasons that we shall see, he took the second and third of these to be no less instrumental than the first in helping us to make ultimate sense of our own moral convictions.

On the other hand, he was deeply suspicious of the emotive and superstitious elements in religion. He abhorred many of its ecclesiastical trappings (creeds and observances alike). He had no patience for anything that was in tension with standard scientific methodology, such as mysticism and the belief in miracles. He was firmly opposed to all attempts to prove God's existence, dealing what many people still regard as the crucial death blow to each of the principal traditional attempts to do so.[3] He was unable to come to terms with the basic soteriological concepts of Christianity such as grace and atonement. He was unable to accede to many of Christianity's sacred texts except under the most radical and contrived of interpretations. And above all he was unable to grant religion anything other than an entirely subordinate role to morality. 'On its own behalf,' he wrote, 'morality in no way needs religion ... but is rather self-sufficient by virtue of pure practical reason.'[4] It was not that he thought religion an irrelevance to morality. On the contrary, he held that 'morality ... inevitably leads to religion' because of 'our natural need ... to think for all our doings and nondoings taken as a whole some sort of ultimate end which reason can justify'.[5] But he was adamant that 'this idea rises out of morality and is not its foundation; ... it is an end which to make one's own already presupposes ethical principles.'[6]

The last of these points is the key to understanding Kant's entire religious philosophy. Everything else in the sketch I have just given was driven by it. Consider, for instance, the violence with which he interpreted so many religious texts. Kant himself commented:

> [Such an] interpretation may often appear to us as forced, ... and be often forced in fact; yet, if the text can at all bear it, it must be preferred to a literal interpretation that either contains absolutely nothing for morality, or even works counter to its incentives.[7]

Again, expressing his discomfort with the idea of grace, he wrote:

> Even to accept it as idea for a purely practical intent is very risky and hard to reconcile with reason; for what is to be accredited to us as morally good conduct must take place not through foreign influence but through the use of our own powers.[8]

And it was because he was so committed to the purity and autonomy of morality, whose practice he took to be nothing other than an exercise of reason, that he recoiled, first, from any kind of emotionalism, specifically religious emotionalism, and, second, from any sense that doing one's duty means obeying the will of another, even a divine other. We saw in Theme One, §2, something of Kant's hostility to the idea that morality is contingent on the will of God, a hostility that was all the fiercer when the idea took the form that our chief or only motive for acting morally must be to avoid divine retribution. The only acceptable motive for acting morally, on Kant's rationalistic conception, was to act morally. He even went as far as to proclaim it a matter of great fortune that we cannot prove God's existence. If we could,

> God and eternity with their awful majesty would stand unceasingly before our eyes... Transgressions of the law would, no doubt, be

avoided: what is commanded would be done; but ... [mostly] from fear, only [occasionally] from hope, and [never] at all from duty... [Human] conduct would thus be changed into mere mechanism in which, as in a puppet show, everything would *gesticulate* well but there would be *no life* in the figures. Now, when it is quite otherwise with us;... when the governor of the world allows us only to conjecture his existence and his grandeur, not to behold them or prove them clearly; when, on the other hand, the moral law within us, without promising or threatening anything with certainty, demands of us disinterested respect;... then there can be a truly moral disposition, devoted immediately to the moral law, and a rational creature can become worthy of the highest good in conformity with the moral worth of his person and not merely with his actions. Thus what the study of nature and of the human being teaches us sufficiently elsewhere may well be true here also: that the inscrutable wisdom by which we exist is not less worthy of veneration in what it has denied us than in what it has granted us.[9]

But Kant's subordination of religion to morality accounted just as much for the favour with which he looked upon the former. If we were purely rational, Kant thought, we would have no need of religion. But we are not purely rational. We are fundamentally at variance with the demands of rationality, which is to say: we are fundamentally evil. (Here we glimpse once again the legacy of Kant's pietistic upbringing. See further §3 below.) What religion is is a psychological-cum-sociological prop which helps us to come to terms with this grim fact about ourselves, first, by sharpening our sense of our own infirmity, as a kind of wickedness, but, second, by sustaining our hope that all is not lost.

Most of the rest of this chapter will be devoted to exploring the second of these. In the next section I shall comment briefly on the first.

§2 Kant's view is that we are to think of moral obligations as divine commands. In fact, he defines religion as 'the recognition of all our duties as divine commands'.[10] Thus Jesus 'sums up all duties ... into one universal rule ... namely, Do your duty from no other incentive except the unmediated appreciation of duty itself, *i.e.* love God (the Legislator of all duties) above all else,' together with 'a particular rule [concerning] the human being's external relation to other human beings as universal duty, Love everyone as yourself.'[11]

To think of moral obligations as divine commands is not to relinquish the autonomy of morality. For 'we will not hold actions to be obligatory because they are God's commands, but will rather regard them as divine commands because we are internally obligated to them'.[12] There *is* a sense in which what is obligatory is obligatory because God wills it; but not because God in particular wills it; only because God is supremely rational and wills what all rational beings will. In so far as we too are rational, we both can and do legislate for ourselves. To regard our self-legislation in a divine light is nothing but a device,[13] a device which, as we shall see, relates back to the hope that religion affords,[14] but which also represents the laws which we impose on ourselves as 'governing and absolutely commanding, hence as pertaining to a ruler'.[15]

The fact that Kant treats the concept of God as (part of) a device in this way does not mean that his more forthright pronouncements about the existence and character of God are disingenuous, nor even that they are meant in anything other than a strict and literal sense. He does believe that morality leads to religion; and he does believe in God, in his own fashion (see further §5 below). Michalson has argued that, whereas Kant is traditionally regarded as laying the foundations for a mediating theology – mediating, that is, between the demands of Christian orthodoxy and the demands of enlightened modernism – in fact he is more appropriately regarded as laying the foundations for nineteenth-century atheism.[16] But even this seems to me something of an exaggeration. What *is* true is that the theology and the religion that he champions are very much Enlightenment theology and Enlightenment religion: that is, theology and religion within the bounds of reason, tempered by reason, and at the behest of reason.

The irony, as I have already indicated, is that the only thing that he thinks gives either theology or (especially) religion any kind of role to play in our lives is our *un*reason. Let us now turn to that.

§3 The second of the three difficulties that I identified for Kant's theory of freedom in Theme Two, §5 was to account for irrationality. And I cited a passage from *Religion Within the Boundaries of Mere Reason* in which Kant simply admits that irrationality (evil) is beyond our comprehension. That is, it is beyond our comprehension how we ever come to exercise our freedom, our noumenal quintessential freedom, by violating the very laws by which, in exercise of that same freedom, we bind ourselves.[17]

Let us give Kant the benefit of any doubt here and agree that the incomprehensibility in question falls short of incoherence. Yet Kant goes further. He insists that our irrationality is not sporadic and superficial. It is pervasive and deep. He writes:

> It will readily occur to anyone to ask ... whether [the human being is (by nature) either morally good or morally evil]; and whether some might not claim that the human being is by nature neither of the two, others, that he is both at once, that is, good in some parts and evil in others. Experience even seems to confirm this middle position between the two extremes.
>
> It is of the greatest consequence to ethics in general, however, to

> preclude, so far as possible, anything morally intermediate...; for with any such ambiguity all maxims run the risk of losing their determination and stability...
>
> On [this strict way of thinking], the answer to the question just posed is based on the morally important observation that freedom of the power of choice [*Willkür*] ... cannot be determined to action through any incentive except *so far as the human being has incorporated it into his maxim* (has made it into a universal rule for himself, according to which he wills to conduct himself)... Now, if the [moral] law fails ... to determine somebody's free power of choice [*Willkür*] with respect to an action relating to it, an incentive opposed to it must have influence on the power of choice [*Willkür*] of the human being in question; and since, by hypothesis, this can only happen because the human being incorporates the incentive (and consequently also the deviation from the moral law) into his maxim (in which case he is an evil human being), it follows that his disposition as regards the moral law is never indifferent (never neither good nor bad).
>
> Nor can a human being be morally good in some parts, and at the same time evil in others. For if he is good in one part, he has incorporated the moral law into his maxim. And were he, therefore, to be evil in some other part, since the moral law of compliance with duty in general is a single one and universal, the maxim relating to it would be universal yet particular at the same time: which is contradictory.[18]

It is not that our rationality is eclipsed altogether, still less that we are in diabolic pursuit of evil for its own sake.[19] Kant later writes,

> The human being (even the worst) does not repudiate the moral law, whatever his maxims, in rebellious attitude (by revoking obedience to it). The law rather imposes itself on him irresistibly, because of his moral predisposition; and if no other incentive were at work against it, he would also incorporate it into his supreme maxim as sufficient determination of his power of choice [*Willkür*], i.e. he would be morally good.[20]

He encapsulates this thought elsewhere in the following wonderful nugget: 'Herein lies [man's] dignity: He can forgive himself nothing.'[21] This vision of human evil as the product of weakness rather than the product of rebellion distances Kant from the Augustinian doctrine of original sin. In fact there is much in that doctrine to give Kant pause. Its chief absurdity, he thinks, is the idea that evil is part of our inherited nature.[22] He writes:

> Whatever the nature ... of the origin of moral evil in the human being,

of all the ways of representing its spread and propagation through the members of our species and in all generations, the most inappropriate is surely to imagine it as having come to us by way of *inheritance* from our parents; for then we could say of moral evil exactly what the poet says of the good: ['Race and ancestors, and those things which we did not make ourselves, I scarcely consider as our own.']²³

Furthermore, what is 'original' in a human being's nature, if this means what is essential to it, is not, on Kant's conception, evil, but, on the contrary, 'the predisposition to good'.²⁴ That any given human being is evil is entirely contingent – indeed, as we shall see, remediable. (Thus one thing in the Genesis account of human evil that Kant welcomes is that 'the human being ... is represented as having lapsed into [evil] only *through temptation*, hence not as corrupted *fundamentally* (in his very first predisposition to the good).'²⁵) The fact remains that in Kant's view this contingency is invariably realized, that is to say we are all evil, and, in so far as this means that we allow non-moral incentives to have ultimate control over our actions, our evil is radical and unmitigated.

Kant may seem guilty here of undue polarization. As he himself says in the long passage quoted earlier, 'experience ... seems to confirm [the] middle position between the two extremes'. Are we not an ugly mishmash of the good and the bad, just as prone to self-denying acts of principle as we are to baseness and atrocity?

But Kant's stark view of these matters is neither unmotivated nor out of keeping with the rest of his philosophy. There are two broadly Kantian arguments for his bleak conclusion, one of which he all but gives, the other of which he looks as if he could give. The argument that he all but gives is as follows. Given that our duty consists in acting solely from duty (this is the rigorist loop that is so characteristic of Kant's moral philosophy), we cannot have a partial commitment to doing our duty. If we have anything less than a total commitment to doing our duty, then doing our duty is not what matters most to us; which means that, if ever we do do our duty, then we cannot be doing it *just because* it constitutes our duty (we are doing it in part because there is no other course of action made more appealing by whatever else matters more to us);²⁶ which means that we must be acting only *in conformity with* duty, not *from* duty.

Why do I say that Kant 'all but' gives this argument?

Because he never quite accedes to the full weight of the conclusion, which the logic of the argument demands, namely that no-one *ever* acts from duty – which is to say, no-one ever does what he or she ought to do.²⁷ The most Kant ever commits himself to is that no-one ever unquestionably acts from duty.²⁸ (This is in contrast with the fact that each of us, often, unquestionably fails to do so.)

Here is what Kant actually says:

> Whether the human being is good or evil ... [does] not lie in the difference between the incentives that he incorporates into his maxim [, whether the moral law or the incentives of his sensuous nature,] ... but in their *subordination*...: *which of the two he makes the condition of the other*... He indeed incorporates the moral law into [his] maxims, together with the law of self-love; ... [but] he makes the incentives of self-love and their inclinations the condition of compliance with the moral law – whereas it is this latter that, as *the supreme condition* of the satisfaction of the former, should have been incorporated into the universal maxim of the power of choice [*Willkür*] as the sole incentive.[29]

And to emphasize the point that this does not preclude our acting in conformity with duty, he continues:

> In this reversal of incentives through a human being's maxim contrary to the moral order, actions can still turn out to be *in conformity to* the moral law as if they had originated from true principles... (For example, when adopted as principle, truthfulness spares us the anxiety of maintaining consistency in our lies and not being entangled in their serpentine coils.)[30]

The second argument, the one Kant looks as if he could give, is grounded in the metaphysics of his theory of freedom. It runs as follows. Since our freedom is noumenal, and since we all unquestionably show *some* deviation from complete rationality, it is not clear what else this can mean but that we are all, in ourselves, simply irrational, and therefore simply bad. For whatever variegation there may be in how we appear, it is not clear what can correspond to this in how we really are, where there is no *here* or *there*, no *now* or *then*.

This is not an argument that Kant ever does give however. Why not? Well, in this version certainly, it is too quick. 'No *here* or *there*, no *now* or *then*' does not preclude *all* articulation. The fact that we have no idea what feature of how we are in ourselves can correspond to the various episodes of more or less apparent blameworthiness in our phenomenal lives, and thus what feature of how we are in ourselves can extricate us from the dichotomy of being fundamentally good or being fundamentally bad, does not mean that no such feature can.

But more importantly, there are in any case reasons for Kant to be resistant to this argument. It establishes too much. For Kant, it is crucial that the moral law should have a motivating impact on any particular person at any particular time. Suppose, however, that this second argument holds. Then the very idea that the moral law can have this kind of impact is under threat. Consider an individual whose past conduct contains manifest lapses into immorality. Then all we can say about this person, granted this second argument, is that he has, in himself, for whatever reason, simply abnegated his own rationality: there is nothing he can any longer do about that. How then can the moral law continue to *direct* him? How can it continue to impact on him with the force of an injunction about what he ought to do, here and now, rather than with that of a contrite reflection about the kind of person that he ought to have been, but now, irremediably, is not?[31] That it does continue to direct him is, for Kant, not only the merest common sense, but also fundamental to his utterly unconditioned conception of these things. The full force of the moral law has to be capable of being felt by any person at any time, irrespective of how things are, have been, or will be elsewhere, and irrespective, in particular, of what that person has done in the past. As Kant himself puts it:

> however evil a human being has been right up to the moment of an impending free action (evil even habitually, as second nature), his duty to better himself was not just in the past: it is still his duty *now*.[32]

What Kant's susceptibility to the first of these arguments and his lack of susceptibility to the second reveal is something crucial about the structure of his conception of human evil. Whereas he thinks that there is no middle ground between our being fundamentally good and our being fundamentally bad, and that what we are is fundamentally bad, he does not think that this is irreversible. Thus it is not that we are, in some tenseless sense, fundamentally bad (as we are, in some tenseless sense, a kind of mammal).[33] Rather we are *now* fundamentally bad. It follows that, whatever the noumenal reality underlying this phenomenal fact, it does not take the form of one single indissoluble act of irrationality on the part of each one of us, manifest the moment the person does anything wrong.

Not that Kant thinks that any of us can suddenly start leading a blameless life. We are too mired in evil for that. Reconsider the case of Herod, which I mentioned in Theme One, §6. Having made a rash promise to give Salome whatever she asks for, Herod is arguably bound to do wrong, at least on Kant's conception, when she asks for the head of John the Baptist.[34] And Herod's case may be but one particularly graphic illustration of a kind of inextricability from evil that afflicts even the most zealous penitent, a possibility that we have to take particularly seriously when we remember the variety of complex social structures which, like the institution of promising, bind individuals to their own histories.[35]

Kant does, however, think that each of us can, at any time, undergo a 'change of heart'[36] and initiate a process of reformation whereby he or she becomes fundamentally good. How so? Well, the word 'becomes' is crucial here. The process that Kant thinks each of us can initiate is precisely that: a *process*.[37]

It helps to think of the relationship between being fundamentally bad and being fundamentally good, on Kant's conception, on the model of the relationship between being finitely big and being infinitely big. There is no middle ground between the two. (The phrase 'almost infinite' makes no sense.) Furthermore, if all increments within time are finite, then nothing that starts off as finitely big can ever cease to be so. Nevertheless, something that starts off as finitely big can, through a never-ending process of growth, increase its size indefinitely, which means that it can, *over* time if not *in* time, manifest a kind of infinitude in its size, the kind that Aristotle would have called potential.[38] True, goodness and badness are not quantitative. The analogy has its limitations. But it does give us a sense of how, on Kant's conception, a reformed sinner who still perpetually does wrong can nevertheless, over time, in a never-ending struggle to break free from the chains of his or her own sinfulness, manifest a new-found total commitment to doing right. Kant himself talks in precisely these terms:

> The distance between the goodness which we ought to effect in ourselves and the evil from which we start is ... infinite, and ... is not exhaustible in any time... [But, although,] according to our mode of estimation,... the deed, as a continuous advance *in infinitum* from a defective good to something better, always remains defective, so that we are bound to consider the good as it appears to us, i.e. according to the *deed*, as *at each instant* inadequate to a holy law [, nevertheless,] ... because of the *disposition* from which it derives..., we can think of the infinite progression of the good towards conformity to the law as ... a perfected whole even with respect to the deed (the life conduct).[39]

Is the process that Kant describes here a kind of redemption? Well, it is certainly not redemption of an orthodox Christian kind. Nor is it anything like it. This is for two reasons. First, it is something that the individual has to achieve alone. Whatever a sinner needs to be liberated from, and whatever constitutes the liberation, if the net effect is that his or her life comes to enjoy approval of the most basic kind, then, on Kant's view, nobody else and nothing else can be responsible for that. For approval of the most basic kind cannot ultimately attach to anything in anyone's life except a rational exercise of the will, something which is, and has to be, completely autonomous and self-sufficient. Redemption of an orthodox Christian kind, by contrast, is impossible without divine assistance.

The second reason why the Kantian process of reformation is unlike redemption of an orthodox Christian kind is that the former does not in any way atone for the preceding wrong-doing, still less annul it. For Kant, it is absurd to suppose that what is done can in any way be undone, or even that it can become *as if* undone. On the orthodox Christian conception, by contrast, it *can* become as if undone. That is, the sinner can become as if sinless. There is justification through the death of Christ. Such is God's grace.[40]

This is why I said earlier that Kant is unable to come to terms with the Christian idea of grace. Once these two fundamental differences between his own conception and the orthodox Christian conception have been run together, what we see in the latter – the idea that, with assistance from elsewhere, we can become as if sinless – is an utter anathema to Kant. ('How can God forgive man,' we almost hear Kant ask, 'if man cannot forgive himself?' – a rhetorical question to which, of course, in a non-Kantian framework, there may be all manner of non-Kantian answers.)[41] Kant writes:

> Whatever his state in the acquisition of a good disposition, and, indeed, however steadfastly a human being may have persevered in such a disposition in a life conduct conformable to it, *he nevertheless started from evil*, and this is a debt which is impossible for him to wipe out. He cannot regard the fact that, after his change of heart, he has not incurred new debts as equivalent to his having paid off the old ones... Moreover, so far as we can judge by our reason's standards of right, this original debt ... cannot be erased by somebody else. For it is not a *transmissible* liability which can be made over to somebody else..., but the *most personal* of all liabilities, namely a debt of sins which only the culprit, not the innocent, can bear, however magnanimous the innocent might be in wanting to take the debt upon himself for the other.[42]

Kant does concede, in some characteristic manoeuvring in *Religion Within the Boundaries of Mere Reason* – manoeuvring about which I shall say a little more in §6 – that there is a morally significant faculty available to us 'only through supernatural help', which he calls 'grace'.[43] But he never relinquishes his basic conviction that nothing ultimately counts in our favour save what results from our own virtuous endeavour. In the final sentence of the book he writes, 'The right way to advance is not from grace to virtue but rather from virtue to grace.'[44]

Kant's insistence on our own effort does not, however, prevent him from having a keen sense of how much our reformation depends on contingencies beyond our control.[45] It is not that our reformation is itself out of our own hands. Rather, the *possibility* of our reformation is out of our own hands. To take a particularly crude but pertinent example, I cannot now initiate a process of reformation if I am about to have my life taken from me. So if we are to have any hope, we must assume that all the relevant contingencies obtain. It is on this basis, as I shall now try to show, that Kant erects the positive part of his philosophy of religion.

§4 Kant, despite his uncompromising rationalism, is well aware that we frail humans need non-rational props to sustain us in any commitment to the demands of reason. In particular, we need assurances of various kinds: assurances that our making sense can itself continue to make a certain kind of sense. Thus, to pursue the example just considered, whether I am about to have my life taken from me makes no difference to whether I ought, now, to respect the demands of reason. Certainly I ought.[46] But whether I *believe* that I am about to have my life taken from me does make a difference to whether I can keep that 'ought' properly in focus; whether, in the terms of the previous section, I can see it as suitably motivating and not just as a pointed reminder of all that I have failed to do and all that I have failed to be. To see the 'ought' as suitably motivating, I must think that there is still some point in respecting the demands of reason. To think that there is still some point in respecting the demands of reason, I must think that respecting them can be part of a new-found total commitment to doing what is right. To think this, I must think that the conditions of the possibility of making such a commitment, the conditions of the possibility of reforming, are satisfied. And to think that the conditions of the possibility of reforming are satisfied, I must think, not merely that I am not about to have my life taken from me, but, granted what was said in the previous section, that I enjoy *some* sort of immortality. Such, broadly speaking, is Kant's primary vindication of the second of the triumvirate of ideas in mainstream Christianity – *freedom*, *immortality*, and *God* – that he is so keen to preserve.[47] (In the next section we shall see a supplementary vindication that he gives of this idea.)

Kant calls these three ideas, or more strictly the three propositions stating that they are instantiated, 'postulates of pure practical reason'. By a 'postulate of pure practical reason' he means a '*theoretical* proposition, though one not demonstrable as such, insofar as it is attached inseparably to an *a priori* unconditionally valid *practical* law'.[48] It is a proposition that we can neither prove nor disprove but that we must assume, in a distinctive sense of 'must' that I shall consider in more depth in §7, if we are to put pure reason to practical use. Just as we cannot act except on the belief that we are free, so too, Kant thinks, there is a sense in which we cannot act except on the belief that we are immortal, and (for reasons that I shall outline in the next section) except on the belief that there is a God.

The vindication that he gives of each of these three postulates is therefore not – repeat, not – a direct argument that the postulate in question holds. It is an indirect argument that we must, in the relevant sense of 'must', *believe* that the postulate in question holds (supplemented by an assurance that this is not an incoherent thing for us to believe). It is a 'practical' vindication. Thus the vindication that he gives of the second of the postulates, sketched above, is not an argument that we are immortal, but rather an argument about what it would cost us not to *believe* that we are immortal. If it were an argument that we are immortal, it would be question-begging. Why, for instance, should the conditions for the possibility of anyone's reformation be satisfied? Perhaps all prospect of reformation is lost.

But we hope not. 'Hope' is the critical word here. The concept of hope lies at the very heart of Kant's system. In *Critique of Pure Reason* he writes:

> All interest of my reason (the speculative as well as the practical) is united in the following three questions.
>
> 1 *What can I know?*
> 2 *What should I do?*
> 3 *What may I hope?*[49]

The postulates of pure practical reason, as well as being things we must believe, are at the same time things we hope.[50] And the reason we must believe them *is* that we hope them: if we did not believe these things, our hope would turn to despair and we would not be able to keep the moral law in focus through the cloud of that despair.

Now in Theme Two we saw the vindication that Kant gives of the first of the three postulates, the postulate that we are free. And I have just sketched the primary vindication he gives of the second postulate, the postulate that we are immortal. Let us turn now to the vindication he gives of the third postulate, the postulate that God exists.

§5 Although Kant holds that the only unqualified good is a good will (see Theme One, §4, and Variations Two, §8), he does not hold that the only good is a good will. He is quite prepared to acknowledge other goods, such as 'power, riches, honour, and health'.[51] These are things that we certainly value, and they are good in a perfectly straightforward sense of 'good'. It is just that they are not good without qualification. This is because they are not always in accord with the demands of reason. (Indeed, when they befall unworthy people, they can become objects of – legitimate – abhorrence.) Kant tends to use the word 'happiness' as a catch-all term to cover all these other goods; or rather, to cover the states of satisfaction to which they conduce.[52]

This leads to his conception of 'the highest good'. By 'the highest good' he means an ideal state of affairs in which the unqualified good of virtue and the qualified good of happiness come together in a harmonious unity.

But there is an important ambiguity here. On the stronger interpretation, each of the two elements needs to be at its highest level: 'harmonious unity' signifies a kind of joint reciprocal maximization. On the weaker interpretation, all that is required is that people be happy *to the extent that* they are virtuous. Kant sometimes defines 'the highest good' in the stronger way, sometimes in the weaker way, and sometimes in a way that is indeterminate between the two.[53] The ambiguity is not completely harmless. But nor is it an insuperable obstacle to our following Kant's argument, which, as we shall see, makes the vacillation understandable.

Now although virtue consists in the autonomous exercise of pure reason, and is to be sharply distinguished from the heteronomous pursuit of happiness,[54] nevertheless, because we cannot but desire our own happiness, nor can we put pure reason to practical use except in a way that reckons with happiness as a desideratum in whatever we do.[55] This is why, for instance, I must not act on a maxim that allows me to disregard the happiness of other people whenever it is convenient for me to do so: I could not will that everyone act on such a maxim because I could not will that my own happiness be similarly disregarded.[56] (This may go some way towards explaining what Kant has in mind when he talks about what I am capable of willing without my will 'contradicting itself': see Theme One, §6.) It follows that, if everyone always acted virtuously, the highest good, even in the stronger sense, would be realized. Here is an important quotation from *Critique of Pure Reason*:

> In the moral world [i.e. the world as it would be if it were in conformity with all moral laws] ... a system of happiness proportionately combined with morality can ... be thought of as necessary, since freedom, partly moved and partly restricted by moral laws, would itself be the cause of the general happiness, and rational beings, under the guidance of such principles, would themselves be the authors of their own enduring welfare and at the same time that of others.[57]

But everyone does not always act virtuously. The highest good, in that strong sense, is no longer attainable. Each of us remains under an obligation to act virtuously, doing whatever will make him or her *worthy* of happiness. But what the actual implications for happiness are, granted our imperfect past, is no longer clear. Perhaps, by holding to some agreement that it was crazy for me ever to have entered into, I am about to heap untold unredeemed misery upon both myself and others. Here is Kant again:

> This system of self-rewarding morality is only an idea, the realization of which rests on the condition that *everyone* do what he should... But since the obligation from the moral law remains valid for each

particular use of freedom even if others do not conduct themselves in accord with this law, how their consequences will be related to happiness is determined neither by the nature of the things in the world, nor by the causality of actions themselves and their relation to morality.[58]

The fact remains, Kant thinks, that we cannot, in the sense of 'cannot' that is relevant to these practical vindications, persevere in acting virtuously unless we cherish some hope that the highest good, in at least its weaker sense, is still attainable. We must believe that *some* alignment of happiness with virtue remains possible. Otherwise virtue itself will no longer make any real sense to us. In *Critique of the Power of Judgment* Kant considers a righteous man with no such belief and no such hope. He asks, 'How would he judge his own inner purposive determination by the moral law, which he actively honours?' And he replies:

> He does not demand any advantage for himself from his conformity to this law, whether in this or another world; rather, he would merely unselfishly establish the good to which that holy law directs all his powers. But his effort is limited... Deceit, violence, and envy will always surround him, even though he is himself honest, peaceable, and benevolent; and the righteous ones besides himself that he will still encounter will, in spite of all their worthiness to be happy, nevertheless be subject by nature, which pays no attention to that, to all the evils of poverty, illnesses, and untimely death, just like all the other animals on earth, and will always remain thus until one wide grave engulfs them all together (whether honest or dishonest, it makes no difference here) and flings them, who were capable of having believed themselves to be the final end of creation, back into the abyss of the purposeless chaos of matter from which they were drawn. – The end, therefore, which this well-intentioned person had and should have had before his eyes in his conformity to the moral law, he would certainly have to give up as impossible... [Only if he believed in some connection between virtue and happiness could he] remain attached to the appeal of his moral inner vocation and not weaken the respect, by which the moral law immediately influences him to obedience, by the nullity of the only idealistic final end that is adequate to its high demand.[59]

We hope and must believe, then, that making ourselves worthy of happiness will bring us happiness; that the world is, in Engstrom's phrase, 'a home for virtue'.[60] We hope that the world makes a certain kind of sense.

This may seem one way of overcoming what Nietzsche calls *ressentiment* (see Variations One, §17). In fact, however, there would be some justice to the complaint that it is merely a way of succumbing to *ressentiment*, a way of not properly facing up to the fact that the world does *not* make sense and that *we* therefore have to make sense *of it*. Kant enjoins us to be worthy of happiness. Deleuze, in a much more Nietzschean vein, enjoins us to be worthy of what happens to us – whatever that may be (see again Variations One, §17). In the next chapter I shall consider whether this Nietzschean alternative may not itself, even so, need to be underpinned by a Kantian hope.

Be that as it may, the question arises what grounds there are for the Kantian hope. Do we have any reason to suppose that the attainability of the highest good, in the weaker sense, survives its attainability in the stronger sense? Kant himself insists not. The hope must be precisely that: a hope. For since there is no conceptual connection aligning happiness with virtue – contra Epicureans, virtue does not consist in the procurement of happiness, and contra Stoics, happiness does not consist in the exercise of virtue[61] – any alignment of happiness with virtue must have something to do with the actual workings of the world. But we have no reason to suppose that the world does in fact work like that. If anything, we have reason to suppose that it does not. For happiness cannot be what motivates virtuous action on pain of abnegating its virtue. Yet nor can happiness be an effect of virtuous action, if 'effect' is understood in anything like its familiar physical sense: physical causes and effects are impervious to the motives with which people act.[62] The only possibility, then, if there *is* an alignment of happiness with virtue of the kind hoped for, is that this alignment is secured at the level of how things are in themselves, beyond anything that we can (empirically) know.[63]

This in turn requires two things. It requires a life beyond this one, in which the alignment can be worked out.[64] (There is therefore independent vindication here – as adumbrated in the previous section – for the second postulate, that we are immortal. Indeed, given that immortality not only allows the alignment to be worked out, but also allows us to embark on an endless process of reformation whereby we become fundamentally good, there is also renewed prospect here for the hope that the highest good can still be realized even in something close to its stronger sense.[65]) The second thing it requires is a being capable of effecting the alignment. That is, it requires 'a *single, most perfect*, and *rational* primordial being', a 'supreme will' which

> must be omnipotent, so that all of nature and its relation to morality in the world are subject to it; omniscient, so that it cognizes the inmost dispositions and their moral worth; omnipresent, so that it is immediately ready for every need that is demanded by the highest good for the world; eternal, so that this agreement of nature and freedom is not lacking at any time, etc.[66]

In a word, the second thing it requires is God.

§6 Such is Kant's vindication of the third postulate of pure practical reason then. In the next section we shall look more closely at the status of the three postulates and at what is involved in such 'practical' vindications. First, I want to say a little more about the second postulate, the postulate that we are immortal.

If Kant is right, then we must think that we have *some* sort of immortality. But this need not be understood in literally temporal terms. It would suit Kant's purposes just as well if what we had, or thought we had, was a dimension of existence beyond the world of space and time (as it were, some other way of appearing to ourselves) in which there could be something *like* an endless process of reformation. How like that? Well, like that in as much as, considered as a whole if not in any of its parts, it was capable of reflecting whatever fundamental commitment on our part to doing our duty was already partly reflected in our reformed efforts, here and now, to break free from the chains of our own past wrong-doing. For what matters on Kant's conception, as he makes clear, is not the precise way in which any such commitment is reflected. It is the commitment itself, as it (atemporally) is in itself.[67]

Very well; but how does Kant himself conceive of our immortality? Perhaps not in any one fixed way. Often he refers to our immortality as if it consisted straightforwardly in an endless afterlife. Sometimes this looks as if it is to be taken at face value. In particular, this is true of what he says in his first major work *Critique of Pure Reason*, where he is primarily interested in our immortality as the arena in which God aligns happiness with virtue.[68] But sometimes when he refers to our immortality as if it consisted in an endless afterlife, this is quite clearly meant as just a convenient and familiar image to convey something of which he himself has, and thinks he cannot in principle help having, a very indeterminate conception.[69] Thus in a much later work, the essay 'The End of All Things', he deals sympathetically with the idea that, when someone dies, he or she goes 'out of time into eternity',[70] and he emphasizes the absurdity of a literal interpretation of the temporal language we naturally use to describe this. He writes:

> This expression would in fact say nothing if *eternity* is understood here to mean a time proceeding to infinity; for then the person would indeed never get outside time but would always progress only from one time into another. Thus what must be meant is an *end of all time* along with the person's uninterrupted duration; but this duration ... as a magnitude ... wholly incompatible with time, of which we are obviously able to form no concept (except a merely negative one).[71]

And later:

> We ... say that we think of a duration as *infinite* (as an eternity) not because we have any determinate concept of its magnitude – for that is impossible, since time is wholly lacking as a measure – but rather because that concept – since where there is no time, *no end* can come about – is merely a negative one of eternal duration.[72]

Elsewhere all that seems to count for Kant is what the belief in immortality does for us; and since what it does for us it does most effectively when we frame it in broadly temporal terms, he seems content to play along with that.[73]

In so far as our commitment to doing our duty does initiate a process of on-going reformation (which, at least in this world, Kant thinks it does quite literally), then it connects with one of the most radical of Kant's interpretations of Christian orthodoxy. As we saw in §3, Kant is adamant that a person's wrong-doing can never be annulled. Someone, he thinks, must suffer for it. Yet once the process of reformation has begun, the person himself no longer deserves to suffer. Indeed, it is as if there are two people. '*Physically*,' Kant writes, 'he is still the same human being liable to punishment... Yet in his new disposition, ... he is *morally* another being.'[74] So in the alignment of happiness with virtue, the reformed sinner suffers as it were vicariously, taking on the burden of those earlier sins. And

> the suffering which the new human being must endure while dying to the old human being throughout his life is depicted in the representative of the human kind [i.e. the Son of God] as a death suffered once and for all.[75]

It is also in this connection that Kant feels able to make his one serious concession to the doctrine of grace. For although the 'new human being' does not deserve to suffer, he never reaches the point of fully deserving what pertains to his reformed disposition either (see above, §3). God's grace consists in the fact that

> what in our earthly life (and perhaps even in all future times and in all worlds) is always only in mere *becoming* (namely, our being a human being well-pleasing to God) is imputed to us as if we already possessed it here in full.[76]

§7 In this final section I want to consider what status the three postulates of pure practical reason have.

I emphasized in §4 that Kant's practical vindications are not intended to establish the truth of these postulates. Indeed, he himself is especially and effectively militant against the idea that their truth can be established – most famously, perhaps, in the case of the third postulate. In his *Critique of Pure Reason* he considers classic arguments for God's existence, and formulates what have since become classic arguments against them. The classic arguments for God's existence which he considers, and which are in his view the only possible arguments for God's existence, are: the 'ontological' argument, which purports to establish *a priori* that failure to exist would be a violation of God's very essence; the 'cosmological' argument, which purports to establish that God is needed to account for the existence of that which might just as easily not have existed; and the 'physico-theological' argument (what would nowadays be called 'the argument from design'[77]), which purports to establish that God is needed to account for the existence of our world as it actually is, 'such an immeasurable showplace of manifoldness, order, purposiveness, and beauty'.[78] Kant argues that the third of these is nothing without the second, that the second is nothing without the first, and that the first rests on a basic logical confusion about existence.[79] So although Kant's God may seem – to echo Pascal – more the God of the philosophers and the learned than the God of Abraham, Isaac, and Jacob,[80] nevertheless He is not the subject of some quasi-mathematical theorem or of some quasi-scientific hypothesis. For Kant, belief in God is a requirement not of theoretical reason but of practical reason. It is needed to play a hope-sustaining, sense-conferring, mist-dispelling role in each of our lives.

This brings us to the sense of 'must' in which I must hold this belief, or rather, more strictly, in which I must hold this belief in order to be suitably motivated to do my duty. It is a 'practical' sense. Indeed, we might almost call it a 'pragmatic' sense.[81] For it pertains to morality; but it also registers a connection between my various faculties that holds precisely because of my *im*morality, and, more generally, because of my imperfection. Anything more demanding, for instance anything that registered some connection of principle – like the conceptual 'must' in 'I must be a brother in order to be an uncle' – would undermine Kant's rationalism. In *that* sense of 'must', all I must do, in order to be suitably motivated to do my duty, is be rational. And, if I were purely rational, this would suffice. But I am not purely rational. Here is Kant:

> [Duty] is based on something that is ... quite independent of [the postulates of pure practical reason] and of itself apodictically certain, namely the moral law; and so far it needs no further support by theoretical opinions as to the inner character of things, the secret aim of the order of the world, or a ruler presiding over it, in order to bind us most perfectly to actions unconditionally conformed to the law. But the subjective effect of this law ... nevertheless presupposes at least

that the latter is *possible*; in the contrary case it would be *practically impossible* to strive for the object of a concept that would be, at bottom, empty and without an object.[82]

There are two corollaries worth noting here. First, the sense of 'must' in which I must believe in God is not (itself) the sense of 'must' in which I must do my duty. It had better not be. For I cannot be duty-bound to believe anything: belief is not subject to the will. As Kant says, 'this ... necessity is ... a need, and not ... itself a duty; for, there can be no duty to assume the existence of anything (since this concerns only the theoretical use of reason)'.[83] The fact that Kant is prepared, even so, to call the necessity a 'moral' necessity is due partly just to its connection with morality, but partly also to the fact that, since I cannot suitably engage with morality unless I believe in God, there *are* some duties hereabouts: for instance, I am duty-bound to cherish my belief and to foster it.[84]

The second corollary is that there is something about the necessity that is at once subjective, because it is rooted in my own imperfect constitution, and objective, because it is rooted there willy-nilly – and also because the constitution is one I share with everyone else.[85] Again, because of the belief's relation to morality, Kant expresses this by describing the belief as a 'moral certainty'. He writes:

> The conviction [that there is a God] is not *logical* but *moral* certainty, and, since it depends on subjective grounds (of moral disposition) I must not even say '*It is* morally certain that there is a God,' ... but rather '*I am* morally certain' etc. That is, the belief in a God ... is so interwoven with my moral disposition that I am in as little danger of ever surrendering the former as I am worried that the latter can ever be torn away from me.[86]

All of these comments apply equally to the sense of 'must' in which I must believe that I am immortal. But they do *not* apply equally to the sense of 'must' in which I must believe that I am free. The first postulate stands apart from the other two in this respect.[87] The sense of 'must' in which I must believe that I am free has nothing to do with my imperfections. This is a belief I would have to hold even if I were purely rational. For there can be no agency at all except under the idea of freedom. (This is connected with the 'fact of pure reason' which we considered in §9 of the previous chapter. I have a kind of practical knowledge concerning my own freedom of which there is no analogue concerning either my immortality or the existence of God.[88] It is not that I know myself to be free. It is rather that I know *how* to be free. That is, I know what it would be properly to exercise my freedom. And I cannot act except on the belief that this knowledge is operative.)

However, there is no difference between the first postulate and the other two as far as Kant's method of protecting them is concerned. Just as he insists that the idea of freedom, if it applies anywhere, applies beyond the bounds of our experience and knowledge (see Theme Two, §3), so too he insists that the ideas of immortality and God, if they apply anywhere, apply beyond the bounds of our experience and knowledge, thereby ensuring that the very thing that deprives the three postulates of the security of proof is also what safeguards them from the threat of disproof.[89] 'I had to deny *knowledge*,' Kant famously declares in the Preface to the second edition of *Critique of Pure Reason*, 'in order to make room for *faith*.'[90]

'Faith' is a word that has not occurred before in this chapter. Kant defines it as follows:

> *Faith* ... is reason's moral way of thinking in the affirmation of that which is inaccessible for theoretical cognition... Faith ... is trust in the attainability of an aim the promotion of which is a duty but the possibility of the realization of which it is not possible for us to have insight into... It is a free affirmation, not one for which dogmatic proofs for the theoretically determining power of judgment are to be found, nor one to which we hold ourselves to be obligated, but one which we assume for the sake of an aim in accordance with the laws of freedom.[91]

That nicely summarizes the relation in which Kant thinks we stand to all three postulates.

It is instructive at this point to compare the use to which we thereby put the three ideas of freedom, immortality, and God with the use to which we put ideas when we adopt regulative ideals (see §11 of the previous chapter). There is a fundamental difference. To have faith in one of the three postulates is to act as if some non-empirical idea has an application which we cannot know it has, but hope it does. To adopt a regulative ideal is to act as if some non-empirical idea has an application which we not only cannot know it has, but know it cannot have. (The application which we hope the former has is beyond the bounds of our experience and knowledge: the application which we know the latter cannot have is within the bounds of our experience and knowledge.) But this difference also signals an equally fundamental similarity, which Kant himself notes. In each case we act as if some non-empirical idea has an application – even though we cannot know it does.[92]

In the former case, to repeat, we *hope* it does. And we must believe it does. This raises one of the most basic questions concerning the three postulates. In so far as we have no alternative but to believe them, can we take an ironic step back and concede that, even so, they may be false?

Yes and no. Yes; we can recognize that our having no alternative but to believe them does not entail their truth.[93] No; we cannot convert that recognition into genuine agnosticism. If we really do have no alternative but to believe them, then we have no alternative but to *believe* them.[94] This helps to explain, I think, why Kant himself, though he often takes the ironic step back, always ends up giving the impression that he has not done so.[95] Indeed, it is worth recalling how much Kant is prepared to concede to our unavoidable belief in the first postulate: 'Every being that cannot act otherwise than under the idea of freedom is just because of that *really free in a practical respect.*'[96]

But is there perhaps more to it than that? Does Kant perhaps think that our having no alternative but to believe the three postulates *does* entail their truth? In general, there is a gap between our being so constituted that we cannot help believing something and its being true. But much of Kant's philosophy involves bridging this gap. In particular, he bridges it for those of our beliefs that concern, not how things are in themselves, but how they appear to us through the 'lens' of our own cognitive equipment (see Theme Two, §3). If we are so constituted that we *must* believe something in such a case, for instance that everything that happens is completely physically determined, then this can only be because of what the lens is like, in which case, since our belief is a belief about how things appear through the lens, what we believe is true. So does Kant perhaps think that the gap can likewise be bridged in the case of the three postulates, so that their practical vindications become arguments for their truth after all?[97]

No. The *only* thing that allows the gap to be bridged in the case of beliefs concerning how things appear to us through the lens is that they concern how things appear to us through the lens – the very thing that is not true of the three beliefs in question. It is vital for Kant, as I emphasized a little earlier, that these three beliefs are not beliefs about anything we can experience and know. The possibility remains and must remain, as Kant would be the first to admit, that they are false.

Appendix

There are certain diachronic aspects of Kant's thinking from which I have on the whole prescinded in this chapter. As a result I may have given the impression that his views have more unity than they do.[98] In this appendix I want very briefly to indicate the extraordinary direction in which his ideas were beginning to take him in work that he was in the throes of producing at the end of his life. This will serve a double function. On the one hand, it will show that Kant's views were not settled, that he never stopped wrestling with these issues. On the other hand, it will hint at some of the things that may have been latent in his thinking all along.

In notes left behind after his death Kant was coming round to the following picture.[99] God and the world are set over against each other, in a relation of mutual implication which is nevertheless not symmetric. The world is subordinate to God. God, as it were, possesses the world. It is as if God is the subject and the world the predicate in some grand cosmic proposition. But, as with any proposition, this requires unity.[100] And that unity has its source in man. Man is the copula in this proposition. Through his animality he is located in the world. Through his personhood God is located in him. Man unites God and the world. And he properly exercises his freedom when, by doing his duty, he at the same time expresses that unity. But this means that God is inseparable from man. 'It cannot be denied that [God] exists; yet it cannot be asserted that [God] exists outside rationally thinking man.'[101] God is as dependent on man as man is on God. Indeed, there is a sense in which man creates God.[102] For man constitutes himself, *as* a person, as a being with pure practical reason, and 'the concept of God is the idea of ... pure practical reason itself in its personhood'.[103]

At one point Kant encapsulates these thoughts in a pithy reference to 'the act of consciousness whereby the subject becomes the originator of itself and, thereby, of the whole object of technical-practical and moral-practical reason in one system – ordering all things in God'.[104] At the beginning of this chapter I took issue with Michalson for representing Kant as laying the foundations for nineteenth-century atheism. However, even if I am right about that, there can be no doubt that the position of God, in at least this late development of Kant's thinking, and perhaps incipiently in the earlier phases too, is highly precarious. (Later on the page from which the quotation above is taken, he writes, '*Religion is conscientiousness* ... To have religion, the concept of God is not required (still less the postulate: "There is a God").'[105]) God has an important part to play in Kant's philosophy. But Kant never quite avoids giving the impression that he begrudges this. And he certainly never accords to God the primordiality that he accords to reason.

Further reading

An outstanding study of Kant's philosophy of religion, written from a broadly sympathetic point of view, is Wood (1970). In Wood (1978) he supplements the earlier book, which deals almost exclusively with the moral aspects of Kant's thinking about religious issues, with a study of the metaphysical aspects. For a much pithier overview, see Wood (1992).

Two excellent books by Michalson are: Michalson (1990), to which I referred in the further reading for Theme Two; and Michalson (1999), the book to which I have referred a couple of times in this chapter, in which he sees Kant as the progenitor of nineteenth-century atheism. (In the case of Michalson (1999), I cannot resist mentioning, as an incidental plaudit, the author's remarkable achievement of managing to write some two hundred pages of completely unforced theological prose without at any point using a pronoun to refer to God and thereby risking offence either to those who do or to those who do not take God to be a 'He'.)

Other books on Kant's philosophy of religion include Despland (1973), England (1929), Reardon (1988), Rossi and Wreen (1991), and Webb (1926). The following chapters/sections from books are also to be recommended: Förster (2000), Chapter 5, to which I referred in note 98; [E.C.] Moore (1912), Chapter II, §1; Neiman (1994), Chapter 4; Walker (1978), Chapters X and XII; and Yovel (1980), Chapter 5. The following articles are likewise to be recommended: Adams (1998); Davidovich (1994); Guyer (2000d); Korsgaard (1996c); O'Neill (1997); Ricoeur (1974); and Silber (1960).

A fine book, whose primary aim is not exegesis but rather, very much like the primary aim of my own book, to make use of Kant's moral and religious ideas, is Green (1978). (Green's execution of this aim, especially in Part I, is also very much like mine.) An equally fine book, which is perhaps more balanced between exegesis and appropriation, is [J.E.] Hare (1996), which explores Kant's use of Christian resources to make sense of the gap between the demands of morality and our capacity to meet them.

For insight into the biographical and historical contexts of Kant's religious views, see Cassirer (1981), Chapter VII; Greene (1960); and Kuehn (2001), especially Chapter 8. All three of these give an account of Kant's one serious brush with authority. *Religion* was published in the reign of the illiberal Friedrich Wilhelm II, who had appointed an anti-Enlightenment figure, Wöllner, as minister of ecclesiastical affairs. At Wöllner's prompting, the King wrote to Kant forbidding him to write any more on religious matters. Kant wrote back complying, but by proclaiming himself 'Your Majesty's most faithful subject', took himself to have licence to publish further work on religion once Friedrich Wilhelm II had died.

Third set of variations

> There was given to me a thorn in the flesh, the messenger of Satan to buffet me... For this thing I besought the Lord thrice, that it might depart from me. And he said unto me, My grace is sufficient for thee: for my strength is made perfect in weakness. Most gladly therefore will I rather glory in my infirmities, that the power of Christ may rest upon me. Therefore I take pleasure in infirmities, in reproaches, in necessities, in persecutions, in distresses for Christ's sake: for when I am weak, then am I strong.
>
> (St Paul, II Corinthians, Chapter XII, verses 7–10)

§1 What may we hope?

That the Basic Idea is true: that there is a nisus in us more fundamental than any other towards rationality. I said at the end of Variations Two that, if we are to accept the Basic Idea, then we must hope that it is true – in the absence of any way of establishing it. But likewise we *may* hope that it is true – in the absence of any way of refuting it.

The fact that we can neither establish nor refute the Basic Idea does not mean that its truth or falsity makes no empirical difference to how the world is, still less that it makes no difference at all. If it is true, it is a deep contingent truth with definite implications concerning what human beings are like: what they yearn for, what they need, and what makes them suffer. But because of its limitless susceptibility to apparent counterexamples, nothing we observe can ever count decisively in its favour (nothing we observe can ever show that there is not *some* apparent counterexample that cannot be accounted for), while because of the limitless susceptibility of apparent counterexamples to being accounted for, nothing we observe can ever count decisively against it either (nothing we observe can ever show that there *is* some apparent counterexample that cannot be accounted for).

To repeat: the Basic Idea, if it is true, is a deep contingent truth. It is founded upon an elaborate network of further contingencies. For instance, given that there could scarcely be a fundamental nisus in us towards rationality if we did not at least have the capacity to be rational, it is founded upon whatever contingencies this capacity is in turn founded upon. There would be no question of our being rational if our brains were no more complex than the brains of earthworms, say. Nor would there be any question of our being rational if our environment were not suitably hospitable to our efforts to make sense of it. No doubt we could survive the shock of waking up to blue grass and green sky. But too much of that sort of thing would mean that eventually we could no longer even have the expectations to be shocked. We could no longer make sense of things at all.[1] And in as much as the Basic Idea requires, not only that we have the capacity to make sense of things, but that we have the capacity, in particular, to make ethical sense of things, then there needs to be all the more refinement and complexity in the underlying network of contingencies. For instance, there would be no question of our making ethical sense of things if there were not some suitable combination of stability and malleability in our conative states allowing us to work them into action-guiding concepts by which we could live.[2]

At the end of Variations One I mentioned the feeling of pleasure we have when contingencies do conspire to enable us to make sense of things, and I alluded to the importance of this feeling in Kant's philosophy. Kant thinks we cannot help seeing such contingencies as an indication of order and purposiveness. This has a clear aesthetic dimension, which is why, as I indicated then, he identifies this feeling of pleasure with a feeling of beauty. But it has an equally clear religious dimension. And this is something else that Kant is keen to probe.[3] He is well aware of nature's capacity to tap a very deep and very primitive sense within us of the Creator God, even though he insists that this has no implications for whether there *is* such a God. This adumbrates ideas that we shall be exploring later. There is one point, however, that is worth making straight away. No-one – whatever pleasure he or she may feel when contemplating how far we and the world seem to be made for each other, whatever relevance he or she may see in this for whether there is some kind of nisus in us towards rationality, whatever religious gloss he or she may put on this[4] – no-one can avoid adopting, towards the contingencies that enable us to make sense of things, something *like* an attitude of faith, some kind of combination of belief and trust and hope. For there is no proof, no *a priori* guarantee, that these contingencies will continue to hold.[5] Every time a person eats bread, or so much as takes a step forward, that person displays a kind of faith in the constancy of nature, a kind of faith without which it would be impossible to function. (Yet the contingencies do continue to hold. Our primeval trust in nature continues to be rewarded. The starry heaven above us, like the moral law within us, continues to declare its fixedness in the scheme of things.[6]) The question is not whether to have faith or not. The question is how much faith to have. We can have faith that our basic expectations will continue to be met: that is a minimum. Or we can go further: we can have faith that we shall continue to be able to make sense of things. Or we can go further still: we can have faith that we shall continue to have an *interest* in making sense of things, in other words that there will continue to be some kind of nisus in us towards rationality. Or we can go as far as to have faith in the Basic Idea. (In due course I shall be urging that we should go even further.) Each of these piles contingencies upon contingencies, but never so many as to make faith, or the hope that goes with it, impossible. If those are attitudes that we are inclined to adopt, or perhaps even cannot help adopting, then we are free, in each case, to do so.[7]

Before delving more deeply into the value of having faith in the Basic Idea (or, in line with what I shall be urging, in an enrichment of it), we need to delve more deeply into the Basic Idea itself. There is a radical indeterminacy, or family of indeterminacies, in the account of it that I have given so far. The time has come to resolve these.

§2 The Basic Idea is that there is a nisus in all of us, more fundamental than any other, towards rationality. But to what extent is this to be understood individualistically, and to what extent corporately?[8] Does it mean that each person's rationality is a supreme value for that person? Does it mean that our collective rationality is a supreme value for each person? Does it mean that our collective rationality is a supreme value, somehow, for all of us collectively?

One natural way of responding to these questions, or at least of initiating a response to them, is by invoking an idea that dominated Variations One: the idea, as I put it in §15 of that chapter, that 'our making individual sense of things and our making collective sense of things should be thought of as two sides of a single coin'; or, in other words, that a life of rationality cannot ultimately be anything but a life of shared rationality with other people (see especially §§11 and 15 of that chapter). This immediately mitigates the indeterminacy. It immediately makes the alternatives seem less stark.

Even so, they remain alternatives. To see how the difference between them might matter, consider a point that is sometimes made to emphasize how non-consequentialist certain non-consequentialist moral outlooks, such as Kant's own brand of rationalism, are. Williams makes the point in the following way:

> We might suppose that some non-consequentialist would consider it a better state of things in which more, rather than fewer, people kept their promises, and kept them for non-consequentialist reasons. Yet consistently with that he could accept, in a particular case,... that X

would do the right thing only if he kept his promise; [and that an effect of *X*'s keeping his promise] would be to provide some inducement to [several other people] which would lead them to break promises which otherwise they would have kept. Thus a non-consequentialist can hold both that it is a better state of affairs in which more people keep their promises, and that the right thing for *X* to do is something which brings it about that fewer promises are kept... If the goodness of the world were to consist in people's fulfilling their obligations, it would by no means follow that one of my obligations was to bring it about that other people kept their obligations.[9]

Granted that there is a fundamental nisus in all of us towards rationality, what follows concerning those unhappy situations, if such there be – call them 'discord' situations – in which the rationality of one person entails the irrationality of others?

One subsidiary question, of course, is whether discord situations are really possible. There is an argument to show that, on Kant's own rationalistic conception, they are not. Consider Williams' case. In order for the other people in this case to keep their promises, there must be no inducement of the relevant kind for them to do otherwise, which in turn means that *X* must break his. But then, if *X* does break his and they keep theirs, they will be acting only *in conformity with* duty, not *from* duty: doing their duty will not be what matters most to them. So their rationality in this affair does not after all depend on what *X* does. And similar considerations apply to any other case of this sort. (This is related to the argument that we considered in §3 of the previous chapter for Kant's conclusion that we are fundamentally bad.)

One problem with this argument, however, is that it is vulnerable to the possibility of a situation whose discord is not simply due to the contingencies of people's motivations, but is somehow intrinsic to the situation. What if one person's rationality *forces* other people into irrationality, say, by bringing about a state of affairs in which they, Herod-like, can do nothing that is not in some respect irrational (see Variations One, §6, and Theme Three, §3)? There may be a Kantian argument to block this possibility. But if so, it remains to be given.

Here is another argument to show that discord situations are not possible, based this time on my reconstruction of Kant's rationalism. Consider someone in what seems to be such a situation. That is, consider someone who possesses a concept which gives her a reason for doing something which, in this particular situation, seems to involve other people in irrationality. Then all that follows is that the reason in question is defeasible (see Variations One, §6), in which case she should adopt a maxim that legitimizes her doing something else in this situation (see Variations One, §9). For instance, to revert again to Williams' case, she should adopt a maxim to break any promise she has made if this will prevent widespread promise-breaking on the part of other people.

A problem with this argument, however, is that there is no guarantee that she *can* adopt a maxim that legitimizes her doing something else in this situation. A maxim can legitimize her doing something else in this situation only if the maxim is capable of becoming a law. And as we saw at different points in Variations One (see especially §§15 and 16), a maxim is capable of becoming a law only if a variety of factors, including sociological, historical, and psychological factors, allow it. (This relates back to the point I made in the previous section about the contingencies that have to be in place if we are to make ethical sense of things.)

This problem, the problem that this person might not be able to find a maxim which legitimizes her doing something else in this situation, will be greatly exacerbated if the situation is of a sort which I considered in §5 of the Introduction, but have said very little about since, a situation in which she has an ethical disagreement with other people that does not involve error on anyone's part. I have in mind a disagreement that results from her possessing different concepts from them. I initially presented such cases as a threat to ethical objectivism, and thereby to rationalism (the second of the three principal objections to rationalism that I considered in that section). But by the end of Variations One it should have been clear that the ethical objectivism to which my version of rationalism commits me can accommodate such cases. The ethical objectivism to which my version of rationalism commits me precludes error-free disagreement about the importance of keeping faith with the concepts one possesses; it likewise precludes error-free disagreement about what constitutes keeping faith with the concepts one possesses; but it does not preclude error-free disagreement about what concepts to possess in the first place, disagreement which, in Mackie's words, '[reflects] people's adherence to and participation in different ways of life'.[10] However, where there *is* such disagreement, it is even harder to see why one person's rationality should not involve the irrationality of others, in a way that cannot be resolved by her adopting a maxim that legitimizes her doing something other than what she would normally have to do. If her concepts clash with theirs – if she 'adheres to and participates in a different way of life' from them – then what guarantee is there that her concepts and their concepts will not impose irresolubly conflicting demands on some situation in which they all find themselves, with the result that if she acts rationally then they are bound not to?

In general, there seems to me to be no good reason to think that discord situations are impossible. And this in turn means that the alternative interpretations of the Basic Idea remain definite alternatives.

But now we run into a problem that I raised in §3 of the Introduction, a problem for any species of conative objectivism. I distinguished between a conative state's *type* and its *content*. And I said that the sense in which we are most likely to share any conative states seems not to be the sense in which any conative states we share are most likely to ground our ethical reasons for doing things. The former sense seems to be that in which we have conative states of the same type. The latter sense seems to be that in which we have conative states with the same content.[11] This problem is relevant to our current quandary in the following way. If the Basic Idea means that each person's rationality is a supreme value for that person, then it ascribes conative states of the same type to us. If it means that our collective rationality is a supreme value for each person, then it ascribes conative states with the same content to us. In the former case, while it is more likely to be true, it is less likely to have the ethical significance that it is supposed to have: this is precisely because of the possibility of discord situations. (To be sure, this is not a consideration that will weigh with an inveterate non-consequentialist who thinks that there can be situations in which the right thing to do is not the thing that minimizes wrong-doing.) In the latter case, the case in which the Basic Idea means that our collective rationality is a supreme value for each person, it is more likely to have the ethical significance that it is supposed to have, but less likely to be true. Discord situations look as if they could pose a real threat to the truth and ethical significance of the Basic Idea.

Admittedly, I am now painting with very broad brush strokes. All sorts of questions remain unaddressed about what 'our collective rationality' consists in, and *a fortiori* about what its being a supreme value for each of us consists in. I have also said nothing about the interpretation of the Basic Idea whereby our collective rationality is a supreme value for all of us together (whatever that in turn might mean). But I take it that I am entitled to use broad brush strokes when what I am doing is making trouble for the truth and ethical significance of something that I myself hold to be both true and ethically significant.

How then do I evade this trouble? In the most direct way possible. Simply by holding, as an addendum to the Basic Idea, that *there are no discord situations*. (All I have been maintaining is that discord situations are possible. I have not been maintaining that there are any. Whether there are or not is a contingent matter of fact.) This means that the indeterminacies with which we began this section are so to speak resolved by not needing to be resolved. So long as there are no discord situations, then the different interpretations of the Basic Idea (in fact) come to the same thing.

But what entitlement do I have simply to say that there are no discord situations? Well, I think I have at least the following minimal entitlement to do so: like the Basic Idea itself, this addendum can never be refuted. For consider someone in what seems to be a discord situation. I do not see how we can rule out the possibility of some radical conceptual innovation (some radical new way of viewing things, or some radical development of an old way of viewing things – see Variations Two, §3) which gives her the wherewithal to be rational without creating difficulties for the rationality of other people.

Even so, to say that the addendum can never be refuted, and that it offers at least that minimal refuge to its own acceptance, is one thing. To say that it is *true*, or that it *merits* acceptance, is quite another, especially if, as I also think, it can never be established either. I take it to be, just like the Basic Idea, a deep contingency, founded upon an elaborate network of further contingencies. To accept it is to incur an additional and considerable burden of hope. What is to be said for doing so?

At the end of Variations Two I sketched an argument to show that whether the Basic Idea itself merits acceptance depends simply on whether it is true. But it is not clear that even this much can be said of the addendum. Suppose the addendum *is* true. That is, suppose there really are no discord situations. Then while we can agree that accepting this has the merit of encouraging us to look for ways out of *apparent* discord situations, there might also be a case for the view that remaining resolutely agnostic about it has the merit of keeping us on our guard against getting into apparent discord situations in the first place.

This is an apt point at which to state the main idea of this chapter, itself a variation on the main idea of the previous chapter. It is this. Imperfect as we are, we cannot abide by our own fundamental nisus towards rationality unless we cherish the hope that that nisus has a place deep in the order of things: a place that protects it from the corrosion of our own irrationality, that makes it impervious to the vicissitudes of our circumstances, and that prevents it from turning in on itself and producing internal conflict. We need to cherish the hope that the Basic Idea is not just true, but *secure*; that there is sufficient harmony between us and the world, and between us and our own values, to guarantee that there will be a nisus in us more fundamental than any other towards making sense for as long as we are here to make it; that we shall always be able to make *this* much sense of our own sense-making.[12]

To accept that there are no discord situations is part of what it is to accept that the Basic Idea enjoys such security. If the Basic Idea is to have as firm a place in the order of things as that, then it must not in any way compromise each person's total commitment to his or her own rationality, nor the harmony of that total commitment with the total commitment of each other person to his or hers. If it did compromise these in any way, there would be a danger that it would tear itself apart. Specifically, there would be a danger that situations in which some of us might as well not have the fundamental nisus towards rationality would multiply to such an extent that eventually some or all of us no longer did.

Much of the rest of this chapter will be concerned with further examples of what accepting the security of the Basic Idea involves; and with the question of why we should accept it. But, first, I want to consider and counter a reason that might be given for why we should not.

§3 I have in mind a variant of an objection to Kant that I mentioned in §5 of the previous chapter, namely that hoping for the attainability of the highest good is a way of succumbing to what Nietzsche calls *ressentiment*. It is a way of abnegating our own responsibility to make sense of things by expecting things to make sense for us, or at least by expecting them to do *some* of our work for us. Is the same not true of hoping for the security of the Basic Idea?

Well, hoping for the security of the Basic Idea is certainly a way of hoping that things are, and will continue to be, hospitable to our own efforts to make sense of them. But for reasons that I gave above, in §1, I do not see how we can avoid *something* like this if we are to get anywhere in our efforts.[13] I do not see how we can avoid *something* like this if we are to get anywhere at all.

Still, it is one thing to hope for sufficient constancy in nature for us to continue to be able to make sense of things. It is far more to hope for the security of the Basic Idea. Even if the former is not a sign of *ressentiment*, is not the latter?

I do not think so. I do not think that hoping for the security of the Basic Idea is a way of hoping that the world itself somehow makes sense on our behalf, nor indeed that it makes sense at all except figuratively and unobjectionably. It is a way of hoping that the world fosters and protects our own sense-making. (See further §9 below.) What I am prepared to concede, however, is that hoping for the security of the Basic Idea shares with *ressentiment* the following very important feature. It is, in Nietzsche's own words, 'born of weakness'.[14] Here no doubt I am closer to Kant than I am to Nietzsche. I see our weakness as a datum, as something that we have to come to terms with, partly indeed by making sense of it, but partly by cherishing the hopes that it leaves us needing to rely upon if we are to sustain any commitment to being rational.

§4 My picture is as follows.

For reasons sketched in Variations Two, §11, we do well to accept the Basic Idea, provided that it is true. To accept the Basic Idea is to accept that we should never give up in our efforts to account for apparent counterexamples to it. And, provided that it is true, this has a number of salutary effects. For instance, it leads us to seek out and to try to understand the forces of corruption that bring us to pursue the irrational over the rational. However, given that we have no way of establishing the truth of the Basic Idea, and given that accepting its truth may be pernicious *unless* it is true, we must, if we do accept its truth, likewise hope for its truth.

But we must hope for more. Or rather, we must hope for more if we are to *abide* by its truth; if we are to sustain a commitment to rationality. We must hope, as I put it in §2, *that the Basic Idea is not just true, but secure*. Thus even if there is an issue about whether it would be corrupt for one person to pursue his or her own rationality at the expense of other people's, or whether, conversely, it would be corrupt for one person to sacrifice his or her own rationality for the sake of other people's, we must hope and believe that the issue never arises. We must hope and believe that the Basic Idea enjoys the kind of security that ensures that the issue never arises. Otherwise, imperfect as we are, we shall find ourselves confronted by constant temptations to rationalize wrong-doing of various kinds: to approve unjustified violations of principle as being in the interest of the greater good, say, or, conversely, to approve unjustified moral self-indulgences as being in the interest of integrity. Only if we have faith that our nisus towards rationality cuts through all such complications can we keep the demands of rationality suitably in focus. Only then can we feel their full force. Only then indeed can we play our own part in maintaining the nisus, which is another way of saying that only then can we play our own part in ensuring the truth of the Basic Idea. (To accept that the Basic Idea is secure is not to accept that its truth has nothing to do with us.)

What else does the security of the Basic Idea involve? Much.[15] It has two aspects in particular to which I want to devote special attention and to which I shall return in the next two sections. The first of these, like the absence of discord situations, is a kind of external condition. It is the absence of what I shall call 'no-win' situations: situations in which we are forced, at some ultimate level, into irrationality. (No-win situations, just like discord situations, would be in danger of multiplying to such an extent that eventually some or all of us no longer had the fundamental nisus towards rationality. Even if this never happened, the mere danger of its happening would be enough to make the Basic Idea insecure.) The second aspect is a simple corollary of the security of the Basic Idea. It is that nothing will ever come to be of greater value to us than rationality; hence that nothing will ever enable us to look back on some current irrationality and be glad of it. Hoping for, and having faith in, each of these further enable us to sustain our commitment to rationality. They give us an assurance that, whatever happens, we shall have a way of making sense, and that, whatever ways we have of failing to make sense, we are never to pursue any of *them* at the expense of *it*.

A third aspect of the security of the Basic Idea, itself a variation on the second, is that the sense in which we have a nisus more fundamental than any other towards rationality is a tenseless sense – just as the sense in which we are a kind of mammal is a tenseless sense. (In other words we do not just have the nisus *now*. This is in contrast to the view which, in §3 of the previous chapter, I said that Kant took of our being fundamentally bad.) But this is not to say that we shall literally be here at all times aspiring to be rational, any more than we shall literally be here at all times suckling our young. Still less is it to say anything of the sort about each of us individually. It is quite possible that people will eventually become extinct; and it is certain that each individual person will. There is no promise of immortality in the security of the Basic Idea. (See below, §9, for what there *is* corresponding to the second of Kant's postulates of pure practical reason.) Relatedly, our assurance that, whatever happens, we shall have a way of making sense is to be understood as an assurance that, whenever we can make a move within the logical space of reasons, we can make a good move there. It is not an assurance that we always shall be able to make a move within the logical space of reasons. Thus even if there are no no-win situations, that is even if there is nothing to force us, at some ultimate level, into irrationality, there are all sorts of things, of which extinction is merely the starkest example, to force us, at some ultimate level, into non-rationality. Death, depression, desolation, dire need, deep unfulfilled desire, and indeed despair – the lack of the very hope that I am currently championing – can all force people out of the logical space of reasons altogether. This is one of the many reasons why we need to be especially assiduous in making sense of *them*. The differences between non-rationality and irrationality can be very slight, and it is important for us to have as clear an understanding as possible of the edges of this space which it is so important, in turn, for us to negotiate. Furthermore, given that our nisus towards making sense involves a nisus towards moving in this space, we do well to recall something that I urged in Variations One, §17: one way of making sense of things is making sense of them as an abomination. The unique value that attaches to movement within the logical space of reasons makes the unjustified exclusion of anyone from that space uniquely wicked. (But it can also make morbid preoccupation with the eventual and inevitable exclusion of anyone from that space a uniquely destructive form of *ressentiment*.)

Before returning, in the next two sections, to the first and second aspects of the security of the Basic Idea, I want to consider a related worry about whether the Basic Idea is secure. This worry is grounded in the thought that there are certain situations in which irrationality fits into larger patterns of rationality, situations in which, as it were, it is rational to be irrational. Call these 'paradoxical' situations. Parfit describes a number of apparently paradoxical situations.[16] Some of these are extremely contrived. (In one a man trying to be impervious to the threats of another man reaches for a drug 'conveniently at hand' which will briefly cause him to be very irrational.[17]) It is doubtful in many of these cases whether anything of the like will ever actually occur. And it is doubtful too, in many of these cases, whether what is really in the interest of large-scale rationality is small-scale irrationality, as opposed to small-scale non-rationality. Even so, there is enough in Parfit's discussion to suggest that paradoxical situations do sometimes occur. More to the point, I myself have already conceded that they do. In particular I have conceded that there are situations in which adopting a maxim that is not capable of being a law helps to subvert some abhorrent concept (see Variations One, §10, and Variations Two, §6: the clearest example is that of the maxim to violate some absurd taboo whenever possible). The worry is that paradoxical situations are just as much of a threat to the security of the Basic Idea as either discord situations or no-win situations. Indeed, discord situations are themselves a kind of paradoxical situation. In a discord situation the irrationality of one person fits into a larger pattern of rationality involving other people. More alarmingly, paradoxical situations appear to be a kind of no-win situation. For if someone is in a paradoxical situation, then she must either accede to some small-scale irrationality or accede to the large-scale irrationality against which the small-scale irrationality militates.

This worry can be appeased, however. In particular we need not agree that paradoxical situations are a kind of no-win situation. (If they were, that would be the end of the matter. The Basic Idea is insecure if there are any no-win situations.) A no-win situation is a situation in which someone is forced, *at some ultimate level*, into irrationality. It is a situation in which all the available moves within the logical space of reasons are, even when considered in the widest relevant scheme of things, bad moves, moves of unredeemed irrationality. This is admittedly vague. But it is not so vague that we cannot apply it to, say, the case where someone adopts a maxim to violate some absurd taboo whenever possible. Though this does indeed involve an element of irrationality, since the person is failing to keep faith with some concept she possesses, there is a deeper level at which it makes very good sense. This is reflected in the fact that, were the person to stop possessing the offending concept, which is after all part of the aim of the exercise, and which is different, remember, from her stopping grasping it altogether (see Variations One, §8), then not only could she look back on her current policy with the kind of detachment that made its irrationality look entirely relative and parochial, but also, more significantly, she could look back on it with the kind of detachment, and with the kind of distaste for the concept involved, that made both regret and remorse look entirely inappropriate, and indeed be entirely inappropriate. This contrasts importantly with how it would be in a discord situation. If, in a discord situation, someone sacrificed her own rationality for the sake of other people's, it would still be appropriate for her to feel regret and remorse at what she had done – even if this was what her nisus towards rationality demanded. True, her irrationality would not be unredeemed. (Discord situations, as I have said, are a kind of paradoxical situation.) But provided that she still possessed the relevant concepts, neither would the fact that she had flouted those concepts be a matter of indifference to her. Or at least, it should not be. (She had *broken a promise*, let us say: *someone had been relying on her*.) In general, paradoxical situations lack that potential for disruption, self-deception, and outright complication which both discord situations and no-win situations have and which I have claimed destabilizes the Basic Idea.[18]

It is worth noting, while we are discussing these unproblematical paradoxical situations, that many apparent discord situations are of this type. In particular, many apparent discord situations that result from a clash of concepts (see above, §2) are of this type. Often, when it seems that people's different concepts impose conflicting demands on a situation in such a way that one person cannot act rationally without forcing others into irrationality, there is an escape route of the kind we have just been considering: that is, via the violation of one of the offending concepts and its eventual subversion. (Having said that, I still see no *a priori* guarantee that an escape route of this kind, or of any other kind, will always be available.)

§5 In this section I want to return to the first of the aspects of the security of the Basic Idea that I mentioned and temporarily shelved in the previous section: the absence of no-win situations. (In the next section I shall return to the second of these aspects: that nothing will ever be of greater value to us than rationality.) To hope that there are no no-win situations is to hope that, whatever we are confronted with, and in particular, crucially, whatever we bring upon ourselves, we never find that every available move in the logical space of reasons is, at some ultimate level, irrational.

The difficulty here is to balance the absence of no-win situations against their possibility. We need both. If they were not possible, their absence would contribute nothing to the security of the Basic Idea. Nor would it be an appropriate object of hope.

It would be easy enough to define 'irrationality' in such a way as to preclude no-win situations. For that matter it would be reasonable enough to do so. Consider what I said in Variations Two, §1, when outlining the Radical Picture. I said that, in circumstances where there is a 'suitably salient possibility' that someone acts rationally, her realizing some other possibility can constitute her acting irrationally. If this were extended and adapted so that irrationality, by definition, had always to be accompanied by some such 'suitably salient possibility', and if the conception of possibility in question were suitably demanding, then no-win situations would be a contradiction in terms. The difficulty arises because, *unless* 'irrationality' is defined in this or some similar way, then there seem to be many clear examples of no-win situations. And here the case of Herod once again comes to mind.

Perhaps Herod *is* in a no-win situation, on Kant's rationalistic conception. But I do not think he is on my reconstruction of Kant's conception. I do not see why Herod cannot rationally act on a maxim to break any promise he has made when the alternative is to take somebody's life (see Variations One, §9).[19] Nor do I see why there should not be *some* such escape route in any apparent no-win situation. (This leaves open the possibility that there is more than one such escape route. Often, I think, there is. For often there is more than one suitable development in the concepts involved.)

I do not deny that obligations sometimes conflict.[20] It is just that, whenever they do, there is a rational way (perhaps not a unique rational way – reconsider the parenthetical point at the end of the previous paragraph) to resolve the conflict. (Obligations, like reasons and resolutions, are defeasible: see Variations One, §§6 and 9.) I am quite happy to say that a situation like Herod's involves conflicting obligations, because I think it is entirely reasonable for a person, in such a situation, even having acted rationally, and even having found himself in the situation through no fault of his own, let alone having culpably got himself into it, *à la* Herod, to feel remorse – and for other suitably affected parties to feel resentment. (The concepts of obligation, remorse, and resentment, like the concept of blameworthiness, are 'superficial': see Variations Two, §1.) Indeed, I do not think that a person would count as fully possessing the concept of a promise, say, if he did not recognize himself as being under a (defeasible) obligation to keep any promise he had made, and hence did not feel some remorse whenever he had deliberately broken one, even if he had done so rationally and justifiably. (And lest my claim that, whenever obligations conflict, there is a rational way to resolve the conflict seems insensitive to the costs that can be incurred in such situations, then I hope that these remarks go some way towards redressing any such impression. A rational way to resolve the conflict, yes; an easy way to do so, no. Often, when obligations conflict, they do so in a way that is unbearably painful.[21])

But now the other horn of the dilemma threatens again: if Herod's case is not an example of the sort of enforced irrationality I have in mind, then why think that such a thing is so much as possible? Even if I am not working with a definition of 'irrationality' that straightway precludes no-win situations, the suspicion remains that I would refuse to count anything, real or imaginary, as one. To deflect this suspicion I need to say how I think such a situation could arise.[22]

I think it could arise in a very alien, hostile world containing enough inconstancy to throw us off conceptual balance, but not so much as to throw us out of the logical space of reasons altogether. If we continually found ourselves having to modify our concepts, or to abandon them in favour of new ones, in an effort to make sense of things, then I do not see why we should not eventually reach the point that, granted our circumstances, granted our modes of interaction with one another, and granted our limitations, the only available moves in the logical space of reasons were unmitigated bad moves. Our hope that there are no no-win situations is of a piece with our hope that the sun will rise tomorrow, on edible bread and green grass. In the nature of the case, it is difficult to describe a no-win situation. To adapt a famous sentence of Strawson's: we lack concepts to say, with any specificity, what it would be to be forced to violate our own concepts.[23] But we do not lack concepts to say this much: given that our rationality is a contingency, resting on all sorts of other contingencies, there is scope for untold horrors, including untold horrors of enforced irrationality, if ever those contingencies begin to break down.

And that is the point. In order to abide by our nisus towards rationality, we must hope that these contingencies are not about to break down; that we can cope, rationally, with whatever is thrown at us and with whatever we throw ourselves at; that, whenever we have a move to make in the logical space of reasons, we have a good move to make there. Otherwise laziness, cowardice, self-deception, and all manner of other weaknesses will make it very easy for us to think that, because we *are* in a no-win situation, only bad moves are available to us, and that, because one of these (the one that tempts us anyway) is no worse than any of the others, we might as well make it.

§6 I turn next to the second of the two aspects of the security of the Basic Idea that I mentioned in §4: that nothing will ever be of greater value to us than rationality. One question that immediately arises is why *hope* is an appropriate attitude to adopt towards this. Indeed, given how steeped in irrationality we are, are there not grounds for hoping for the very opposite, namely that something *will* eventually be of greater value to us than rationality, allowing us, in retrospect, to acquiesce in all this violence against reason, and perhaps even to celebrate it? Are there not grounds in fact for trying to *bring this about* (in so far as that is an intelligible aim)? Would that not be the ultimate redemption?[24]

Well, let us not forget that the answers to these questions depend on our conative states. And this whole discussion is based on the assumption that we do in fact have a nisus, more fundamental than any other, towards rationality; that the Basic Idea is at least true, if only temporarily, if only insecurely. What is at issue is what we must hope if we are to abide by this nisus; if we are not to lose sight of its demands in the glare of the various enticements of irrationality. The issue is not what grounds there are for *optimism*. The hope that nothing will ever be of greater value to us than rationality may provide little in the way of cheer, conscious as we are of precisely that feature of our current situation that prompted the questions above: how steeped we are in irrationality. What it will provide is a counter-balance to various temptations that were visible in those questions, temptations to rationalize the irrational by anticipating some future perspective from which our most fundamental values will be different – whether because they are better informed, or because they are more mature, or because they are less servile, or whatever. Thus consider the all too familiar temptation, when confronted with some manifest injustice, not only to connive at it, but to justify doing so, at least to oneself, on the grounds that it is for some greater good (an easy life for the majority of those affected, say, or the smooth running of the corporation, or perhaps even a diminished risk of further similar injustices). This temptation, considerable as it is, will be much exacerbated by the thought that our most fundamental moral sensibility, against which the injustice offends, may in any case change.

But here a worry arises in connection with something I emphasized in §4, namely that, even if the Basic Idea is secure, this does not mean that we shall never be forced out of the logical space of reasons altogether. Sooner or later we shall, individually if not collectively. Moreover, advances in technology have greatly multiplied the ways in which this might happen. No doubt they will continue to do so. The worry is that our knowing this undoes whatever good is done by our hoping that the Basic Idea is secure. Any security that the Basic Idea enjoys, we realize, is relative to our remaining in the logical space of reasons. So all sorts of temptations of rationalization come to the fore again. Thus we may be tempted to justify certain irrational indulgences (however tacitly, however unselfconsciously – I am not suggesting that we are likely to think about what we are doing in just these terms) on the grounds that these indulgences induce some state of more or less literal analgesia, or even that they bring us closer to some brave new world, in which we *are* no longer in the logical space of reasons, in which nothing is properly of *value* to us at all, in which we are simply 'happy'.[25] Or we may be tempted to justify certain irrational risks (again, however tacitly, however unself-consciously) on the grounds that, if we end up annihilating ourselves, *nothing* will then matter to us, never mind the fact that taking those risks made no sense.

We may. I do not pretend that the hope which I am championing is some kind of panacea. Nevertheless, I think the worry expressed above is an overreaction, to at least the following extent: even if some of the good done by this hope is undone by the knowledge that there is space for us beyond the logical space of reasons, not all of it is. I *hope* not all of it is. That hope, the hope that not all of it is, is itself a self-referential part of the hope which I am championing, the hope that the Basic Idea is secure. For the security of the Basic Idea requires the effectiveness of whatever props we need to live by it. (Come to that, the security of the Basic Idea requires that, where those props are threatened, as they are here, we have other resources that we can draw on, say, an abhorrence of leaving the logical space of reasons which is deep enough that it cannot be treated as mere squeamishness, and deep enough, in fact, that it can counteract these various temptations.)

In sum, then, we must hope that nothing – not happiness, not some glorious enterprise of any kind, not the march of history, not the will of God – will ever place greater demands on us than the demand to make sense. Unless we hope this, we cannot feel the full force of that demand. We cannot resist various temptations of rationalization. To use a helpful slogan that is sometimes bandied about in discussions of this nature, we must hope that *the right thing to do is always the thing that is right*; or, to cast it in terms of our own discussion, that *making sense is always what makes sense*.

§7 Let us take stock. How is the picture that I have been painting in the last three sections a variation, to revert to my guiding metaphor, on the Kantian theme of the previous chapter?

First, and most basically, it begins with our imperfection. Kant's philosophy of religion has as its starting point the fact that, although we are essentially rational, and although our rationality can be used to determine us to action, it does not (in fact) find its most basic expression by being used in that way: it finds its most basic expression by being *ab*used to determine us to action. (See §3 of the previous chapter.) This leaves us needing various non-rational props to become fully (re-)attuned to our own essence, to 'become those that we are'.[26] In particular, we need various reassurances that there is still something, and always will be something, that meaningfully counts as 'becoming those that we are'. It is these reassurances that religion provides.

In my picture, too, our imperfection means that we need various reassurances that there is still something, and always will be something, that meaningfully counts as 'becoming those that we are' – that is, as abiding by our fundamental nisus towards rationality. In due course I shall address the question of whether I too see religion as providing these reassurances. That will enable me to play out further variations on the Kantian theme.

But first I want to pick up briefly on Kant's bleak view of human nature. Is our irrationality – our evil – as deep and as pervasive as Kant takes it to be? This is a huge question of course. It merits a book of its own. All I can do here is to gesture at the answer I am inclined to give, and to highlight one aspect of that answer which I think is especially relevant to this discussion.

I am inclined to agree with Kant. In some ways I am inclined to go further than Kant. At one point when he is discussing human evil he fastens on 'the vices of culture and civilization'.[27] (These prompt him to make one of his most memorably caustic comments, namely that when we attend to 'human nature ... in its civilized state ... we shall have enough of [these vices] ... to make us rather turn our eyes away from the doings of human beings, lest we be dragged ourselves into another vice, namely that of misanthropy'.[28]) But I think he makes too little, in this part of his discussion, of something that is nowadays all too clear: the depths of evil to which corporate action enables us to sink. As Nagel says, 'the great modern crimes are public crimes'.[29]

However, it is notoriously difficult to motivate the view that we are radically evil, and I am not even going to sketch what a motivation would look like. Part of the difficulty lies in giving clear sense to the view without making it, like the view that people only ever pursue their own interests, either an uninteresting conceptual truth or an even less interesting empirical falsehood. Suffice to say that I see it as neither. I see it as being, like the Basic Idea itself, a deep contingency.[30] And it is this aspect of my answer that I think is especially relevant to this discussion.

It is because of the combination of this contingency – the contingency of our radical involvement with irrationality – and the contingency of the Basic Idea that the hope which I have been discussing, the hope that the Basic Idea is secure, finds its *raison d'être*. Our radical involvement with irrationality both extends and aggravates the range of temptations, including temptations of rationalization and self-justification, to which we are subject. This leaves us in need of something to (re-)appropriate our own most fundamental nisus, something to bring the demands of rationality back into focus. And this in turn is what we find in the hope, the hope that the nisus, along with its demands, has a place deep in the order of things from which it cannot be dislodged. But of course, that same radical involvement with irrationality also represents one of the most rigorous tests for the hope. Not even that is to dislodge the nisus, whether by creating a no-win situation, or by sheer corruption, or in any other way. This highlights a striking ambivalence that exists within the hope. On the one hand, it is a hope that the world is immune to what we are like and what we get up to: despite our worst efforts, we never wreak sufficient damage to force ourselves into irrationality. On the other hand, it is a hope that the world is in tune with what we are like and what we get up to: our most basic expectations are sufficiently accurate for us always to be able to make sense of things (grass is green, for instance, not grue).

The contingency of our radical involvement with irrationality, in other words the contingency of our radical failure to abide by the Basic Idea, is thus delicately intertwined with the contingency of the Basic Idea itself. Each of these contingencies is a deep contingency, resting on an elaborate network of further contingencies (as also, *a fortiori*, is their combination). But there are significant differences between them. Not least of these is the fact, to put it graphically, that whereas the first contingency positively assaults us, the second keeps hidden in the background. Belief in neither can be instilled by any simple argument. In neither case is simple argument enough to persuade anyone to view things in the relevant way. But whereas belief in our radical irrationality can be reinforced by attention to what is constantly before us, belief in the Basic Idea has to be reinforced by something more like faith (see above, §1).

This is a good cue to return to the character of the Basic Idea, about which I have already said a little, but about which the theme of the previous chapter enables me to say more. In Variations Two, §11, I likened the Basic Idea to a Kantian regulative ideal. To accept it, I said, is to accept, among other things, that we are never to give up in our efforts to account for cases in which we place greater value on what is irrational than we do on what is rational. Even more fundamentally, to accept it is to accept that we are always to make sense of things. However, I also pointed out that the Basic Idea is unlike a Kantian regulative ideal in being either true or false. (A regulative ideal is neither true nor false. It is a rule to act as if some non-empirical concept has an empirical application, which, in the nature of the case, it cannot have.) If we do accept the Basic Idea, then clearly, as I have already remarked a couple of times, we must hope that it is true. In view of this, the material of the previous chapter, in particular §7, provides a better Kantian analogue of the Basic Idea. *The Basic Idea is akin to a postulate of pure practical reason.*

More fully, the Basic Idea is akin to a postulate of pure practical reason in each of the following four respects. First, it is either true or false (true, we may hope). Second, it can never be established or refuted. (The fact that it can never be refuted is what entitles us to hope that it is true.) Third, although it can never be established, it can be given a 'practical' vindication. That is to say, there is an argument to show that we must believe it if we are to engage properly with the demands of reason, coupled with an assurance – itself part of the fact that it can never be refuted – that it is at least not an incoherent thing for us to believe. And, fourth, we can recognize a logical gap between our having to believe it and its being true (though obviously we cannot both believe it and at the same time convert that recognition into genuine agnosticism). Here, certainly, is a variation on a Kantian theme.

There is, moreover, another obvious variation on the same theme. All four of these features, according to the picture that I was painting in §§4–6 above, belong likewise to the proposition that the Basic Idea is secure. So *the proposition that the Basic Idea is secure is likewise akin to a postulate of pure practical reason.*

In §7 of the previous chapter I drew a distinction between the first of Kant's three postulates, the postulate that we are free, and the other two, the postulate that we are immortal and the postulate that God exists. This distinction had to do with the third of the features identified above. Specifically, it had to do with the necessity involved in that feature, the necessity of our believing the postulate if we are to engage properly with the demands of reason. In the case of each of the second and third postulates, the necessity is grounded in our imperfection, and, in particular, in our radical tendency *not* to engage properly with the demands of reason. The same is not true of the first postulate.

How does this distinction apply to my two variations on Kant's theme? Well, the Basic Idea is like the first postulate in this respect; and the proposition that the Basic Idea is secure is like the other two. The Basic Idea is like the first postulate because accepting that nothing is of greater value to us than rationality is like acting under the idea of freedom: it is a simple precondition of any proper rational activity at all. (This is assuming that the Basic Idea *is* true. I have never denied the element of question begging in my account of these matters. See again Variations Two, §11.) The proposition that the Basic Idea is secure, on the other hand, is like the second and third postulates, because precisely what leaves us needing to hope and believe that this proposition is true is our radical involvement with irrationality.

In §9 below I shall develop these ideas. But first, I want to consider in what other ways the picture I have been painting might be expected to include religious elements.

§8 It is not hard to envisage ways in which familiar religious ideas could be used to sustain both the hope and the belief that the Basic Idea is secure. In particular, it is not hard to envisage ways in which the idea of God could be used to sustain them. If we are to hope and believe that our fundamental nisus towards rationality is suitably fixed in the scheme of things, then one obvious way of doing so is to think of it as having been so fixed by God; to acknowledge a divine order whereby we and our environment are so organized as to preserve our nisus, be the antics and vicissitudes of either what they may. Kant himself, despite his opposition to the 'physico-theological' argument for God's existence, or what would nowadays be called 'the argument from design' (see §7 of the previous chapter[31]), thinks that we cannot regard the organization that we and our environment exhibit *except* as involving some such divine order. In *Critique of Pure Reason* he writes, 'Reason bids us consider every connection in the world according to principles of a systematic unity, hence *as if* they had all arisen from one single all-encompassing being, as supreme and all-sufficient cause.'[32]

To be sure, unless we accept the argument from design, then we shall not see any prospect here of a proof that God exists. I certainly do not want to suggest that acknowledging a divine order is the *only* way to sustain the hope that the Basic Idea is secure. But it is one obvious way. And it is a natural way. As Michalson puts it, 'belief in God and confidence in morality grow out of the same metaphysical soil'.[33] More generally, belief in God and confidence in our continuing ability to make sense of things grow out of the same metaphysical soil. Belief in God is of a piece with belief in the rationality of reality – to give the point a Hegelian twist.[34]

But does this not reduce belief in God to mere wishful thinking, or to a kind of renunciation?

Not at all. To think it does is like thinking that belief in the rationality of reality, or belief that reality, to that figurative extent, makes sense, is a way of succumbing to *ressentiment*. And, as I urged in §3, it need not be. It can be part of a commitment to making (our own) sense. The same is true, I suggest, of belief in God.

People sometimes distinguish between *belief in God* and *belief that God exists*.[35] There are all sorts of things that might be intended by this. One simple possibility is that the distinction is to be understood on the model of the distinction between belief in justice, say, and belief that justice exists. Someone can, in a given context, believe in justice, in as much as he or she can believe that it is important for justice to prevail there, even while recognizing that it does not (yet). On this model belief in God would be, roughly, belief that it is important to promote and cherish whatever bespeaks God; belief that God exists would be belief that whatever bespeaks God speaks truly. Though I did not have exactly this distinction in mind in the previous paragraph, I did deliberately use the phrase 'belief in God', rather than 'belief that God exists', in order to convey the idea of a belief that was, as I put it there, part of a *commitment*, a commitment to making sense, and not simply some metaphysical conjecture. Belief in God, on this way of construing it, is to be characterized by what it enables us to do, not by its content. To quote Deleuze and Guattari, 'Kierkegaard's "knight of faith" ... [and] Pascal's gambler ... are concerned no longer with the transcendent existence of God but only with the infinite immanent possibilities brought by the one who believes [in God]'.[36] A quotation from Murdoch is also pertinent:

> No existing thing could be what we have meant by God. Any existing God would be less than God. An existent God would be an idol or a demon. (This is near to Kant's thinking.) God does not and cannot exist. But what led us to conceive of him does exist and is *constantly* experienced and pictured. That is, it is real as an Idea, and is *also* incarnate in knowledge and work and love. This is the true idea of incarnation, and is not something obscure. We *experience* both the reality of perfection and its distance away, and this leads us to place our idea of it outside the world of existent being as something of a different unique and special sort. Such experience of the reality of good ... is a discovery of something independent of us, where that independence is essential. If we read these images aright they are not only enlightening and profound but amount to a statement of a belief which most people unreflectively hold.[37]

But is belief in God rational?

Is belief in justice 'rational'? Is belief in someone we love 'rational'? Is belief that the sun will rise tomorrow 'rational'?[38] Each of these makes a certain kind of sense. Or better, each of them can play a role in our making a certain kind of sense. That is to say, each of them can play a role in our being rational. (Not 'purely' rational, perhaps; but as I tried to make clear in the course of Variations One, there is room for doubt about the very idea of 'pure' reason.) Can belief in God not do the same?

Not, it might be said, if belief in God involves believing *that* all sorts of things are the case which anyone who believes in God must have some inkling are not the case. Consider, for instance, the problem of reconciling belief in God with awareness of the social and psychological needs that are served by that very belief.[39] Consider for that matter the notorious problem of reconciling belief in God with awareness of suffering.[40] Nor, it would seem, can belief in God help us to make any kind of sense if the very concept of God is incoherent. But is it not? For how are we to conceive of God? Not in any determinate way, lest we fall foul of the point that Murdoch was making at the beginning of the quotation above: no being that we can conceive of in any determinate way would be great enough to count as God. On the other hand, unless we can conceive of God in some determinate way, then we surely cannot conceive of God at all.

Obviously I cannot hope to address all of these concerns here. Even so, I do want to comment briefly on the last of them, the concern that the very concept of God is incoherent. This connects further with my decision to talk about belief in God rather than belief that God exists. For, it seems to me, any incoherence in the concept of God is damaging to the latter in a way in which it need not be damaging to the former.

I have in mind the Kantian notion of a regulative principle, a rule directing us to act as if some supposition held, even though that supposition might not be capable of holding. (A regulative ideal is a particular sort of regulative principle: see Variations Two, §11.) It seems to me that we can view belief in God as the embracing of such a rule. Belief in God, on this way of viewing it, consists in acting *as if* God exists. And this need not be compromised by knowledge that there is an incoherence in the very concept of God.[41]

This in turn connects with ideas that I have tried to develop elsewhere and that I shall take the liberty of sketching here. Often, when it is appropriate for us to adopt such a rule, that is to act in accord with a given supposition, our knowing *how* to act in this way is an example of what I take to be ineffable knowledge, that is to say knowledge which does not answer to reality in such a way that it can be put into words. And often, when this is true, it is further true that, if we were to attempt (unsuccessfully, of course) to put the knowledge into words, then what we would do is to give voice to the supposition in question. In this case, which I take to be a case in point, we would say that God exists. Moreover, if we were to attempt to put related ineffable knowledge into words, then we would use related religious language. What this means is that such language, without being an expression of the relevant knowledge, could, in the right contexts, help to identify it. Furthermore it could, in the right contexts, help to celebrate, nurture, proclaim, or even impart it.[42]

The knowledge here, in common with all ineffable knowledge, is practical. It is knowledge how to cope with various situations. It is manifest in the ways in which a person directs his or her life. This relates back to what I said earlier, about belief in God being part of a commitment to making sense. To believe in God is to know how to sustain various hopes, hopes that are in turn needed to sustain that very commitment: the hope, for example, that making sense is always what makes sense. (But to echo a point I made earlier, I do not want to suggest that there is no other way to sustain these hopes. What I am proffering here is not only not an argument for God's existence. It is not even an argument that we should believe in God.) To believe in God is itself to make a certain sense of things.

In general, being able to make a certain sense of things, and thus possessing certain concepts, is a form of ineffable knowledge. (It does not answer to anything: there is no question of 'right' or 'wrong' about the concepts we possess. But it is knowledge. It is knowledge, for instance, of what it is for the concepts to apply, or at least it includes this knowledge.) Moreover, the language that results from attempting to put such knowledge into words is very often of a religious kind.[43] 'Very often' is an important qualifier. I do not claim that attempts to put our ineffable knowledge into words result *only* in such language; nor, for that matter, that such language results *only* from attempts to put our ineffable knowledge into words. It would be a serious depreciation of both ineffability and religion to think that there was complete overlap here. But there is significant overlap, both in the sense that there is overlap that counts for much and in the sense that there is much of it.

In particular, no matter what sense we make of things, we are liable, when trying to put the associated knowledge into words, to treat that sense as if it had been awaiting our discovery, as if it were literally God-given. We are liable to say that *God invests things with sense*. Even if we do say this, however, and even if it is an appropriate thing for us to say (in this context), it by no means follows that the concept of God is coherent. What is required of a concept for exercise of that concept to be apt in attempting (unsuccessfully) to put ineffable knowledge into words is very different from what is required of a concept for exercise of that concept to be apt in attempting (successfully) to put effable knowledge into words. In the former case what is required may be, precisely, incoherence of a sort.

Making play with incoherence of that sort may have just the right resonances and associations for the task in hand.

(There is a related point that is worth noting parenthetically. If what I have been arguing is right, then the following situation may well occur: there may be ineffable knowledge such that the result of attempting to put it into words could with complete indifference be said to be either a particular sentence or its negation. For whatever features of the one sentence allow it to be put to this effect – the images it conjures up, the associations it has, the lines of thought it suggests – negating it may well leave them intact. Thus consider the famous sentence from Wittgenstein's *Tractatus Logico-Philosophicus* that I quoted in Variations Two, §3: 'The world of the happy man is a different one from that of the unhappy man.'[44] Fogelin, commenting sceptically on this sentence, remarks, 'A competing sage might say that the world of the happy man is no different from that of the unhappy man (and this too has a ring of profundity).'[45] But suppose that Wittgenstein's sentence is the result of an attempt to express the inexpressible.[46] Then any unclarity about what makes it better suited to this role than its denial, indeed any intimation that it is no better suited to this role than its denial, need occasion neither suspicion nor surprise. Who knows but that both Wittgenstein's sentence and Fogelin's reversal of it, each in a suitable context, may be apt to achieve the same broad effect? Certainly they have something important and relevant in common which neither shares with, say, 'The world of the happy man is a *funnier* one than that of the unhappy man,' or 'The *brain* of the happy man is a different one from that of the unhappy man.' – It is also worth thinking in this connection about the creative use of contradiction in mystical and religious writing. Examples abound. They can be found in the writings of Plato, the Psalmists, Lao Tze, Nicholas of Cusa, Kierkegaard, and countless others.)

In sum, whatever absurdities and inconsistencies may be built into the concept of God, they cannot impugn its suitability to be used either as part of adopting a regulative principle or as part of attempting to express inexpressible knowledge. And each of these in turn may be a significant creative exercise, keeping alive certain hopes in us, sustaining a commitment in us to making sense. Each of them may reinforce our confidence in the contingencies that enable us to carry on telling our stories. Each of them may reinforce our belief that these contingencies are in some sense necessary, just as the contingencies that enable the earth to carry on spinning on its axis are in some sense necessary: utterly steadfast, utterly to be relied upon.

§9 In this final section I want to draw together the main ideas of this chapter by returning to the question of how they constitute variations on a Kantian theme. In particular I want to show that there is something here corresponding to each of Kant's three postulates of pure practical reason.

Corresponding to the first postulate, the postulate that we are free, there is the Basic Idea itself. Kant's hope and belief that we are free, and that our freedom finds supreme expression in the exercise of reason, are matched by the hope and belief that the exercise of reason is what is of supreme value to us. Our rationality constitutes our most fundamental worth. We can be, we must be, and at some deep level we are, *noble in reason*.

Corresponding to the second postulate, the postulate that we are immortal, there is that aspect of the security of the Basic Idea whereby, come what may, provided only that we can still make moves within the logical space of reasons, then we can still make good moves there: we can still make sense of things. Both in Kant's picture and in the picture that I have been painting there is the hope and there is the belief that we have infinite room in which to manifest our fundamental commitment to being rational. In Kant's picture this room may take the form of an infinite range of times, or it may take some analogous form (see §6 of the previous chapter). In the picture that I have been painting it takes the form of an infinite range of possibilities. We have an unlimited capacity, not just to live by concepts, but, where appropriate, to develop old concepts and to create new ones (see Variations One, §§15–17, and Variations Two, §§2–3). We are *infinite in faculty*.

Corresponding to the third postulate, the postulate that God exists, there is that aspect of the security of the Basic Idea whereby we can always make sense of our own sense-making: that aspect whereby the world is 'a home for rationality'.[47] Kant's hope and belief that there is a being who will effect a suitable alignment of happiness with virtue are matched by the hope and belief that the world is both immune to us and in tune with us, in whatever ways and to whatever extent are necessary for our fundamental nisus towards rationality never to be dislodged (see above, §7). And, as I tried to argue in the previous section, we may be able to afforce this hope and this belief by making suitable play with the concept of God. To quote Murdoch again: 'We tend to feel that ... dissimilar demands and states of mind must somehow connect, there must be a deep connection, it must all somehow make a unified sense; this is a religious craving, God sees it all.'[48] 'God sees it all': God is a *constant companion*.

It is frequently urged nowadays that there is no 'metanarrative'.[49] (Lyotard, in the introduction to *The Postmodern Condition*, defines '*postmodern*' as 'incredulity towards metanarratives'.[50]) What this means, very roughly, is that there is no preordained story about the human condition to which all our own individual stories must be subordinated: things, to that extent, do not make sense.

Perhaps not. But we must hope that there is whatever enables *us* to make sense *of things*. We must hope that there is whatever enables us to carry on telling our own individual stories. And this already requires something like providence.[51] It requires something at least enough like providence for us to be assured that grass will not turn blue overnight, without any explanation, or that eating bread will not all of a sudden become lethal. Does it require God? Not unless we accept the argument from design. Certainly not if we think that the argument from design is outweighed by compelling arguments *against* the existence of God. If we are persuaded that God does not exist, then that is itself one of the things that we have to make sense of. And one of the paradoxes inherent in the distinction between belief in God and belief that God exists is that belief in God may be a crucial prop in helping us to make such sense, that is in helping us to make sense of the fact that God does not exist.[52]

Let us return to our 'infinitude in faculty'. We have an unlimited capacity to become worthy of what happens to us, to use Deleuze's phrase; or to be worthy of happiness, to use Kant's. In §5 of the previous chapter I contrasted these. Latterly I have been arguing in such a way as to highlight what they share. But is it possible that they can in any case be aligned? Does our unlimited capacity include an unlimited capacity to be happy, at some level, with whatever happens to us? Does it include an unlimited capacity to adapt our conative states to our circumstances? Is that what the development and creation of concepts that will enable us to make sense of things fundamentally involve? Deleuze talks of '*amor fati*'.[53] And Kant says:

> It is ... possible, under all want and affliction, to retain one's peace and contentment. We can be sad and yet content, although not through the senses. We can perceive by reason ... that the ruler of the world does nothing that would have no purpose, and may thus have comfort in the evils of life.[54]

Well, yes; but as I emphasized in Variations One, §17, making sense of what happens is not the same as revelling in it. One way of making sense of what happens is making sense of it as an atrocity, the like of which must never be allowed to happen again. To do this is to locate it in the ongoing story of one's own life, acting out that story in such a way that the only continuation from here that makes sense is a continuation in which one strives to ensure that nothing of the like *will* ever be allowed to happen again. Deleuze writes:

> What does it mean ... to will the event? Is it to accept war, wounds, and death when they occur?... If willing the event is, primarily, to release its eternal truth,... this will would reach the point at which war is waged against war, the wound would be the living trace and the scar of all wounds, and death turned on itself would be willed against

all deaths... 'To my inclination for death,' said Bousquet, 'which was a failure of the will, I will substitute a longing for death which would be the apotheosis of the will.' From this inclination to this longing there is, in a certain respect, no change except a change of the will, a sort of leaping in place ... of the whole body which exchanges its organic will for a spiritual will. It wills now not exactly what occurs, but something *in* that which occurs, something yet to come which would be consistent with what occurs... The splendour and magnificence of the event is sense. The event is not what occurs (an accident), it is rather inside what occurs, the purely expressed... [It] is what must be understood, willed, and represented in that which occurs.[55]

There are echoes here of the views of the early Wittgenstein, to which I alluded in Variations Two, §3. Wittgenstein writes:

The sense of the world must lie outside the world.[56] In the world everything is as it is, and everything happens as it does happen: *in* it no value exists – and if it did exist, it would have no value.

If there is any value that does have value, it must lie outside the whole sphere of what happens and is the case. For all that happens and is the case is accidental.

What makes it non-accidental cannot lie *within* the world, since if it did it would itself be accidental...

If the good or bad exercise of the will does alter the world, it can only alter the limits of the world, not the facts...

In short the effect must be that it becomes an altogether different world. It must, so to speak, wax and wane as a whole.

The world of the happy man is a different one from that of the unhappy man.[57]

In arguing that we must hope for the security of the Basic Idea I am not arguing that we must acquiesce in whatever happens then. We must actively and rationally engage with whatever happens. We must make sense of things. It is precisely because there is nothing of greater value to us than this that the hope has the rationale it has. The hope is that it will always be possible for us to make sense of things. But it is up to us to do so. (See §3 above.)

Kant sometimes gives the impression that he advocates acquiescence. In his *Lectures on Ethics* he says:

Renunciation (resignation) in regard to the divine will is our duty. We renounce our own will, and leave things to another, who understands the matter better, and means us well. Hence we have cause to leave it all in God's hands, and let the divine will take control.[58]

But he immediately corrects this impression:

> [That] does not mean that we ought to do nothing, and let God do it all; rather, we should resign to God what does not lie within our power, and do those things of ours which are within our compass. And this is resignation to the divine will.[59]

Later he embellishes this as follows.

> We take faith ... to mean that we should do the best that lies in our power, and this in the hope that God, in His goodness and wisdom, will make up for the frailty of our conduct... This is the faith ... which is associated with resignation. Such faith prescribes nothing [*sc.* to God], but does what duty requires to the best of its ability, and hopes, without defining it, for support; and of such a person one may say that he has an unconditional faith, and that it is practical. So practical faith ... lies in this, that we in no way prescribe anything to God through our will, but resign the matter to His will, and hope that if we have done what lies within our natural capacity, God will repair our frailty and incapacity by means that He knows best.[60]

One thing that I have been trying to accomplish in this final set of variations is a way of making sense of things, including our own yearning to make sense of things, that allows us to say 'Amen' to this sentiment in Kant.

Notes

Introduction

1. On various aspects of making sense of things see [B.] Williams (2002), Chapter 10. See also Gibbard (1990), pp. 6–7, 36–38, and 156 ff.
2. Mackie (1977), p. 15. The phrase 'argument from queerness' first occurs in the title of Chapter 1, §9.
3. Ibid., p. 38.
4. Smith (1994), especially §1.3.
5. See ibid., especially Chapters 5 and 6.
6. Korsgaard (1996a), p. 166.
7. Williams makes this point in [B.] Williams (1972), p. 50.
8. Aristotle (1941d) and Aristotle (1941e), *passim*.
9. In what follows cf. [A.W.] Moore (1999), §IV.
10. [B.] Williams (1995d), pp. 109–110. (I have replaced 'suggests' in the third sentence by 'suggest'.) Cf. [B.] Williams (1972), p. 76.
11. Ansell Pearson (1999), pp. 13–14. For discussion of the phrase 'become those that we are', see Variations Three, note 26.
12. See especially Variations Two, §7.
13. See above, note 10.
14. Cf. Wittgenstein (1974b), Part I, §240.
15. Hollis (1985), p. 1. (I have corrected the misspelling 'opposible'.)
16. For comments on the significance of this result, see Maor (1987), pp. 49–52.
17. Sellars (1963), p. 169. McDowell has been keen to pick up on this idea: see McDowell (1994), pp. 5–13, 70–86, and 180.
18. Cf. Brandom (1994) and Brandom (2000) (the latter a compendium of the former).
19. *A fortiori* there is a question about whether it uniquely has it. The first objection may pose more of a threat, and certainly poses as much of a threat, to other versions of objectivism.
20. Mackie (1977), p. 36.
21. See e.g. Wittgenstein (1978), Parts II and V respectively.
22. Mackie (1977), p. 36.
23. Hume (1978), p. 415.
24. Murdoch (1993), p. 34.
25. See Wittgenstein (1974b), Part I, §124. Marx said, 'The philosophers have only *interpreted* the world...; the point, however, is to change it,': Marx and Engels (1968), 'Theses on Feuerbach', §XI, his emphasis.
26. Lewis (1991), p. 59
27. See e.g. Rotman (1993).

28 See e.g. Plato (1961c), Book IV.
29 The following pointers for where especially to look may be helpful:
   i   *passim*;
   ii Variations Two, §8;
   iii Variations One, §17;
   iv Variations Two, §11, and Variations Three, *passim*;
   v   Variations Two, §7;
   vi Variations One, *passim*, especially §15;
   vii Variations One, *passim*, and Variations Three, §2;
   viii *passim*.
30 More than one reader of an earlier draft of this book urged me to be clearer about what is supposed to be Kant and what is supposed to be me. An impatient response would be that this is precisely to miss the point of the themes and variations format. But that would be too brusque: after all, some uses of this format are more concerned with exploring the themes, others with developing the variations. Even so, the best I can offer without going into absurd and unhelpful detail is the following very rough-and-ready rule: in the three chapters presenting the main themes I take myself to be primarily responsible to what Kant says, and in the three chapters presenting the variations on those themes I take myself to be primarily responsible to the moral and religious issues themselves. I hope that, as the book proceeds, there are enough indicators of incidental shifts of emphasis for this crude guideline not to be worse than useless.

First theme: morality

1 'Enlightenment', 8: 35, his emphasis. '*Sapere aude!*' translates literally as 'Dare to be wise!'
2 *Groundwork*, 4: 414.
3 Wittgenstein (1965), p. 5.
4 Williams famously gives them separate meanings: see especially [B.] Williams (1985), p. 6 and Chapter 10.
5 There is a point of terminology that needs to be registered. I have been treating the phrase 'categorical imperative' as if it could properly be pluralized ('categorical imperatives'). And I shall continue to do so. But Kant himself hardly ever does so, going as far as to insist, in *Groundwork*, 4: 421, that there is 'only a single categorical imperative'. (The few exceptions include: *Groundwork*, 4: 425 and 454; 2nd *Critique*, 5: 41; and *Metaphysics of Morals*, 6: 221. Cf. also 2nd *Critique*, 5: 20–21.) This is because he nearly always reserves the phrase 'categorical imperative' for what I shall later be calling the *fundamental* categorical imperative, that which grounds all the others (see e.g. §4 below). But I hope and believe that this terminological departure from Kant does not represent a distortion of his views. (See further *Groundwork*, 4: 421 – where, having said that there is 'only a single categorical imperative', Kant gives it an alternative name, 'the universal imperative of duty', and suggests that 'all imperatives of duty [in the plural] can be derived from [it] as from their principle.' See also *Metaphysics of Morals*, 6: 221–228.)
6 *Groundwork*, 4: 389.
7 For classic treatments, see Genesis, Chapter XXII, verses 1–18, to which Kant alludes in *Religion*, 6: 87; Plato (1961a), where the main issue is presented especially crisply at 10a; and Kierkegaard (1954), especially the Panegyric on Abraham and Problems I and II.

8 *Groundwork*, 4: 408–409, his emphasis, '*a priori*' italicized by me. This is the passage to which Murdoch refers in the quotation at the head of this chapter: Murdoch (1985), p. 80. The biblical passage to which Kant refers is St Matthew, Chapter XIX, verse 17.
9 2nd *Critique*, 5: 26, '*a priori*' italicized by me. Cf. *Groundwork*, 4: 425.
10 Ibid., 4: 395.
11 Ibid., 4: 396, his emphasis.
12 Ibid., 4: 404. Cf. ibid., ff.; and cf. 1st *Critique*, A807/B835.
13 2nd *Critique*, 5: 36, his emphasis. (I have replaced 'unpracticed' by 'unpractised.')
14 Ibid., 5: 161–162.
15 Ibid., 5: 8, footnote.
16 See e.g. ibid., Part II; and *Metaphysics of Morals*, Part II ('Metaphysical First Principles of the Doctrine of Method'), §§49–52.
17 Not that this is a difficulty only for rationalism: cf. Introduction, note 19. For a marvellous attempt to address it in a decidedly non-rationalist context see Hume (1975), *An Enquiry Concerning the Principles of Morals*, 'A Dialogue'.
18 See especially *Religion*, Parts One and Two. For the concession (i.e. that immorality is inexplicable) see in particular ibid., 6: 43–44. For the explanations (i.e. of immorality's manifestations) see in particular ibid., 6: 33 ff.
19 *Pietism* was an evangelical movement within the German Lutheran Church which originated in the seventeenth century and which dominated Kant's upbringing. It was intended, above all, to revive practical Christianity. It emphasized repentance, Bible study, personal devotion, the priesthood of all believers, and a rigorous and austere morality. For more on Kant's relations to pietism, see Theme Three.
20 *Groundwork*, 4: 417.
21 'Irrational' is not a Kantian label. (I am grateful to Iskra Fileva for emphasizing this point to me.) But the concept of irrationality is a Kantian concept, with a great deal of work to do in Kant's moral philosophy: see e.g. *Groundwork*, 4: 413–414 and *Religion*, 6: 21–22. See also Theme Two, §2, for discussion of how this concept relates to that of freedom, as construed by Kant.
22 Cf. 1st *Critique*, A84–85/B116–117.
23 *Groundwork*, 4: 393–394. Cf. 2nd *Critique*, 5: 21; 3rd *Critique*, 5: 442–443; and *Metaphysics of Morals*, 6: 213–214.
24 *Groundwork*, 4: 397–400.
25 2nd *Critique*, 5: 62–64.
26 He gives many clear applications of the formula, e.g. in ibid., 5: 30, 36–37, and 143, footnote. See also *Opus Postumum*, 21: 16 (=p. 223), where the formula is stated more or less explicitly.
27 Cf. 2nd *Critique*, 5: 37.
28 Cf. [B.] Williams (1993), *passim*.
29 In *Groundwork*, 4: 428, Kant defines a *person* as a rational being (cf. *Metaphysics of Morals*, 6: 223). Elsewhere he uses 'person' in its more idiomatic sense, as synonymous with 'human being' (e.g. 2nd *Critique*, 5: 60, and *Religion*, 6: 80, footnote). See below, Variations Two, §8, for further discussion of some of the problems that arise in this connection.
30 *Groundwork*, 4: 429, his emphasis. See further ibid., 4: 428–431. And cf. 2nd *Critique*, 5: 76–77.
31 See above, note 5.
32 Cf. Nozick (1981), p. 408.
33 It is well exposed in Blackburn (1998), Chapter 8, especially §3.

34 See e.g. *Groundwork*, 4: 444 and 457–458; 2nd *Critique*, 5: 22 ff. and 118; and *Metaphysics of Morals*, 6: 405–408.
35 See e.g. *Groundwork*, 4: 421, footnote. (In §6 we shall come back to the question of what Kant means by a 'maxim'.) Cf. in this paragraph what Allison famously calls Kant's 'Incorporation Thesis': this is a thesis which Allison culls from *Religion*, 6: 23–24, and which he characterizes, in Allison (1996b), p. 109, as 'the view that [conative states] do not of themselves constitute an incentive or sufficient reason to act but do so only insofar as they are "taken up" or "incorporated" into a maxim'. Cf. Allison (1990), pp. 39–41; and see further ibid., *passim*, for extended discussion of the thesis and its significance.
36 Cf. *Groundwork*, 4: 434 and 438.
37 Ibid., 4: 401, footnote, and 421, footnote; and 2nd *Critique*, 5: 19.
38 *Groundwork*, 4: 421, his emphasis. See also ibid., 4: 401–402 and 420–421; and 2nd *Critique*, 5: 19–41. And cf. *Groundwork*, 4: 434 and 438–439.
39 Ibid., 4: 403.
40 Ibid., 4: 423, his emphasis.
41 2nd *Critique*, 5: 65, emphasis removed, '*a priori*' italicized by me.
42 *Groundwork*, 4: 430, footnote.
43 Chesterfield (1973), letter dated 16 October 1747.
44 *Groundwork*, 4: 424.
45 For some remarks in connection with this see *Metaphysics of Morals*, 6: 391–392.
46 Cf. O'Neill (1989c), pp. 86–87.
47 St Mark, Chapter VI, verses 17–25.
48 E.g., *Metaphysics of Morals*, 6: 224.
49 1st *Critique*, A508–515/B536–543 and A669/B697 ff.
50 Ibid., A312–320/B368–377 and A567–571/B596–599.
51 This example is taken from Blackburn (1998), p. 218.
52 This qualm is a focus of Herman (1993c), which relates closely to much of what I shall be arguing in the next chapter. Other related discussions include: Allison (1990), pp. 39–40 and 86 ff.; Beck (1960), pp. 70 ff., 80 ff., and 118 ff.; Herman (1993a), *passim*; McCarty (2002); O'Neill (1989d), especially pp. 150 ff.; Walker (1998), pp. 33 ff.; [T.C.] Williams (1968), Chapter 2; Wood (1970), pp. 44 ff.; and Wood (1999), pp. 51 ff. Cf. also Scanlon (1998), p. 53.
53 *Groundwork*, 4: 421, footnote, his emphasis. Cf. ibid., 4: 401, footnote; 2nd *Critique*, 5: 19; and *Metaphysics of Morals*, 6: 225 and 389. Cf. also the distinction between explanatory reasons and normative reasons to which I referred in §5.
54 *Groundwork*, 4: 434.
55 Cf. [B.] Williams (1985), pp. 61–63.
56 Of the many attempts to do something similar, two that are especially interesting are in Allison (1990), pp. 87 ff., and Korsgaard (1996a), §3.3.5.
57 *Groundwork*, 4: 445, his emphasis, '*a priori*' italicized by me.

First set of variations

1 Cf. [B.] Williams (1985), pp. 140 ff., which provides the principal model for what I have in mind – what Williams famously calls 'thick' ethical concepts.
2 Cf. *Groundwork*, 4: 402, where Kant writes that 'the concept of the action [of being truthful] in itself already contains a law for me'. Cf. also Brandom (1994), pp. 245–249; Brandom (1998), p. 128; Harman (1999), p. 219; Mackie

(1977), Chapter 3, §4; McDowell (1998a), p. 87; and [B.] Williams (1998), p. 569.
3 Cf. Brandom (1994), Chapter 4, where he argues that what logical vocabulary does is to enable people to make explicit various features of the process of offering and asking for reasons. Cf. also in this connection Korsgaard (1996g); and Scanlon (1998), pp. 73–74 and 371–372.
4 Cf. Korsgaard (1996a), p. 134, and Nagel (1986), p. 160. But contrast Korsgaard (1996g), p. 301, which, though undoubtedly at variance with what I say here, may differ more in letter than in spirit.
5 This distinction is related to the distinction that Nagel draws, in Nagel (1970), pp. 90 ff., between 'subjective' reasons and 'objective' reasons. (Cf. Williams (1973c), pp. 260 ff.) But the two distinctions are not aligned.
6 For an excellent discussion of this see [B.] Williams (1995c). See also Bennett (1995), *passim*.
7 Goodman (1979), especially Chapters III and IV.
8 I have slightly and inconsequentially adapted Goodman's own definition: see ibid., p. 74.
9 See [B.] Williams (1981c). See also [B.] Williams (1995b) and [B.] Williams (1995f), pp. 186–194, the latter of which is a response to McDowell (1995). For further contributions to the debate see Hollis (1987), especially Chapter 6, and Millgram (2001).
10 Cf. Crisp (2000).
11 Cf. Scanlon (1998), Chapter 1. (Scanlon's opening sentence in that chapter is: 'I will take the idea of a reason as primitive.')
12 There is a large literature on the nature of reasons. Parts of it that I have found especially helpful and thought-provoking, in addition to those already cited, are: Foot (1978), to which McDowell replies in McDowell (1998a); Lenman (1996); Parfit (1984); Raz (1978); Skorupski (1999b); Smith (1994); Smith *et al.* (1989); and Wiggins (1998).
13 Cf. McDowell's discussion of 'second nature' in McDowell (1994), pp. 84 ff., and McDowell (1998b), *passim*. McDowell in turn rightly indicates an Aristotelian source for these ideas: see especially Aristotle (1941d), Book II. Also very relevant to this discussion is Anscombe (1981a), and Lovibond (2002), especially Chapter 3.
14 Cf. Wittgenstein (1974a), p. 54; and Hacker (1986), Chapter VII, §3.
15 [B.] Williams (1981b), p. 81. Cf. [B.] Williams (1985), pp. 113–114. Cf. also Wittgenstein (1974b), Part I, §289, and Wittgenstein (1969), §612.
16 The work of Peacocke is relevant here: see especially Peacocke (1992). (For an application of Peacocke's ideas to action-guiding concepts, see Wedgwood (2001), especially §5.)
17 It is a distinction that Williams draws in a number of places. See e.g. [B.] Williams (1985), pp. 141–142; [B.] Williams (1986); [B.] Williams (1995f), p. 206; and [B.] Williams (1998), p. 569.
18 Diamond (1991c), pp. 331–332, her emphasis. (The whole of Diamond (1991c) can be seen as an exploration of concept possession in the sense I intend.)
19 Wittgenstein (1978), Part VII, §67. Cf. Wittgenstein (1974b), Part II, §xii.
20 See e.g. Wittgenstein (1974b), Part I, §§19, 23, and 241, and Part II, p. 226.
21 Cavell (1976), p. 52.
22 *Metaphysics of Morals*, 6: 423. Cf. *Groundwork*, 4: 421–422 and 429; and 2nd *Critique*, 5: 44 and 69.
23 *Metaphysics of Morals*, 6: 423–424. The king in question was Frederick the Great.

24 *Groundwork*, 4: 422.
25 For a suggestion that Kant could have been more alive to the complexities of defeasibility see Korsgaard (1996e), pp. 135–137. But see also ibid., pp. 137 ff.
26 Cf. Goodman (1979), Chapter IV, §5, and Brandom (1998), §IV. Cf. also [S.G.] Williams (1989/90).
27 But I yet again disclaim simple exegesis.
28 Cf. Kant's own claim in 2nd *Critique*, 5: 157, that '*principles* must be built on concepts', his emphasis.
29 2nd *Critique*, 5: 30. See also Allison (1990), pp. 40–41, and Walker (1998), pp. 24 ff. And cf. 1st *Critique*, A666/B694 ff., where Kant discusses maxims in a theoretical context.
30 St Matthew, Chapter V, verses 33–37.
31 Hegel (1942), §135, his emphasis.
32 Ibid. See further Hegel (1942), §§105–141, and Hegel (1977), §§596–671. See also Taylor (1975), pp. 370 ff.
33 See Einstein (1960), §I and Appendix V; and Ryckman (1998).
34 1st *Critique*, Introduction; and *Prolegomena*, §§1–5.
35 Cf. various currents of thought in MacIntyre (1988).
36 Lemmon (1965), p. 103.
37 See e.g. *Groundwork*, 4: 411–412, and 2nd *Critique*, Part I, Book II, Chapter II, §III.
38 It is worth recalling in this connection Kant's own (almost uniform) tendency to reserve the phrase 'categorical imperative' for this one fundamental instance: see note 5 of the previous chapter.
39 Cf. Romans, Chapter VII, verse 7. Incidentally, on my reconstruction of Kant, to say that the maxim never to accept a tip could not be a law is to say, in effect, that the concept of a tip does not encompass the practice of never accepting a tip. It was with this in mind that I made the parenthetical remark, in §7 of the previous chapter, that I hoped to be able to bypass certain awkward questions that would otherwise arise about why such a maxim could not be a law.
40 There may be elements of this idea in Hegel's philosophy of history: see e.g. Hegel (1942), §§341 ff. For discussion, see Wood (1990), pp. 234–236; and for a brief counter, see Skorupski (1999a), footnote 40.
41 For excellent discussions of the issues see Mackie (1977), Chapter 3, §1, and [B.] Williams (1985), Chapter 7.
42 Hume (1978), p. 469.
43 Searle (1967), p. 102. He has had more to say about such derivations in Searle (2001): see especially Chapter 6 (much of which relates to my project in this chapter, some of it in accord, some of it not).
44 Searle (1967), pp. 102–103.
45 [R.M.] Hare (1967), p. 126.
46 Mackie (1977), p. 71.
47 Searle (1967), pp. 108–109.
48 Ibid., p. 113, footnote.
49 This is not to say that there are any action-guiding concepts that human beings must possess. Whether there are or not is a question that need not detain us here. In any case, it is a question that cannot be addressed until we have been told more about how strong the 'must' is and about how stringent the criteria of identity for concepts are. In §14 below I shall suggest a sense in which human beings must possess the concept of a *need*. In Variations Two, §8, I shall suggest a sense in which they must possess the concept of a *person*.

Other plausible candidates, on suitable interpretations of the claim, include various concepts relating to trust, such as that of a *lie*. (I am indebted here to Gordon Davis and Bernard Williams.)

50 Respectively, Aristotle (1941d), 1098a, and Aristotle (1941e), 1253a.
51 For some indication of Aristotle's difficulties see Aristotle (1941d), Book X, Chapters 7–8. Many people would regard this inseparability as a very Wittgensteinian motif. See e.g. Wittgenstein (1974b), Part I, §§240–242. Cf. also Davidson (1984), especially the essays in the section entitled 'Radical Interpretation'.
52 Cf. [B.] Williams (1972), pp. 62 ff. For a discussion of Stoic thinking about the roles we play, a discussion that connects at several points with this chapter, see Annas (2001–2).
53 It is what Hare thought: see [R.M.] Hare (1963), Chapter 10, §1.
54 E.g. McDowell (1998c), pp. 200–203, and [B.] Williams (1985), pp. 141–142.
55 Ibid.
56 For a discussion that has an interesting bearing on this section see Anscombe (1981a).
57 Cf. Wittgenstein (1974b), Part II, §xii. For further important reservations about the idea of pure reason see Putnam (1981), *passim*; Sacks (2000), Chapter 4, §4; and Skorupski (1999a), §§3–4. (But note that Skorupski's reservations, which owe much to Hegel, have to do with what pure reason can achieve rather than with the very idea of pure reason.)
58 Cf. Crisp and Slote (1997).
59 Cf. Ricoeur (1992), especially the Seventh Study, where he argues that ethics is concerned with both of these in reciprocal combination.
60 This is a very Nietzschean motif: see especially Nietzsche (1974).
61 See e.g. Plato (1961c), 352d; and cf. Aristotle (1941d), 1103b.
62 As far as questions about what sorts of concepts we are capable of possessing are concerned, I could have added 'the logical'. For there are certain concepts whose joint possession is ruled out on straightforwardly logical grounds. Consider, for instance, the concept of greenness and that of grueness; or the concept of chastity and that of free love.
63 Cf. Deleuze and Guattari (1994), and Diamond (1991b), pp. 312–313. Cf. also Coleridge (1997), Vol. I, Chapter XIII, where he draws his celebrated, and Kant-influenced, distinction between the 'fancy' and the 'imagination'. (I am grateful to Bernard Williams for drawing my attention to the relevance of Coleridge's distinction.) See further Variations Two, §3.
64 Of great relevance to the next three sections is [B.] Williams (2000).
65 Nietzsche (1990), 'Expeditions of an Untimely Man', §5, his emphasis.
66 Anscombe (1981b), pp. 26 and 30, her emphasis, some emphasis removed.
67 MacIntyre (1981).
68 Ibid., p. 1.
69 Ibid.
70 Ibid., p. 2.
71 Austin (1970), p. 185.
72 Ibid., his emphasis, some emphasis removed.
73 In the ethical case, cf. again Jesus on promising: see above, note 30 and accompanying text.
74 In the ethical case, cf. [B.] Williams (1985), pp. 17 and 117. (I say 'conversely', but these may in fact be two variations on a single theme: cf. Turetzky (1998), pp. 200–201.)

75 Lovibond is very insightful on these issues, as indeed she is on many of the issues that we are addressing in this chapter: see Lovibond (1983), *passim*, but especially §§4, 16, 28–32, 37, and 38.
76 Korsgaard (1996a), pp. 76–77, her emphasis.
77 Anscombe (1963), p. 77.
78 The notion of *confidence* is one that Williams uses in a related connection: see [B.] Williams (1985), pp. 170–171.
79 See further Thomson (1987), and Wiggins (1987). And see note 49 above.
80 Hume (1978), pp. 521–522, his emphasis.
81 For discussion of the necessity that has been thought to attach to certain institutional identities, including that of slavery, see [B.] Williams (1993), especially Chapter 5.
82 Cf. note 51 above. And cf. the issues raised by Wittgenstein's so-called 'private language argument' in Wittgenstein (1974b), Part I, §§243–315, an excellent discussion of which is McGinn (1984).
83 For a fuller discussion of these matters, see [A.W.] Moore (1997a), Chapter 8. (I there argue that the knowledge in question is ineffable. For echoes of this idea in Kant see 1st *Critique*, A132–136/B171–175, and especially *Religion*, 6: 137.)
84 Neiman (1994), p. 3.
85 Cf. Hacker (1996), p. 110, where he writes that 'if one had to choose one single fundamental insight from the whole corpus of Wittgenstein's later work, it might well be argued that it should be the insight that philosophy contributes not to human knowledge, but to human understanding'. (Hacker too is talking about knowledge of the latter kind.) For more on the relevance of Wittgenstein to my argument see Wittgenstein (1967), §§357, 358, and 364; Wittgenstein (1974a), §68; Wittgenstein (1974b), Part II, §xii; and Wittgenstein (1978), Part I. See further Hacker (1986), Chapter VII, §2.
86 Cf. Brandom (1979), and McDowell (1994), *passim*. Cf. also Wolf (1990), *passim*, with a different but related emphasis on the importance, for freedom, of susceptibility to constraints of rationality.
87 Cf. Quine (1961), p. 79; and cf. again the passages from Wittgenstein cited above in note 85.
88 Cf. Baker and Hacker (1985), pp. 303–307. Cf. also Wittgenstein (1974b), Part I, §83.
89 Cf. Brandom (1999), p. 169, where he writes, 'To be a self – a locus of conceptual commitment and responsibility – is to be taken or treated as one by those one takes or treats as one: to be recognized by those one recognizes.' Cf. also Korsgaard (1996a), §4.2.
90 Cf. Taylor (1975), pp. 377 ff., taking off from Hegel's criticisms of Kant's moral theory (see above, notes 31 and 32 and accompanying text).
91 Quine (1960), p. 3.
92 [B.] Williams (1985), p. 178. Note: if the suggestion in this paragraph is correct, then it goes some way towards answering the challenge that Williams issues in ibid., p. 63: 'Why should I think of myself as a legislator and ... at the same time a citizen of a republic governed by ... notional laws?' Cf. note 55 of the previous chapter, and accompanying text.
93 See e.g. the sections in *Metaphysics of Morals* on 'rights of persons': 6: 276 ff.
94 See Introduction, §4.
95 Wittgenstein (1974b), Part I, §258.
96 Cf. Gibbard (1990), pp. 6–7, 36–38, and 156 ff.
97 Shakespeare, *Hamlet*, Act II, Scene II, ll. 323–324.

98 Cf. Aristotle (1941d), 1120a, 23.
99 2nd *Critique*, 5: 162, transposed from the first person singular to the first person plural. (I have also taken the liberty of replacing the translator's 'personality' by 'personhood': the German word is '*Persönlichkeit*'.)
100 *Groundwork*, 4: 424, his emphasis. The first two ellipses occur because Kant talks here of 'laws of nature' rather than just 'laws'; but for our purposes this is an inessential difference based on a variant formulation of the fundamental categorical imperative that he gives (ibid., 4: 421). The two kinds of duty belong to a semi-scholastic taxonomy that Kant develops elsewhere (see especially *Metaphysic of Morals*, 6: 390–391).
101 Cf. Wittgenstein (1978), Part VI, §49. Cf. also McDowell (1993), pp. 282 ff.
102 See e.g. Nagel (1997), pp. 55 ff.
103 *Groundwork*, 4: 421–422; cf. ibid., 4: 402–403. But see Nell (1975), pp. 62–83, and Korsgaard (1996d). See also Wood (1999), pp. 87 ff.
104 *Groundwork*, 4: 403, transposed from the first person to the third person.
105 Cf. Walker (1998), p. 35, and Wood (1999), pp. 88–89. Cf. also the brief discussion of tipping in Theme One, §7.
106 Elford (2000), p. 4.
107 Holloway (1999), *passim*.
108 See above, note 65 and accompanying text.
109 For effective rebuttal of this claim see further Elford (2000), especially Chapters 4 and 5.
110 Holloway (1999), p. 34.
111 Ansell Pearson (1999), p. 14.
112 Cf. McDowell's discussion of the shaping of our 'second nature' by our 'first nature', in McDowell (1998b), pp. 190–191 and 193. Cf. also Lovibond (2002), especially Chapter 3, and more especially pp. 56–57.
113 Cf. again the passage from Diamond (1991c) cited above: see note 18 and accompanying text.
114 Locke (1965), p. 291.
115 Gödel (1967).
116 Peacocke (1993), p. 184.
117 Cf. Diamond (1991a). I try to develop this view in [A.W.] Moore (1998).
118 Nietzsche (1969), Part Two, 'Of Redemption'.
119 Nietzsche (1969), and Nietzsche (1974), in each case *passim*.
120 Deleuze (1969), p. 149: this is the source of the quotation at the head of this chapter.
121 Nietzsche (1967b), 'Why I Am So Wise', §6.
122 Deleuze (1969), pp. 72–73. For a helpful account of Deleuze's ethics, with significant resonances in what is to come, see Buchanan (2000), Chapter 3.
123 Turetzky (1998), pp. 211 and 245, note 1.
124 Spinoza (1959), Part III, Definition. II. See further Spinoza (1959), *passim*, but especially Parts III and IV.
125 See Lloyd (1996), especially Chapter 3.
126 [B.] Williams (1985), p. 57, his emphasis.
127 Voltaire (1990).
128 See Deleuze (1969), p. 149.
129 Camus (1971), p. 11.
130 I have unfortunately been unable to trace the source of this quotation.
131 *Religion*, 6: 24–25, footnote, his emphasis. For the importance of joy in Spinoza (i.e. what Spinoza calls '*laetitia*'), see Spinoza (1959), Parts III and IV, *passim*; see also Lloyd (1996), pp. 83–97. For the importance of joy in

Nietzsche, see Nietzsche (1969), Part IV, 'The Intoxicated Song', §§11–12. For some remarks by Kant in opposition to Spinoza, see 3rd *Critique*, 5: 452–453 (we shall return to this passage in Theme Three: see note 59 of that chapter, and accompanying text).
132 3rd *Critique*, 5: 294.
133 Ibid., 5: 295.
134 Ibid., 5: 179.
135 Ibid., 5: 307–308, his emphasis.
136 See e.g. ibid., §61.
137 Ibid., Part I, *passim*.
138 'Enlightenment', 8: 37–38.
139 Ibid., 8: 39.

Second theme: freedom

1 Cf. also in this connection [B.] Williams (1981a), pp. 20–21, footnote 1; and Wolf (1990), pp. 62–66.
2 Tertullian (1942), Chapter 5.
3 Cf. [S.G.] Williams (1989/90). And cf. Davidson's account of weakness of the will in Davidson (1980a). For a general discussion of these and related matters, see Pears (1984).
4 Davidson (1980b), p. 221. (Davidson has 'consistency' where I have inserted 'rationality', but I think I have preserved the essence of his view.) See further Davidson (1980c) and Davidson (2001), pp. 124–125.
5 See Introduction, §4.
6 Cf. Variations One, §15. And see Wolf (1990) for a sustained development of a conception of freedom along these lines.
7 E.g. 2nd *Critique*, Part One, Book One, Chapter I, Problem I and Remark.
8 E.g. *Groundwork*, 4: 461.
9 2nd *Critique*, 5: 4, footnote, his emphasis, some emphasis removed. Cf. 3rd *Critique*, §76; and *Religion*, 6: 49, footnote.
10 Cf. what Allison calls 'the Reciprocity Thesis' in Allison (1990), *passim*, especially Chapter 11. For a further clear indication of the connection in Kant see, in 2nd *Critique*, alongside Problem I mentioned in note 7 above, Problem II and the discussion of it.
11 *Groundwork*, 4: 412. Cf. Aristotle (1941c), Book IX, Chapter 5.
12 *Groundwork*, 4: 446–447. Cf. Brandom (1999), e.g. pp. 170–171. And for a discussion that bears importantly if indirectly on the two kinds of causality being mooted here, see Davidson (1980b).
13 *Groundwork*, 4: 448.
14 E.g. 1st *Critique*, A538–541/B566–569, and §II, Chapter II, §I ('On the Ultimate End of the Pure Use of Our Reason'); *Groundwork*, Chapter III, *passim*; 2nd *Critique*, Introduction, and 5: 29–30; *Metaphysics of Morals*, 6: 405–408; and the passage from the letter to Reinhold quoted by Allison in Allison (1990), p. 133, = 6: 226. Cf. in this connection that familiar phrase 'Whose service is perfect freedom', which occurs in the second collect for Matins in *The Book of Common Prayer*.
15 See Theme One, notes 33 and 34 and accompanying text.
16 *Groundwork*, 4: 448.
17 Ibid., some emphasis removed.

18 2nd *Critique*, 5: 32. Cf. also 3rd *Critique*, 5: 448–449, footnote; and *Religion*, 6: 22, footnote.
19 See e.g. Allison (1990), Chapter 7, §I, and Silber (1960), §III.
20 *Metaphysics of Morals*, 6: 213, his emphasis. (I have taken the liberty of leaving '*Wille*' and '*Willkür*' untranslated.) Cf. also ibid., 6: 225–226, and *Religion*, 6: 26 ff.
21 Allison (1990), p. 129.
22 *Groundwork*, 4: 421, footnote. Cf. *Religion*, 6: 23–24.
23 2nd *Critique*, 5: 22, and *Religion*, Part One, §III.
24 *Groundwork*, 4: 449. Cf. ibid., 4: 453–454, 2nd *Critique*, 5: 32–33, and *Religion* 6: 36.
25 For helpful pithy summaries of Kant's views on these matters, and indeed of some of the other aspects of his theory of freedom which we shall consider in this chapter, see Beck (1960), Chapter XI, especially §§2 and 11; Schneewind (1992), §§VIII and IX; and Sullivan (1994), Chapter 10. For more sustained discussions see the material in the bibliography at the end of the chapter. For a very helpful and concise placing of Kant's theory of freedom within the context of his moral philosophy see Thomson (2000), Chapter 8.
26 1st *Critique*, §I, Part Two, Division One, Book II, Chapter II, §III.3.B ('the Second Analogy'). Cf. *Prolegomena*, Part II, *passim*.
27 NB. There is no single standard usage for the label 'libertarianism'. Not all writers mean by it the doctrine that we are free. Some mean by it the joint doctrine that we are free *and* that determinism is incompatible with our freedom; others again, the doctrine that determinism is incompatible with our freedom and false.
28 2nd *Critique*, 5: 95.
29 See e.g. Hume (1975), *An Enquiry Concerning Human Understanding*, §VIII. Cf. Dennett (1984) and [P.F.] Strawson (1974).
30 Quine (1990b), pp. 69–70.
31 Hume (1975), *An Enquiry Concerning Human Understanding*, p. 95, emphasis removed. But note: Hume's 'will' here is much closer to Kant's '*Willkür*' than to his '*Wille*'; the comparison is less striking than it first appears.
32 2nd *Critique*, 5: 96–97, his emphasis. Note: for a freer but somewhat more accessible translation of this passage – as of many other passages in 2nd *Critique* – see Beck (1956).
33 Quine (1990b), p. 70.
34 1st *Critique*, §I, Part Two, Division Two, Book II, Chapter II, §IX.III ('Resolution of the Cosmological Idea of the Totality in the Derivation of Occurrences in the World from their Causes'); and *Groundwork*, 4: 455 ff.
35 For a related conception, which adumbrates some of what is to come, see Nagel (1986), Chapter VII. Cf. also Bok (1998); Cockburn (1997), Chapter 9; Ricoeur (1966); and O'Shaugnessy (1980). (For discussion of Kant's influence on Ricoeur, see Anderson (1993).) That it would also be appropriate in this connection to re-cite [P.F.] Strawson (1974), cited above in note 29, serves to emphasize that the line between absolute compatibilism and relativistic compatibilism is sometimes very fine.
36 *Groundwork*, 4: 448, transposed from the third person to the second person.
37 See above, note 11 and accompanying text.
38 2nd *Critique*, 5: 48. Cf. 1st *Critique*, A550/B578.
39 2nd *Critique*, 5: 49–50.
40 See again *Groundwork*, 4: 446–447.
41 This picture helps to explain why Kant believes that there is but one faculty of reason at work in both theoretical reasoning and practical reasoning: see e.g.

Groundwork, 4: 391. For further discussion of this issue, see Beck (1960), Chapter IV, §4; Neiman (1994); and O'Neill (1989b).
42 [A.W.] Moore (1997a), pp. 261–269 *passim*. For uses of the label or its cognates in Kant himself see 1st *Critique*, A307/B364, and *Groundwork*, 4: 432.
43 [A.W.] Moore (1997a), especially Chapters 1 and 4. Note: even if Kant could be made to agree that one of these ways of making sense of things was from no point of view at all, he would certainly then disagree about which one it was. See further ibid., Chapter 6, §§1 and 2; and see further below, note 52 and accompanying text.
44 *Groundwork*, 4: 459.
45 Ibid., 4: 455–456.
46 2nd *Critique*, 5: 4.
47 Ibid., 5: 30, my emphasis. (See also Theme One, note 26 and accompanying text.) The discussion preceding this sentence gives a very graphic illustration of Kant's point to which I shall return in §4 of the next chapter.
48 2nd *Critique*, 5: 103, and 3rd *Critique*, 5: 195. This is related to what Kant calls, in 2nd *Critique*, 5: 31, 'the sole fact of pure reason': see further §9 of the next chapter.
49 Cf. 2nd *Critique*, Part I, Book II, Chapter II, §§VII and VIII.
50 Cf. *Groundwork*, 4: 456 and 459. Cf. also 1st *Critique*, A557–558/B585–586.
51 *Groundwork*, 4: 450–452, his emphasis. (I have taken the liberty of replacing the translator's 'standpoints' by 'points of view', in line with the translation in Paton (1964): the German word is '*Standpunkte*'. Note: Paton (1964) stands in the same sort of relation to *Groundwork* as does Beck (1956) to 2nd *Critique* (see above, note 32).) For my insertion of 'concepts of reason' in place of the original 'ideas' see 1st *Critique*, A320/B377.
52 This is why I said in note 43 that, if Kant could be persuaded that either way of making sense of ourselves was from no point of view, then it would be the one in terms of the logical space of reasons.
53 1st *Critique*, §I, Part Two, Division One, Book I, Chapter II.
54 Beck (1956), 5: 46. (In 2nd *Critique*, which is the translation that I have used in every other citation, this is rendered as 'one cannot hope to get on so well': the German is '*darf man nicht so gut fortzukommen hoffen*'.)
55 1st *Critique*, A444/B472 ff.
56 Cf. 2nd *Critique*, 5: 55 ff.
57 1st *Critique*, Bxxvi and B146.
58 2nd *Critique*, 5: 55. Cf. ibid., 5: 48 ff., and *Groundwork*, 4: 458–459. Cf. also 2nd *Critique*, 5: 141, where he goes as far as to suggest that this vindication of our faith in our own freedom is the main benefit of the hard work in the Transcendental Deduction. And in connection with the overall project, cf. 1st *Critique*, Bxxx, where he says that he 'had to deny *knowledge* in order to make room for *faith*', his emphasis.
59 *Groundwork*, 4: 463, his emphasis. (This is the very last sentence of *Groundwork*.)
60 Cf. 1st *Critique*, A251.
61 Cf. ibid., A539–541/B567–569.
62 2nd *Critique*, 5: 123. Cf. *Religion*, 6: 24–25 and 36.
63 *Religion*, 6: 25. (I have taken the liberty of replacing the translator's 'first' by 'ultimate'. This is in line with Greene and Hudson (1960): the German word is '*erste*'.) See further ibid., *passim*, but especially Part One and Part Two, §I. See also Allison (1990), Chapter 7, §II, and Silber (1960), §III.vi.

64 *Groundwork*, 4: 458, transposed from the third person to the first person.
65 Cf. Herman (1993b), especially pp. 11–17.
66 But see again Theme One, notes 33 and 34 and accompanying text.
67 2nd *Critique*, 5: 98. It is interesting to compare this with the views of Chrysippus: see Cicero (1991), §§39–44.
68 Walker (1989), p. 65, his emphasis. The passage from Plato to which Walker refers is Plato (1961c), 617d–621d.
69 Cf. Descartes (1984), 7: 69–70.
70 1st *Critique*, A79/B105 ff.
71 Ibid., A320/B377. Cf. ibid., A408–409/B435.
72 Ibid., A642/B670. Cf. ibid., A295–298/B351–B355.
73 Ibid., A409/B436.
74 Ibid., A497/B525 ff., and 2nd *Critique*, 5: 107–108.
75 1st *Critique*, A503–505/B531–533. Cf. the discussion of the concept of the infinite in Theme One, §6.
76 Ibid., A468/B496.
77 2nd *Critique*, 5: 108.
78 For example, ibid., 5: 30 and 49, from the latter of which the phrase 'objective and undoubted reality' is taken. Cf. above, note 48 and accompanying text.
79 For an extended discussion of the idea of freedom as a deep illusion see Smilansky (2000). And for further material pertaining to this first difficulty see Theme Three, §7.
80 Cf. in this connection 3rd *Critique*, 5: 195–196, footnote.
81 Cf. Lear (1984), p. 137, and [B.] Williams (1985), p. 69. See further 'the second way' in §10 of the next chapter.
82 *Religion*, 6: 43. For a Pauline attempt to grapple with the same mystery see Romans, Chapter VII, verses 7–25. For comments by Kant on this passage see *Religion*, 6: 29 ff.
83 1st *Critique*, A551/B579, footnote.
84 Ibid., A554–555/B582–583. Cf. 2nd *Critique*, 5: 97–98.

Second set of variations

1 There is an old joke that helps to illustrate Kant's extraordinary ambitions here. Two people are in bitter dispute with each other about whether some proposed course of action can be justified. They consult a sage. To the one who says that the course of action can be justified the sage says, 'You are right.' To the one who says that it cannot be justified the sage says, 'You are right.' A bystander protests, 'But they can't both be right: their views are incompatible.' Turning to the bystander, the sage says, 'And you are right too.'
2 I have been helped in what follows by discussions with Thomas Startup.
3 'A Discovery', 8: 251, translation adapted by Langton (see Langton (1998), p. 1). Cf. 1st *Critique*, A314/B370, where he writes, 'It is not at all unusual to find that we understand [an author] even better than he understood himself, since he may not have determined his concept sufficiently and hence sometimes spoke, or even thought, contrary to his own intention.'
4 1st *Critique*, A547/B575, his emphasis.
5 2nd *Critique*, 5: 94.
6 Ibid., 5: 97. See further ibid., 5: 94–103. See also 1st *Critique*, Bxxvii–xxix, A549–550/B577–578, and A552–553/B580–581; and *Opus Postumum*, 21: 16 (=p. 223).

7 This is a summary allusion to a huge debate that I cannot properly enter into here. For a small sample of contributions to this debate see, in addition to the material cited in Theme Two, notes 29 and 35: Berofsky (1966); Honderich (1988); Honderich (1978); Klein (1990); Searle (2001), Chapter 9; [G.] Strawson (1986); van Inwagen (1983); Watson (1982); and [B.] Williams (1995a). For a brief discussion of these issues specifically in relation to Kant, see Korsgaard (1996a), pp. 94–95. For a very insightful discussion of what may well be the most serious threat to our freedom, see Cockburn (1997), pp. 239 ff.

8 For further development of this picture see [A.W.] Moore (1990). Cf. Romans, Chapter VII, verses 14–25; Adams (1985); Nagel (1979a), pp. 32–33; Schlossberger (1986); Skorupski (1999a); and Sher (2001). For hints of the picture in Kant himself see *Metaphysics of Morals*, 6: 405–408. The suggestion that succumbing to temptation means losing control of oneself is famously ridiculed by Austin in Austin (1970), p. 198, footnote. Contrasting views can also be found in Aristotle (1941d), Book II, Chapter 5; Book III, Chapters 1 and 5; and Book VII, Chapters 3 and 4. A striking quotation in connection with these issues is Winston's famous diary entry in Orwell (1987), p. 84: 'Freedom is the freedom to say that two plus two make four. If that is granted, all else follows.'

9 For a small sample of the feminist recoil from this kind of picture see Gatens (1991); Irigaray (1977); Irigaray (1993); and Lloyd (1984). Cf. also Anzaldúa (1987), which, on p. 49, includes the following provocative passage:

> Why does she have to go and try to make 'sense' of it all? Every time she makes 'sense' of something, she has to 'cross over,' kicking a hole out of the old boundaries of the self and slipping under or over, dragging the old skin along, stumbling over it. It hampers her movement in the new territory, dragging the ghost of the past with her.

10 Cf. Deleuze (1969), pp. 132–133; Nietzsche (1974), p. 38; Smilansky (2000), Chapter 7; [B.] Williams (1993), pp. 66–68; and Wittgenstein (1974b), Part I, §§90 ff.
11 Cf. [P.F.] Strawson (1974).
12 Cf. [B.] Williams (1985), p. 194.
13 Cf. various currents of thought in Ryle (1949), Chapter III.
14 For example, *Groundwork*, 4: 448 ff.
15 Cf. again that familiar phrase 'Whose service is perfect freedom', quoted in Theme Two, note 14.
16 The Radical Picture, along with much else that I defend in this enquiry, has clear echoes in Stoic thought. See e.g. Epictetus (1916), Book I, Chapters 1–2, and Book IV, Chapter 1.
17 *Groundwork*, 4: 463.
18 See again the passage from 2nd *Critique*, 5: 96–97, quoted in Theme Two, §3, where Kant says:

> Some ... let themselves be put off by this [wretched] subterfuge [sc. (Humean) compatibilism] and so think they have solved, with a little quibbling about words, that difficult problem on the solution of which millennia have worked in vain and which can therefore hardly be found so completely on the surface.

19 See again note 7 above: I make no pretence that these dogmatic assertions

contribute to this huge debate into which, as I have said, I cannot properly enter here. For something less dogmatic see the next section.
20 This is related to Gödel's theorem, discussed in Variations Two, §17: see further [A.W.] Moore (2001), pp. 172–176.
21 It is worth noting, however, that the antecedent to this conditional – 'if the solution to the problem is s' – is less innocuous than it looks. Since the hypothesis in question is mathematical, its use to speculate about possible future outcomes in this way hides some extremely deep questions in the philosophy of mathematics about whether mathematics is a matter of 'creation' or 'discovery'. See Wittgenstein (1978), *passim*. Cf. also Wittgenstein (1974b), Part I, §§352 and 578; and cf. the discussion in the next section.
22 Cf. Quine (1990a). And cf. again the material cited in Variations One, note 63 (where, among other things, I referred to Coleridge's distinction between the 'fancy' and the 'imagination').
23 This echoes ideas in Bergson and Deleuze. See e.g. Bergson (1975) and Deleuze (1994). See further Turetzky (1998), Chapters XIII and XIV.
24 Consider e.g. the use of ordinal numbers to prove Goodstein's theorem: see Henle (1986), pp. 45–48, 91–93, and 137–139, and Isaacson (1996). But consider also in this connection Wittgenstein's important dictum, 'One can often say in mathematics: let the proof teach you *what* was being proved': Wittgenstein (1974b), p. 220, his emphasis.
25 See e.g. ibid., Part I, §67.
26 This is a context-specific point. Disputes about such matters *can* be very deep: see above, note 21, and see again the material cited in note 23.
27 See again Quine (1990a).
28 Cantor (1955).
29 In distinguishing between 'sense' and 'meaning' here I am presupposing a notion of sense which is broadly Fregean and a notion of meaning which includes what Dummett, on behalf of Frege, calls 'tone' (where tone is precisely what distinguishes swear words from their non-taboo synonyms): see Frege (1967), pp. 22–23, and Dummett (1980), Chapter 1.
30 Once again I am gliding over an area of fierce philosophical debate. I try to say more about these issues in [A.W.] Moore (1997a), Chapter 3. For further contributions to the debate see Jackson (1986), Lewis (1990), and Nemirow (1990). I am also reminded of how, on one reading of Quine's views about indeterminacy – see e.g. Quine (1960), Chapter II – Quine combines the most extreme physicalism with the view that physical facts leave certain matters unresolved, in other words that there are more refined ways of slicing the possibilities than physics affords: see further [A.W.] Moore (1997b).
31 2nd *Critique*, 5: 43, his emphasis.
32 Spinoza (1959), Part III, Definition II.
33 Lloyd (1996), p. 85.
34 Wittgenstein (1961).
35 Ibid., 1.
36 Ibid., 6.43. See further 6.4 ff., and cf. Wittgenstein (1979), pp. 76–89. And for further discussion of relations between Kant and the early Wittgenstein see [A.W.] Moore (1987). Note that Wittgenstein himself denies that it properly makes sense to say these things: see Wittgenstein (1961), 6.54. For further discussion of some of the issues that this raises, see Variations Three, §§8–9.
37 2nd *Critique*, 5: 30.
38 Cf. McDowell (1998a).
39 This is a significant point of continuity between his earlier work and his later

work: see e.g. respectively Wittgenstein (1961), 4.003, and Wittgenstein (1974b), Part I, §38.
40 Wittgenstein (1974b), Part I, §111, his emphasis.
41 Hacker (1996), p. 112. Cf. Russell's comment in Russell (1975), p. 330:

> [Wittgenstein] used to come to see me every evening at midnight, and pace up and down my room like a wild beast for three hours in agitated silence. Once I said to him: 'Are you thinking about logic or about your sins?' 'Both,' he replied, and continued his pacing.

42 Wittgenstein (1978), Part II, §22.
43 Cf. what I call in [A.W.] Moore (1997a) our craving for infinitude: see especially Chapter 11, §6. Cf. also Lear (1988), Chapter 1.
44 Aristotle (1941d), 1095a30–b13, and Book I, Chapter 7, *passim*. See further Lear (1988), p. 193; and Nussbaum (2001), especially Chapter 8.
45 Aristotle (1941d), Book II, *passim*. For Kant's views on education and upbringing see again the material cited in Theme One, note 16 – though see also, for a hint of something more Aristotelian, *Lectures on Ethics*, 27: 1429–1430 (=pp. 72–73).
46 See in this connection *Religion*, Part One, §I.
47 Cf. Wood (1999), pp. 121–122.
48 Cf. Korsgaard (1996a), §4.4.
49 Compare what I say in this section with currents of thought in Wiggins (1995) and Wiggins (1998).
50 *Groundwork*, 4: 393, his emphasis.
51 3rd *Critique*, 5: 442–443, his emphasis. Cf. *Groundwork*, 4: 393 ff. and 428–429; and 2nd *Critique*, 5: 60 ff.
52 2nd *Critique*, 5: 86–87, first emphasis his, second emphasis mine.
53 This is an allusion to Wittgenstein (1974b), Part I, §217.
54 Wittgenstein (1974b), Part II, §iv. Cf. Blackburn (1998), p. 320, where he says that 'the verdict that a person's behaviour does or does not make sense ... expresses an attitude'. (Note, however, that Blackburn goes on to make claims that are in conflict with what I am saying. This is because he accepts a narrower conception of rationality than I do.)
55 See again Theme One, note 29.
56 For pertinent discussions see Korsgaard (1996a), §4.4, and Wood (1998), pp. 98–199.
57 Cf. again the material cited in Variations One, note 89. And see again Variations One, note 49. I try to develop some of the connections that I am tracing here between the concept of a person and the point of view of a person in [A.W.] Moore (1997a), especially Chapters 10 and 11. Cf. in this connection Korsgaard (1996a), p. 124.
58 Korsgaard (1996a), p. 166.
59 Cf. Wiggins (1995).
60 See 3rd *Critique*, §42.
61 For a fascinating exchange on some of Kant's views about various non-rational parts of creation, and particularly about non-human animals, see Wood (1998) and O'Neill (1998).
62 This question is not entirely rhetorical. See e.g., in relation to Kant, Haezrahi (1969) and Wood (1999), Chapter 4. See also, at a more general level, Gaita (2000). For scepticism, not about whether people have a special value, but about whether the concept of a person is robust enough to serve as a 'founda-

tion for ethical thought', as these reflections seem to suggest, see [B.] Williams (1985), p. 114. (Note, however, that Williams is talking about a scalar concept of a person. His use of 'person' is less like my use of 'person' than like my use of 'normally functioning, fully developed person'.)
63 2nd *Critique*, 5: 47.
64 *Groundwork*, 4: 460, his emphasis. (I have corrected the misspelling 'fulfillment'.) It is very interesting to compare this with Wittgenstein (1961), 6.422.
65 *Groundwork*, 4: 460.
66 Ibid., 4: 461, his emphasis.
67 Ibid., 4: 401, footnote, transposed from the first person singular to the first person plural.
68 Ibid., 4: 400 ff.; and 2nd *Critique*, Part One, Book One, Chapter III. See further Allison (1990), Chapter 6; Beck (1960), Chapter XII; and Reath (1989).
69 2nd *Critique*, 5: 72.
70 Ibid., 5: 76, my emphasis.
71 Ibid., 5: 31, '*a priori*' italicized by me.
72 See e.g. ibid., 5: 6, 42, 43, 55, and 104. Also very significant is 3rd *Critique*, 5: 468.
73 See further [A.W.] Moore (1997a), Chapter 8, §1. See also Stanley and Williamson (2001) – though, unlike me, they assimilate all 'knowledge how' to 'knowledge that'.
74 For further discussion of this second idea see Allison (1990), Chapter 13; Beck (1960), Chapter X; and O'Neill (1989b), especially the very brief appendix on pp. 64–65, which, though it calls into question the suggestion that Kant takes the fact of reason to be a datum, is less in conflict with my gloss than it appears to be. The knowledge in question here seems to me to be a prime example of what I have elsewhere argued to be ineffable knowledge: see [A.W.] Moore (1997a), especially Chapters 8 and 11 (and see again Variations One, note 83, for related Kantian references). For further discussion of ineffable knowledge see Variations Three, §8. And for opposition, see again Stanley and Williamson (2001), cited in the previous note.
75 Compare the discussion in this section with that of §3 of the Introduction.
76 Cf. in this connection 2nd *Critique*, 5: 160–161. Cf. also Dostoyevsky (1958), Part Two, Book Five, Chapter 5 ('The Grand Inquisitor'), e.g. p. 298, where the inquisitor says, 'Man has no more agonizing anxiety than to find someone to whom he can hand over with all speed the gift of freedom with which the unhappy creature is born.' And cf. finally Sartre's famous cry that 'I am condemned to be free,' in Sartre (1957), p. 439.
77 For example, *Groundwork*, 4: 451–452. For Aristotle's views see Aristotle (1941a), Chapters 1 and 5; and cf. Aristotle (1941d), 1097b23–1098a19.
78 *Groundwork*, 4: 461, my emphasis.
79 Ibid., his emphasis. See further ibid., 4: 461–463; and cf. [B.] Williams (1985), p. 64.
80 Spinoza thinks there is, at least on one plausible interpretation: see Spinoza (1959), Part III, Props VI and VII. But his proof of this does not take him any deeper in the order of explanation than I am claiming we can go: see ibid., pp. 83–91.
81 See [A.W.] Moore (1999), §VI. See also Watt (1975).
82 [B.] Williams (1985), pp. 55–56.
83 Korsgaard (1996a), §§3.4.9–3.4.10.
84 Concerning the possibility that we cannot coherently deny it, cf. again Wittgenstein (1974b), Part II, §iv; and Wittgenstein (1969), §§341–344.

85 Cf. [B.] Williams (1995f), the sentence straddling pp. 186–187. What I am saying here is also relevant, I think, to Williams' claim in ibid., p. 220, footnote 3, that 'it best preserves the point of the internalism/externalism distinction [i.e. the distinction between the view that normative reasons *are* suitably grounded in conative states and the view that they are not] to see [Kant's view] as a limiting case of internalism'. Cf. Korsgaard (1996a), §3.1.1.
86 For a fuller discussion of these matters, with important qualifications, see [A.W.] Moore (1999), especially §V. As I intimate in the penultimate sentence of that piece, to the extent that I think that what I call 'conative transcendental arguments' are worth pursuing in connection with the Basic Idea, then it is with a view to deriving other propositions from it (or from some variation on it), not with a view to deriving it from other propositions.
87 *Groundwork*, 4: 395, his emphasis.
88 This is an allusion to St John, Chapter XV, verse 13. (Of course, as Bernard Williams has reminded me, there is the familiar reductivist point that, if his 'friends' were sufficiently closely related to him, and if there were sufficiently many of them, then laying down his life for them would in fact be another good way of passing on his genes. But the point in the main text would hold even if we stipulated that his friends did not satisfy these conditions.)
89 Nagel (1986), p. 230.
90 Paton (1964), 4: 396. (In *Groundwork*, which is the translation that I have used in every other citation, this is rendered as 'true vocation': the German is '*wahre Bestimmung*'. Another interesting and related use of '*Bestimmung*' in Kant is in his *Religion Innerhalb der Grenzen der Bloßen Vernunft*, 6: 26, where we find the phrase '*Bestimmung des Menschen*'. This is rendered in *Religion* as 'determination of the human being', and in Greene and Hudson (1960) as 'fixed character and destiny of man'.)
91 3rd *Critique*, Part Two ('Critique of the Teleological Power of Judgment').
92 E.g. ibid., §§66–68.
93 [B.] Williams (1995d), pp. 109–110.
94 Ibid.
95 How can it *not* be intended to do that, if these ideas are to have any real content? I hope that Variations Three will go some way towards addressing this question. (But I should perhaps add that keeping my distance from Aristotle is not one of my highest priorities.) See in this connection Nussbaum (1995), to which Williams replies in [B.] Williams (1995f), pp. 194–202.
96 Nietzsche (1967a).
97 [B.] Williams (2002), especially Chapter 2.
98 Nietzsche (1967a).
99 Hume (1978), Book III, Part II, §II.
100 Craig (1990).
101 [B.] Williams (2002).
102 In fact, I do this in [A.W.] Moore (1997a): see especially pp. 210 and 254.
103 Contrast ibid., p. 224. 'We', there, are people who have been corrupted in a certain way: see further ibid., pp. 274–276.
104 1st *Critique*, A508–515/B536–543 and A669/B697 ff.
105 Cf. ibid., A568–569/B596–597. An example of a regulative principle that is not a regulative ideal is the principle 'never to assume anything empirical as unconditioned': see ibid., A616–617/B644–645. (This is an opportunity for me to correct the definition of 'regulative principle' that I give in [A.W.] Moore (1997a), p. 249. I there define the term in such a way as effectively to preclude regulative principles that are not regulative ideals.)

Third theme: religion

1 See Theme One, note 19. I do not say that he retained a pietistic understanding of that outlook. Much in this chapter will reveal that he did not – a further indication of the ambivalence.
2 'Immortality' is the standard translation of '*Unsterblichkeit*'. For many, 'eternal life' might have a more appropriate ring.
3 But see below, note 98 and accompanying text.
4 *Religion*, 6: 3. See above, note 1: this was a very non-pietistic understanding of the relation between religion and morality.
5 Ibid., 6: 6 and 6: 5.
6 Ibid., 6: 5.
7 Ibid., 6: 116.
8 Ibid., 6: 191. See further below, §6.
9 2nd *Critique*, 5: 147–148, his emphasis, some emphasis removed.
10 *Religion*, 6: 153–154. See also the accompanying footnote. And cf. 2nd *Critique*, 5: 129; 3rd *Critique*, 5: 481; and *Opus Postumum*, pp. 200–256, *passim*.
11 *Religion*, 6: 160, my emphasis, some emphasis removed. Cf. 2nd *Critique*, 5: 83. The biblical passage to which Kant refers is St Mark, Chapter XII, verses 29–31.
12 1st *Critique*, A819/B847.
13 Cf. ibid., A771/B799.
14 Cf. 2nd *Critique*, 5: 129. Cf. also Palmquist (1992), p. 139.
15 *Opus Postumum*, 22: 130 (=p. 209).
16 Michalson (1999).
17 See §10 of the previous chapter. (Note that there is no equivalent difficulty on the Radical Conception, because, on the Radical Conception, there are no free acts of irrationality.)
18 *Religion*, 6: 22–25, his emphasis, some emphasis removed. See further ibid., Part One, especially the empirical observations at 6: 32–34. And cf. the ancient idea of the unity of the virtues, see e.g. Plato (1961b), 329 ff.
19 *Religion*, 6: 37.
20 Ibid., 6: 36. Cf. *Anthropology*, 7: 293–294.
21 *Opus Postumum*, 22: 124 (=p. 205).
22 See e.g. St Augustine (1972), Book XIII, Chapter 14.
23 *Religion*, 6: 40, his emphasis. (The quotation is from Ovid (1986), Book XIII, ll. 140–141.) But see also *Religion*, 6: 32, where he allows that our evil is 'somehow entwined with humanity itself and, as it were, rooted in it'. Cf. also ibid., 6: 25.
24 Ibid., Part One, §I.
25 Ibid., 6: 44, his emphasis.
26 Cf. ibid., 6: 38–39. Cf. also McDowell (1998a), §9.
27 Here I part company with Wood: see Wood (1970), pp. 222 ff.
28 See e.g. 1st *Critique*, A551/B579, footnote; *Groundwork*, 4: 407–408; and *Religion*, 6: 63.
29 *Religion*, 6: 36, his emphasis.
30 Ibid., 6: 36–37, his emphasis. See also ibid., ff.
31 Cf. 1st *Critique*, A553–554/B581–582.
32 *Religion*, 6: 41, his emphasis.
33 Cf. ibid., 6: 32. (But see again the passage from ibid. quoted above in note 23.)
34 For further discussion of this case see [A.W.] Moore (1990), especially §II. Cf. *Religion*, 6: 41. And see further §5 of the next chapter.

35 Cf. in this connection *Religion*, 6: 47–48.
36 Ibid., 6: 47.
37 Ibid., 6: 75. Cf. also *Metaphysics of Morals*, 6: 446.
38 Aristotle (1941b), Book III, Chapters 6–8.
39 *Religion*, 6: 66–67, his emphasis. Cf. 2nd *Critique*, 5: 123–124; and 'The End', 8: 335.
40 See e.g. Romans, Chapter VII, verse 24–Chapter VIII, verse 2.
41 See further Michalson (1990), Chapter 5; [A.W.] Moore (1990); Quinn (1986); Silber (1960), pp. cxxxi ff.; Vossenkuhl (1987–8); [B.] Williams (1985), p. 195; Wolterstorff (1991); and Wood (1970), pp. 234 ff. For a somewhat opposed reading of Kant, see Mariña (1997).
42 *Religion*, 6: 72, his emphasis. Cf. ibid., 6: 70, footnote, and 6: 116–117.
43 Ibid., 6: 190. See also ibid., ff.
44 Ibid., 6: 202.
45 For a quite different (but complementary) angle on the importance of contingency in Kant's moral and religious philosophy see Michalson (1990), p. 142.
46 Cf. *Religion*, 6: 162, footnote.
47 2nd *Critique*, Part One, Book II, Chapter II, §IV.
48 Ibid., 5: 122, his emphasis, '*a priori*' italicized by me.
49 1st *Critique*, A804–805/B832–833, his emphasis. For an interesting discussion of the importance of hope in Kant's philosophy, see Stratton-Lake (1993).
50 See e.g. 1st *Critique*, A805/B833 ff., and *Religion*, 6: 48.
51 This list is taken from *Groundwork*, 4: 393. (I have replaced 'honor' by 'honour'.)
52 See e.g. ibid., 4: 393 and 405; 2nd *Critique*, 5: 41 and 120; 3rd *Critique*, §83; and *Metaphysics of Morals*, 6: 480. (But see also below, note 63.)
53 Examples of the first are: 3rd *Critique*, 5: 453; and the passage from his metaphysics lectures, 28: 337, cited by Guyer in Guyer (2000b), pp. 93–94; cf. also 2nd *Critique*, 5: 122. Examples of the second are: 1st *Critique*, A810/B838; and 2nd *Critique*, 5: 110–111. An example of the third is 3rd *Critique*, 5: 450. For discussion of this ambiguity see Beck (1960), pp. 268 ff., and Rawls (2000), pp. 313 ff.
54 *Groundwork*, 4: 433. Cf. 2nd *Critique*, 5: 64.
55 2nd *Critique*, 5: 61, and 3rd *Critique*, 5: 450.
56 Cf. *Groundwork*, 4: 423; 2nd *Critique*, 5: 34–35; and *Metaphysics of Morals*, 6: 385–388.
57 1st *Critique*, A809/B837. (The elucidatory clause in square brackets is taken from ibid., A808/B836.) Cf. once again the passage from Kant's metaphysics lectures referred to in note 53 above; and cf. 1st *Critique*, A316/B373; *Lectures on Ethics*, 27: 470 (=p. 221); and the passage from Kant's *Reflexionen*, 19: 181, cited by Guyer in Guyer (2000c), p. 122.
58 1st *Critique*, A809–810/B837–838, his emphasis. Cf. 2nd *Critique*, 5: 130 ff. and *Religion*, 6: 97–98.
59 3rd *Critique*, 5: 452. (I have replaced 'honors' with 'honours') Cf. ibid., §88, concluding 'Remark'. (Note: Kant likens the righteous man he considers here to Spinoza. Whatever the appropriateness of this, it is interesting to reflect in this connection on Spinoza's definition of hope, as 'an uncertain pleasure arisen from the idea of a thing past or future, the event of which we still doubt to some extent': Spinoza (1959), Part III, Definition XII. Cf. Romans, Chapter VIII, verses 24–25.)
60 Engstrom (1996), p. 133.
61 2nd *Critique*, 5: 111.

62 Ibid., Part One, Book II, Chapter II, §I.
63 Ibid., 5: 114–115 and 119. For a careful analysis of various subtleties in Kant's conception of the relation between virtue and happiness, passed over here, see Guyer (2000c). See further *Metaphysics of Morals*, 6: 377–378.
64 1st *Critique*, A810–811/B838–839. For a more nuanced account of the relationship between the highest good, this life, and the life beyond this life, see Mariña (2000).
65 2nd *Critique*, 5: 122. Cf. Michalson (1990), p. 21.
66 1st *Critique*, A814–815/B842–843, his emphasis. Cf. 2nd *Critique*, Part One, Book II, Chapter II, §V; 3rd *Critique*, 5: 444 and 450; and more generally, 3rd *Critique*, §§85–91.
67 *Religion*, 6: 66–67. This of course raises the question whether it need be reflected at all: see Allison (1990), p. 174.
68 For example, 1st *Critique*, A811/B839.
69 Cf. Perovich (1991), and Wood (1970), pp. 180–182 and 230.
70 'The End', 8: 327, emphasis removed.
71 Ibid., his emphasis.
72 Ibid., 8: 334, his emphasis.
73 For example, *Religion*, 6: 69–71, footnote. It is interesting to compare this with Nietzsche's doctrine of eternal recurrence, whereby we must live our lives as if every event will recur in exact detail infinitely many times and must do whatever we need to do in order to treat this prospect with joy rather than dismay (see Nietzsche (1969), Part Three, 'Of the Vision and the Riddle').
74 *Religion*, 6: 74, his emphasis.
75 Ibid., 6: 75, emphasis removed.
76 Ibid., his emphasis. Cf. also ibid., 6: 76. And cf. Palmquist (1992), pp. 141 ff. That our lives are properly to be assessed as wholes, perhaps even as wholes that continue after our deaths, is an ancient idea, though Kant's peculiarly retributive eschatology gives it a highly distinctive modern twist: see *Religion*, 6: 70, footnote; and cf. both Aristotle (1941d), 1098a17–19 and – very differently – Ovid (1986), Book III, ll. 136–137.
77 Some philosophers prefer to call it 'the argument *to* design' on the grounds that design is more properly viewed as a feature of its conclusion than of any of its premises.
78 1st *Critique*, A622/650.
79 Ibid., §I, Part Two, Division Two, Book II, Chapter III ('The Ideal of Pure Reason'). For Kant's opposition to the idea that the first postulate can be established, see ibid., Chapter II, §IX.III ('Resolution of the Cosmological Idea of the Totality in the Derivation of Occurrences in the World From Their Causes'); and, for his opposition to the idea that the second postulate can be established, see ibid., Chapter I ('The Paralogisms of Pure Reason').
80 Pascal (1960a), p. 203.
81 But perhaps not on Kant's understanding of 'pragmatic': see 1st *Critique*, A824/B852.
82 2nd *Critique*, 5: 142–143, first emphasis his, second emphasis mine. Cf. 3rd *Critique*, §91.
83 2nd *Critique*, 5: 125, emphasis removed. See also ibid., 5: 126 and 144, the latter of which includes the claim that 'a belief that is commanded is an absurdity.' And cf. 3rd *Critique*, 5: 451–452. For the idea that belief is not subject to the will see [B.] Williams (1973a).
84 2nd *Critique*, 5: 125 and 143. Cf. 1st *Critique*, A828/B856, and 3rd *Critique*, 5: 450.

85 See e.g. 2nd *Critique*, 5: 4. Cf. 1st *Critique*, A820–821/B848–849; 3rd *Critique*, 5: 450–451, especially the footnote; and ibid., §90. Cf. also Kant's views about the character of beauty: see especially 3rd *Critique*, §22 and Part One, §II ('The Dialectic of the Aesthetic Power of Judgment').
86 1st *Critique*, A829/B857, his emphasis.
87 As indeed it does in a number of other, related respects: see 2nd *Critique*, 5: 3–5, and 3rd *Critique*, 5: 474.
88 Cf. 2nd *Critique*, 5: 103.
89 Ibid., Part One, Book II, Chapter II, §§VI and VII.
90 1st *Critique*, Bxxx, his emphasis.
91 3rd *Critique*, 5: 471–472, his emphasis, some emphasis removed. See further the whole of ibid., §91; and cf. 1st *Critique*, §II, Chapter II, §III ('On Having an Opinion, Knowing, and Believing'). Cf. also Hebrews Chapter X, verse 39–Chapter XI, verse 1, which likewise merits comparison with the material cited in note 59.
92 See e.g. 2nd *Critique*, 5: 48–49, and 3rd *Critique*, §76. Cf. also *Religion*, 6: 71, footnote. And consider once again the comparison with Nietzsche: see above, note 73. See Vaihinger (1935) for further exploration of this theme.
93 Cf. the first difficulty for Kant considered in Theme Two, §5. And cf. again Descartes (1984), 7: 69–70, cited in footnote 69 of that discussion.
94 Cf. Moore's paradox (that even though it is possible for me to believe something false, there is an incoherence in my saying, of any given proposition, both that I believe it and that it is false): see Sorensen (1988), Chapter 1.
95 E.g. 2nd *Critique*, 5: 144, footnote.
96 *Groundwork*, 4: 448, my emphasis, some emphasis removed.
97 Cf. Beck (1960), Chapter XIV, §2, and Walker (1978), p. 139.
98 For a useful corrective (which perhaps errs in the other direction) see Förster (2000), Chapter 5. A particularly graphic illustration of the changes in Kant's thinking to which I am referring is provided by an early work, 'The Only Possible Argument', in which he attempts to prove God's existence.
99 *Opus Postumum*, especially pp. 200–256. And see Förster (2000), pp. 137–147.
100 See Bell (2001).
101 *Opus Postumum*, 22: 55 (=p. 214).
102 Ibid., 21: 83 (=p. 248).
103 Ibid., 22: 118 (=pp. 201–202). (I have taken the liberty of replacing the translator's 'personality' by 'personhood': the German word is '*Persönlichkeit*'.)
104 Ibid., 21: 78 (=p. 245).
105 Ibid., 21: 82 (=p. 248), his emphasis.

Third set of variations

1 Cf. Harrison (1974), Chapter 3.
2 See Variations One, e.g. §§7 and 17. And see again the material cited in Variations One, note 112.
3 3rd *Critique*, Part Two, *passim*.
4 See e.g. Walker (1978), Chapter XII, and Walker (1989), Chapter XI. And see further below, §8.
5 See Hume (1975), *An Enquiry Concerning Human Understanding*, §§IV and V. See also [P.F.] Strawson (1952), Chapter 9, §II; Wittgenstein (1974b), Part I, §§472–486; Wittgenstein (1969), §§508–509; and, with particular reference to Kant, Walker (1999). Cf. 1st *Critique*, A669–679/B697–707.

6 This is another allusion to the famous passage in the conclusion to 2nd *Critique*, 5: 161–162, to which I referred in Theme One, §3.
7 Cf. here, and indeed throughout this chapter, Hursthouse (1999), pp. 260–265.
8 Cf. the question posed (and the answer given) in [A.W.] Moore (1997a), pp. 220–221.
9 [B.] Williams (1973d), pp. 88–89.
10 See Introduction, note 22 and accompanying text. For an expression of such relativism from a perhaps unlikely source see Romans, Chapter XIV. For an approach to such relativism that is comparable to mine (though certainly not identical to it) see Hume (1975), *An Enquiry Concerning the Principles of Morals*, 'A Dialogue', where he writes, on p. 333, (his emphasis):

> The Rhine flows north, the Rhone south; yet both spring from the *same* mountain, and are also actuated, in their opposite directions, by the *same* principle of gravity. The different inclinations of the ground, on which they run, cause all the difference of their courses.

11 Cf. 2nd *Critique*, 5: 28.
12 This hope has an almost Hegelian ring to it: see e.g. Hegel (1977), §V ('The Certainty and Truth of Reason').
13 See again in this connection Wittgenstein (1969), §§508–509.
14 Nietzsche (1967b), p. 231.
15 One fascinating and very large question that I shall not address is how it relates to what has come to be known as 'moral luck'. See [B.] Williams (1981a), to which Nagel replies in Nagel (1979a), and which Williams himself supplements in [B.] Williams (1995e). See also, with a broader sweep, Nussbaum (2001).
16 Parfit (1984), Chapter 1, *passim*, especially §§5–6. See also Parfit (2001).
17 Parfit (1984), pp. 12–13.
18 Consider here the following wonderful quotation from Nietzsche (1973), §280: '"Bad! Bad! What? Is he not going – backwards?" – Yes! But you ill understand him if you complain about it. He goes backwards as everyone goes backwards who wants to take a big jump.'
19 Not that this is what he does, notoriously. As St Mark puts it, 'for his oath's sake, and for their sakes which sat with him, he would not reject [Salome]': St Mark, Chapter VI, verse 26.
20 Cf. [B.] Williams (1973b) and [B.] Williams (1985), pp. 174 ff. (Note that this is a non-Kantian notion of obligation. See e.g. *Metaphysics of Morals*, 6: 224. But the difference may be, as that very discussion suggests it is, terminological.)
21 Consider the agonizing choice faced by Sophie in Styron (1992).
22 We might think that various familiar paradoxes of rationality show how such a situation could arise: see e.g. Priest (2002) and Sainsbury (1995), Chapter 3. My worry is that, if they do, then they also show that such a situation sometimes does arise. I do not think, however, that they show either, although arguing for this would involve a case-by-case discussion of each relevant paradox that would be beyond the scope of this book.
23 [P.F.] Strawson (1966), p. 273. The original is 'We lack words to say what it is to be without them.'
24 Cf. Nietzsche (1969), Part Two, 'Of Redemption'. (But Nietzsche is advocating something importantly different from this: see Variations One, §17.)
25 It is worth recalling in this connection the passage from Williams that I quoted in Variations One, §17, where he says, 'We may sometimes think that we are dismally constrained to be rational agents, and that in a happier world it would

not be necessary. But that is a fantasy (indeed it is *the* fantasy),': see Variations One, note 126 and accompanying text.
26 This is a Nietzschean phrase: see e.g. the motto to Nietzsche (1967b), p. 215, and Nietzsche (1974), §§270 and 335. (The phrase is taken from Pindar (1980), Pythian 2, l. 71, which contains the injunction 'Listen, and become what you are.' It also occurs in the quotation from Ansell Pearson that I gave in Introduction, §3.) But I do not say that I am putting the phrase to Nietzschean use.
27 *Religion*, 6: 33–34.
28 Ibid.
29 Nagel (1979b), p. 75. Cf. [B.] Williams (1985), p. 46, where he says that the modern world 'has made evil ... a collective enterprise.' Cf. also Camus (1971), pp. 146 ff.
30 For reservations about this, with reference to Kant, see Allison (1990), pp. 154 ff., and Michalson (1990), Chapters 2 and 3 *passim*. I find myself much more sympathetic to the account given in Wood (1970), which very helpfully locates our evil in the conflict between our finitude and our rationality: see 'Introduction' and 'Conclusion'. For further brief discussion of how our finite craving for rationality becomes perverted, see [A.W.] Moore (1997a), Chapter 11, §6; and cf. Emmett (1994), pp. 74–75, and Taylor (1989), pp. 137 ff.
31 See in particular note 77 of that chapter.
32 1st *Critique*, A686/B714, his emphasis. Cf. 3rd *Critique*, 5: 413–414. The tell-tale phrase 'as if' in this quotation from 1st *Critique* indicates that Kant is talking about a regulative principle: see ibid., A687/B715. (Regulative principles, remember, are the genus of which regulative ideals are a species. See Variations Two, §11, and see further below.)
33 Michalson (1990), p. 25.
34 See Hegel (1975), §6; and cf. again the material cited in note 12 above. Cf. also Lucas (1984), Chapter I, especially pp. 12–13; and the paragraph from Michalson from which the quotation above was taken (see previous note).
35 E.g. Price (1966). I myself draw such a distinction in [A.W.] Moore (1997a), p. 278.
36 Deleuze and Guattari (1994), p. 74. (I have inserted 'in God' in place of 'that God exists' to fit with the distinction that I am drawing: I trust that this does not do undue violence to the text.) For the references to Kierkegaard and Pascal, see respectively Kierkegaard (1954), pp. 49 ff., and Pascal (1960b), §418.
37 Murdoch (1993), p. 508, her emphasis. Cf. Wittgenstein (1961), 6.432. Note: the first five sentences of this quotation almost supplement Kant's rejection of the 'ontological' argument that God exists (see §7 of the previous chapter) with an 'ontological' argument that God does not exist.
38 See again the material cited in note 5 above.
39 Cf. [B.] Williams (1985), pp. 32–33. And see e.g. Marx and Engels (1957); and Freud (1962).
40 See Hume (1948), Parts X and XI; Dostoyevsky (1958), Part Two, Book Five, Chapter 5 ('The Grand Inquisitor'); and Adams and Adams (1990).
41 Not that Kant himself would be entirely comfortable with this: see §7 of the previous chapter.
42 [A.W.] Moore (1997a), especially Chapters 7–9, and, for the connection with regulative principles, Chapter 10, §5. See also ibid., pp. 277–278. (But see the disclaimer in Variations Two, note 105.)
43 In what follows I am drawing on [A.W.] Moore (2003), in which I try to pursue these issues in greater depth.
44 Wittgenstein (1961), 6.43.

45 Fogelin (1987), p. 103.
46 Cf. in this connection Wittgenstein (1961), 6.5–6.54.
47 This is a variation on the phrase I borrowed from Engstrom in the previous chapter: see note 60 of that chapter and accompanying text.
48 Murdoch (1993), p. 483.
49 See e.g. Michalson (1990), pp. 134 ff.
50 Lyotard (1979), p. xxiv.
51 Cf. again the material from Hursthouse (1999) cited above in note 7.
52 Cf. again [A.W.] Moore (1997a), p. 278.
53 Deleuze (1990), Series 21. This is another Nietzschean phrase: see e.g. Nietzsche (1967b), p. 258, and Nietzsche (1974), §276.
54 *Lectures on Ethics*, 27: 319 (=p. 105). Cf. 2nd *Critique*, 5: 116–117; and Wittgenstein (1961), 6.422. NB. I am taking something of a liberty in ascribing quotations from *Lectures on Ethics* to Kant himself, since these are lecture notes taken by his students.
55 Deleuze (1990), p. 149, his emphasis. (I have replaced 'splendor' by 'splendour'.)
56 For the tension between Deleuze's 'inside' and Wittgenstein's 'outside' cf. the parenthetical discussion above about the role of contradiction in attempts to express the inexpressible. In any case, the crucial point, for both Deleuze and Wittgenstein, is that the sense of what happens is not itself something that happens.
57 Wittgenstein (1961), 6.41 and 6.43, his emphasis. See further ibid., the whole of the 6.4s.
58 *Lectures on Ethics*, 27: 320 (=p. 106). But see again the caveat in note 54 above.
59 Ibid.
60 Ibid., 27: 320–321 (=pp. 106–107).

Bibliography

(a) Works by Immanuel Kant: main versions cited

1st *Critique* = *Critique of Pure Reason*, trans. and ed. Paul Guyer and Allen W. Wood (Cambridge: Cambridge University Press, 1998).

2nd *Critique* = *Critique of Practical Reason*, trans. Mary J. Gregor, in Immanuel Kant, *Practical Philosophy*, trans. and ed. Mary J. Gregor (Cambridge: Cambridge University Press, 1996).

3rd *Critique* = *Critique of the Power of Judgment*, trans. Paul Guyer and Eric Matthews and ed. Paul Guyer (Cambridge: Cambridge University Press, 2000).

'A Discovery' = 'On a Discovery according to which any New Critique of Pure Reason has been made Superfluous by an Earlier One', in *The Kant-Eberhard Controversy*, trans. Henry E. Allison (Baltimore: The Johns Hopkins University Press, 1973).

'A Supposed Right' = 'On a Supposed Right to Lie From Philanthropy', trans. Mary J. Gregor, in Immanuel Kant, *Practical Philosophy*, trans. and ed. Mary J. Gregor (Cambridge: Cambridge University Press).

Anthropology = *Anthropology From a Pragmatic Point of View*, trans. Mary J. Gregor (The Hague: Nijhoff, 1974).

'Enlightenment' = 'An Answer to the Question: What Is Enlightenment?', trans. Mary J. Gregor, in Immanuel Kant, *Practical Philosophy*, trans. and ed. Mary J. Gregor (Cambridge: Cambridge University Press, 1996).

Groundwork = *Groundwork of the Metaphysics of Morals*, trans. Mary J. Gregor, in Immanuel Kant, *Practical Philosophy*, trans. and ed. Mary J. Gregor (Cambridge: Cambridge University Press, 1996).

Lectures on Ethics = *Lectures on Ethics*, trans. Peter Heath and ed. Peter Heath and J.B. Schneewind (Cambridge: Cambridge University Press, 1997).

Metaphysics of Morals = *The Metaphysics of Morals*, trans. Mary J. Gregor, in Immanuel Kant, *Practical Philosophy*, trans. and ed. Mary J. Gregor (Cambridge: Cambridge University Press, 1996).

Opus Postumum = *Opus Postumum*, trans. Eckart Förster and Michael Rosen and ed. Eckart Förster (Cambridge: Cambridge University Press, 1993).

Perpetual Peace = *Toward Perpetual Peace: A Philosophical Project*, trans. Mary J. Gregor, in Immanuel Kant, *Practical Philosophy*, trans. and ed. Mary J. Gregor (Cambridge: Cambridge University Press, 1996).

Prolegomena = *Prolegomena to Any Future Metaphysics*, trans. Lewis White Beck (Indianapolis: The Bobbs-Merrill Co., 1950).
Religion = *Religion Within the Boundaries of Mere Reason*, trans. George di Giovanni, in Immanuel Kant, *Religion and Rational Theology*, trans. and ed. Allen W. Wood and George di Giovanni (Cambridge: Cambridge University Press, 1996).
'The End' = 'The End of All Things', trans. Allen W. Wood, in Immanuel Kant, *Religion and Rational Theology*, trans. and ed. Allen W. Wood and George di Giovanni (Cambridge: Cambridge University Press, 1996).
'The Only Possible Argument' = 'The Only Possible Argument in Support of a Demonstration of the Existence of God', trans. David Walford and Ralf Meerbote, in Immanuel Kant, *Theoretical Philosophy, 1755–1770*, trans. and ed. David Walford and Ralf Meerbote (Cambridge: Cambridge University Press, 1992).
'Theory and Practice' = 'On the Common Saying: That May Be Correct in Theory, But it is of No Use in Practice', trans. Mary J. Gregor, in Immanuel Kant, *Practical Philosophy*, trans. and ed. Mary J. Gregor (Cambridge: Cambridge University Press, 1996).

(b) Works by Immanuel Kant: alternative versions cited

Beck (1956) = *Critique of Practical Reason*, trans. Lewis White Beck (Indianapolis: The Bobbs-Merrill Co.).
Greene and Hudson (1960) = *Religion Within the Limits of Reason Alone*, trans. Theodore M. Greene and Hoyt H. Hudson (New York: Harper & Row).
Paton (1964) = *Groundwork of the Metaphysic of Morals*, trans. H.J. Paton (New York: Harper & Row).

(c) Works by other authors

Acton, H.B. (1970) *Kant's Moral Philosophy* (London: Macmillan).
Adams, Robert M. (1985) 'Involuntary Sins', *The Philosophical Review* 94.
Adams, Robert M. (1998) 'Introduction', in Immanuel Kant, *Religion Within the Boundaries of Mere Reason and Other Writings*, ed. Allen W. Wood and George di Giovanni (Cambridge: Cambridge University Press).
Adams, Robert M. and Adams, Marilyn M. (eds) (1990) *The Problem of Evil* (Oxford: Oxford University Press).
Allison, Henry E. (1983) *Kant's Transcendental Idealism: An Interpretation and Defense* (New Haven, CT: Yale University Press).
Allison, Henry E. (1990) *Kant's Theory of Freedom* (Cambridge: Cambridge University Press).
Allison, Henry E. (1996a) *Idealism and Freedom: Essays on Kant's Theoretical and Practical Philosophy* (Cambridge: Cambridge University Press).
Allison, Henry E. (1996b) 'Kant on Freedom: A Reply to My Critics', reprinted in his Idealism and Freedom (Cambridge: Cambridge University Press).

Anderson, Pamela Sue (1993) *Ricoeur and Kant: Philosophy of the Will* (Atlanta, GA: Scholars Press).
Annas, Julia (2001–2) 'My Station and its Duties: Ideals and the Social Embeddedness of Virtue', *Proceedings of the Aristotelian Society* 102.
Anscombe, G.E.M. (1963) *Intention* (Oxford: Basil Blackwell).
Anscombe, G.E.M. (1981a) 'On Promising and its Justice, and Whether it Need be Respected *in Foro Interno*', reprinted in her *Ethics, Religion and Politics: Collected Philosophical Papers*, Vol. III (Oxford: Basil Blackwell).
Anscombe, G.E.M. (1981b) 'Modern Moral Philosophy', reprinted in her *Ethics, Religion and Politics: Collected Philosophical Papers*, Vol. III (Oxford: Basil Blackwell).
Ansell Pearson, Keith (1999) *Germinal Life: The Difference and Repetition of Deleuze* (London: Routledge).
Anzaldúa, Gloria (1987) *Borderlands/La Frontera: The New Mestiza* (San Francisco: Aunt Lute Books).
Aristotle (1941a) *Categoriae* (=*Categories*), trans. E.M. Edghill, in Richard McKeon (ed.), *The Basic Works of Aristotle* (New York: Random House).
Aristotle (1941b) *Physica* (=*Physics*), trans. R.P. Hardie and R.K. Gaye, in Richard McKeon (ed.), *The Basic Works of Aristotle* (New York: Random House).
Aristotle (1941c) *Metaphysica* (=*Metaphysics*), trans. W.D. Ross, in Richard McKeon (ed.), *The Basic Works of Aristotle* (New York: Random House).
Aristotle (1941d) *Ethica Nicomachea* (=*Nicomachean Ethics*), trans. W.D. Ross, in Richard McKeon (ed.), *The Basic Works of Aristotle* (New York: Random House).
Aristotle (1941e) *Politica* (=*Politics*), trans. Benjamin Jowett, in Richard McKeon (ed.), *The Basic Works of Aristotle* (New York: Random House).
Augustine, St (1972) *The City of God*, trans. J. O'Meara (Harmondsworth: Penguin).
Aune, Bruce (1979) *Kant's Theory of Morals* (Princeton, NJ: Princeton University Press).
Austin, J.L. (1970) 'A Plea for Excuses', reprinted in his *Philosophical Papers*, ed. J.O. Urmson and G.J. Warnock (Oxford: Oxford University Press).
Auxter, Thomas (1982) *Kant's Moral Teleology* (Macon, GA: Mercer University Press).
Baker, G.P. and Hacker, P.M.S. (1985) *Wittgenstein: Rules, Grammar and Necessity, Volume 2 of An Analytical Commentary on the Philosophical Investigations* (Oxford: Basil Blackwell).
Baron, Marcia W. (1995) *Kantian Ethics Almost Without Apology* (Ithaca, NY: Cornell University Press).
Beck, Lewis White (1960) *A Commentary on Kant's Critique of Practical Reason* (Chicago: The University of Chicago Press).
Bell, David (2001) 'Some Kantian Thoughts on Propositional Unity', *Proceedings of the Aristotelian Society* Supp. Vol. 75.
Bennett, Jonathan (1974) *Kant's Dialectic* (Cambridge: Cambridge University Press).
Bennett, Jonathan (1995) *The Act Itself* (Oxford: Oxford University Press).
Bergson, Henri (1975) *An Introduction to Metaphysics: The Creative Mind*, trans. Mabelle L. Andison (Totowa, NJ: Littlefield, Adams & Co.).

Berofsky, Bernard (ed.) (1966) *Free Will and Determinism* (New York: Harper & Row).
Blackburn, Simon (1998) *Ruling Passions: A Theory of Practical Reasoning* (Oxford: Oxford University Press).
Bok, Hilary (1998) *Freedom and Responsibility* (Princeton, NJ: Princeton University Press).
Brandom, Robert (1979) 'Freedom and Constraint by Norms', *American Philosophical Quarterly* 16.
Brandom, Robert (1994) *Making It Explicit: Reasoning, Representing, and Discursive Commitment* (Cambridge, MA: Harvard University Press).
Brandom, Robert (1998) 'Actions, Norms, and Practical Reasoning', in James E. Tomberlin (ed.), *Philosophical Perspectives* 12: *Language, Mind and Ontology*.
Brandom, Robert (1999) 'Some Pragmatist Themes in Hegel's Idealism: Negotiation and Administration in Hegel's Account of the Structure and Content of Conceptual Norms', *European Journal of Philosophy* 7.
Brandom, Robert (2000) *Articulating Reasons: An Introduction to Inferentialism* (Cambridge, MA: Harvard University Press).
Buchanan, Ian (2000) *Deleuzism: A Metacommentary* (Edinburgh: Edinburgh University Press).
Camus, Albert (1971) *The Rebel*, trans. Anthony Bower (Harmondsworth: Penguin).
Cantor, Georg (1955) *Contributions to the Founding of the Theory of Transfinite Numbers*, trans. Philip E.B. Jourdain (New York: Dover).
Carnois, Bernard (1987) *The Coherence of Kant's Doctrine of Freedom*, trans. David Booth (Chicago: The University of Chicago Press).
Cassirer, Ernst (1981) *Kant's Life and Thought*, trans. James Haden (New Haven, CT: Yale University Press).
Cavell, Stanley (1976) 'The Availability of Wittgenstein's Philosophy', reprinted in his *Must We Mean What We Say?* (Cambridge: Cambridge University Press).
Chesterfield, Philip Dormer Stanhope, Earl of (1973) *Letters to His Son* (London: Folio Society).
Cicero (1991) *On Fate*, ed. and trans. R.W. Sharples (Warminster: Aris & Phillips Ltd).
Cockburn, David (1997) *Other Times: Philosophical Perspectives on Past, Present and Future* (Cambridge: Cambridge University Press).
Coleridge, S.T. (1997) *Biographia Literaria*, ed. Nigel Leask (London: Everyman).
Craig, Edward (1990) *Knowledge and the State of Nature: An Essay in Conceptual Synthesis* (Oxford: Oxford University Press).
Crisp, Roger (2000) 'Particularizing Particularism', in Brad Hooker and Margaret Little (eds), *Moral Particularism* (Oxford: Oxford University Press).
Crisp, Roger and Michael Slote (eds) (1997) *Virtue Ethics* (Oxford: Oxford University Press).
Davidovich, Adina (1994) 'How to Read Religion Within the Limits of Reason Alone', *Kant Studien* 85.
Davidson, Donald (1980a) 'How is Weakness of the Will Possible?', reprinted in his *Essays on Actions and Events* (Oxford: Oxford University Press).
Davidson, Donald (1980b) 'Mental Events', reprinted in his *Essays on Actions and Events* (Oxford: Oxford University Press).

Davidson, Donald (1980c) 'Psychology as Philosophy', reprinted in his *Essays on Actions and Events* (Oxford: Oxford University Press).
Davidson, Donald (1984) *Inquiries into Truth and Interpretation* (Oxford: Oxford University Press).
Davidson, Donald (2001) 'The Emergence of Thought', reprinted in his *Subjective, Intersubjective, Objective* (Oxford: Oxford University Press).
Deleuze, Gilles (1969) *The Logic of Sense*, trans. Mark Lester and Charles Stivale and ed. Constantin V. Boundas (New York: Columbia University Press).
Deleuze, Gilles (1994) *Difference and Repetition*, trans. Paul Patton (New York: Columbia University Press).
Deleuze, Gilles and Guattari, Félix (1994) *What Is Philosophy?*, trans. Hugh Tomlinson and Graham Burchall (New York: Columbia University Press).
Dennett, Daniel (1984) *Elbow Room: Varieties of Free Will Worth Wanting* (Cambridge, MA: The MIT Press).
Descartes, René (1984) *Meditations on First Philosophy*, in his *The Philosophical Writings*, Vol. II, trans. John Cottingham, Robert Stoothoff, and Dugald Murdoch (Cambridge: Cambridge University Press).
Despland, Michel (1973) *Kant on History and Religion* (Montreal: McGill-Queen's University Press).
Diamond, Cora (1991a) 'The Face of Necessity', reprinted in her *The Realistic Spirit: Wittgenstein, Philosophy, and the Mind* (Cambridge, MA: The MIT Press).
Diamond, Cora (1991b) 'Missing the Adventure: Reply to Martha Nussbaum', reprinted in her *The Realistic Spirit: Wittgenstein, Philosophy, and the Mind* (Cambridge, MA: The MIT Press).
Diamond, Cora (1991c) 'Eating Meat and Eating People', reprinted in her *The Realistic Spirit: Wittgenstein, Philosophy, and the Mind* (Cambridge, MA: The MIT Press).
Dostoyevsky, Fyodor (1958) *The Brothers Karamazov*, trans. David Magarshack (Harmondsworth: Penguin).
Dummett, Michael (1980) *Frege: Philosophy of Language*, 2nd edn (London: Duckworth).
Duncan, A.R.C (1957) *Practical Reason and Morality: A Study of Immanuel Kant's Foundations for the Metaphysics of Morals* (London: Nelson and Sons).
Einstein, Albert (1960) *Relativity: The Special and the General Theory*, trans. Robert W. Lawson (London: Methuen).
Elford, R. John (2000) *The Ethics of Uncertainty: A New Christian Approach to Moral Decision-Making* (Oxford: Oneworld Publications).
Emmett, Dorothy (1994) *The Role of the Unrealisable: A Study in Regulative Ideals* (New York: St Martin's Press).
England, F.E. (1929) *Kant's Conception of God: A Critical Exposition of its Metaphysical Development, Together with a Translation of the Nova Dilucidatio* (London: Allen & Unwin).
Engstrom, Stephen (1996) 'Happiness and the Highest Good in Aristotle and Kant', in Stephen Engstrom and Jennifer Whiting (eds) *Aristotle, Kant and the Stoics* (Cambridge: Cambridge University Press).
Engstrom, Stephen and Whiting, Jennifer (eds), *Aristotle, Kant and the Stoics: Rethinking Happiness and Duty* (Cambridge: Cambridge University Press).

Epictetus (1916) 'Discourses', in his *The Discourses and Manual*, trans. P.E. Matheson (Oxford: Oxford University Press).
Fogelin, Robert J. (1987) *Wittgenstein*, 2nd edn (London: Routledge & Kegan Paul).
Foot, Philippa (1978) 'Morality as a System of Hypothetical Imperatives', reprinted in her *Virtues and Vices and Other Essays in Moral Philosophy* (Oxford: Basil Blackwell).
Förster, Eckart (2000) *Kant's Final Synthesis: An Essay on the Opus Postumum* (Cambridge, MA: Harvard University Press).
Frede, Michael (1999) 'On the Stoic Conception of the Good', in Katerina Ierodiakonou (ed.), *Topics in Stoic Philosophy* (Oxford: Oxford University Press).
Frege, Gottlob (1967) 'The Thought: A Logical Inquiry', trans. A.M. and Marcelle Quinton and reprinted in P.F. Strawson (ed.), *Philosophical Logic* (Oxford: Oxford University Press).
Freud, Sigmund (1962) *The Future of an Illusion*, trans. W.D. Robson-Scott and James Strachey and ed. James Strachey (London: Hogarth Press).
Gaita, Raimond (2000) *A Common Humanity: Thinking about Love and Truth and Justice* (London: Routledge).
Gatens, Moira (1991) *Feminism and Philosophy: Perspectives on Difference and Equality* (Cambridge: Polity Press).
Gibbard, Allan (1990) *Wise Choices, Apt Feelings: A Theory of Normative Judgment* (Oxford: Oxford University Press).
Gödel, Kurt (1967) 'On Formally Undecidable Propositions of *Principia Mathematica* and Related Systems I', trans. Jean van Heijenoort, in Jean van Heijenoort (ed.), *From Frege to Gödel: A Source Book in Mathematical Logic, 1879–1931* (Cambridge, MA: Harvard University Press).
Goodman, Nelson (1979) *Fact, Fiction, and Forecast*, 3rd edn (Brighton: The Harvester Press).
Green, Ronald M. (1978) *Religious Reason: The Rational and Moral Basis of Religious Belief* (Oxford: Oxford University Press).
Greene, Theodore M. (1960) 'The Historical Context and Religious Significance of Kant's *Religion*', in Immanuel Kant, *Religion Within the Limits of Reason Alone*, trans. Theodore M. Greene and Hoyt H. Hudson (New York: Harper & Row).
Gregor, Mary (1963) *Laws of Freedom: A Study of Kant's Method of Applying the Categorical Imperative in the Metaphysic der Sitten* (Oxford: Basil Blackwell).
Guyer, Paul (1993) *Kant and the Experience of Freedom: Essays on Aesthetics and Morality* (Cambridge: Cambridge University Press).
Guyer, Paul (ed.) (1998) *Kant's Groundwork of the Metaphysics of Morals: Critical Essays* (Lanham, MD: Rowman & Littlefield).
Guyer, Paul (2000a) *Kant on Freedom, Law, and Happiness* (Cambridge: Cambridge University Press).
Guyer, Paul (2000b) 'The Unity of Reason: Pure Reason as Practical Reason in Kant's Early Conception of the Transcendental Dialectic', reprinted in his *Kant on Freedom, Law, and Happiness* (Cambridge: Cambridge University Press).
Guyer, Paul (2000c) 'Freedom as the Inner Value of the World', in his *Kant on Freedom, Law, and Happiness* (Cambridge: Cambridge University Press).
Guyer, Paul (2000d) 'From a Practical Point of View: Kant's Conception of a

Postulate of Pure Practical Reason', in his *Kant on Freedom, Law, and Happiness* (Cambridge: Cambridge University Press).
Hacker, P.M.S. (1986) *Insight and Illusion: Themes in the Philosophy of Wittgenstein*, revised edn (Oxford: Oxford University Press).
Hacker, P.M.S. (1996) *Wittgenstein's Place in Twentieth-Century Analytic Philosophy* (Oxford: Basil Blackwell).
Haezrahi, Pepita (1969) 'The Concept of Man as End-in-Himself', reprinted in R.P. Wolff (ed.), *Foundations of the Metaphysics of Morals with Critical Essays* (Indianapolis: The Bobbs-Merrill Co.).
Hare, John E. (1996) *The Moral Gap: Kantian Ethics, Human Limits, and God's Assistance* (Oxford: Oxford University Press).
Hare, R.M. (1952) *The Language of Morals* (Oxford: Oxford University Press).
Hare, R.M. (1963) *Freedom and Reason* (Oxford: Oxford University Press).
Hare, R.M. (1967) 'The Promising Game', reprinted in Philippa Foot (ed.), *Theories of Ethics* (Oxford: Oxford University Press).
Harman, Gilbert (1999) '(Non-Solipsistic) Conceptual Role Semantics', reprinted in his *Reasoning, Meaning, and Mind* (Oxford: Oxford University Press).
Harper, William A. and Meerbote, Ralf (eds) (1984) *Kant on Causality, Freedom, and Objectivity* (Minneapolis: The University of Minnesota Press).
Harrison, Ross (1974) *On What There Must Be* (Oxford: Oxford University Press).
Hegel, G.W.F. (1942) *Philosophy of Right*, trans. T.M. Knox (Oxford: Oxford University Press).
Hegel, G.W.F. (1975) *The Encyclopædia of the Philosophical Sciences*, Part I ('Logic'), trans. William Wallace (Oxford: Oxford University Press).
Hegel, G.W.F. (1977) *Phenomenology of Spirit*, trans. A.V. Miller (Oxford: Oxford University Press).
Henle, James M. (1986) *An Outline of Set Theory* (Heidelberg: Springer-Verlag).
Herman, Barbara (1993a) *The Practice of Moral Judgment* (Cambridge, MA: Harvard University Press).
Herman, Barbara (1993b) 'On the Value of Acting From the Motive of Duty', reprinted in her *The Practice of Moral Judgment* (Cambridge, MA: Harvard University Press).
Herman, Barbara (1993c) 'The Practice of Moral Judgment', reprinted in her *The Practice of Moral Judgment* (Cambridge, MA: Harvard University Press).
Hill, Thomas E., Jr (1992) *Dignity and Practical Reason in Kant's Moral Theory* (Ithaca, NY: Cornell University Press).
Hill, Thomas E., Jr (2000) *Respect, Pluralism, and Justice: Kantian Perspectives* (Oxford: Oxford University Press).
Hollis, Martin (1985) *Invitation to Philosophy* (Oxford: Basil Blackwell).
Hollis, Martin (1987) *The Cunning of Reason* (Cambridge: Cambridge University Press).
Holloway, Richard (1999) *Godless Morality: Keeping Religion out of Ethics* (Edinburgh: Canongate).
Honderich, Ted (ed.) (1978) *Essays on Freedom and Action* (London: Routledge & Kegan Paul).
Honderich, Ted (1988) *A Theory of Determinism: The Mind, Neuroscience, and Life-Hopes* (Oxford: Oxford University Press).
Hudson, Hud (1994) *Kant's Compatibilism* (Ithaca, NY: Cornell University Press).

Hume, David (1948) *Dialogues Concerning Natural Religion*, ed. Henry D. Aiken (New York: Hafner Publishing Co.).
Hume, David (1975) *Enquiries Concerning Human Understanding and Concerning the Principles of Morals*, ed. L.A. Selby-Bigge, revised P.H. Nidditch, 3rd edn (Oxford: Oxford University Press).
Hume, David (1978) *A Treatise of Human Nature*, ed. L.A. Selby-Bigge, revised P.H. Nidditch (Oxford: Oxford University Press).
Hursthouse, Rosalind (1999) *On Virtue Ethics* (Oxford: Oxford University Press).
Irigaray, Luce (1977) *This Sex Which is Not One*, trans. Catherine Porter and Carolyn Burke (Ithaca, NY: Cornell University Press).
Irigaray, Luce (1993) *An Ethics of Sexual Difference*, trans. Catherine Porter and Gillian C. Gill (London: Athlone Press).
Isaacson, Daniel (1996) 'Arithmetical Truth and Hidden Higher-Order Concepts', reprinted in W.D. Hart (ed.), *The Philosophy of Mathematics* (Oxford: Oxford University Press).
Jackson, Frank (1986) 'What Mary Didn't Know', *The Journal of Philosophy* 83.
Jones, W.T. (1940) *Morality and Freedom in the Philosophy of Immanuel Kant* (Oxford: Oxford University Press).
Kierkegaard, Søren (1954) under the pseudonym Johannes de Silentio, *Fear and Trembling*, in his *Fear and Trembling and The Sickness Unto Death*, trans. Walter Lowrie (Princeton, NJ: Princeton University Press).
Klein, Martha (1990) *Determinism, Blameworthiness, and Deprivation* (Oxford: Oxford University Press).
Körner, S. (1967) 'Kant's Conception of Freedom', *Proceedings of the British Academy* 53.
Korsgaard, Christine M. (1996a) *The Sources of Normativity* (Cambridge: Cambridge University Press).
Korsgaard, Christine M. (1996b) *Creating the Kingdom of Ends* (Cambridge: Cambridge University Press).
Korsgaard, Christine M. (1996c) 'An Introduction to the Ethical, Political, and Religious Thought of Kant', reprinted in her *Creating the Kingdom of Ends* (Cambridge: Cambridge University Press).
Korsgaard, Christine M. (1996d) 'Kant's Formula of Universal Law', reprinted in her *Creating the Kingdom of Ends* (Cambridge: Cambridge University Press).
Korsgaard, Christine M. (1996e) 'The Right to Lie: Kant on Dealing With Evil', reprinted in her *Creating the Kingdom of Ends* (Cambridge: Cambridge University Press).
Korsgaard, Christine M. (1996f) 'Aristotle and Kant on the Source of Value', reprinted in her *Creating the Kingdom of Ends* (Cambridge: Cambridge University Press).
Korsgaard, Christine M. (1996g) 'The Reasons We Can Share: An Attack on the Distinction Between Agent-Relative and Agent-Neutral Values', reprinted in her *Creating the Kingdom of Ends* (Cambridge: Cambridge University Press).
Korsgaard, Christine M. (1997) 'Introduction', in Immanuel Kant, *Groundwork of the Metaphysics of Morals*, ed. Mary Gregor (Cambridge: Cambridge University Press).
Kuehn, Manfred (2001) *Kant: A Biography* (Cambridge: Cambridge University Press).

Langton, Rae (1998) *Kantian Humility: Our Ignorance of Things in Themselves* (Oxford: Oxford University Press).
Lear, Jonathan (1984) 'Moral Objectivity', in S.C. Brown (ed.), *Objectivity and Cultural Divergence* (Cambridge: Cambridge University Press).
Lear, Jonathan (1988) *Aristotle: The Desire to Understand* (Cambridge: Cambridge University Press).
Lemmon, E.J. (1965) *Beginning Logic* (London: Thomas Nelson and Sons).
Lenman, James (1996) 'Belief, Desire and Motivation: An Essay in Quasi-Hydraulics', *American Philosophical Quarterly* 33.
Lewis, David (1990) 'What Experience Teaches', in W.G. Lycan (ed.), *Mind and Cognition: A Reader* (Oxford: Basil Blackwell).
Lewis, David (1991) *Parts of Classes* (Oxford: Basil Blackwell).
Lloyd, Genevieve (1984) *The Man of Reason: 'Male' and 'Female' in Western Philosophy* (London: Methuen).
Lloyd, Genevieve (1996) *Spinoza and the Ethics* (London: Routledge).
Locke, John (1965) *Essay Concerning Human Understanding* (London: Dent).
Louden, Robert B. (1986) 'Kant's Virtue Ethics', *Philosophy* 61.
Louden, Robert B. (2000) *Kant's Impure Ethics: From Rational Beings to Human Beings* (Oxford: Oxford University Press).
Lovibond, Sabina (1983) *Realism and Imagination in Ethics* (Oxford: Basil Blackwell).
Lovibond, Sabina (2002) *Ethical Formation* (Cambridge, MA: Harvard University Press).
Lucas, J.R. (1984) *Space, Time, and Causality: An Essay in Natural Philosophy* (Oxford: Oxford University Press).
Lyotard, Jean-François (1979) *The Postmodern Condition: A Report on Knowledge*, trans. Geoffrey Bennington and Brian Massumi (Minneapolis: Minnesota University Press).
McCarty, Richard (2002) 'The Maxims Problem', *The Journal of Philosophy* 99.
McDowell, John (1993) 'Wittgenstein on Following a Rule', reprinted in A.W. Moore (ed.), *Meaning and Reference* (Oxford: Oxford University Press).
McDowell, John (1994) *Mind and World* (Cambridge, MA: Harvard University Press).
McDowell, John (1995) 'Might There Be External Reasons?', in J.E.J. Altham and Ross Harrison (eds), *Mind, World, and Ethics: Essays on the Ethical Philosophy of Bernard Williams* (Cambridge: Cambridge University Press).
McDowell, John (1998a) 'Are Moral Requirements Hypothetical Imperatives?', reprinted in his *Mind, Value, and Reality* (Cambridge, MA: Harvard University Press).
McDowell, John (1998b) 'Two Sorts of Naturalism', reprinted in his *Mind, Value, and Reality* (Cambridge, MA: Harvard University Press).
McDowell, John (1998c) 'Non-Cognitivism and Rule-Following', reprinted in his *Mind, Value, and Reality* (Cambridge, MA: Harvard University Press).
McGinn, Colin (1984) *Wittgenstein on Meaning: An Interpretation and Evaluation* (Oxford: Basil Blackwell).
MacIntyre, Alasdair (1981) *After Virtue: A Study in Moral Theory* (London: Duckworth).

MacIntyre, Alasdair (1988) *Whose Justice? Which Rationality?* (London: Duckworth).
Mackie, J.L. (1977) *Ethics: Inventing Right and Wrong* (Harmondsworth: Penguin).
Maor, Eli (1986) *To Infinity and Beyond: A Cultural History of the Infinite* (Stuttgart: Birkhäuser).
Mariña, Jacqueline (1997) 'Kant on Grace: A Reply to His Critics', *Religious Studies* 33.
Mariña, Jacqueline (2000) 'Making Sense of Kant's Highest Good', *Kant Studien* 91.
Marx, Karl and Engels, Friedrich (1957) *On Religion* (Moscow: Foreign Languages Publishing House).
Marx, Karl and Engels, Friedrich (1968) *Selected Works in One Volume* (London: Lawrence and Wishart).
Michalson, Gordon E. (1990) *Fallen Freedom: Kant on Radical Evil and Moral Regeneration* (Cambridge: Cambridge University Press).
Michalson, Gordon E. (1999) *Kant and the Problem of God* (Oxford: Basil Blackwell).
Millgram, Elijah (ed.) (2001) *Varieties of Practical Reasoning* (Cambridge, MA: The MIT Press).
Moore, A.W. (1987) 'Beauty in the Transcendental Idealism of Kant and Wittgenstein', *British Journal of Aesthetics* 27.
Moore, A.W. (1990) 'A Kantian View of Moral Luck', *Philosophy* 65.
Moore, A.W. (1997a) *Points of View* (Oxford: Oxford University Press).
Moore, A.W. (1997b) 'The Underdetermination/Indeterminacy Distinction and the Analytic/Synthetic Distinction', *Erkenntnis* 46.
Moore, A.W. (1998) 'More on "The Philosophical Significance of Gödel's Theorem"', in Johannes L. Brandl and Peter M. Sullivan (eds), 'New Essays on the Philosophy of Michael Dummett', *Grazer Philosophische Studien* 55.
Moore, A.W. (1999) 'Conative Transcendental Arguments and the Question Whether There Can Be External Reasons', in Robert Stern (ed.), *Transcendental Arguments: Problems and Prospects* (Oxford: Oxford University Press).
Moore, A.W. (2001) *The Infinite*, 2nd edn (London: Routledge).
Moore, A.W. (2003) 'Ineffability and Religion', *European Journal of Philosophy* 11.
Moore, E.C. (1912) *An Outline of the History of Christian Thought Since Kant* (London: Duckworth).
Munzel, G. Felicitas (1999) *Kant's Conception of Moral Character: The 'Critical' Link of Morality, Anthropology, and Reflective Judgment* (Chicago: The University of Chicago Press).
Murdoch, Iris (1985) 'The Sovereignty of Good Over Other Concepts', reprinted in her *The Sovereignty of Good* (London: Ark Paperbacks).
Murdoch, Iris (1993) *Metaphysics as a Guide to Morals* (Harmondsworth: Penguin).
Nagel, Thomas (1970) *The Possibility of Altruism* (Princeton, NJ: Princeton University Press).
Nagel, Thomas (1979a) 'Moral Luck', reprinted in his *Mortal Questions* (Cambridge: Cambridge University Press).
Nagel, Thomas (1979b) 'Ruthlessness in Public Life', reprinted in his *Mortal Questions* (Cambridge: Cambridge University Press).

Nagel, Thomas (1986) *The View from Nowhere* (Oxford: Oxford University Press).
Nagel, Thomas (1997) *The Last Word* (Oxford: Oxford University Press).
Neiman, Susan (1994) *The Unity of Reason: Rereading Kant* (Oxford: Oxford University Press).
Nell (=O'Neill), Onora (1975) *Acting on Principle: An Essay on Kantian Ethics* (New York: Columbia University Press).
Nemirow, Laurence (1990) 'Physicalism and the Cognitive Role of Acquaintance', in W.G. Lycan (ed.), *Mind and Cognition: A Reader* (Oxford: Basil Blackwell).
Nietzsche, Friedrich (1967a) *On the Genealogy of Morals*, trans. and ed. Walter Kaufman, in his *On the Genealogy of Morals and Ecce Homo* (New York: Random House).
Nietzsche, Friedrich (1967b) *Ecce Homo*, trans. and ed. Walter Kaufman, in his *On the Genealogy of Morals and Ecce Homo* (New York: Random House).
Nietzsche, Friedrich (1969) *Thus Spoke Zarathustra*, trans. R.J. Hollingdale (Harmondsworth: Penguin).
Nietzsche, Friedrich (1973) *Beyond Good and Evil*, trans. R.J. Hollingdale (Harmondsworth: Penguin).
Nietzsche, Friedrich (1974) *The Gay Science*, trans. Walter Kaufmann (New York: Random House).
Nietzsche, Friedrich (1990) *Twilight of the Idols*, trans. R.J. Hollingdale, in his *Twilight of the Idols and The Anti-Christ* (Harmondsworth: Penguin).
Nozick, Robert (1981) *Philosophical Explanations* (Cambridge, MA: Harvard University Press).
Nussbaum, Martha C. (1995) 'Aristotle on Human Nature and the Foundations of Ethics', in J.E.J. Altham and Ross Harrison (eds), *World, Mind, and Ethics: Essays on the Ethical Philosophy of Bernard Williams* (Cambridge: Cambridge University Press).
Nussbaum, Martha C. (2001) *The Fragility of Goodness: Luck and Ethics in Greek Tragedy and Philosophy*, 2nd edn (Cambridge: Cambridge University Press).
O'Neill, Onora (1989a) *Constructions of Reason: Explorations of Kant's Practical Philosophy* (Cambridge: Cambridge University Press).
O'Neill, Onora (1989b) 'Reason and Autonomy in *Grundlegung* III', reprinted in her *Constructions of Reason* (Cambridge: Cambridge University Press).
O'Neill, Onora (1989c) 'Consistency in Action', reprinted in her *Constructions of Reason* (Cambridge: Cambridge University Press).
O'Neill, Onora (1989d) 'Kant After Virtue', reprinted in her *Constructions of Reason* (Cambridge: Cambridge University Press).
O'Neill, Onora (1997) 'Kant on Reason and Religion', *The Tanner Lectures on Human Values* 18.
O'Neill, Onora (1998) 'Necessary Anthropomorphism and Contingent Speciesism' (=Part II of 'Kant on Duties Regarding Nonrational Nature'), *Proceedings of the Aristotelian Society* Supp. Vol. 72.
Orwell, George (1987) Volume 9 (=*Nineteen Eighty-Four*) of Peter Davison (ed.), *The Complete Works of George Orwell* (London: Secker & Warburg).
O'Shaugnessy, Brian (1980) *The Will: A Dual Aspect Theory* (Cambridge: Cambridge University Press).
Ovid (1986) *Metamorphoses*, trans. A.D. Melville (Oxford: Oxford University Press).

Palmquist, Stephen (1992) 'Does Kant Reduce Religion to Morality?', *Kant Studien* 83.
Parfit, Derek (1984) *Reasons and Persons* (Oxford: Oxford University Press).
Parfit, Derek (2001) 'Bombs and Coconuts, or Rational Irrationality', in Christopher W. Morris and Arthur Ripstein (eds), *Practical Rationality and Preference: Essays for David Gauthier* (Cambridge: Cambridge University Press).
Pascal, Blaise (1960a) *Pensées and Notes on Religion and Other Subjects*, ed. Louis Lafuma and trans. John Warrington (London: Dent).
Pascal, Blaise (1960b) *Pensées*, in his *Pensées and Notes on Religion and Other Subjects* (London: Dent).
Paton, H.J. (1947) *The Categorical Imperative: A Study in Kant's Moral Philosophy* (London: Hutchinson).
Peacocke, Christopher (1992) *A Study of Concepts* (Cambridge, MA: The MIT Press).
Peacocke, Christopher (1993) 'Proof and Truth', in John Haldane and Crispin Wright (eds), *Reality, Representation, and Projection* (Oxford: Oxford University Press).
Pears, David (1984) *Motivated Irrationality* (Oxford: Oxford University Press).
Perovich, Anthony M. (1991) '"For Reason... Also Has Its Mysteries": Immortality, *Religion*, and "The End of All Things"', in Philip J. Rossi and Michael Wreen (eds), *Kant's Philosophy of Religion Reconsidered* (Bloomington and Indianapolis: Indiana University Press).
Pindar (1980) *Pindar's Victory Songs*, trans. Frank J. Nisetich (Baltimore: The Johns Hopkins University Press).
Plato (1961a) *Euthyphro*, trans. Lane Cooper, in his *The Collected Dialogues*, ed. Edith Hamilton and Huntington Cairns (Princeton, NJ: Princeton University Press).
Plato (1961b) *Protagoras*, trans. W.K.C. Guthrie, in his *The Collected Dialogues*, ed. Edith Hamilton and Huntington Cairns (Princeton, NJ: Princeton University Press).
Plato (1961c) *Republic*, trans. Paul Shorey, in his *The Collected Dialogues*, ed. Edith Hamilton and Huntington Cairns (Princeton, NJ: Princeton University Press).
Price, H.H. (1966) 'Belief "In" and Belief "That"', *Religious Studies* 2.
Priest, Graham (2002) 'Rational Dilemmas', *Analysis* 62.
Proust, Marcel (1983) *Remembrance of Things Past*, trans. C.K. Scott Moncrieff, Terence Kilmartin, and Andreas Mayor, 3 vols (Harmondsworth: Penguin).
Putnam, Hilary (1981) *Reason, Truth and History* (Cambridge: Cambridge University Press).
Quine, W.V. (1960) *Word and Object* (Cambridge, MA: The MIT Press).
Quine, W.V. (1961) 'Identity, Ostension, and Hypostasis', reprinted in his *From a Logical Point of View: Logico-Philosophical Essays* (New York: Harper & Row).
Quine, W.V. (1990a) 'Creation', in his *Quiddities: An Intermittently Philosophical Dictionary* (Harmondsworth: Penguin).
Quine, W.V. (1990b) 'Free Will', in his *Quiddities: An Intermittently Philosophical Dictionary* (Harmondsworth: Penguin).
Quinn, Philip L. (1986) 'Christian Atonement and Kantian Justification', *Faith and Philosophy* 3.

Rawls, John (1999) *A Theory of Justice*, 2nd edn (Oxford: Oxford University Press).
Rawls, John (2000) *Lectures on the History of Moral Philosophy*, ed. Barbara Herman (Cambridge, MA: Harvard University Press).
Raz, Joseph (ed.) (1978) *Practical Reasoning* (Oxford: Oxford University Press).
Reardon, Bernard M.G. (1988) *Kant as Philosophical Theologian* (London: Macmillan).
Reath, Andrews (1989) 'Kant's Theory of Moral Sensibility: Respect for the Moral Law and the Influence of Inclination', *Kant Studien* 80.
Ricoeur, Paul (1966) *Freedom and Nature: The Voluntary and the Involuntary*, trans. Erazim Kohak (Evanston, IL: Northwestern University Press).
Ricoeur, Paul (1974) 'Freedom in the Light of Hope', trans. Robert Sweeney, in his *The Conflict of Interpretations: Essays in Hermeneutics*, ed. Don Ihde (Evanston, IL: Northwestern University Press).
Ricoeur, Paul (1992) *Oneself as Another*, trans. Kathleen Blamey (Chicago: The University of Chicago Press).
Ross, W.D. (1954) *Kant's Ethical Theory: A Commentary on the Groundwork of the Metaphysics of Morals* (Oxford: Oxford University Press).
Rossi, Philip J. and Wreen, Michael (eds) (1991) *Kant's Philosophy of Religion Reconsidered* (Bloomington and Indianapolis: Indiana University Press).
Rotman, Brian (1993) *Ad Infinitum... The Ghost in Turing's Machine: Taking God Out of Mathematics and Putting the Body Back in: An Essay in Corporeal Semiotics* (Stanford, CA: Stanford University Press).
Russell, Bertrand (1975) *Autobiography* (London: Allen & Unwin).
Ryckman, Thomas (1998) 'Geometry, Philosophical Issues in', in Edward Craig (ed.), *Routledge Encyclopedia of Philosophy* (London: Routledge).
Ryle, Gilbert (1949) *The Concept of Mind* (London: Hutchinson).
Sacks, Mark (2000) *Objectivity and Insight* (Oxford: Oxford University Press).
Sainsbury, R.M. (1995) *Paradoxes*, 2nd edn (Cambridge: Cambridge University Press).
Sartre, Jean-Paul (1957) *Being and Nothingness: An Essay on Phenomenological Ontology*, trans. Hazel E. Barnes (London: Methuen).
Scanlon, T.M. (1998) *What We Owe to Each Other* (Cambridge, MA: Harvard University Press).
Schlossberger, Eugene (1986) 'Why We Are Responsible for Our Emotions', *Mind* 95.
Schneewind, J.B. (1992) 'Autonomy, Obligation, and Virtue: An Overview of Kant's Moral Philosophy', in Paul Guyer (ed.), *The Cambridge Companion to Kant* (Cambridge: Cambridge University Press).
Searle, John R. (1967) 'How to Derive "Ought" From "Is"', reprinted in Philippa Foot (ed.), *Theories of Ethics* (Oxford: Oxford University Press).
Searle, John R. (2001) *Rationality in Action* (Cambridge, MA: The MIT Press).
Seidler, Victor J. (1986) *Kant, Respect and Injustice: The Limits of Liberal Moral Theory* (London: Routledge & Kegan Paul).
Sellars, Wilfrid (1963) 'Empiricism and the Philosophy of Mind', reprinted in his *Science, Perception and Reality* (London: Routledge & Kegan Paul).
Sher, George (2001) 'Blame for Traits', *Noûs* 35.
Sherman, Nancy (1997) *Making a Necessity of Virtue: Aristotle and Kant on Virtue* (Cambridge: Cambridge University Press).

Sidgwick, Henry E. (1962) *The Methods of Ethics* (London: Macmillan).
Silber, John R. (1960) 'The Ethical Significance of Kant's *Religion*', in Immanuel Kant, *Religion Within the Limits of Reason Alone*, trans. Theodore M. Greene and Hoyt H. Hudson (New York: Harper & Row).
Skorupski, John (1999a) 'Freedom, Morality, and Recognition: Some Theses of Kant and Hegel', in his *Ethical Explorations* (Oxford: Oxford University Press).
Skorupski, John (1999b) 'Irrealist Cognitivism', in Jonathan Dancy (ed.), *Normativity* (Oxford: Basil Blackwell).
Smilansky, Saul (2000) *Free Will and Illusion* (Oxford: Oxford University Press).
Smith, Michael (1994) *The Moral Problem* (Oxford: Basil Blackwell).
Smith, Michael, Lewis, David, and Johnston, Mark (1989) 'Dispositional Theories of Value', *Proceedings of the Aristotelian Society* Supp. Vol. 63.
Sorensen, Roy A. (1988) *Blindspots* (Oxford: Oxford University Press).
Spinoza, Baruch (1959) *Ethics*, trans. Andrew Boyle (London: Dent).
Stanley, Jason and Williamson, Timothy (2001) 'Knowing How', *The Journal of Philosophy* 98.
Stratton-Lake, Philip (1993) 'Reason, Appropriateness and Hope: Sketch of a Kantian Account of a Finite Rationality', *International Journal of Philosophical Studies* 1.
Stratton-Lake, Philip (2000) *Kant, Duty and Moral Worth* (London: Routledge).
Strawson, Galen (1986) *Freedom and Belief* (Oxford: Oxford University Press).
Strawson, P.F. (1952) *Introduction to Logical Theory* (London: Methuen).
Strawson, P.F. (1966) *The Bounds of Sense: An Essay on Kant's Critique of Pure Reason* (London: Methuen).
Strawson, P.F. (1974) 'Freedom and Resentment', reprinted in his *Freedom and Resentment and Other Essays* (London: Methuen).
Styron, William (1992) *Sophie's Choice* (London: Picador).
Sullivan, Roger J. (1989) *Immanuel Kant's Moral Theory* (Cambridge: Cambridge University Press).
Sullivan, Roger J. (1994) *An Introduction to Kant's Ethics* (Cambridge: Cambridge University Press).
Taylor, Charles (1975) *Hegel* (Cambridge: Cambridge University Press).
Taylor, Charles (1989) *Sources of the Self: The Making of Modern Identity* (Cambridge, MA: Harvard University Press).
Teale, A.E. (1951) *Kantian Ethics* (Oxford: Oxford University Press).
Tertullian, Quintus Septimus Florens (1942) *De Carne Christi* = A. Kroymann (ed.), Corpus Scriptorum Ecclesiasticorum Latinorum Vol. 70 (Vienna: Tempsky).
Thomson, Garrett (1987) *Needs* (London: Routledge & Kegan Paul).
Thomson, Garrett (2000) *On Kant* (Belmont: Wadsworth).
Turetzky, Philip (1998) *Time* (London: Routledge).
Vaihinger, Hans (1935) *The Philosophy of 'As If': A System of the Theoretical, Practical and Religious Fictions of Mankind*, trans. C.K. Ogden (London: Routledge & Kegan Paul).
van Inwagen, Peter (1983) *An Essay on Free Will* (Oxford: Oxford University Press).
Velkley, Richard L. (1989) *Freedom and the End of Reason: On the Moral Foundations of Kant's Critical Philosophy* (Chicago: The University of Chicago Press).

Voltaire (1990) *Candide*, trans. Roger Pearson, in his *Candide and Other Stories* (Oxford: Oxford University Press).
Vossenkuhl, Wilhelm (1987–8) 'The Paradox in Kant's Rational Religion', *Proceedings of the Aristotelian Society* 88.
Walker, Ralph C.S. (1978) *Kant* (London: Routledge & Kegan Paul).
Walker, Ralph C.S. (1989) *The Coherence Theory of Truth: Realism, Anti-Realism, Idealism* (London: Routledge).
Walker, Ralph C.S. (1998) *Kant and the Moral Law* (London: Phoenix).
Walker, Ralph C.S. (1999) 'Induction and Transcendental Argument', in Robert Stern (ed.), *Transcendental Arguments: Problems and Prospects* (Oxford: Oxford University Press).
Watson, Gary (ed.) (1982) *Free Will* (Oxford: Oxford University Press).
Watt, A.J. (1975) 'Transcendental Arguments and Moral Principles', *Philosophical Quarterly* 25.
Webb, C.C.J. (1926) *Kant's Philosophy of Religion* (Oxford: Oxford University Press).
Wedgwood, Ralph (2001) 'Conceptual Role Semantics For Moral Terms', *The Philosophical Review* 110.
Wiggins, David (1987) 'Claims of Need', in his *Needs, Values, Truth* (Oxford: Basil Blackwell).
Wiggins, David (1995) 'Categorical Requirements: Kant and Hume on the Idea of Duty' in Rosalind Hursthouse, Gavin Lawrence, and Warren Quinn (eds), *Virtues and Reasons: Philippa Foot and Moral Theory* (Oxford: Oxford University Press).
Wiggins, David (1998) 'In a Subjectivist Framework, Categorical Requirements and Real Practical Reasons', in Christoph Fehige and Ulla Wessels (eds), *Preferences: Perspectives in Analytical Philosophy* (Berlin: Walter de Gruyter).
Williams, Bernard (1972) *Morality: An Introduction to Ethics* (Cambridge: Cambridge University Press).
Williams, Bernard (1973a) 'Deciding to Believe', reprinted in his *Problems of the Self* (Cambridge: Cambridge University Press).
Williams, Bernard (1973b) 'Ethical Consistency', reprinted in his *Problems of the Self* (Cambridge: Cambridge University Press).
Williams, Bernard (1973c) 'Egoism and Altruism', in his *Problems of the Self* (Cambridge: Cambridge University Press).
Williams, Bernard (1973d) 'A Critique of Utilitarianism', in J.J.C. Smart and Bernard Williams, *Utilitarianism: For and Against* (Cambridge: Cambridge University Press).
Williams, Bernard (1981a) 'Moral Luck', reprinted in his *Moral Luck* (Cambridge: Cambridge University Press).
Williams, Bernard (1981b) 'Conflicts of Values', reprinted in his *Moral Luck* (Cambridge: Cambridge University Press).
Williams, Bernard (1981c) 'Internal and External Reasons', reprinted in his *Moral Luck* (Cambridge: Cambridge University Press).
Williams, Bernard (1985) *Ethics and the Limits of Philosophy* (London: Fontana).
Williams, Bernard (1986) contribution to 'Making Ends Meet: A Discussion of *Ethics and the Limits of Philosophy*', *Philosophical Books* 27.

Williams, Bernard (1993) *Shame and Necessity* (Berkeley, CA: The University of California Press).
Williams, Bernard (1995a) 'How Free Does the Will Need to Be?', reprinted in his *Making Sense of Humanity and Other Philosophical Papers* (Cambridge: Cambridge University Press).
Williams, Bernard (1995b) 'Internal Reasons and the Obscurity of Blame', reprinted in his *Making Sense of Humanity and Other Philosophical Papers* (Cambridge: Cambridge University Press).
Williams, Bernard (1995c) 'Acts and Omissions, Doing and Not Doing', reprinted in his *Making Sense of Humanity and Other Philosophical Papers* (Cambridge: Cambridge University Press).
Williams, Bernard (1995d) 'Evolution, Ethics, and the Representation Problem', reprinted in his *Making Sense of Humanity and Other Philosophical Papers* (Cambridge: Cambridge University Press).
Williams, Bernard (1995e) 'Moral Luck: A Postscript', reprinted in his *Making Sense of Humanity and Other Philosophical Papers* (Cambridge: Cambridge University Press).
Williams, Bernard (1995f) 'Replies', in J.E.J. Altham and Ross Harrison (eds), *World, Mind, and Ethics: Essays on the Ethical Philosophy of Bernard Williams* (Cambridge: Cambridge University Press).
Williams, Bernard (1998) 'Ethics', in A.C. Grayling (ed.), *Philosophy 1: A Guide Through the Subject* (Oxford: Oxford University Press).
Williams, Bernard (2000) 'Philosophy as a Humanistic Discipline', *Philosophy* 75.
Williams, Bernard (2002) *Truth and Truthfulness: An Essay in Genealogy* (Princeton, NJ: Princeton University Press).
Williams, S.G. (1989/90) 'Belief, Desire, and the Praxis of Reasoning', *Proceedings of the Aristotelian Society* 90.
Williams, T.C. (1968) *The Concept of the Categorical Imperative: A Study of the Place of the Categorical Imperative in Kant's Ethical Theory* (Oxford: Oxford University Press).
Wittgenstein, Ludwig (1961) *Tractatus Logico-Philosophicus*, trans. D.F. Pears and B.F. McGuiness (London: Routledge & Kegan Paul).
Wittgenstein, Ludwig (1965) 'A Lecture on Ethics', *Philosophical Review* 74.
Wittgenstein, Ludwig (1967) *Zettel*, ed. G.E.M. Anscombe and G.H. von Wright and trans. G.E.M. Anscombe (Oxford: Basil Blackwell).
Wittgenstein, Ludwig (1969) *On Certainty*, ed. G.E.M. Anscombe and G.H. von Wright and trans. Denis Paul and G.E.M. Anscombe (Oxford: Basil Blackwell).
Wittgenstein, Ludwig (1974a) *Philosophical Grammar*, ed. Rush Rhees and trans. Anthony Kenny (Oxford: Basil Blackwell).
Wittgenstein, Ludwig (1974b) *Philosophical Investigations*, trans. G.E.M. Anscombe, revised edn (Oxford: Basil Blackwell).
Wittgenstein, Ludwig (1978) *Remarks on the Foundations of Mathematics*, ed. G.H. von Wright, Rush Rhees, and G.E.M. Anscombe and trans. G.E.M. Anscombe, 3rd edn (Oxford: Basil Blackwell).
Wittgenstein, Ludwig (1979) *Notebooks: 1914–1916*, ed. G.H. von Wright and G.E.M. Anscombe and trans. G.E.M. Anscombe (Oxford: Basil Blackwell).
Wolf, Susan (1990) *Freedom Within Reason* (Oxford: Oxford University Press).

Wolff, Robert Paul (1973) *The Autonomy of Reason: A Commentary on Kant's Groundwork of the Metaphysics of Morals* (New York: Harper & Row).
Wolff, Robert Paul (ed.) (1969) *Foundations of the Metaphysics of Morals with Critical Essays* (Indianapolis: The Bobbs-Merrill Co.).
Wolterstorff, Nicholas P. (1991) 'Conundrums in Kant's Rational Religion', in Philip J. Rossi and Michael Wreen (eds), *Kant's Philosophy of Religion Reconsidered* (Bloomington and Indianapolis: Indiana University Press).
Wood, Allen W. (1970) *Kant's Moral Religion* (Ithaca, NY: Cornell University Press).
Wood, Allen W. (1978) *Kant's Rational Theology* (Ithaca, NY: Cornell University Press).
Wood, Allen W. (1984) 'Kant's Compatibilism', in Allen W. Wood (ed.), *Self and Nature in Kant's Philosophy* (Ithaca, NY: Cornell University Press).
Wood, Allen W. (1990) *Hegel's Ethical Thought* (Cambridge: Cambridge University Press).
Wood, Allen W. (1992) 'Rational Theology, Moral Faith, and Religion', in Paul Guyer (ed.), *The Cambridge Companion to Kant* (Cambridge: Cambridge University Press).
Wood, Allen W. (1998) 'Kant on Duties Regarding Nonrational Nature', *Proceedings of the Aristotelian Society* Supp. Vol. 72.
Wood, Allen W. (1999) *Kant's Ethical Thought* (Cambridge: Cambridge University Press).
Yovel, Yirmiyahu (1980) *Kant and the Philosophy of History* (Princeton, NJ: Princeton University Press).

Index

abnormality *see* normality and abnormality
Abraham 164
action-guiding concepts: defined and explored xv, 39–51, 56–7, 63–6, 70, 76, 83, 89, 92–3, 96, 117, 133, 171, 173–4, 201n.16, 202–3n.49; requiring practices xv, 51–6, 60, 77; *see also* concepts encompassing practices
active, being xvi, 29–30, 39, 57, 60, 75, 85, 90–6 *passim*, 103, 116, 125–7, 195–6; *see also* autonomy
aesthetics 13, 37, 87–8, 122, 131, 164, 171
affirmation 66, 84–5; *see also amor fati*
Allison, Henry E. 96, 200nn.35 and 36
amor fati 194, 221n.53; *see also* affirmation
'An Answer to the Question: What is Enlightenment?' 20, 89
Anscombe, G.E.M. 67–71, 82
Ansell Pearson, Keith 10, 19, 83, 220n.26
answerability: of concepts to nothing *see* concepts have nothing to answer to; of resolutions to practices *see under* resolutions
Anzaldúa, Gloria 210n.9
appearance/reality distinction, Kant's xvii, xix, 79, 103–12 *passim*, 114–15, 119–20, 124–5, 132, 135–8 *passim*, 153–5, 161–2, 167, 208nn.43 and 52
a priori concepts in Kant 33–4, 37, 101–5, 109, 145, 166, 187, 189, 208n.51; *see also* regulative ideals
Archimidean point 69
arguments for the existence of God 1, 147–9, 157, 164, 166–7, 171, 188, 191, 194, 217n.77, 218n.98, 220n.37; *see also* 'The Only Possible Argument in Support of a Demonstration of the Existence of God', third postulate of pure practical reason
Aristotle vi, 7–9, 37, 63, 129, 133, 138, 142–3, 155, 201n.13, 214n.95
astrology 48, 74
atonement and redemption 84, 147–8, 155–6, 163, 180, 183, 196, 219n.24; *see also* grace
Augustin, St 151
Austin, J.L. 69, 210n.8
authority xiv, xvi, 2, 5, 14, 20, 22, 25, 134, 136
autonomy 20, 22, 25, 73, 87–88, 90, 94–8, 101, 110, 119, 125, 132, 135–8, 148–50, 155, 159; *see also* being active, concepts have nothing to answer to, freedom

babies and children 46–8, 54–6, 69, 83, 86, 130, 133, 143–5
bagging 62–3
Baptist, the *see* John the Baptist
Basic Idea xviii, xx, 29, 128, 130–1, 136–7, 141–6 *passim*, 170, 176–8, 183, 187, 193; contingency of xix, 140, 170–2, 176, 183, 186; meaning of xviii–xix, 128–35 *passim*, 139, 142–5, 172–9 *passim*, 214n.95; security of xix–xx, 172, 175–88 *passim*, 193, 195, *see also* making sense fostered by the world, providence; significance of if true xviii, 128, 130–1, 139–46 *passim*, 170, 175, 188, 214n.86; whether it can be established xviii, 7–8, 131–46 *passim*, 170, 177, 186–7; whether it

Basic Idea *continued*
  can be refuted 129–30, 141–2, 145–6, 170, 175, 187; *see also* good will as supreme value, rationality as a value
  becoming those that we are 10, 83, 185, 220n.26
belief in God (as opposed to belief that God exists) xx, 188–91, 194; *see also* faith, third postulate of pure practical reason
Bergson, Henri 85
Bible 148, 152, 199n.19; *see also* St Paul, Psalmists
biological necessity 7–8, 10, 23, 51, 66, 71, 79, 83, 205n.112; *see also* conative states as non-rational forces, needs
Blackburn, Simon 212n.54
blame and blameworthiness vi, xvii, 6, 95, 105, 111–12, 115–18, 128, 153–4, 182; *see also* evil and wrong-doing, guilt, Radical Picture, responsibility
blameworthiness *see* blame and blameworthiness
Bousquet, Joe 195
Brandom, Robert 90, 201n.3, 204n.89

Camus, Albert 86, 147
Cantor, Georg 123, 128
categorical imperatives xiv–xv, 21–31 *passim*, 57, 79, 198n.5; transcendental vindication of *see* transcendental vindication of categorical imperatives; *see also* duty, fundamental categorical imperative, moral law, obligations
Catholicism 50–1
causation 85, 94–112 *passim*, 114–15, 125, 135, 160–1, 188, 206n.12; *see also* determinism, Newtonian mechanics
Cavell, Stanley 51
character and disposition 87, 106–8, 111–12, 127, 151–6 *passim*, 161–3, 165; *see also* strength and weakness of character
children *see* babies and children
Christ *see* Jesus Christ
Christianity 67, 82–3, 89, 91, 147–8, 150, 155–6, 163, 169, 199n.19; *see also* Catholicism, pietism
Chrysippus 209n.67
Coleridge, S.T. 203n.63, 211n.22
commands, divine *see* God's commands

commitment to morality and rationality xix–xx, 116, 152, 155, 157, 162–3, 176–178, 183–193 *passim*
communal in relation to individual xvi, 34–5, 51, 63, 73–78, 87–9, 119, 124–5, 133–4, 159–160, 172–83 *passim*, 186, 204nn.82, 89, and 92, 212n.54, 220n.29; *see also* discord situations, general reasons, reasons must be in the public domain, shared conative states, shared reasons
compassion 40, 45–7, 83; *see also* love
compatibilism: Kant's version of xvii, 97–117 *passim*, 207n.35, 208n.58, 209n.1, 210n.18; relativistic *see* Kant's version of compatibilism; *see also* whether determinism is compatible with freedom, Incommensurability Thesis
conative states: as non-rational forces vi, 30, 32, 57, 94–7 *passim*, 107, 110, 115, 125–7, 132, 153, 179, *see also* relation of irrationality to non-rationality, being passive; content of *see* content of a conative state; ethically productive *see* ethically productive conative states; relation of to reasons 5–6, 8–9, 17, 43, 45–6, 126, 139–40, 183, 200n.35, 214n.85; *see also* conative objectivism, ethically productive conative states; shared *see* shared conative states; type of *see* type of a conative state
conative objectivism xiii, 6–11, 16–17, 19, 23, 131, 146, 174–5; relation of rationalism to *see under* rationalism; *see also* ethically productive conative states
concept of God, whether it is coherent *see under* God
concepts: action-guiding *see* action-guiding concepts; *a priori* in Kant *see a priori* concepts in Kant; development of *see* development of concepts; disengaged grasp of *see* disengaged grasp of concepts; encompassing practices 54–6, 77, 202n.39; engaged grasp of *see* possession of concepts; grasp of *see* grasp of concepts; have nothing to answer to 73–4, 191; living by *see* living by concepts; possession of *see* possession of concepts; radically

new *see* radically new concepts; resolutions involving *see under* resolutions; subversion of *see* subversion of concepts and practices; superficial *see* superficial concepts; 'thick' ethical *see* 'thick' ethical concepts; vague *see* vague concepts; vicarious versus non-vicarious applications of *see* vicarious versus non-vicarious applications of concepts; *see also* conceptual space, whether the concept of God is coherent
conceptual space 66, 72, 78, 118, 121–3; *see also* logical space of reasons, possibilities
conclusion-directed objectivity xiii, 5–6, 11–17 *passim*
confidence 70, 78, 188, 192, 204n.78
consequentialism and non-consequentialism 154, 172–3, 175; *see also* utilitarianism
conservatism 68–9, 75–6, 127–8
constancy of nature xix, 42, 55, 97, 160–1, 171, 177, 182–3, 190, 192
content: of a conative state 8–9, 26, 174–5; of a reason 41, 201n.5
contrition *see* remorse and contrition and penitence
corruption and depravity 110–11, 129, 134, 141, 145–6, 152, 177, 186, 214n.103; *see also* evil and wrong-doing, normality and abnormality, self-love
courage 20, 87–9
cowardice 40, 53, 107, 183
Craig, Edward 143
creation and creativity xvii, 10, 15, 72–88 *passim*, 120–2, 168, 171, 192–4, 211n.21; *see also* imagination, genius, radically new concepts, unpredictability
creativity *see* creation and creativity
Critique of Practical Reason 23–4, 32, 57, 79, 93–110 *passim*, 114–15, 124–6, 132, 135–6, 148–9, 157, 164–5, 202n.28, 207n.32, 208nn.48, 51, and 58, 210n.18, 217n.83, 218n.6
Critique of Pure Reason 104, 108–12 *passim*, 114, 149, 158–6 *passim*, 188, 208nn. 51 and 58, 209n.3, 214n.105; *see also* Transcendental Deduction

Critique of the Power of Judgment 87–8, 102, 131, 142, 160, 166

Darwinism 9–10, 140–2, 214n.88; *see also* evolution, teleology
Davidson, Donald 91, 206nn.3 and 12
death vi, 10, 35, 50–1, 53–4, 58, 113, 126, 130, 135, 141, 156–63 *passim*, 179, 184, 194–5, 214n.88, 217n.76; *see also* immortality, suicide
Deduction, Transcendental *see* Transcendental Deduction
defeasibility: of obligations 182; of reasons xv, 26, 43–5, 53–5, 70, 74, 92–3, 127, 135, 173–4, 182; of resolutions 53, 182
Deleuze, Gilles 10, 19, 39, 83, 85, 161, 189, 194–5, 221n.56
depravity *see* corruption and depravity
determinism xvii, 97–9, 101–2, 107, 113, 120, 123–4, 167; whether it is compatible with freedom xvii, 96–102, 108, 111–12, 113–15, 120, 207nn.27 and 35; *see also* Incommensurability Thesis, Kant's version of compatibilism, Newtonian mechanics
development of concepts xv, 54–6, 77–84 *passim*, 88–9, 122, 130, 175–6, 182, 193–194; *see also* concepts encompassing practices
Diamond, Cora 49–50, 201n.18
dignity 83, 113, 151; *see also* nobility
disagreement 2–3, 15–16, 58, 174; socially grounded ethical *see* second objection to rationalism
discord situations 173–181 *passim*
discovery xviii, 1, 6, 17, 22–23, 32, 73, 85, 111, 122, 189, 191, 211n.21
disengaged grasp of concepts 48–51, 57, 60, 63–5, 72, 74–5, 180; *see also* vicarious versus non-vicarious applications of concepts
disposition *see* character and disposition
Dostoyevsky, Fyodor 213n.76
Dummett, Michael 211n.29
duty 20, 24, 31, 56, 79–80, 87, 89, 132, 135, 151–2, 154, 162–168 *passim*, 196, 198n.5, 205n.100, *see also* categorical imperatives, fundamental categorical imperative, moral law, obligations;

242 Index

duty *continued*
difference between acting in conformity with and acting from 27, 149, 152–3, 173; motive of acting from *see* motive of acting from duty

education and upbringing 24–5, 35, 43, 45–6, 51, 67, 83, 111–12, 129, 144
Elford, John 82
encompassing of practices by concepts *see* concepts encompassing practices
engaged grasp of concepts *see* possession of concepts
English, the 67
Engstrom, Stephen 160, 221n.47
enlightenment 20, 67, 88–9, 150, 169; *see also* 'An Answer to the Question: What Is Enlightenment?'
Epicureans 161
eternal life *see* immortality
ethical concepts, 'thick' *see* 'thick' ethical concepts
ethical disagreement, socially grounded *see* second objection to rationalism
ethical expertise *see* first objection to rationalism
ethically productive conative states 6–9, 16, 131, 140, 175; *see also* conative objectivism
ethics: ground-level *see* normative ethics; normative *see* normative ethics; upper-level *see* meta-ethics
Euclidean and non-Euclidean geometry 15–16, 58–60, 68, 74
evil and wrong-doing xviii–xix, 24–5, 33, 87, 96, 106–12 *passim*, 126–7, 134, 149–56, 162–4, 173, 175, 178–9, 185–8, 212n.41, 220n.29; *see also* blame and blameworthiness, corruption and depravity, guilt, self-love
evolution 9–12; *see also* Darwinism, teleology
expertise, ethical *see* first objection to rationalism
explanatory reasons 6, 30, 43, 91, 94, 96, 100–1, 135, 151, 200n.53

fact of pure reason xviii, 24, 93, 102, 110, 124, 126, 136–7, 146, 165, 208n.48, 213n.74
faith 25, 51, 102–3, 108, 166, 171–2, 178, 187, 189, 196, 208n.58; *see also* belief in God, hope, trust
first objection to rationalism *see under* rationalism
first postulate of pure practical reason *see under* postulates of pure practical reason
Fogelin, Robert J. 192
forms of life xvi, 9, 11, 15–16, 47, 51, 56, 66–80 *passim*, 172, 174; *see also* living by concepts
freedom: as a value 94–5, 118–19, 128, 132, 137–9, 213n.76; how to be understood 94–105 *passim*, 113–26 *passim*, 132, 193, 206n.14, 210n.8, *see also* Incommensurability Thesis, Radical Conception, whether determinism is compatible with freedom; relation of to morality *see* 'ought' implies 'can'; whether determinism is compatible with *see under* determinism; whether it is compatible with irrationality *see* Radical Conception; *see also* being active, autonomy, first postulate of pure practical reason, *Wille*, *Willkür*
Frege, Gottlob 211n.29
Friedrich II (= Frederick the Great) 54, 201n.23
Friedrich Wilhelm II 169
fundamental categorical imperative 27, 29, 31, 36–7, 90, 198n.5, 202n.38, 205n.100; in the form of acting only on maxims that one can will to be laws xiv, 28–37, 57–8, 60, 77–81 *passim*, 88, *see also* golden rule; in the form of treating humanity as an end xiv, 28–9, 36–7, 134; *see also* categorical imperatives, duty, moral law
future vi, 66, 71–2, 76–87 *passim*, 121, 154, 163, 171–2, 177–85 *passim*, 195, 211n.21, 216n.59, 217n.73; *see also* unpredictability

genealogy (of a Nietzschean kind) 70–1, 142–3
general reasons xv, 43–4; *see also* shared reasons
genius 88
geometry *see* Euclidean and non-Euclidean geometry

Index 243

God xix–xx, 1, 11, 22–3, 27, 61, 67, 85, 106, 133, 147, 149–50, 155–69 *passim*, 170–1, 185–96 *passim*; arguments for the existence of *see* arguments for the existence of God; belief in *see* belief in God; His commands xviii, 22, 67, 106, 148–50, *see also* relation of morality to religion; whether the concept of is coherent xx, 157–8, 164–6, 187, 190–2; *see also* third postulate of pure practical reason
Gödel, Kurt 84
golden rule 32; *see also* fundamental categorical imperative in the form of acting only on maxims that one can will to be laws
good, highest *see* highest good
Goodman, Nelson 42, 68; *see also* 'grueness'
good will as supreme value xiv, xviii, 23, 27–28, 131, 155–6, 158; *see also* Basic Idea
grace 147–8, 156, 163, 170; *see also* atonement and redemption
grasp of concepts xv, 12, 48–51, 72, 119, 123, 180; disengaged *see* disengaged grasp of concepts; engaged *see* possession of concepts
ground-level ethics *see* normative ethics
Groundwork of the Metaphysics of Morals 20–37 *passim*, 54, 79–81, 94–108 *passim*, 131, 135, 138, 140, 142, 158, 167, 198n.5, 199n.29, 200n.2, 205n.100, 208nn.51 and 59, 214n.90
'grueness' 42, 49, 56, 59, 66, 68, 74–5, 82, 171, 186, 194, 203n.62
Guattari, Félix 189
guilt 28, 86, 111, 156, 163, 182; *see also* blame and blameworthiness, evil and wrong-doing, responsibility

Hacker, P.M.S. 127, 204n.85
Hamlet 78
happiness and welfare xix, 27, 70, 125, 131, 147, 158–63, 184–5, 192–5; *see also* highest good, utilitarianism
Hare, R.M. 62–4
Hegel, G.W.F. 57–8, 189, 202n.40, 203n.57, 219n.12
Herod 33, 52, 154, 173, 181–2, 219n.19
highest good xix, 148–9, 158–63, 177, 193

Hollis, Martin 13
Holloway, Richard 82–3
hope xviii–xx, 11, 19, 45, 131, 146, 149–50, 156–66 *passim*, 170–2, 176–96 *passim*, 216n.59, 219n.12; *see also* faith, optimism
Hume, David 17, 38, 61, 70, 98–100, 113, 143, 199n.17, 207n.31, 210n.18, 219n.10
hypothetical imperatives xiv, 21–30 *passim*, 34, 57–8; *see also* means-end reasoning

ideals, regulative *see* regulative ideals
illusion, morality as an *see* under morality
imagination 64, 66, 71, 74, 77, 91, 124, 203n.63, 211n.22; *see also* creation and creativity
immorality *see* evil and wrong-doing
immortality xix, 147–8, 157, 161–3, 166, 179, 215n.2; *see also* second postulate of pure practical reason
impairments, mental *see* mental impairments
imperatives: categorical *see* categorical imperatives; hypothetical *see* hypothetical imperatives; *see also* fundamental categorical imperative
imperfection *see* perfection and imperfection
Incommensurability Thesis 114–15
incentives *see* motives and incentives
individual, communal in relation to *see* communal in relation to individual
ineffability 190–2, 204n.83, 213n.74, 221n.56
infinitude 15, 18, 33–4, 78–9, 106, 123, 128, 145, 155, 161–3, 189, 193–4, 212n.43, 217n.73; *see also* Georg Cantor
involvement of concepts by resolutions *see* resolutions involving concepts
irrationality: in the context of (a broader) rationality 60–1, 91–2, 129, 134, 141, 145–6, 151, 179–80, 184, 185, 187, *see also* paradoxical situations, rationalization of what is not rational; relation of to non-rationality xviii, 92, 94–7, 107, 110, 116, 118–19, 125–9, 179–80, *see also* irrationality in the context of rationality; whether it is

irrationality *continued*
  compatible with freedom *see* Radical Conception
'is'/'ought' distinction xvi, 61–5, 114
Isaac 164

Jacob 164
Jesus Christ 20, 22–3, 57, 149, 156, 163, 170, 203n.73
John the Baptist 33, 154
joy vi, 87, 205–6n.131, 217n.73
Judaism 48–9, 59, 67

Kant, Immanuel: *a priori* concepts in *see a priori* concepts in Kant; his appearance/reality distinction *see under* appearance/reality distinction; his rigorism *see under* rigorism; his version of compatibilism *see under* compatibilism; his version of rationalism *see under* rationalism; his version of rationalism reconstructed *see under* rationalism; his works *see* 'An Answer to the Question: What Is Enlightenment?', *Critique of Practical Reason*, *Critique of Pure Reason*, *Critique of the Power of Judgment*, *Groundwork of the Metaphysics of Morals*, *Lectures on Ethics*, 'On a Discovery according to which any New Critique of Pure Reason has been made Superfluous by an Earlier One', *Opus Postumum*, *Religion Within the Boundaries of Mere Reason*, 'The End of All Things', *The Metaphysics of Morals*, 'The Only Possible Argument in Support of a Demonstration of the Existence of God'; *see also* categorical imperatives, duty, fact of pure reason, fundamental categorical imperative, good will as supreme value, highest good, hypothetical imperatives, moral law, motive of acting from duty, postulates of pure practical reason, Transcendental Deduction, unconditionedness, *Wille*, *Willkür*
Kierkegaard, Søren 189, 192
knowledge vi, xviii, 12, 33, 73, 102–5, 109, 120, 123–4, 136–7, 143, 145, 158, 161, 165–7, 189–92, 204nn.83 and 85, 208n.58, 213 nn.73 and 74

Korsgaard, Christine 4–5, 19, 69–70, 134, 138–9, 200n.56, 201n.4

language 61–2, 68–71, 74–5, 86, 123, 127, 168, 190–2, 204n.82, 211n.29; *see also* nonsense
Lao Tze 192
Lectures on Ethics 194–6, 221n.54
Leibniz, G.W. 85
Lewis, David 18
living by concepts 13, 46–51, 66, 127, 171, 193; *see also* forms of life, possession of concepts
Lloyd, Genevieve 125
Locke, John 83
logical space of reasons 13, 77, 92, 95, 100–1, 103, 118–20, 179–85, 193, 208n.52; *see also* conceptual space
love 83, 129–30, 149, 189–90; of self *see* self-love; *see also* compassion
Lyotard, Jean-François 193

McDowell, John 201n.13, 205n.112
MacIntyre, Alasdair 67–71 *passim*, 82
Mackie, J.L. 4–5, 11, 15–16, 19, 62, 134, 174
making sense: equivalent to being rational xvi, 78–81, 87–8, 107, 119, 128–9, 172, 190, 212n.54; fostered by the world xix–xx, 88, 157, 171–89 *passim*, 193–6, *see also* providence, security of the Basic Idea; not something the world does xvi, xix, 10, 85, 160–1, 177, 189, 193, 195, 221n.56
Manichaeus 129
Marx, Karl 17–18, 197n.25
mathematics 5, 11–18, 24–5, 58, 84, 120–3, 128, 164, 210n.8, 211nn.21 and 24; *see also* Georg Cantor, Euclidean and non-Euclidean geometry, Kurt Gödel
maxims xiv–xvi, 30–6, 39, 51–60 *passim*, 66, 76–81, 88, 96, 107, 110, 122, 151, 153, 159, 173–4, 180, 182, 200n.35, 202nn.29 and 39; *see also* fundamental categorical imperative in the form of acting only on maxims that one can will to be laws, resolutions
means-end reasoning 17, 25–6, 140; *see also* hypothetical imperatives
mental impairments 133, 143–4

meta-ethics 1–2, 4, 11, 17, 32, 61
Michalson, Gordon E. 150, 168–9, 188
Moore, G.E. 218n.94
morality: as an illusion 22, 37, 109–10; commitment to *see* commitment to morality and rationality; relation of to freedom *see* 'ought' implies 'can'; relation of to religion xviii–xix, 67–8, 89, 148–50, 157–69 *passim*, 188, 199n.19, 215n.4; *see also* God's commands
moral law xviii, 23–4, 32, 76, 79, 87, 93, 102, 105–6, 110, 124, 126, 132, 135–6, 138, 148–60 *passim*, 164, 171; *see also* categorical imperatives, duty, fundamental categorical imperative, obligations
motive of acting from duty 27, 32, 97, 126, 135–6, 148–9, 151–3, 157–60 *passim*, 164, 173; *see also* difference between acting in conformity with duty and acting from duty, Kant's rigorism
motives and incentives 32–3, 35, 71, 90–4, 126, 135–6, 138, 148, 151–3, 161, 164, 172–3, 200n.35; *see also* explanatory reasons, motive of acting from duty, normative reasons, 'So what?'
Murdoch, Iris 17, 20, 189–90, 193, 220n.37

Nagel, Thomas 186, 201n.15
nature, constancy of *see* constancy of nature
narrative and stories 9, 11, 70–1, 75–6, 84–6, 147, 192–4; *see also* genealogy
necessity, biological *see* biological necessity
needs 9, 69–70, 82, 95, 97, 142, 148, 165, 170, 177, 179, 186, 188, 190, 202n.49; *see also* biological necessity, conative states as non-rational forces
Neiman, Susan 73
Nero 54
Neurath, Otto 76
Newtonian mechanics 97
Nicholas of Cusa 192
Nietzsche, Friedrich 67–71 *passim*, 82–7 *passim*, 142–3, 160–1, 177, 203n.60, 205–6n.131, 217n.73, 219nn.18 and 24, 220n.26, 221n.53; *see also* genealogy
nobility 20, 78–9, 113, 132, 193; *see also* dignity
non-consequentialism *see* consequentialism and non-consequentialism
non-Euclidean geometry *see* Euclidean and non-Euclidean geometry
non-rationality: relation of irrationality to *see under* irrationality; *see also* being passive, conative states as non-rational forces, rationalization of what is not rational
nonsense 88, 118, 127–8, 162, 192, 211n.36
non-vicarious applications of concepts *see* vicarious versus non-vicarious applications of concepts
normality and abnormality 7–8, 23–4, 82, 92, 133–4, 143–4, 146, 213n.62; *see also* corruption and depravity, irrationality in the context of rationality, mental impairments
normative ethics 1–4, 11, 16–17, 32, 61
normative reasons xv, 6, 30, 41, 43–7, 53, 91, 96, 100–1, 135, 139, 200n.53, 214n.85
no-win situations 33, 178–83, 186

obligations 21–2, 48, 61, 67, 97, 149–50, 159–60, 166, 173, 182, 219n.20; defeasibility of *see under* defeasibility; *see also* categorical imperatives, duty, fundamental categorical imperative, moral law
objections to rationalism *see under* rationalism
objectivism 2–18 *passim*, 135, 142, 174, 197n.19, 199n.17; conative *see* conative objectivism; queerness of *see* queerness of objectivism
objectivity xiii, 1–5, 9–11, 15–16, 19, 135, 142, 197n.19; conclusion-directed *see* conclusion-directed objectivity; world-directed *see* world-directed objectivity; *see also* objectivism
omissions xv, 41
'On a Discovery according to which any New Critique of Pure Reason has been made Superfluous by an Earlier One' 114

optimism 183; *see also* hope
Opus Postumum 150–1, 167–8
Orwell, George 210n.8
'ought': distinguished from 'is' *see* 'is'/'ought' distinction; implies 'can' 28, 30, 93–4, 102, 109, 126, 147, 154, 199n.26
Ovid 152

Pangloss, Dr 86
paradoxical situations 35–6, 60–1, 129–30, 179–81, 219nn.18 and 22
Parfit, Derek 179–80
Pascal, Blaise 113, 164, 189
passive, being 17, 29–30, 85, 87, 94–5, 99–100, 116, 125–30, 152
past vi, 66–69, 71, 82–5, 99, 107–8, 153–6 *passim*, 159, 162, 210n.9, 216n.59
Paul, St 170, 219n.10
Peacocke, Christopher 84, 201n.16
penitence *see* remorse and contrition and penitence
people (as rational beings in general) xviii, 5, 7, 19, 28–9, 37, 79, 83, 131, 133–5, 139, 143–6, 168, 199n.29, 202n.49, 204n.93, 212n.57, 212–213n.62, 214n.103
perfection and imperfection xix–xx, 23, 34, 39, 95, 119, 121, 155, 159, 161, 164–5, 170, 176, 178, 185–6, 188–9, 206n.14, 210n.15
physical objects and properties xvii, 5, 9, 12–13, 16, 33, 58–9, 68, 97–124 *passim*, 145, 160–1, 163, 167, 211n.30
pietism 25, 147, 149, 199n.19, 215nn.1 and 4
Pindar 220n.26
Plato 18, 108, 192
points of view xvii, 99–107 *passim*, 113, 129, 133–4, 137, 146, 208nn.43, 51, and 52, 212n.57
politics 37–8, 63, 66, 71–2, 112
possession of concepts: defined and explored xv, 40, 42, 47–65 *passim*, 72–6, 87, 92–3, 100–1, 117, 122, 126, 180–2, 191; question which concepts we are to possess xv–xvi, 57–89 *passim*, 130, 174, 180, 182–3, *see also* subversion of concepts and practices; *see also* living by concepts
possibilities xviii, 10, 19, 22, 56, 66, 71–2, 76–7, 80–1, 121–5, 133, 174, 181–3, 189, 193, 203n.62, 211nn.21 and 30; suitably salient *see* suitably salient possibilities; *see also* conceptual space
post-modernism 193
postulates of pure practical reason xix–xx, 157, 187, 192; first (that we are free) xvii, xix–xx, 73, 75, 86–7, 90–112 *passim*, 132, 136, 139, 147, 157–8, 165–7, 187–8, 193, 217n.79, 218n.87, *see also* autonomy, freedom; second (that we are immortal) xix–xx, 147, 157–66 *passim*, 179, 187–8, 193, 217n.79, 218n.87, *see also* immortality; status of xix–xx, 102, 108, 136–7, 156–67 *passim*, 187–8, 208n.58, 217n.79; third (that God exists) xix–xx, 147, 157–168 *passim*, 187–8, 193, 218n.87, *see also* belief in God, God
practices: action-guiding concepts requiring *see under* action-guiding concepts; answerability of resolutions to *see under* resolutions; concepts encompassing *see under* concepts; subversion of *see* subversion of concepts and practices
principles, regulative *see* regulative principles
privacy 39, 44–5
promising 17, 30–4 *passim*, 39, 46–7, 51–7 *passim*, 60–6, 70–2, 77, 81, 97, 106, 126, 154, 172–4, 181–2, 203n.73, 219n.19
Proust, Marcel vi
providence 86, 149, 160–2, 164, 171, 188, 191–6 *passim*, 217n.77; *see also* highest good, making sense fostered by the world, security of the Basic Idea
Psalmists 192
pure reason: fact of *see* fact of pure reason; whether it can be practical *see* third objection to rationalism; whether there is such a thing xvi, 36, 59, 65, 203n.57, 78, 81–2, 90, 97, 190; *see also* being rational, postulates of pure practical reason, rationality

queerness of objectivism 4–6, 11–12, 15–16

question: which concepts we are to possess *see under* possession of concepts; 'So what?' *see* 'So what?'; who 'we' are *see under* we
Quine, W.V. 76, 98, 113, 211n.30

Radical Conception xvii, 57, 90, 94–7, 110–11, 115–16, 119, 128, 132, 137–9, 147, 199n.21, 204n.86, 215n.17; *see also* Radical Picture
radically new concepts xvi–xvii, 66, 72, 121–3, 128, 175–6
Radical Picture xvii, 115–29 *passim*, 181; *see also* Radical Conception
rational, being: equivalent to making sense *see* making sense equivalent to being rational; *see also* pure reason, rationality
rationalism xiii–xiv, 11, 13–14, 17–18, 20, 25, 57, 78, 81–2, 95, 115, 131, 144; first objection to (that it allows for ethical expertise) xiii–xiv, 14–15, 17, 19, 24–5, 197n.19, 199n.17; Kant's version xiv, xvi, 18–19, 20–37 *passim*, 57–8, 61, 65, 77–82, 87–8, 93, 95, 135–6, 148–50, 157, 159, 164, 172–3, 182, *see also* Kant's version reconstructed; Kant's version reconstructed xv–xvi, 35–6, 41–2, 51–60 *passim*, 76–88 *passim*, 173–4, 182, 202n.39; relation of to conative objectivism xiii, xviii, 11, 17, 19, 29, 131, 139; second objection to (that it makes a mystery of socially grounded ethical disagreement) xiii–xiv, 14–17, 19, 25, 77, 174; third objection to (that pure reason cannot be practical) xiii–xiv, xvi–xvii, 14, 16–17, 19, 25–6, 36–7, 90–3, 97
rationality: as a value 20, 90–2, 118–19, 128–46 *passim*, 171–2, 179, 183–4, *see also* Basic Idea; as supreme value *see* Basic Idea; commitment to *see* commitment to morality and rationality; irrationality in the context of *see under* irrationality; relation of religion to *see under* religion; *see also* being rational, irrationality, non-rationality, pure reason, rationalization of what is not rational

rationalization of what is not rational 178, 183–6; *see also* irrationality in the context of rationality, paradoxical situations
reason *see* pure reason
reasoning, means-end *see* means-end reasoning
reasons: content of *see* content of a reason; defeasibility of *see under* defeasibility; explanatory *see* explanatory reasons; general *see* general reasons; logical space of *see* logical space of reasons; must be in the public domain 40–1, 201n.3; normative *see* normative reasons; relation of conative states to *see under* conative states; shared *see* shared reasons; type of *see* type of a reason
redemption *see* atonement and redemption
reform xix, 26, 87, 152–63 *passim*; *see also* remorse and contrition and penitence
regulative ideals 33–4, 145–6, 166, 187, 190, 214n.105, 220n.32; *see also* regulative principles
regulative principles 33–4, 145, 190–2, 214n.105, 220nn.32 and 42; *see also* regulative ideals
relativism 15–16, 58–60, 64, 174, 180–1, 219n.10; *see also* Kant's version of compatibilism
relativistic compatibilism *see* Kant's version of compatibilism
religion: relation of morality to *see under* morality; relation of to rationality xviii–xix, 149–50, 157, 164, 166, 168, 171, 185, 188–93 *passim*; *see also* Catholicism, Christianity, Judaism, pietism
Religion Within the Boundaries of Mere Reason 87, 107, 110–11, 148–63 *passim*, 169, 185–6, 214n.90, 215n.23
remorse and contrition and penitence 84, 154, 180–2; *see also* atonement and redemption, reform
renunciation *see* resignation and renunciation
resignation and renunciation 85–6, 127, 189, 195–6

resolutions xiv–xv, 30, 34–5, 52–3, 60, 66, 71, 76, 182; answerability of to practices, xv, 52–6, 77; defeasibility of *see under* defeasibility; involving concepts xv, 52, 55, 60, 182
respect xviii, 37, 47, 58, 83, 92, 132, 135–6, 149, 157, 160
responsibility 20, 95, 106–7, 110–12, 137, 177, 204n.89; *see also* blame and blameworthiness, guilt
ressentiment 85–6, 160–1, 177, 179, 189
Ricoeur, Paul 203n.59
rigorism, Kant's 33, 151–4, 173
roles 49, 63–4, 89, 203n.52, 204n.81
romanticism 130
Russell, Bertrand 212n.41

salient possibilities *see* suitably salient possibilities
Salome 33, 52, 154, 219n.19
Sartre, Jean-Paul 213n.76
Satan 170
Scanlon, T.M. 201n.11
science 2, 15, 18, 24, 58–9, 67–8, 70, 83, 101–2, 117, 147, 164; *see also* Darwinism, Euclidean and non-Euclidean geometry, Newtonian mechanics
Searle, John 61–4, 75, 202n.43
second objection to rationalism *see under* rationalism
second postulate of pure practical reason *see under* postulates of pure practical reason
security of the Basic Idea *see under* Basic Idea
self-love 136, 141, 153, 186
Sellars, Wilfrid 13
Seneca, Lucius Annaeus 54
sense *see* making sense
sexism 7, 59, 69–70, 78, 116, 143, 169
Shakespeare, William vi
shame vi, 28, 112
shared conative states xiii, 6–9, 23, 29, 41, 45, 48, 51, 131, 134, 142, 172, 175; *see also* ethically productive conative states
shared reasons xv, 40–5 *passim*, 51, 165, 201n.4; *see also* general reasons
sin *see* evil and wrong-doing
situations: discord *see* discord situations; no-win *see* no-win situations; paradoxical *see* paradoxical situations
Skorupski, John 203n.57
Smith, Michael 4–5
socially grounded ethical disagreement *see* second objection to rationalism
Socrates 24
Sophie 219n.21
'So what?' xvii, 90–1, 94–5, 118–19, 130
space: conceptual *see* conceptual space; of reasons *see* logical space of reasons
Spinoza, Baruch 85, 87, 125, 205–6n.131, 213n.80, 216n.59
Stanhope, Philip 32
Stoics 37, 67, 85, 161, 203n.52; *see also* Chrysippus
stories *see* narrative and stories
Strawson, P.F. 183, 219n.23
strength and weakness of character 107, 116, 126, 149, 151, 170, 177, 183, 196, 206n.3, 210n.8; *see also* character and disposition
subversion of concepts and practices 36, 60, 68, 76, 129, 180–1
suicide 53–54
suitably salient possibilities 116–17, 126, 181
superficial concepts xvii, 98–9, 117, 119, 182, 210n.18
supreme value xviii, xx, 20, 70, 129, 131, 141, 175; good will as *see* good will as supreme value; *see also* Basic Idea, highest good
swearing 39–45 *passim*, 49, 64–5, 123, 211n.29

taboos 49–51, 60, 63–4, 123, 129, 180, 211n.29
teleology 7, 9–10, 70, 131, 140–3 *passim*, 148, 160, 164, 171, 194, 214n.90; *see also* Darwinism, evolution
temptation 152, 178, 183–6, 210n.8
Tertullian, Quintus Septimus Florens 91
'The End of All Things' 162–3
The Metaphysics of Morals 53–4, 96
'The Only Possible Argument in Support of a Demonstration of the Existence of God' 218n.98
'thick' ethical concepts 200n.1; *see also* action-guiding concepts
third objection to rationalism *see under* rationalism

third postulate of pure practical reason *see under* postulates of pure practical reason
time vi, 18, 44, 71, 98–9, 104–11 *passim*, 113–14, 122, 153–5, 161–3, 178–9, 193, 217n.73; *see also* future, past
tipping 36, 60, 129, 202n.39, 205n.105
transcendence 11, 20, 103–12 *passim*, 120, 124–5, 131, 142, 161–2, 189, 195
Transcendental Deduction 104–5, 208n.58
transcendental vindication of categorical imperatives xiv, 26–7, 29, 37, 138
trust vi, 31, 52, 71, 81, 166, 171; *see also* faith
Turetzky, Philip 85
type: of a conative state 8–9, 174–5; of a reason 41, 201n.5

unconditionedness 101, 105, 109, 154, 157, 164, 196, 214n.105
unpredictability xvii–xviii, 72, 88, 120–4
upbringing *see* education and upbringing
upper-level ethics *see* meta-ethics
utilitarianism 70; *see also* consequentialism and non-consequentialism

vague concepts 43, 48–50, 54–5, 190, 213n.62
value: freedom as a *see under* freedom; good will as supreme *see* good will as supreme value; rationality as a *see under* rationality; supreme *see* supreme value; *see also* worthiness
vicarious versus non-vicarious applications of concepts 49, 64, 89
vindication of categorical imperatives *see* transcendental vindication of categorical imperatives
virtue and virtues xix, 24, 45, 67, 87, 156, 158–63, 193, 215n.18; *see also* highest good, worthiness
virtues *see* virtue and virtues

Walker, Ralph C.S. 108
we: becoming those that we are *see same*; question who 'we' are 5, 7–8, 29, 63, 66, 82, 128–30, 137–9, 143–5, 214n.103; *see also* becoming those that we are
weakness of character *see* strength and weakness of character
welfare *see* happiness and welfare
Wille 96–7, 119, 207n.31
Williams, Bernard 9–12, 19, 43, 46, 76, 83, 86, 138–9, 142–3, 172–3, 198n.4, 200n.1, 201n.17, 204nn.78, 81, and 92, 212–13n.62, 214n.85, 219n.25, 220n.29
willing and its limits xiv–xv, 30–3, 56, 79–81, 135–6, 159, 165, 194–5; *see also* good will as supreme value, *Wille, Willkür*
Willkür 96–7, 110, 119, 151, 153, 207n.31
Wittgenstein, Ludwig 1, 17–18, 21, 51, 77, 122, 125, 127–8, 133, 192, 195, 203n.51, 204nn.82 and 85, 211nn.24 and 36, 211–12n.39, 212n.41, 221n.56; *see also* forms of life
Wolf, Susan 204n.86
Wöllner, J.C. 169
world-directed objectivity xiii, 4–6, 10–17 *passim*, 189
worthiness 39, 85, 132, 149, 158–61, 194; *see also* highest good, virtue and virtues
wrong-doing *see* evil and wrong-doing